BORN IN THE CHICKEN HOUSE

(DON'T TRY N GIT BOVE YER RASIN')

BY WILEY TAYLOR

Photo by Brooke Cagle on Unsplash

Dedicated to:
Sue, Tim, and Mary

Contents

1. WHY IS WEDNESDAY'S CHILD FULL OF WOE?

Information for this page from:
"reference.com/world-new/Wednesday's-child-full-woe…"

"As the chief god of the Norse pantheon, Odin was not only a fierce king and warrior but also a poet who loved traveling the earth disguised as a traveler. Seeking knowledge above all else, Odin was a serious personality who even sacrificed one of his eyes in the pursuit of enlightenment. It's possible that the woe of Wednesday's child could be a reflection of some of the more serious attributes of Odin, the weekday's namesake. "Woe" may not be quite as tragic as it sounds and may have simply indicated a more serious demeanor—or even a longing to understand the deeper mysteries of life.

Interestingly, however, there are a variety of different versions of "Monday's Child," some of which tell a much different story about Wednesday babies. In a Scottish version of the poem, Wednesday's child is "merry and glad," while Thursday's child is "wise and sad."

2. CHIP OFF THE OLD BLOCK

The United States had been involved in fighting World War II with its Allies for over two years— over two years, two months, and one week, to be more precise. The world had gone crazy! The sacrifices, the countless useless deaths, and lessons from World War I seemed to have had no meaning. Lessons learned from that war had been forgotten. Memories of all that anguish and suffering seemed to have vanished and were languishing somewhere in the past. And now, the youngest and maybe even some of the brightest and perhaps those with the most potential were being trained and sent to become fodder to this new great war machine. This had happened here in the United States after the Japanese attacked Pearl Harbor on December 7, 1941, in Hawaii. Those brave and patriotic farm boys and ranchers' sons, youngsters hardly out and many not even out of high school, kids from all walks of life were quick to heed the call of their country and were eager to fight for freedom, anxious for the opportunity to show their patriotism. They would go over and show those Japs and Nazis what they had let themselves in for messing around with America. Many of those brave, fearless souls would never return! Others would return maimed for life with limbs missing or scars that would never really heal. The horrors of war they had endured would haunt them until their dying days. Families from all over the country were being hit hard. Countless lives would be lost on both sides of that devastating war. It would not be an easy victory as time would sort it out.

***

[SPECIAL NOTE: The first portion of this Memoir describes events in my childhood which took place mostly in the hills of Kentucky. The early settlers, mainly from the United Kingdom, settled along the Atlantic Coast in the 17th and 18th centuries. Then, they gradually migrated to what later became West Virginia, Tennessee, and Kentucky, often becoming isolated in the Appalachian mountain's backwoods and hollers of those states, maintaining, and embellishing some of their customs, folklores, and tales. My ancestors were part of that early migration. I've attempted to document some of those stories and experiences handed down to me by my grandparents in the vernacular of the language I heard spoken in my formative years and added my own experiences growing up in that area.]

Dad and Mom

Bert Taylor
4/14/1914 – 2/24/2006
Fannie Bishop
5/6/1917 - 9/10/1008

Married
6/5/1935

The date of the startin' interest here wuz February 17, 1943, ah WEDNESDAY. We war located in Owsley County, Kentucky on the South Fork of Island Creek which in turn emptied in ta the Kentucky River in jest 'bout ah mile and ah half further down. Ar domain wuz a two-room structure (house) built by mah Daddy with the assistance of his brothers and some neighbors. The house had neither plumbin' nor electricity and wuz located on mah Grandma Taylor's property, about seventy-five yards from her main house at the end of her orchard. The orchard included several varieties of apple trees 'cept fer one lone pear tree and three beehives. Hit ended eastward towards the barnyard that had a steep hill which made fer nice sleddin' whenever thar wuz a little snow or ice coverin' the surface of the hill, but the hillside provided little pasturin' fer the livestock.

The barn sat at the bottom of the hill. I thank thar war three stalls fer the livestock, may'ave been four. Not shore. Don't 'member 'xactly. In the winter, the barn stalls could get really mucky and smelly, and hit could be a real chore ta do the milkin'. Drainage in the stalls wuz practically nonexistent and muckin' 'em out wuz a real chore. Thar wuz a hog lot that covered the lower side of the mountain jest beyond the barnyard and hit abutted up ta the cliff.

The top of the cliff wuz covered with trees, mostly deciduous, that went all the way up the mountain as fur up as the eye could see. Thar wuz a couple of black walnut trees inside the hog lot but hit wuz a competition with the hogs as ta who would get ta the walnuts first; us'ens or the hogs. The hogs usually won out. Fer if'n ya warn't thar wen the walnuts fell offen the trees, or ya shook the walnuts off yerself, ferget hit. The hogs would make shore thar warn't nothin' left. Next ta, and jest afore gettin' ta the hog lot, wuz ar outhouse smellin' somethin' awful in the summertime and cold as heck in the wintertime; neither condition encouraged lingerin' fer any length of time. Discarded Sears Roebuck catalogs provided whatever sanitation that would be available atter doin' one's business as I don't recall ever seein' or usin' what today we ar used ta referring ta as toilet paper. In lieu of discarded catalogs in an emergency, corncobs or foliage (weeds or leaves), as long as they warn't poison ivy (don't laugh, hit had been known ta happen) could still get the job done.

Grandma Taylor's fruit trees war still fairly young, not mature, and war placed fur enough apart so that some gardenin' or a corn crop could still be tended round the trees. The back side of the house wuz twenty feet or so from the hillside, whar the orchard took a stiff climb up the mountainside while the front side wuz on sandstone hewed stilts ta keep hit somewhat (mostly) level. The front of the house looked out over the gravel road that ran 'tween the house and the family garden that wuz jest beyond the road. In dry spells, every passin' vehicle raised a cloud of dust that sprayed the house and yard and surroundin' area. Fortunately, thar wuz not an abundance of traffic in those days. Thar wuz still mostly foot-traffic, horse riders, or horse-drawn wagons, and a few buggies. Mechanized traffic included the mail carrier, the school bus, an occasional peddler, and thar war a few folks who owned motor vehicles who used the gravel road.

Cross the road wuz the family garden, and beyond hit wuz Island Creek, and on the other side of the creek a steep mountainside which towered straight up into the sky and wuz covered with the stark skeletons of thousands of deciduous trees with their naked branches reachin' towards the heavens. Should thar be enough snow, the mountain would become white and blend in with the sky. Come springtime, the mountain would be covered with splotches of pink redbuds and white dogwoods before turnin' into the lush shades of green of late spring and summer. And then, as fall encroached, hit would seem as if the hills would become mostly ablaze as the mountainside took on the fiery reds, yallers, and burnt browns afore abandonin' their covers, indifferently each leaf, then all the leaves, seemingly in concert, would float earthwardly ta cover the forest floor in preparation fer winter's approach.

The house hit self wuz divided inta two rooms. In the room whar I wuz being held in abeyance wuz Mommy and Daddy's bedroom and hit wuz purty sparsely decorated. In addition, ta the double bed thar wuz a small crib waitin' fer me and a cot fer Mary Jane, who wuz about two and a half years older than me, and a large wooden crate (chest) Mommy used fer storin' what few clothes the family wuz not wearin' at the time along with other odds and ends. Durin' most of mah childhood, we war lucky ta own two sets of clothin', one ta wear and one usually waitin' ta be warshed. The walls war austere, completely bare—no artwork, no pictures, no family photos. The second room wuz the kitchen furnished with the kitchen stove, a dinin' table, a bed fer William David, and a bed fer Cosetta and Fern. Fern wuz frequently hospitalized in Lexington recuperatin' or in therapy rehabilitatin' from her bout with polio. What few chairs Daddy had managed ta scrounge war shared 'tween both rooms.

On that particular day, the weather couldn't seem ta make up hits mind whether ta snow or ta rain—so hit wuz doin' both, and at the same time. The temperature wuz hoverin' round thirty degrees Fahrenheit, but the icy wind make hit feel much colder. The patter on the tin roof would, on a normal day, would'ave been soothin', conducive ta nappin'—but not that day. Occasionally the wind could be heard howlin' round the corner of the house, then hit would die down inta a low moan as if hit wuz tryin' ta tell everyone somethin'—a secret perhaps, or an omen of thangs ta come, or jest who knows what?

Daddy wuz busily tendin' ta the fire in the pot-bellied stove, which had a big tub of water heatin' on hits top. Every now and agin he'd throw in a block or two of coal and stir up the fire with the poker. The little stove wuz keepin the room fairly warm. Daddy wuz anxious; he'd alla's ben a little high-strung. Grandma Taylor, a certified midwife, wuz calmly tendin' ta Mommy and intermittently sewin' on a quilt. She would hum snatches of some tune that didn't make much sense, but she wuz alert ta all of the goin's on. Ever so often she'd git up and check on Mommy and maybe give her a sip of water, push on her belly and once in a while checked down thar. Then she might take ah looksee outsides, all the while keepin' her eagle eyes on Daddy, afore goin' back ta her quiltin. Mommy sorta wuz grittin' her teeth, clenchin' the covers and lettin' out low moans as the birthin' cramps came and went; pains came and then slowly subsided. Mommy had ben sufferin' through the pangs of childbirth through most of the night, and now daybreak wuz only a few hours away. Her brow wuz covered with a thin film of sweat as she morphed along with the birthin' pains and contractions. Mommy actually wuz gettin' ta be an old hand at this—she already had birthed four older young'uns and had had one miscarriage—after her last live birth, mah older sister, Mary Jane. No worries either.

Mommy's midwife (Grandma Taylor) wuz the most experienced midwife in the county and probably in the entire area. Grandma Taylor had delivered dozens of babies—perhaps even hundreds—alla's called in ta assist with the most difficult cases. She had assisted Mommy in deliverin' three of the four older young'uns mentioned earlier: Cosetta, seven years older; William David, named fer both grandfathers (William fer William Taylor and David fer David Bishop), four years older; and Mary Jane, named fer both grandmothers (Mary for Mary Elizabeth Bishop and Jane fer Nancy Jane Taylor). Grandma Taylor had not delivered Fern, six years older, who had had polio wen she wuz two. Well, these siblings of mine war down at the main house bein' looked atter by some of Daddy's kinfolk. Me? I didn't know nothin'. I wuz jest waitin' ta be born—or should I say in the process of bein' born?

Hit wuz jest round 7 a.m. wen the heavens opened up! Wen hit happened!! Afore I had ben happily ridin' round or I had ben bein' carried round in mah own little coach, insulated from the rest of the world, bein' gently rocked to and fro with jest the smallest of jolts ever now and agin. Wenever I wuz bored, I could kick mah lags back and forth or sometimes even sideways or flail mah hands ever which way. Maybe I thought I wuz goin' be a boxer, and I could butt mah head somethin' fierce. Other times, I took long, leisure naps. But wen I wuz wide awake, I tried some locomotion and tried ta turn over or do flips but found that I wuz tied down by this big ropey thangy.

But now thangs war takin' on a different hue. Somethin' else wuz going on. Somethin' weird! I could feel hit in mah bones. I warn't shore I wuz up ta the way thangs war turnin' out. A squeeze! And another squeeze! I wuz bein' crushed from all sides, on mah top, and on mah bottom! Everythang seemed ta be in a turmoil. I warn't shore what I wuz supposed ta do. Help! Would I be able ta survive all of this? I didn't thank so. Then thar would be a small reprieve, and jest wen I thought everythang wuz goin' ta be gettin' better, the squeeze would come agin, and the squeezes seemed ta be comin' on more often and stronger, much stronger! Jest wen I thought I couldn't survive any more, thar wuz a big push, and I felt mah whole being bein' crushed and moved outta mah coach. Mah head wuz squeezed so hard I swear I could feel mah eyeballs bein' pushed ta the back of mah head! Then, another push! And all of ah sudden the brightest lights in the universe completely overwhelmed me. Grandma Taylor grabbed mah heels and whacked me on the rump. I did not like that ah' tall! I'm shore I warn't 'spectin' such harsh treatment, and anyway hit hurt. Darn it!

I protested and drew in this great big gust of air— mah first breath—and hit hurt even worse! Then, I cried out with all mah might. A simple snip, and Mommy and I war separated, detached ferever, and

I wuz bein' manhandled all over—a bit of rubbin' and cleanin' and wipin' stuff out of mah eyes and nose. I wuz wrapped in flannel and handed over to mah daddy. Grandma said to Daddy, "Bert, he looks jest like ya. He's yer spittin' image, an he's got yer lungs ta boot." And she chuckled—laughed right out loud. She did. Then she gave a reassuring hand ta Mommy and told her she did good and that everything was good and goin' ta be alright.

Daddy gingerly took me in his arms, looked down at me, and then held me close and smiled down at me. A small tear slowly trickled down from his red eyelashes, down his face, and down his cheeks, and landed rite on mah blanket. I don't know if hit wuz from tenderness or guilt fer all the times that he had 'ccused Mommy that I warn't his'en. That he warn't mah daddy. Mommy's and Daddy's futile attempts at birth control jest hadn't worked. After four young'uns, and Fern's terrible ordeal with polio they had decided to pause the child production mill. Figured they'd had enough fer the time bein'. Hadn't worked though. Whatever the cause that let me slip through, thar had been a lot of suspicion and some terrible arguments!

The peculiar thang wuz that of all thar ten kids, I am the one who most physically looked like ar Daddy. Personality-wise, I am the least like 'em, or so I thank and honestly believe. The few times Daddy and I would be out together in public, an acquaintance of Daddy's would look at him and then look at me and relook at me and on more than one occasion, I have heard 'em say, "Bert, you'll never die, as long as that 'young'un' is alive." But that moment I just described wuz possibly the closest mah Daddy and I ever war ta each other throughout ar lives.

I wuz jest a few days old and still had not been given mah name. Mah brother and sisters had been brought up from Grandma Taylor's house, and atter takin' a curiosity peek at me nestled in Grandma's arms, had settled round the stove ta keep warm, quickly lost interest in me, and then generally 'nored me completely. Grandma Taylor queried them as ta what their new baby brother should be called. She got back blank stares but no suggestions. Why wuz she askin' them, anyhow? Whar wuz the authority comin' from ta consult that lot fer a name fer ME? Then she sat down by William David and axed 'em, "What about namin' yer new baby brother fer one of yer uncles, William David?" Not wishin' ta show partiality ta either side of the families, she offered, "Murphy (Daddy's brother) or Wiley (Mommy's brother)?" Fer some reason she didn't offer Alfred or Floyd, mah other uncles. William David kinda bit his lip and wrinkled his brow and actually seemed ta ponder the decision fer a few minutes and responded, "I thank he should be called Wiley." So, I'm told that wuz how I wuz named by mah four-year-and-two-month-old older brother.

An aside: Wen ar family moved back from Cincinnati, Ohio, ta Island Creek, Kentucky, in April 1947, wen I wuz four, we all moved inta Grandma Taylor's abandoned house, whar Daddy had mostly grown up and whar he had taken his new bride in 1935 ta take up residence with Grandpa and Grandma Taylor, along with the remainder of his brothers and sisters, who war still livin' at home.

The house whar Mommy and Daddy and the rest of ar family lived wen I wuz born had now been converted into a storage/corn crib in one room, and the room whar I wuz actually born had been converted into ar **chicken house**. Tharfore, I have gone round fer most of mah life known (or at least teased by the others) as the one who wuz born in the chicken house. Fer most of mah younger years, I wuz a towhead—as mah Grandma Bishop described mah hair as "hair as white as cotton."

3. ODE TO DAD

Mah earliest, most memorable memory of Daddy wuz him grabbin' me up roughly, pullin' up mah dress, throwin' me cross his knees, and beatin' mah rump soundly with his hand. I had on nothin' 'neath mah dress. Yes, in ar culture, little boys wore dresses 'til they war fully potty-trained. I don't 'member 'xactly how old I wuz at the time, but I 'spect I may'ave been 'bout one, maybe nearin' one and a half. I don't recall the indiscretion fer which I wuz bein' punished. However, upon the first smack, I let out a howl that probably could'ave ben heard clear over ta the next street, and I didn't let up on the next several slaps neither.

Our very pregnant Mommy looked in from the kitchen and yelled over at Daddy, askin' if'n he couldn't get me ta hesh up ah little bit. Upon hearin' Mommy's voice, I really turned up the volume. Daddy picked me up and shook me good and proper and told me ta shut hit up! I wuz sobbin' and slobberin' so hard I could barely breathe, which really set Daddy off. I mean, I had *really* set Daddy off!

Daddy alla's had a very bad temper and a very short fuse. I larned in later life that when Daddy's short fuse got lit and he went off, thar wuz no stoppin' 'em. He shifted inta another gear as his personality changed. The vessels in his neck would bulge and start throbbin' and his face would turn red, red, and redder, almost matchin' the color of his hair.

So, over his lap agin, up the dress agin, and this time he began beatin' me in earnest. Mah rump wuz hot—

pepper hot. Hit felt like hit wuz burnin' up in flames with every smack of his hand feelin' like fire—I wuz shore mah backsides war turnin' black and blue, even though I didn't know what black and blue wuz back then. Daddy then throwed me on the floor and dared me ta make a sound or ta move ah muscle. I tried mah best not ta make any more noises and held mah breath as best as I could and cried silently ta mahself 'til thar wuz no more tears left and somehow still sobbed mahself ta sleep.

Do babies hate? I jest really wanted ta love mah daddy, and I dearly wanted mah daddy ta love me, too. I can't say that wuz the first time that I experienced mah daddy's wrath fer shore, but I can say with certainty hit would not be the last.

In his defense, Daddy wuz kind, hardworkin', and most of the time a lovin' Daddy. He tried ta be the best daddy he knew how ta be. At that time, he wuz sharin' his love and attention with five kids, one of whom had polio and wuz in and out of the hospital and rehabilitative care. He also had a very fertile and demandin' (some would describe Mommy as passive-aggressive) wife. The number of offspring would increase from the current five ta ten in the next six years. Perhaps this wuz not mah first memory of mah daddy but hit wuz certainly the one that lingers in mah mind the strongest. In all that time, we would'ave been considered well below the poverty line, so hit wuz a struggle fer Daddy ta keep us clothed and food on the table. One of the reasons fer our struggle wuz that Mommy and Daddy believed in follerin' the biblical guidance of tithin'. In spite of Daddy's meager salary, they attempted ta tithe 10 percent of their salary ta the church and usually did.

August 10, 1944, Cosetta, the oldest (8) sister, had William David (5), Mary Jane (4), and me (18 months) all huddled on the bed in the kitchen while Dr. Jackson our family doctor, with her big black bag, wuz holdin' court with Mommy and Daddy in the main bedroom. (We only had two rooms, agin.) Fern (7), my sister who had contracted polio wen she wuz two, wuz in the hospital or rehab. Dr. Jackson wuz an interestin' person. She wuz a little dowdy, short, and a somewhat plain-lookin' woman who wore these big black glasses. Atter what seemed ferever, I heard a screechin' noise' that could'ave ben a baby cryin'. I didn't thank hit sounded like Mommy or Daddy and couldn't thank hit would be Dr. Jackson. I really didn't know what the sound wuz, or what all the commotion wuz 'bout. Sometime later, Dr. Jackson left, and we war all told—or so I wuz led ta believe, and I'm shore I didn't really understand—that she had brought Henry in her big black doctor's bag. The reason she wuz with Mommy and Daddy so long wuz cause Henry wuz so big—weighed over eleven pounds—and they had a hard time gettin' em out of the doctor's bag 'cause he got stuck and he started cryin' wen he seed that everybody kept on lookin' at 'em and he didn't like that a bit so he started in cryin' and wuz jest cryin' his eyes out! Go figger.

Mah aunt and uncle Burton, who lived over in Bellevue, Kentucky cross the Ohio River, often came ta visit us with their daughter, Thelma Jean (two years older than me). On one such visit, Daddy and Uncle Elvin Burton decided ta run an errand in downtown Cincinnati, or perhaps they war jest goofing off—gettin' away from the brood and all the confusion and noise? Too far back ta 'member all the particulars now. Anyway, I do 'member I wanted ta go with 'em, in the worst way possible. I wanted ta go explorin', too. Of course, they didn't care ta invite me, nor did they even want me ta go with 'em, I reckon, even though I really bagged 'em, hard. So, I waited 'til they left the 'partment and then I simply follered 'em. I guess that wuz mah first effort at sleuthin'. Mind ya, I wuz barely three at the time. I wuz very careful they didn't see me, so I would stay 'bout a block behind 'em, and I tried ta stay hidden from 'em as best I could. Thank goodness, they war too engrossed in enjoyin' each other's company and never thought ta look backards or they woulda probably found me out. This worked fer several blocks, but I got held up by a red light. I mean, I knowed 'bout red lights—not shore how, but spect that maybe mah older brother or sisters had taken me cross the streets and larnt me 'bout the red and green lights and stop and go and watchin' out fer cars and such.

I wuz purty clever even at that age. Skeptical? Well, jest ask me. Ya couldn't cross the street if'n the light wuz red. Ya had ta wait 'til hit turned green. That wuz the rules. Imagine that! So, ya can guess what happened atter follerin' 'em like a baby Dick Tracy fer several blocks. Mah speedy little lags failed ta allow me ta keep up. A red light caught me, and wen I hurried cross the street, wen the light finally turned green, I could barely see 'em turnin' round the corner of a distant buildin' way up ahead of me. Wen I got ta the corner, I couldn't see which a'way of the street they had went. I'm a purty good guesser, so I chose the street I thought looked best and wound up near the public library (which, in later years, I would become an adamant patron of when we moved back to Cincinnati the second time).

Atter wonderin' round aimlessly fer some time, I got picked up by the Cincinnati police in their cruiser—

mah first run-in with the police force. "Whar ar ya going, Sonny?" one of the policemen had rolled his car winder down and stuck out his big head and axed me in this really gruff, loud voice. Hit scared me a little at first, but now we war from Kentucky, and we hadn't got the speech 'bout not talking ta strangers. So. heck, we're a friendly lot and we talk ta jest 'bout anybody and everybody.

"I ben goin' with mah Daddy and mah Uncle Elvin," I told 'em. (Which wuz almost true.) "But I kinda got left behind and I ain't shore which away they went." By this time, I wuz gettin' a little worried that Daddy might not like hit that I had follered 'em and they hadn't knowed hit, plus I warn't too shore I really knowed how ta git back home by mahself. I hadn't left no breadcrumbs ta foller back ta ar 'partment.

I could feel tears building up all round mah eyeballs, but I didn't want ta show those big policemen I might be afeared, or they might thank I wuz a lost little baby, or a fraidy cat. They axed me who wuz mah mommy and daddy. Well, I knowed Mommy wuz called Fannie and Daddy wuz called Bert from mah aunt and uncle and the folks from ar church, but I didn't know anythang 'bout no Christian names that they wuz axing me 'bout. I mean, Mommy and Daddy went ta church all ah the time and took us young'uns with 'em some of the time, so I shore reckoned they were Christians all right. I did thank they war God's children 'cause I'd heard 'em say so, so that would make 'em Christians. Right?

"Do I know whar I live? Shore, I live on Clay Street," I said ta the officers. Everybody knowed that.

"Yes, but whar 'bouts on Clay Street do you live?"

Huh? That wuz a puzzlement. I knowed if'n ya turned right from ar 'partment and went down ta the next street and turned another right, thar wuz a little store 'bout halfway down the block and if'n ya had a nickel ya could buy a popsicle from the nice old lady who alla's wore a big white apron, a funny little hat on her red hair, and she had these funny little glasses and worked behind the counter thar. I knowed 'xactly whar we lived when I wuz thar, but how ta tell these policemen wuz a different story.

"Well, do ya thank ya would know hit if'n we took ya thar?"

I wuz shore I did, or I could find hit. The policeman in his shiny blue uniform told me first that we needed ta go ta the police station ta see if thar war any reports of missing little boys. I guess he meant me? This wuz ta be my first, last, and only visit inside a jail!

Wen we got ta the jail, thar war no reports of missing little boys. However, the kind policeman thought that I should have an ice cream cone 'fore we started out tryin' ta find mah home, and I agreed. I mean I did agree, but I didn't say nuthin'. I jest stood thar all quiet like, 'til the nice policeman handed me this mouth-waterin' lookin' ice cream cone. That wuz probably the best ice cream cone I ever had in mah whole, entire life. Hit wuz a biggen too, and 'fore I could lick hit all up, hit started in meltin' and runnin' down the sides of the ice cream cone and onto mah fangers, and mah arm. But never ya mind, fer I jest matter of factly started lickin' hit right up, off of mah arm, mah fangers, and then the rest of the ice cream cone, quick as I could with alternatin' licks—arm, fangers, ice cream cone—'til hit wuz all gone. Nuttin' wuz goin' ta waste thar. "Waste not, want not," mah Grandma alla's told me.

By mah side, I heard the friendly policeman kinda chuckle—the man wuz chuckling ta his self and as I finished mah ice cream cone, I glanced up at 'em; he wuz jest smilin' as big as ya please from ear to ear, with this funny twinkle in his eyes. I guess he musta thought I wuz kinda funny, but I liked 'em anyways. The policemen then loaded me back into their police cruiser and took me fer a drive ta Clay Street. I didn't even have ta ponder whar I lived, fer wen we got ta Clay Street, the whole family wuz scattered about searchin' fer me, includin' mah aunt, mah uncle, and mah cousin. Mah mommy came a runnin' and grabbed me and gave me a great big hug and I could see she had been cryin'. I told her, "I'm OK, Mommy." And she jest gave me another big hug.

Another time, I 'member ridin' on Daddy's shoulders ta a baptizin' that wuz held down on the Ohio River near the old L & N Bridge so's I could see the preacher man dunkin' all those folks in the river like he wuz tryin' ta give 'em a quick bath or somethin'. Guess they warn't all that dirty after all, 'cause hit went purty quick. First, they had a quick dunk in the murky, muddy water, and the preacher man wuz yellin' somethin' at 'em while everybody round wuz sangin' somethin' ta Jesus. Then the dunked person walked out of the water, shakin' themselves a bit, with thar hands wavin' up in the air, and then they casually strolled onta the paved ground jest a grinnin' and lookin' all happy and a shoutin', "Amen! Praise the Lord!" Then 'nother somebody would hand 'em a towel ta dry off.

And I 'member Daddy cryin' wen he larned Grandma Taylor had died (December 13, 1945). Everett wuz born a couple of days later (December 15, 1945) and subsequently got double pneumonia. So, Daddy couldn't even go ta Grandma's funeral. Can't even imagine how awful he musta felt. Ya know, he wuz alla's her baby as long as she lived. I've been told she pampered him somethin' awful all his life. Ruined him right rotten, she did!

Atter the war (WWII) ended, Uncle Wiley (I'm his namesake, as ya might 'member) wuz on furlough and stopped by on his way ta visit Grandpa and Grandma Bishop, who lived back in the mountains in Kentucky. He somehow persuaded Mommy ta let him take me with 'em on the train ta visit 'em (I wuz approachin' three at the time). Not sure how that happened. He wuz suppose ta brang me back with 'em wen he returned on his way back through Cincinnati, as his furlough wuz drawin' ta an end. However, fer whatever reason, he left me down in the hills of Kentucky with Grandma and Grandpa!

I've been told Mommy wuz really upset with Uncle Wiley fer leavin' me down thar. She had a hard time believin' he would do such a thang. Atter Uncle Wiley came in the house Mommy ran outside lookin' fer me, thankin' he wuz jest playin' a trick on her, and wuz hidin' me outside somewhar. Turned out he warn't.

I guess Grandma had ben purty persuasive 'bout Uncle Wiley leavin' me with her, and as fer me, I wuz treated royally by bein' left behind. I didn't have ta compete with all those other young'uns. The only thang left ta do wuz to retrieve me by takin' the whole family by train from Cincinnati ta Beattyville, Kentucky, which wuz the closest train stop, then hire a taxi ta take the family ta the head of Buffalo and walk the rest of the way on ta the head of Wolf Creek, whar Grandma and Grandpa lived.

Grandma and I had really bonded—I had one whole grown-up all ta mahself (Grandpa wuz just kinda a bonus)—and I didn't have ta share anythang with nobody. I know that sounds a little selfish, but Grandma loved me so much, and I loved her so much, too. Almost whatever I wanted ta do wuz all right with her. I had really larned ta like that.

Grandma and I war in the kitchen when we heard 'em (the family) comin' atter me, and I knowed they war comin' atter me, and I warn't too happy 'bout that. I wuz very willful and really wanted ta stay with Grandma and Grandpa. Grandma wuz strangin' and breakin' up green beans ta cook fer dinner (I had helped her pick 'em in the garden earlier in the morning. I had ben real careful and pulled one bean by hit self offen the vine else the hole bean vine might come up or I could 'stroy the younger beans that warn't full (mature), yet). Now I wuz tellin' her one of mah stories—I wuz good at tellin' stories—that wuz wen we first heard this God-awful racket way up the holler and I knowed right away hit wuz them fer shore. They would be thar in no time a'tall—those screamin' babies and everyone else vyin' fer attention. I'd rather jest stay thar with mah grandma and be her little boy. So, without a second thought, I scooted mahself right under the kitchen table and hid beneath the droopin' tablecloth, hopin' they wouldn't find me, so's they'd ferget 'bout me, and would go back ta Clay Street without me, leavin' me alone ta enjoy mah Grandma and Grandpa.

Alas, hit wuz not ta be. As soon as they got in the door, hit didn't take a minute fer them ta find me under the table. Henry happily pointed me out—much ta mah chagrin. He waddled over ta the kitchen table and stooped down jest a little and peeked under the tablecloth whar I thought I wuz well-hidden and yelled out in his squeaky little voice, "He's rite thar, hiddin' under the table! I can see 'em. I ken see 'em, he' all hunched over and squattin' rite thar." all the while pointin' his accusin' dirty, little fanger at me, almost in mah face. If looks could've killed, that would've been the end of the story fer Henry. (Sorry, Henry.) Took no time fer Daddy ta sprang into action and he squatted down and reached under the table, and roughly grabbed me, and dragged me out screamin' and kickin', and whupped me real good—warmed mah behind somethin' fierce, agin. Hit would've been much worse, but Grandma interceded and told Daddy that wuz enough! Daddy gave Grandma a really dirty look wen she told him that wuz enough, but he did stop whupping me. However, I did have ta return with the family back ta Cincinnati, anyhow.

And, another time, the whole family wuz traipsin' up Wolf Creek ta go visit Grandma and Grandpa, and I, of course, wuz overeager ta see mah Grandma and against better advice and good judgment wuz runnin' on ahead on the narrow path on a steep embankment above a rather overflowing Wolf Creek when mah foot got caught on a tree root stickin' up by the side of the path and I stumbled, fell right down, tumbled down the steep embankment, and rolled right into the rushin' waters. This time hit wuz Daddy ta mah rescue! Daddy wuz carryin' Everett, who wuz maybe almost one at the time. He handed Everett over ta Mommy quickly, scooted down the embankment, and pulled me from what I thought wuz the icy waters. I wuz shore I would'ave drowned had hit not been fer mah daddy even though the rushin' waters wuz only a few anches deep. Daddy soothed me by pickin' me up, rubbin' me off, and dryin' me with his shirtsleeves aided by Mommy's head rag (scarf) and told me everythang wuz goin' to be all right, and hit wuz. Then he set me back down on the trail and we war all on our way to Grandma's house once more, without further incident.

Wen I wuz five and in the first grade, I 'member how important and proud I felt wen Daddy let me climb up on his knees and read him mah new Dick and Jane book shortly atter I started school. And, wen mah first tooth got loose, Daddy pulled hit with a strang tied round the offendin' tooth and yanked hit out with jest one big quick jerk. I hardly even felt hit and didn't even mind the little bit of blood nether. Daddy jest told me ta spit hit out in the fireplace. Atter, he pulled the tooth, he baked me an Irish Tater in the ashes 'neath the fireplace grate fer mah first thang ta eat after losin' mah first tooth. He peeled the tater and fed me the Irish Tater with his pocketknife and fangers.

I recall tusslin' with Daddy on the porch along with Henry and Everett. He would take all three of us on at the same time and beard our bare tummies and blow frog croaks on our bellies. We would yell, squeal, kick, and laugh 'til we all war out of breath. Mommy would yell out, "Bert, you're bein' too rough with those boys, one of 'em's goin' git hurt fer shore." We jest loved hit, though. Gettin' time with Daddy wuz alla's a treat! I do fondly 'member the good times.

Snippets of Remembrances

Daddy takin' me ta Aunt Rachel's fer haircuts, and it alla's seemed hair would be left stickin' ta mah neck and mah back and itchin' me like crazy. Hit wuz like a million needles stickin' me all over, at the same time.

Ridin' on the back of old Betsy (our horse—actually a mule) bareback behind William David, behind Daddy ta Grandma's house.

Ole Betsy fartin' with every other step—and me bouncin' up and down with every step of the way until mah rear end wuz properly sore with the hide on mah crack rubbed raw, but I didn't complain. We war taught complainin wouldn't get ya very fur. I'm shore I had blisters and no skin left thar. I'd walk round like one of them bow legged cowboys fer days atterwards.

Daddy heftin' me up on top of Ole Silver, Grandpa's old nag, as they cleared the "New Ground" fer the planned new corn crop. I wuz scared ta death I wuz goin' ta fall off but I wuz not goin' ta let anybody thank I wuz a sissy (I wuz all of four now). "New Ground" wuz a forested area, and ta make hit ready fer plantin' the crops, in this case corn, all the trees and brush had ta be removed along with their roots whenever possible. Trees of any size that war usable war culled fer lumber or firewood and the rest war cut and piled inta large stacks ta be later burned; the burned wood/brush wuz considered fertilizer or soil conditioner. Hit wuz an arduous task, especially if done by hand, which wuz the case for mah Grandpa and Daddy.

October 7, 1950, Daddy wuz in the vegetable garden doin' some work and I wuz with 'em along with Ole Betsy, our mule, who wuz grazin' on some leftover sweet corn stalks at the fur end of the garden. Hit wuz atter school and wuz a pleasant sunny day that hadn't been 'specially eventful up until that time. Don't 'member 'xactly what I wuz doin'. Just messin' round, I reckon, but I wuz with Daddy, who wuz doin' somethin' in the garden—don't 'member what, though. Daddy told me ta fetch Ole Betsy as hit wuz gettin' on ta suppertime. Shore, I could do that. However, Ole Betsy wuz loathe ta leave her munchies on the cornstalks, and all mah attempted cajolin' fell on deaf ears. So, I picked up a loose cornstalk and hit her with hit, and she reluctantly moved away from her feastin'—somewhat hesitantly and purty slowly.

I herded her towards Daddy, but then she hesitated and decided she would like another go at the cornstalks. Mind ya, I wuz right behind her at that time, so I gave her I good wallop with the cornstalk I wuz still carryin'—the best I could. The very next thang I knowed, I found mahself flyin' through the air. Ole Betsy said enough was enough, ya nasty, little squirt—no more hittin' her with that ole cornstalk. She let out with both hind feet right at my head. Caught me right in the mouth and sent me flyin' in the air whar I landed on the drag with mah right ear almost torn off and six of mah front teeth knocked up into mah gums and a big gash in mah chin. I wuz a bloody mess—bleedin' like there wuz no tomorrow, and probably a little hysterical!

Daddy came runnin' back ta me ta see what in the world had happened and found me layin' flat on the ground, bleedin' like a stuck hog and screamin' my head off. I thought shorely I wuz dyin'. He scooped me up and carried me cryin' and moanin' ta the kitchen door all the time tryin' ta calm me down. The rest of the family came pilin' out of the house and circled round us. Daddy yelled, "Don't look, Fannie, stay in the house!" All I wanted wuz mah Mommy, but unbeknownst ta me, hit wuz jest 'bout time fer the twins ta make thar entry inta this world—I jest thought Mommy wuz getting really, really fat. I knowed that as of late the onlyest chair she could sit in wuz the big black rockin' chair, so all of us young'uns had ta be careful ta save hit fer Mommy.

Daddy told Cosetta ta get a pan of water and some rags ta warsh me off. He left me with her ta clean me up and bandage me as best she could with what she had available, which warn't much, and she had ta consider the condition I wuz in. In addition ta the blood all over mah face and in mah hair, mah shirt wuz soaked with blood and blood wuz drippin' down on my britches, too. Daddy ran down ta the garden, bridled up Ole Betsy—didn't even take the time ta saddle her—and rode up the road as fast as he could ta go git Hardin Hensley (ar cousin) ta take us ta Booneville ta see Dr. Gibson—the only doctor in town. Hardin had a pickup truck. Daddy held me in his lap all the eleven miles ta Booneville and carried me inta Dr. Gibson's office. By that time, I had calmed down somewhat. I still hurt like heck, but I felt numb and wuz probably in some degree of shock. Atter examinin' and bandagin' me up as best he could, Dr. Gibson told Daddy this boy wuz goin' ta need surgery and need surgery right now, in a hospital. Then, Daddy took me ta the bus station/restaurant, whar we caught the Greyhound Bus ta Lexington, Kentucky.

I don't 'member much 'bout the trip ta Lexington. I thank Dr. Gibson probably gave me somethin' ta ease mah pain 'cause I felt kinda woozy or maybe I wuz in shock. I thank I wuz purty much out of hit and I slept most of the way ta Lexington. Wen I wuz awake I 'member bein' fascinated by all of the electric lines I could see along the highway whippin' by us as we sped through the night. Hit seemed like thar wuz jest lines whizzin' by—lines like on my tablet writin' paper. I 'member thankin', *how can you write 'tween those lines?*

Wen we got ta the hospital in Lexington, I do 'member how bright hit wuz once we got inside. Hit wuz just like hit wuz still daylight with the sun shining inside the building. How could that be? Daddy left me at the hospital atter checkin' me in with the doctors and nurses, and I'm shore he told me a bunch of other stuff, but I don't 'member any of hit. Daddy had ta turn round and go back home 'cause Mommy wuz 'specting ta deliver babies any day, unbeknownst ta me. I don't think I understood why Daddy had ta leave me, but hadn't Fern had ta be away from the family all those years? Was this ta be somethin' like that? I guess I understood that Daddy needed ta be with Mommy and the rest of the children. I would be OK by mahself. And then, I wuz all alone. But hit seemed thar war all kinds of people everywhar.

Almost immediately, someone came ta remove mah clothes and sprayed me down with water. (I tried ta cover mah privates, but hit didn't seem to matter ta nobody, and anyhow, I hurt too much ta care that much.) They throwed me on a table that had wheels on hit and rolled me down all these hallways whar we met other folks doin' the same thang—that wuz they too war bein' rolled round on tables, the strangest thang I had ever seed. I guessed ridin' tables wuz better than ridin' horses 'specially round here? Maybe, 'cause I didn't see no horses. Guess horses or mules war not allowed in hospitals. Hit might have been fun if'n I hadn't been so skeered, hurtin' so much and kinda out of hit. I thank I wuz dozin' off and on, even though I mighty hard wanted ta see what wuz goin' on all 'bout me. Plus, they had a bottle of water on a pole thang with a sorta small rope danglin' down to a board, and the one end of the ropey thang wuz stuck in mah arm and they told me I must'en move or I might tare the thang right out of mah arm, and that would be really bad.

Atter awhile, we got ta this room whar they put on the brakes and grabbed me off the wheelie table and sot me right down in the middle of another table with no wheels. I 'spected we warn't goin' ta do any more ridin' round—at least not fer now. (I had probably gone to X-ray afore that, but fer whatever reason, I don't 'member the X-rayin'.) Atter they got me settled on the table; they axed me if'n I knowed mah numbers up ta a hundred. Shore, I knowed mah numbers way past a hundred—way past a thousand, even. Then they stuck this black thang over my face and told me to count backards from one hundred and to jest breathe normally.

Well, first, I didn't know if'n I could breathe a'tall with that thang coverin' all over mah face, and anyway, what wuz breathin' normally? But I started in tryin' ta do what I thought they war tellin' me ta do, one hundred, ninety-nine, ninety-eight, ninety-seven, ninety...

Thangs started ta get foggy, like really foggy, really quick, like the kind of foggy that rolls up from the creek bed in the fall of the year when ya can't hardly see whar ya're goin'—can't recognize nothin'; can't even see the trees and certainly can't see the stars or the sky. The voices, too, round the table became fainter and fainter. I could hardly hear 'em a'tall. Seemed everybody wuz whisperin' and mumblin'. Then I couldn't hear nuttin'.

I had this funny feelin' like I wuz sittin' out on Grandma's porch watchin' her churn in that ole white churn twixt her lags, makin' her some butter. Her little bantam rooster wuz scratchin' in the grass at the end of the porch huntin' fer grubs, and ever now and then he'd rare back and crow fer the longest time. 'Cept thar wuz no noise comin' out. The sun wuz shinin', but hit wuz funny, in spite of the sun, I felt the cold settlin' all over me and thar wuz a cold wind blowin' rite down on me.

The next thang I knowed, somebody wuz shakin' me, but I wuz still feelin' really cold. I opened mah eyes, and I wuz shore I must have died and gone ta heaven fer thar wuz this most beautiful angel starin' right down at me. She had the most breathtakin' blue eyes and her hair wuz like spun gold, and her smile jest melted mah heart. She wuz dressed all in white and had a funny-lookin' little white cup perched on top of her head—not a halo, much ta mah surprise! And, too, she smelled soooo good, like a flower.

"Wake up, honey. Wake up! Ya'ra back from surgery and I need ya ta wake up." I thought she said get up and so I tried mah best ta get up but I wuz very dizzy, and I couldn't get mahself up. But anyway, she gently pushed me back down. She really jest wanted ta wake me up, I reckoned. "I jest need ta take yer vitals right now," she told me. I thought she must be kiddin' me 'cause I hadn't had a bite to eat since Lord I couldn't 'member wen. It 'peers that warn't what she meant a'tall—they talked different down thar. She told me to scoot on mah side and stuck what appeared ta be a glass stick up mah bunghole and pumped up this rag on mah arm until hit hurt and did some maneuvers and told me I wuz doin' jest fine under the circumstances. Could ya imagine? She later told me she wuz Nurse Lily—jest like the flower. Maybe that's why she smelled so good.

Atter she left, I quickly dozed back off. I didn't even ax her 'bout mah family 'cause I wuz still in purty much of a daze from the anesthesia. When I did wake up agin, thar wuz no one round but I still hurt all over. Thar wuz certainly no family thar. I didn't know hit at the time, but I would not hear anythang from mah family—not a peep—fer two whole weeks. I wuz completely on mah own; well, on mah own within the confines of the pediatric ward of the hospital—but I would quickly larn ta adapt.

Like I said, I wuz hurtin' all over. Mah head really hurt. They had reattached mah right ear by sewin' hit back together. Imagine that! And the big cut in mah chin, well, they had sewed that together too with what looked kinda like sewin' thread. The only thang now wuz that I wuz completely missin' six of mah front teeth: four upper and two lower ones. Those they had taken out during mah surgery, said they war impacted into mah gums and had ta be removed, and consequently, I would have no front teeth fer the next seven and half years and would be called "that snaggle toothed boy."

Larnin' ta talk with no front teeth would become a real challenge, I wuz later ta find out. But, back ta the time when I wuz comin' out of the anesthesia. I could feel the roof of mah mouth disintegratin'. Strings of fiber or somethin' wuz comin' loose and I warn't shore what ta do with hit. I 'membered Grandpa had a spit paper at night fer he wuz alla's coughin' and spittin' somethin' fierce at night. He suffered from bronchitis. Well, I had no paper, but I had ta spit, so spit I did. I spit by the side of the bed. I spit, and I spit, and I spit. I couldn't swaller that stuff, and anyhow, mah throat wuz too sore to swaller much of anythang.

Here came pretty blue eyes, Miss Nurse Lily, and guess what? She wuz not pleased ta find all that spit by the side of mah bed. As a matter of fact, she almost slid and busted her fanny right thar by me. She kinda scolded me and told me I wuz not ta spit on the floor anymore. We jest didn't do that in the hospital. Instead, she gave me this funny-looking dipper thang or cup and told me that wuz what I wuz suppose ta use ta spit in.

Atter that, Nurse Lily and I got along jest fine. She wuz kinda mah special nurse, and whenever she wuz on duty, she wuz the one responsible fer mah care. She got me up and walkin' 'bout in no time and would take me down ta visit with her friends on some of the other wards. They would jest talk and talk with me. They said they loved ta hear me talk—wuz jest the cutest thang, they said! They wanted ta hear all 'bout mah life in the hills, 'bout my family, but most of all, they liked hearin' what they called mah "ax-cent."

I also got ta know other people on the ward, too. Thar wuz this black cleanin' lady, Miss Beula, who found a soft spot in her heart fer me. She kinda adopted me fer those two weeks. I would look forward ta her time on the ward, and she would sometimes let me run the dust broom and dust in the hard-ta-git-ta places. She liked ta hum little ditties, as she called 'em while she worked, but she said her back hurt whenever she had ta stoop down real low that's why she would let me help her. Hit wuz almost like helpin' mah grandma. Every day, she would slip me a small packet of M&Ms. First time I ever had those little round chocolate multicolored candy thangs. I don't thank I ever tasted any thang that sweet afore, and they jest melted in mah mouth. Hit wuz our secret.

My doctor wuz the kind of man that books war written 'bout. Every day he would come and check me all over and tell me what a good boy I wuz and how well I wuz doing, and wen he left, thar would be a dime on mah pillow. I never knew why but I wuz most grateful.

Thar were several other children on mah ward. I seemed ta be the most mobile, though. Thar wuz a little girl called Christina confined ta her bed or a wheelchair. She had no stomach. She had somehow swallered some lye and I wuz told she wuz really lucky ta still be alive. I would act as messenger or gopher fer her by fetchin' her tricks or helpin' her.

An' then thar was Toby at the end of the ward, who had some kind of cancer and wuz bedridden but had lots of comics. I would play checkers with 'em and he sold me some of his comics fer a nickel each. Of course, thar were other kids on the ward, but I don't 'member much 'bout 'em.

At the end of the two weeks, Daddy reappeared and told me hit wuz time ta go home. However, he told me now I had a new baby brother and a new baby sister born October 13, 1950, Bobbie Jean and Bonnie Lou. I mean, what wuz two more babies? I would be able ta help tend ta 'em, feed 'em, nuss 'em, warsh their dirty diapers, play with 'em, etc.

I thank hit musta been a Saturday. I woulda been 7 or even 8. We war all, at least most (of mah siblings), cross the creek at mah Uncle Alfred's. We wuz playin' and messin' round with ar cousins—kick-the-can, tag, blind man's bluff, and so forth. The day wuz wearin' on and I wuz really gettin' thirsty and really, really hongry and dirty and sweaty. At that age, I wuz purty shy. We war taught ta never ask fer thangs. However, everybody wuz goin' inta the kitchen fer a drank of water. Thar wuz a bucket of water settin' on a small table with a dipper in hit. Finally, I, too, went inside and took a quick swig of the water, but thar wuz also a big pan of cornbread (cornpone) on the nearby table. Hit looked so tasty, and I wuz SOOO hongry. I could smell the aroma of the cornpone waffling over past the water bucket, temptin' me, and I could hear mah stomach growlin' at me, jest baggin' fer one little bite. And, on the other hand hit was like the cornpone wuz whisperin' ta me, "Here I am, and I taste really, really good. Go on and 'ave a taste, let me know what ya thank."

Mah mouth wuz really waterin', real bad. Now, I knowed what wuz right and what wuz wrong. One should never take somebody else's property without askin' or bein' told hit wuz all right ta do so. That's stealin'. Says so in the Bible. But jest a little bitty piece wouldn't hurt nuttin', would it? Anyway, nobody else wuz round. The devil wuz fightin' hard in mah head, and he shore 'nuff wuz winnin' and aggin' me on, and I reached over ta the cornpone and broke off jest the tiniest corner and popped hit quickly inta mah mouth. I hardly chewed hit a'tall and swallered hit right down, jest as Mary Jane, mah sister, popped in through the screen door and caught me takin' the cornpone. "I seed that, and I'm gonna tell Daddy! You'ar goin' catch hit, now!"

Oh, Lord. If only the earth could have opened up and swallered me right then and there, all mah troubles would 'ave been over. The guilt. The shame. The disappointment. I'd probably taken and eaten mah cousins' supper. The whuppin' I wuz going ta get. My life as I had knowed hit wuz goin' ta be over. Don't know if hit wuz worse fer havin' stolen or fer bein' caught at stealin'—both really bad! I ran away from everybody, didn't let the screen door hit mah hind end as I slipped away, and hid down by the old swimmin' hole. Long forgotten wuz all mah honger pains. I had stolen. I wuz a sinner, and I wuz goin' ta Hell fer shore. Not only would I be gettin' a well-deserved beatin', but Mommy and Daddy would probably send me away ta a home fer wayward children. I wuz shore I'd never see mah brothers and sisters agin, ferever and no matter how much we fought and sassed each other, I really did love 'em. What would I do without 'em? I shore would miss 'em all. Mah family wuz all I had in this whole world. Maybe I could run away ta Grandma and Grandpa's house. Would Grandma and Grandpa even let me live with 'em atter they found out 'bout mah stealin'? I wuz evil incarnate!

As hit began ta get dark (and mind ya, I warn't particularly brave—and the darkness warn't goin' ta help), I even thought 'bout hidin' in the bushes and waitin' fer some varmint ta come up in the night an' catch me and eat me all up. But then I thought 'bout how terrible that might be, so's I got mahself up and sneaked inta ar smokehouse and climbed up on the meat shelf (the meat wuz long gone—had been eaten up a long time ago) and as hit wuz gettin' colder and as I had no covers ta help keep me warm, I pulled up mah lags ta mah body as close as I could and I cried mahself ta sleep. Sometime after dark, Daddy come in and found me in the smokehouse asleep and carried me inta the house and put me ta bed and covered me up, and I didn't even wake up. And better yet, I didn't get that whuppin' I had so dreaded and nuttin' else wuz said, at least that I 'member.

William David is mah oldest brother, older than me by four years, two months, and six days. He wuz the one who wuz given the honor of namin' me, 'member? By mah measure, I have been close ta all mah brothers and sisters growin' up, but William David has been

the one I have looked up ta the most. The followin'
small narrative wuz but one of the many reasons...

Hit started in the early spring when I wuz seven.
Barbra Ann wuz a baby and Fern wuz home and she
wuz on the porch babysittin' Barbra Ann while I wuz
kinda helpin' her, or at least lookin' on. Or jest
standin' by in case Fern needed me ta help her with
somethin'. Henry and Everett war runnin' round in
the front yard at first, and then scooted under the
house playin'. Actually, they had found a toad, and
they war pushin' hit round with a stick. Fern warned
'em if'n that frog (which was actually a toad) peed on
'em, they war goin' ta get a whole bunch of warts all
over themselves. They jest laughed at her and kept
right on tormentin' that pore ole frog. Ole Blackie ar
dog came over and gave the toad a sniff or two but
wen the toad gave 'em a squirt on the snout he
quickly lost interest and shuffled over near whar Fern
was tendin' ta Barbara Ann, curled up, and went ta
sleep.

Mom's ole dominecker rooster wuz over by the
smokehouse corner. He stretched his neck and let out
with a gosh-a-mighty cocker-doodle-do. Ya had to
watch that ole fool of a rooster or he could run atter ya
and peck ya and/or spur ya real bad. He wuz a mean
'un. He shore looked atter Mommy's hens right well,
though. He made shore they war mindin' their P's an'
Q's, else he'd run right atter 'em, jump on their backs,
and grab their heads with his beak until they cried
uncle, jump off, and crow real loud again as if ta say "I
tole ya so!" I tell ya he, that ole rooster, better mind
his own P's and Q's, else he would 'ave gone and
wound up like one of his brothers in Mommy's ole
black stew pot as chicken and dumplings fer Sunday
dinner.

Anyhow, hit wuz a beautiful sprang day with a lazy, calm, soothing breeze blowing in on us on the porch whar we war tendin' ta Barbara Ann. The temperatures wuz probably in the mid-seventies. The rest of the family wuz down in the garden workin' on early sprang plantin'. Sprang wuz fairly bustin' out all over. Thar wuz a redbird couple (cardinals) tryin' ta build a nest in the apple tree in the corner of the yard comin' and goin' with twigs and grass in thar beaks whar they would scooch around in the forks of that old tree and thar war a few early butterflies flittin' round hither and yon lookin' fer some flowers. The apple tree's buds war jest beginnin' ta try ta break open—not quite in blossom yet. The hillsides wore splotches of red and white, due ta the dogwoods and redbuds blossomin' out. Hit wuz a real purty sight and an excitin' time. Lettuce had already surfaced underneath the white coverlet (mesh) in the northeast corner of the garden. And thar war onions bein' set and peas bein' planted and the earth wuz bein' prepared fer all of the vegetables that would tide us over fer the summer plus those that Mommy would can in reserve wen the garden's offerings would be depleted.

About this time, Charles, who was my favorite cousin livin' in the country near us, jest cross the creek, came saunterin' by and axed me and Fern if'n I couldn't go ta the store with 'em. Charles wuz three years older than me and sometimes led me astray (accordin' ta Mommy) but I really liked 'em and enjoyed his company anyhow. The store warn't fur, and Fern didn't really need help watching Barbra Ann, anyhow. "Please, Fern," I bagged. So, what if Charles wuz the only one round my age? Didn't make no difference ta me. Fern said if she talked Mommy and Daddy inta lettin' me go, I had ta get her a pack of Juicy Fruit gum. "Shore!" I quickly agreed. I'd do that! I thought she'd give me a nickel fer buyin' the gum, but she didn't do that. I didn't have the heart or the gumption ta tell her she wuz fergettin' somethin'. I'm not shore why I didn't. That confused me fer I warn't shore what I wuz supposed ta do then.

Anyhow, off Charles and I went, and I worried 'bout what I wuz goin' ta do 'bout the gum all the way ta the store. In retrospect, the store warn't much of a store anyways. Hit wuz more of a makeshift sort of a thang. Ruth and Corney Taylor, not actual kinfolk—different set of Taylors—war ar neighbors. I guess Ruth wuz a bored middle-aged housewife and had persuaded Corney ta let her set up a little country store in what had been thar smokehouse. So, while Charles and Ruth war busy doin' their tradin', I saw mah chance.

The box of Juicy Fruit gum wuz right down on the counter 'neath the bench, and as quick as the bat of an eye, one pack of Juicy Fruit gum jumped rite out of that box, rite into mah pocket! Can you believe that? I felt purty clever, but I didn't say much ta Charles on ar way back home. As a matter of fact, I stayed purty quiet all the way back while Charles chattered all the time, soundin' like a magpie. And wen we got ta ar house ya know Fern didn't even wait fer Charles ta leave afore she asked me fer the gum. Don't reckon I knowed why she wuz in such a hurry fer the gum. Charles looked at me kinda funny cause he hadn't seed me take the gum. I musta turned fifty shades of red cause I wuz caught red-handed, so thar warn't nuttin' left fer me ta do but fumble in mah pocket and hand over the gum ta Fern.

Fern wuz no fool, purty smart she wuz, and realized at once that I had took the gum and hadn't paid fer hit! Actually, she asked me if'n I had charged hit ta

Daddy's tab. I shore didn't even know what she wuz talkin' 'bout. Now, what she had meant wuz fer me to charge the gum and put it on Daddy's tab (account). I didn't even know Daddy had a tab. Matter of fact, I didn't even know what a tab wuz, and I wouldn't have known what a tab wuz even if she had told me. Maybe if'n she had really splained hit ta me. Many times, communication or lack of communication leaves a lot ta be desired and, throughout mah life, has led ta more complications than thar is time fer me ta tell ya.

So, I told her I hadn't charged the gum. Atter all, thar warn't nuttin' else fer me ta do. Then, I started in jest bawlin' even though I tried ta hold it back as best as I could—another whuppin' fer me fer shore! Fern called Daddy up from the garden and told 'em what had happened—what I had done—that I had taken the Juicy Fruit gum without payin' fer hit—that I had stolen hit. I wuz cryin' so hard by this time I could hardly breathe, and I could not look at Daddy ta save mah life. Visons of the two thieves on thar crosses on the sides of Jesus wen he wuz crucified wuz bobbin' afore mah eyes. This wuz shore ta be the worst beatin I had ever got. I can't 'member what Daddy said ta me, but he called William David up from the garden. I thought fer shore hit wuz ta watch me get that whuppin'. But no, hit wuz worse! Daddy gave me a nickel and told me I had ta go back ta the store and pay Ruth fer the Juicy Fruit gum and William David wuz going with me ta make shore I did jest that! Lordy, I warn't shore I could do hit!

That wuz the longest half-mile walk of mah life. I cried and whimpered with every step of the way. I'm shore I wuz plumb out of tears long afore we got ta Ruth's little country store. If only the world would 'ave jest opened up and swallered me—that wuz the miracle I wuz prayin' fer—but no such luck. Ya can't imagine the shame and guilt I felt. I felt about the size of a piss ant. I felt that life as I had known hit had come ta an end. I drug mah feet tryin' ta make the walk last as long as possible, but as I wuz barefooted, I could only drag 'em so much. Maybe if I held my breath I could faint (would that make me die?), but I wuz never very good at faintin'.

Too soon we war almost thar. And then a miracle did happen. At least hit wuz a miracle fer me. William David stopped us, turned ta me, and told me ta give him the nickel, that **he** would go pay Ruth fer the gum while I waited fer him on the road a little distance from Ruth's store. I don't know how he handled Ruth, or what he told her, but fer me, I don't know if I have ever felt more relief in mah life. Even though thar war many times, William David and I have not seen eye ta eye and we have had ar differences. He, in his way, has alla's looked out fer me. I don't thank I could've ever loved him more than I did fer what he did fer me that day, or 'ave been more grateful. This wuz but one example of why mah big brother has always been mah hero.

Time has a way of takin' the edges off memories. I believe this one happened on a Saturday afternoon. I had a wheelie I wuz putterin' round with and wuz jest goin' up Cane Brick Hill when hit happened. (A wheelie wuz that little iron ring that comes off the hub of a wagon wheel. Ya used a long cross stick ta keep the little wheelie rollin' over potholes, through gravels and ditches, up and down hills and all kinds of obstacles. The trick wuz ta see how long ya could keep the wheelie rollin' without wreckin' hit.) I thank William David and I may 'ave been fussin' 'bout somethin'. He probably had told me ta do somethin' and I probably warn't quite ready ta do hit, or thought hit warn't mah job. William David wuz pretty good at tellin' me what ta do, but he warn't the boss of me, and if'n I wanted ta do hit, I would do hit. And, I would do hit when I wuz good and ready ta do hit, and not afore I wuz ready ta do hit! Otherwise, I jest might do hit a'tall.

Anyway, I wuz in the process of givin' him the old E nore's. William David wuz on the overhang rock cross the gravel road in the hog lot when *BANG!* I felt this big rock—felt like a boulder—hit mah head rite above mah right eye. Blood started streamin' from mah head like a stuck hog jest goin' everywhar, and I started screamin' like a banshee! William David thought he had killed me 'cause I immediately fell ta the ground. (Don't think dead people scream and cry, though.) He came runnin' 'cross the road, grabbed me up, and half carried, and half dragged me back ta the house. Mommy and Cosetta cleaned me up, bandaged me up, and put cold compresses on mah head. I had a great big gash over mah right eye and probably should've had stitches. I still have a scar up over mah eye ta this day. Also, I got a fierce headache, and wen Daddy got home, he took his leather belt off and gave both William David and me a good whuppin'. Never understood why I got a beatin' too. I guess Daddy's thought wuz that hit took two ta tango.

Daddy worked hard, takin' in whatever work he could find ta support us, but even at that, we barely made ends meet. He farmed, he did day labor, he worked the coal mines (he would come home with his clothes, his hands, his head, any part of 'em that wuzn't completely covered with coal dust—black! Had we not known hit wuz him we wouldn't 'ave recognized him. We kids would confiscate some of the carbide from his lamp supplies ta make miniature explosions ta set off tin cans in the front yard. The goal wuz ta see who could get the cans ta go the highest in the air), and he did some loggin'. He had a temporary job wen they war buildin' the Booneville Bridge cross the Kentucky River. He took in whatever work he could find, wenever he could find hit. Finally, things got so bad atter the twins war born, wen thar wuz little or no work available fer Daddy. and debts war mountin' so high thar seemed ta be no easy solution fer ar dilemma, so Mommy insisted Daddy leave the family on Island Creek and return ta Cincinnati ta find steady work. This would have occurred late November or early December 1950—more details discussed elsewhere.

(NOTE: The remaining portion of this chapter occurred approximately fifty years after our migration from the Kentucky mountains and the lapse is covered in much greater details in later chapters. Therefore, for the remainder of this chapter I'm abandoning the Appalachian vernacular.)

Years passed too quickly, and about the second week of February 2006, Mom had William David call to tell me Dad was not doing well and was not expected to live much longer and that if I wanted to see him alive, I needed to come home right away. Sue and I had moved to Grand Prairie, Texas, after we retired from a forty-one-plus-year career in the Air Force. At the time, I was employed by the Veterans Administration in Arlington, Texas, not far from where we were living in the Greater Dallas, Texas, area. Both our adult kids were living in the Greater Dallas area as well. I alerted them, and then Sue, Tim, and I flew back to Kentucky. Mary was pregnant with August (second grandson) at the time and was having other medical issues, and it was not safe, or possible for her to travel with us.

The prognosis for Dad was so grim, we went "home" expecting the worst, expecting to have to attend Dad's funeral. After deplaning, we went directly to Mom and Dad's house. Mom was holding up quite well in spite of the situation—her life partner of almost seventy-one years was expiring fast. In addition to their long-married partnership, they had dated off and on for three years prior to their actually getting married.

When we got in to see Dad in the hospital, he was hardly recognizable—an imitation of his former self. He had shrunk—lost a considerable amount of weight. I hugged him but he was skin and bones. I barely recognized him. This was hardly the towering strength of a man who so many times put the fear of God into me for the tiniest of infractions or even sometimes for the hint of one. Who, to me, had almost seemed abominable, whose word had always been law. Who bided no sass from me nor any of my siblings, less we gambled on being knocked clear into Kingdom Come—or so he had threatened! His flaming red hair was gone. What hair was left was sparse and had turned to snow. His piercing blue eyes were almost lifeless, and the color had deserted his blushing jowls. His face was sunken and had an almost alien pallor. Bones could be observed wherever his clothes left them exposed.

Time had ravaged my Daddy and replaced him with this stranger. I found it hard just looking at him as he lay in the bed that appeared much too big for him. He smiled up at me and seemed genuinely glad to see us. I recognized a glimmer of the man that I grew up with—the man whose faults were still far outweighed by his many goodness's, who worked hard all his life to give the ten kids he had sired the best life he knew how.

He wanted to know who all was there. So, everyone crowded around and said hello. It was very difficult looking at Dad, knowing that he was nearing the end. This was the man who had given me life, who had provided for me and tried his best to guide me in my formative years, and whom I had always loved (mostly). We hadn't been as close as I would have liked; I guess it had been no one's fault. It was just the way it was. I know Dad did the best he could to raise us ten kids in the "right" way, to keep us from getting too big for our britches, for getting above our raising, for knowing our place, for minding our elders, for honoring our mother and father, and for raising us in the righteous path, God's Way. Perhaps his most memorable phrase was, "If folks don't like the way I look, well, they can just turn their heads, I reckon!"

Of course, there were lots of other idiosyncrasies and special characteristics that made Dad the person he was. Dad tended to think he knew something about everything and would argue until he was blue in the face about what he thought was true. Logic or science had little, or no place in his reasoning, and I can't recall him ever admitting he was wrong. Dad could not manage money, though. Don't know whose fault that was. He was Grandma and Grandpa Taylor's baby, and I've heard Grandma spoiled him rotten. When Mom and Dad got married, I think the task fell to Mom even though Dad completed eight grades while Mom completed only four.

Dad was always a follower. As soon as he was old enough, William David (oldest brother) took on the alpha role. Dad had a bad temper and a short fuse and could let his temper get away from him quickly. He not only beat us kids unmercifully, sometimes, but he also treated his animals in the same manner. At least after beating us kids, he would often be so remorseful he would go lie down on the bed and just sob. On the other hand, Dad was a kind and generous person. He was quick to help almost anyone. Sometimes giving up on his own responsibilities, perhaps to the detriment of his own welfare, to help out someone else—like his brother, Alfred, for instance. He was the kind of person that a lot of people took advantage of. He loved children. Was always a bit of a child at heart himself, even until the day he died.

On the call alerting us to Dad's condition, we were warned that Dad might not make it until our arrival, so we packed attire so we would be ready to attend his funeral, just in case—God forbid. I took my best suit that Sue had given me as a gift—not to be crass, but it was rather expensive for us (costing upwards of a thousand dollars). After a few days, Dad seemed to be holding his own, and we decided to return to Texas, but rather than pack and repack my suit, I decided to leave it hanging in Mom and Dad's wardrobe. Dad's demise seemed imminent, and it appeared only to be a matter of time until we would need to return.

Sure enough. I got the call on February 26, 2006, that Dad had passed. Quick arrangements and a flight back to Kentucky were made, our bags mostly already packed. After returning to Kentucky and settling in a bit and consoling Mom, the next thing I did was go upstairs to check on my suit, to see if it needed pressing or anything. Lo and behold, it wasn't there! I couldn't imagine what had happened. I knew exactly where I had left the suit along with my shirt and tie. The shirt and tie were there, but no suit. I searched all around the room, but there was absolutely nowhere my suit could be. I just couldn't understand it. It was a puzzle, and I was bewildered and a little confused as to where it could be, or to what might have happened to it.

In a bit of a panic, I went downstairs and queried Mom. She told me that Bonnie Lou, my youngest sister, had retrieved the suit that Mom had purchased for Dad's burial. Unbeknownst to me, I had left my suit hanging in the vicinity of the one that Mom had selected for Dad's burial. So, when Bonnie Lou went to find Dad's suit, she found mine. Mom described Dad's suit to me, and I went back up to their room and checked their wardrobe and found the suit that Mom had described to me, which was still hanging in the wardrobe. When I brought it downstairs Mom verified it was the suit she had purchased for Dad's burial.

Then it dawned on me what had happened. My sister had provided **my** suit to the funeral home.

I made a quick call to the funeral home to see if it might still be possible to switch out the suit Mom had bought for Dad's burial for mine. It appeared the staff had already fitted my suit to Dad, which consisted of cutting, tucking, and pinning. My suit was in no condition to be retrieved! There could be no exchange. What to do??? I made a quick call to the manager of the not-too-local Menswear, and after explaining my predicament, I was able to purchase a decent suit and the manager was able to provide a seamstress to make the required alterations in time for Dad's funeral the following day. In the interim, I think I lost ten pounds. However, when I walked past Dad's coffin for the last time and I took his cold, lifeless hand in mine to say my final goodbye, he looked good, like he was sleeping—so peaceful, with no pain, no worries.... At complete rest!

In all honesty, the suit never looked that good on me.

4. MOM BACK TO ISLAND CREEK

We war in the kitchen (one room of the two-room apartment ar family occupied on Clay Street, Cincinnati, Ohio), and Mommy wuz busy bakin'. I 'member an apron, an apron dusted with flour and Mommy hummin' and sangin'. She wuz sangin' 'bout the "Sweet By and By" and then somethin' 'bout an undertaker drivin' by. I didn't know what an undertaker wuz, but I just thought Mommy sounded so happy. Do undertakers make people happy? I don't thank hit wuz the song, but the joy of sangin' and the approachin' situation that wuz sparkin' Mommy's *joie de vivre.*

Grandma Bishop and ar Aunt Cassie war comin' fer a visit. Everythang had been cleaned up, and Grandma and Aunt Cassie war going ta get ta sleep in the bed that wuz located in the kitchen. I didn't know whar the rest of the family wuz at that time, but I 'spect Daddy wuz at work. Daddy had a job at Kroger's and worked in the meat processin' portion, whar he wore arctic gear all day 'cause hit wuz so cold all the time, freezing. Brrrrrrrr!

The kids older than me war in school, I thank. Cosetta and William David. Fern, who had contracted polio wen she wuz two, wuz in rehabilitation. Mary Jane, who wuz nearly three years older than me, wuz in kindergarten. Henry, eighteen months younger than me, wuz in his crib asleep, thank goodness. Me? I musta ben somewhar over two at the time.

I know I wuz quite a handful wen I wuz a wee 'un; everyone who 'members me from that time ar quick to remind me that wuz true. However, I thank I must have ben kinda poorly, too; a sickly one. I 'member Mommy forcing a daily dose of cod liver oil down mah throat; big spoonfuls—gag a maggot. YUCK!!! Plus, I seemed ta have ben prone ta have ben easily stricken with tonsillitis (more 'bout that later).

One day, I recall I wuz playin' outside ar door, and this ole black man comes up and knocks on the door— *BAM! BAM! BAM!* —carryin' this great big (to me) coffee sack over his shoulder. Scared the wits outta me. I ran screamin' and cryin' inta the 'partment ta Mommy. I warn't used ta seein' black people, and I wuz shore that this person carryin' his big sack wuz the Booger Man come ta carry me away in that big ole sack of his'en 'cause I had ben so bad!

I hid behind Mommy's skirt and wrapped mahself around her knees, and I warn't 'bout ta sneak a peek round ta look at 'em neither. I wuz alla's bein' threatened by mah older brother and sisters that I wuz goin' ta be carried away by the Booger Man 'cause I wuz so mean and contrary and ornery. I jest knew this time, this wuz hit! **He** had come fer me! I wuz shore this must be the real Booger Man and he wuz thar fer me! I wuz mutterin' under mah breath, "I'm goin' ta be good! I promise I'm goin' ta be good! I promise I'm goin' ta be good! I'll be real good! I'll be good all'ah the time, I promise!" Turns out he wuz jest an old maintenance man (plumber maybe) and wuz thar ta unstop the community toilet located outside of ar 'partment and wuz jest wantin' ta check in with Mommy 'fore he got started. However, I wuz on mah best behavior after he left, at lest fer a little while. Didn't last too long though.

Mommy's other sister, Etta Burton, lived 'cross the Ohio River from Cincinnati in Bellevue, Kentucky. Mommy would often take a couple of us young'uns with her when she would go ta visit her sister. This involved takin' the streetcar down ta the Union Bus Station whar we would catch a Green Line Bus ta continue ar journey ta Mommy's sister's house in Bellevue, Kentucky. Cincinnati still had streetcar service in those days. Long gone now. The Green Line Bus Service provided service ta most of the local Northern Kentucky area.

Mommy and Daddy did not have a car, not that hit would 'ave done 'em any good 'cause neither of 'em could drive, nor did they ever larn. Ta mah knowledge, Mommy never drove a car, never even tried fer all I knowed. Daddy tried drivin' in later years of his life, but he wuz jest too high-strung. He tried and tried ta larn ta drive a car, but he jest couldn't do hit. Finally gave hit up as a bad effort. Daddy did buy a car, though. Hit just sat in front of his house, an eyesore. But I digress.

On this one occasion 'bout which I'm going ta tell ya, Mommy had taken me and Mary Jane with her ta visit Aunt Etta. 'Member, Mary Jane wuz nearly three years older than me, so at that time she would have been 6, and I would have been maybe 3, making ar cousin Thelma Jean 5 (Aunt Etta's daughter).

While we young'uns war playin' in thar livin' room (Aunt Etta actually had a livin' room), we heard 'em talkin' 'bout some crazy ole black lady who had bitten off some young'un's ear. Well, that put me on high alert right thar and then! But, the day went on, and nothin' extraordinary happened fer the rest of the mornin'.

After lunch, though, Aunt Etta gave the three of us—
Mary Jane, Thelma Jean, and me—a nickel each ta go
ta the little family grocery store jest down and cross
the street and round the corner ta treat arselves ta a
Popsicle. We tootled off ta the store real quick 'fore
Aunt Etta changed her mind or Mommy said we
couldn't go.

I suppose we war a sight goin' ta the store cause we
had ta cross a street; looked both ways, checked hit
twice, hurry but didn't run, and when we got inside
the store, we had an awful dilemma tryin' ta select jest
the best and right Popsicle flavor (I got cherry,
Thelma Jean got orange, and Mary Jane got grape).
We unwrapped ar Popsicles and war greedily feedin'
ar faces as we started ar return trip home. We war
bout ta recross the street but not 'fore, we checked
very carefully ta make shore thar war no cars in sight,
and as afore, looked both ways, checked hit twice,
hurry but didn't run.

Wen, lo and behold, this little ole black lady popped
up rite in front of us. She didn't look like nobody I'd
never seen afore. She wuz kinda squat, warn't a lot
taller than Mary Jane, and had on clothes that looked
really strange ta me. She had on a dark purple head
rag, that not only covered her head, but went way past
her bosoms, clear down past her kneecaps. Her bright
red dress swept down ta, and swirled round her shoes,
almost ta the ground. And she looked rite at me with
this dangerous-lookin' gleam in her eyes (I thought),
and then she gave me this great big grin showin' me a
mouth full of pearly white teeth, 'cept she had two
really big gold teeth in the very front and they all war
jest a shinin'. Her lips war bright red, even though I
didn't see no blood drippin' from 'em, I felt certain

they could bite real hard and could easily bite through mah ear.

I could hardly breathe 'cause then I knowed, I shorely knowed right that minute. She had ta be the one who had bitten that poor young'un's ear right off. She wuz the one Aunt Etta had been tellin' everybody 'bout. I knowed hit wuz her! I nearly wet mah pants rite then and thar, on the sidewalk. I started in screamin', and then we all three started in a screamin' and a cryin' at the top of ar lungs, "It's her! It's her! It's her!" We war yellin'! And we flew back ta Aunt Etta's house as fast as we could go. We didn't want our ears bitten off, too. No siree!!

We fergot 'bout checkin' this way and that away and checkin' hit twice. We war runnin' fer our lives! I thought I heard a soft chuckle as we fled and left the poor lady standin' thar wonderin' what in the world wuz goin' on. She looked atter the somewhat raggedy-taggedy trio of wide-eyed, not-yet-school-age innocents who looked like they war refugees from the Kentucky mountains and had never seed a black woman afore. Lordy, hit shore wuz a crazy world. The poor lady would have a good laugh tellin' folks 'bout this little incident later over supper, probably wonderin' what in the world had gotten into those crazy young'uns: *What is the matter with 'em?* Jest goes to show ya what a little overheard rumor and the overactive imaginations of three wee youngsters can generate!

In April 1947, Daddy moved the whole family back ta Island Creek, Kentucky, from Cincinnati to Grandma Taylor's old homeplace. This wuz the same house that Dad's family had moved ta when he wuz 7 from Harlan, Kentucky. A few weeks atter we moved back to Kentucky, Earnest Moore, who wuz married ta

Mommy's first cousin Ruth (Bishop) Moore, daughter of Janie Bishop, Grandpa's sister, stopped by and he axed Mommy, "Fannie, ar y'all gettin' ready ta move back to Cincinnati?"

Hit appeared that fer some unknown reason, somethin' had upset me—got mah dander up—and I wuz havin' a hissy fit at Mommy. Mommy, fer her part, wuz busy tendin' ta other thangs and wuz givin' me the silent treatment and 'norin' me. I wuz havin' none of that, so everythang I could lift, carry, or drag I had taken out of the house and thrown off the porch inta the yard. Hence, the question from Earnest Moore wen he saw all the paraphernalia in the yard. I had told Mommy that I warn't goin' ta live thar with 'em anymore and they warn't goin' ta live thar neither. They needed ta get themselves back ta Cincinnati. I don't recall mah rationale fer insistin' the family return ta the big city, but I had managed ta throw an assortment of thangs out into the yard; almost everythang I could, evidently. Don't 'member why. Remains a mystery ta this day.

Another day when Daddy wuz off workin' and atter a big rain Mommy thought hit would be a treat ta take us all fishin' down ta the creek. The best place wuz the Deep Hole, located jest beyond the end of the garden whar ar fork of Island Creek takes a big bend, and thar wuz a nice sandy beach on the other side. We later discovered hit made a great place ta play. So, the Deep Hole wuz whar we went ta set up fer ar fishin' expedition.

Because of the recent rains, the creek wuz all muddy and swollen and the water wuz runnin' purty swift. We had cane poles with a hook and thread tied ta the end with worms fer fishin'. Worms war plentiful. All a person had ta do wuz go ta the barnyard. The manure-rich dirt made a nice breedin' ground fer worms and with jest a little effort, a few strokes of the hoe, a person could get a whole can full of wiggly worms within minutes. William David dug up a whole bunch of 'em and put 'em in a tin can with a little bit of dirt to keep 'em from dryin' out.

Our fishin' wuz more fer recreation and ta keep us busy than fer sport, I reckoned. If'n we caught any fish, well, that would ah been icin' on the cake. I tried puttin' one of them worms on mah hook but hit wuz jest too dern wiggly, so William David came to mah rescue. He grabbed that ole worm and squished its mouth open, and wen he started ta stick the sharp end of the hook in its open mouth, I thought shorely that ole worm wuz going ta start throwin' up. No siree. William David wuz too quick fer 'em. He pushed that hook right down his throat and I thought that worm was going ta wiggle his tail right off 'cause he wuz wigglin' so hard. Then William David threaded that ole worm on mah hook as simple as ya please, scooched hit down all the way ta the end of the hook with the tail of the worm still wigglin' at the other end.

Anyway, we war lined up along the bank of the creek with ar cane poles and fishin' lines waitin' ta catch a great big'en. I got jest a few nibbles but enough ta get me all excited fer any minute I wuz goin' ta show 'em who the real fisherman wuz. Once, I even thought I had a big fish on mah line. I could see mah fishin' line bobbin' up and down and I felt the slightest jerk on mah cane pole, but when I jerked up mah cane pole, he got away real fast. Aw, shucks! A little doubt then began to creep up in mah mind that maybe, jest maybe, this might not be mah day to catch the big'en.

Everett wuz still jest a toddler so he wuz attached to Mommy's side. Henry, on the other hand, wuz bound he wuz goin' ta help me fish! I wuz purty shore I could handle the job all by mahself and wuz already disgruntled that I hadn't caught even one fish a'tall. However, Mommy said I had ta let Henry help me fish. Now we war always told ta share and help each other, but I warn't always the placid, kind, gracious, loving person that y'all sees today. And I honestly felt I could do a better job by mahself of catchin' a big fish. So, I wuz torn as ta what I wuz told ta do and supposed ta do, and what I shore nuff didn't want ta do.

So, on Mommy's instructions, I had ta let Henry sit in mah lap and let him help me fish. Now I warn't real happy 'bout hit, and I knowed the devil his self wuz settin' right on mah shoulder while Henry wuz tuggin' on my cane pole. I somewhat disgruntledly allowed Henry the satisfaction of imposing on mah fishin' rights fer awhile, but wen I wuz shore no one ('specially Mommy) wuz lookin' in mah direction, I quickly gave Henry a great big push with all mah might, and only Henry's guardian angel, or maybe mah guardian angel, kept Henry from bein' swallered by the ragin' waters below us and carried away ta Kingdom Come. (He didn't actually fall inta the creek.)

However, that wuz the end of mah fishin' fer that day. Henry jest started in bawlin' his head off. Of course, hit warn't mah fault Henry wuz so clumsy that he had almost fallen inta the creek. Me, why I would never push mah little baby brother into the muddy waters, now would I? Heavens forbid! Henry wuz jest a big crybaby tryin' ta get me in trouble all ah the time, warn't he? And he usually did succeed. Shore did that time, too. Thar war witnesses who war more than willin' ta come ta his help and ta share what they'd seed, and point their fangers at me, and say hit wuz all mah fault. Everybody agreed. Time fer some willer switch tea fer me. Sometimes Mommy could jest dish hit out almost as well as Daddy, and I don't know if ya've ever had willer switch tea, but hit stangs like heck, and I don't recommend hit. Don't even ever recommend ya even try hit!

Now that Mommy wuz back near Grandma Bishop, she wuz spected ta go and help her out. I recall Mommy takin' Cosetta, Mary Jane, and me with her on a trip to Grandma and Grandpa's. We stopped fer a little rest at the end of Island Creek and Highway 11, whar now the bridge spans Island Creek. Thar wuz no bridge at that time. However, workers had prepared the apron fer the impendin' bridge, so Mary Jane and I attempted ta slide down the apron 'cause hit looked like a good slidin' place. The rough concrete almost took the skin right off ar bones and we almost lost some of ar clothing in the process. Fer ar unsuccessful efforts, we got a good tongue-lashing from Mommy but no whuppins.

Wen we got ta Grandma's, Mommy started in sewin' fer Grandma. Grandma's stash of sewin' materials consisted of feed sacks and flour sacks which came in colors and designs and war used fer the majority of Grandma's and Aunt Cassie's clothes. Many poor families made use of those materials. Manufacturers of flour and livestock feed used this material as a marketin' ploy ta sell their products. Grandma had saved up a whole bunch of these sacks fer Mommy ta work on. Mommy started right in makin' dresses and bonnets and all kinds of paraphernalia.

Grandma's and Aunt Cassie's bonnets war most interestin'. Grandma and Aunt Cassie never went outside without their bonnets on thar heads. Wen they came inside, they would hang 'em on a post beside the door. Wen they went ta town, visitin' or somewhar outside the holler they would wear hats instead of thar bonnets. Grandpa alla's wore some kind of head coverin wen he wuz outside, too. He had a straw had fer summer and a felt hat fer dress up and a cap with ear flaps fer cold weather. They made shore I had a cover fer my head as well, wenever I wuz stayin' at thar house. They didn't want me gettin' brain fever! When I would stay with 'em, I would have a straw hat ta wear that grandma would buy me. Should I forget ta put hit on, I would be quickly reminded that if'n I wuz goin' ta be outside, I should be wearin' mah hat like mah grandpa. Thar wuz somethin' 'bout catchin' brain fever and hit wuz supposed ta be somethin' very, very bad.

Mommy began her life not fur from whar Grandpa and Grandma war livin' wen I first met 'em. She wuz born in a little house on Bee Branch near what wuz called the head of Buffalo, which wuz a mile or so on the other side of the ridge (over the mountain) on a small farm given to Grandpa and Grandma as a wedding present by Grandpa's mom and dad, John and Catherine (Cat) Bishop. This wuz the same house that Mommy and Daddy war married in on June 5, 1935. Grandpa had mortgaged the property ta buy Uncle Floyd (their oldest child/son) a horse. Grandpa wuz unable ta pay off the mortgage and, tharfore, lost the farm. The house they war livin' in wen I first stayed with 'em wuz bought by Uncle Wiley, the uncle fer whom I am named. Uncle Wiley wuz their third child, second son, and wuz two years older than Mommy.

Mommy and Daddy courted fer some time afore they actually got hitched; I believe from the time Mommy wuz 14 and Daddy wuz 17. Daddy lived four miles away and church seemed ta be a way ta help light the fire fer their attraction. Daddy almost alla's came a courtin' ah ridin' on his mule.

However, as I understand hit, hit was not all smooth sailin'. Somewhar durin' that interim, Uncle Floyd persuaded Mommy ta go ta Ohio and join him whar he was livin' fer a spell. She accepted a position as a maid that Uncle Floyd had found fer her through some contacts of his. I don't know how long that lasted and whether Mommy found bein' a maid wuz not fer her, if she felt out of place, or maybe she missed the callin's of the mountains, the sounds of the whip-poor-wills at night, or the presence of Daddy. Maybe she wuz yearnin' fer her beloved, or perhaps she wuz lonely or jest homesick.

Anyway, she came back to Bee Branch atter jest a few months. *But* if they say absence makes the heart grow fonder, I'm not shore what they say about absence in relationship ta the little green monster. I don't thank Daddy realized Mommy had returned from Ohio fer when Mommy arrived fer church services jest after she returned, what did she see but Daddy and her first cousin gettin' ready ta go into church services. And they war holdin' hands and lookin' real cozy together! I'm told Mommy gave a loud piercin' scream and ran right twixt 'em jest as fast as she could go—breakin' them right apart, knockin' their hands asunder. I believe Daddy and Mommy's cousin war in fer a big shock.

However, unknown war the reactions of Daddy and Mommy's cousin ta Mommy's outburst. Atter all, Mommy had had first dibs on Daddy, but I'm not shore what kind of understandin' Mommy had left Daddy with when she took off fer Ohio. Daddy and Substitute Sweetheart war both lucky they didn't get a good thrashin' from Mommy even though I've never known Mommy ta be that violent. However, when she got her dander up, she could hold her own with the best of 'em even though she often deferred ta Daddy ta fight her main battles. Atter the church incident, Mommy and Daddy picked up from whar they had ben afore Mommy's escapade ta Ohio. They didn't miss a beat atter Mommy's somewhat rude and rather physical breakup twixt Daddy and her cousin.

(As an aside, Mommy wuz also supposed ta have courted Bradley Kinkaid, who lived near Booneville and who wuz later to become a fairly well-known country and western sanger. [I have one of his LPs and a CD.] I believe that wuz afore Daddy.)

When Mommy wuz 16 and Daddy wuz 19, he asked her ta marry 'em. However, Grandma wuz a formidable force (and in truth, Daddy wuz skeered of her), so Daddy persuaded Henry Clay, the minister, ta go fer 'em ta ax Grandma fer Mommy's hand in marriage. Grandma said no—not just no, but heck no—that Mommy wuz jest too young, plus Grandma needed her help at home. (Note: It wuz Grandma's permission Daddy sought, not Grandpa's; a small point 'bout who held the authority in the family.)

For his troubles, Reverend Henry Clay wuz bitten by Grandma and Grandpa's dog. Grandma told me hit wuz God's will and jest payment fer preacher man Henry Clay's trouble fer trying ta interfere whar he ought not ta be. Daddy, bein' somewhat devious and perhaps havin' an ulterior motive, offered ta get Mommy pregnant so Grandma would be forced ta let 'em get married. Now, Mommy has all her life ben a very religious person, and thar wuz no way she would 'ave gone alone with Daddy's generous offer. Hit made no difference how much she wuz enamored by ar Daddy or how persuasive he wuz.

But Daddy stayed true ta Mommy and patiently waited, and they did get married at Grandma and Grandpa's house on Bee Branch. Henry Clay, the same minister who wuz bitten by the family dog for his earlier efforts, still stuck by 'em and officiated at thar marriage ceremony on June 5, 1935. Mommy wuz 18 and Daddy wuz 21 at that time. (By the by, when Henry, my younger brother by eighteen months, wuz born, he wuz named Henry Clay Taylor, honorin' the minister who had attempted ta intercede fer Mommy and Daddy.)

Mommy started her married life livin' with Daddy and his mom and dad. She got pregnant with Cosetta that first month of wedded bliss in spite of limited privacy. In her final stages of pregnancy, she went ta stay with Grandpa and Grandma Bishop. Grandpa Taylor wuz havin' severe medical problems and actually passed on April 7, 1936, seventeen days atter Cosetta's birth. Durin' the birthing process, the midwife assistin' Mommy ran into difficulties; hit was goin' ta be a breach birth. Grandma Taylor, who wuz considered ta be the expert in that entire area, had ta be called in ta assist with her birthin'.

Cosetta wuz born March 21, 1936, on Grandma and Grandpa Bishop's twenty-ninth anniversary. Grandma Taylor handed her ta Daddy, and he clasped her ta his self and kissed her even afore they had a chance ta clean her up. Of course, everybody thar war aghast that Daddy would do sech a thang, but he war so enamored and burstin' with so much pride that he jest couldn't help his self. Mommy and Daddy later moved ta Uncle Murphy's place in Pebworth, Kentucky, near Booneville, Kentucky (Fern wuz born thar July 13, 1937).

They then moved briefly back ta the Taylor homestead (where William David wuz born December 11, 1938), then ta a log cabin up in Haunty Holler, whar Mary Jane wuz born July 22, 1940. Atter Haunty Holler, they moved ta the Chicken House jest a stone's throw from Grandma Taylor's, whar I wuz born, and then ta Clay Street, Cincinnati, whar I have discussed elsewhere. (Just a note: Of the oldest five of us young'uns, Grandma Taylor delivered all except Fern. I have the honor of bein' the last one of us young'uns Grandma Taylor delivered.)

Durin' the early months of their marriage, Mommy had a hankerin' ta go back and visit her folks up on Upper Wolf Creek. Well, hit was only a little over four miles ta whar they lived, so Mommy and Daddy set out on foot. At that time, Mommy wuz only mildly pregnant with Cosetta. A problem arose when they got ta the Kentucky River, fer hit had been rainin' a lot in the last several days and the river wuz purty swollen. The water wuz over waist high on Daddy, or so they said. Mommy didn't know how ta swim, and Daddy didn't want her gettin' wet in her delicate condition. The solution wuz fer Daddy ta carry Mommy cross the muddy waters at the shoals at the foot of Upper Wolf Creek. However, nothin' wuz simple.

Daddy had on his best overalls and didn't want ta get 'em all wet. The next part of the solution wuz ta remove 'em and have Mommy hold 'em while he carried her cross the swollen, muddy river. Another problem though: Daddy didn't have no swimming trunks ta wear, and worse yet, he warn't even wearin' no underwear. What if'n someone came up unannounced and saw 'em with no clothes on—only in his birthday suit? What would they thank?

The continuin' solution turned out ta be fer Mommy ta strip off her bloomers and Daddy ta put 'em on fer the trip cross the ragin', murky waters. Jest goes ta prove the old adage that true love has no boundaries.

The rest of the journey continued without incident. I suppose the bloomers war wrung out and Mommy either put 'em back on, or they war jest stowed away and both Mommy and Daddy war without anythang on, down there. (Au natural?) Of course, they still had on their outside clothes.

Mommy wuz a carin' and lovin' mother, and she took care of us the best she could. We all war more than a handful, and wen I look back, I wuz probably the brattiest of the whole bunch. Later, Barbra Ann may have come in a close second, not shore. While Daddy wuz the main disciplinarian, Mommy did her share. She would send us down ta the creek bed ta fetch ar own switches fer punishment, and should they be insufficient ta suit her, we would be sent back fer somethin' more appropriate. There would be no approval of short, flimsy switches selected that might break easily or not be up ta the demands of a proper switchin'. Her favorites war willer switches (hence my earlier alludin' to willer switch tea). Fer more serious infractions, she would defer punishment ta Daddy and his belt. We would have ta wait 'til he got home fer that belt and his temper—and sweat and squirm while we waited, sometimes most of the day. Sometimes the anticipation wuz worse than the actual punishment, certainly lasted longer and alla's gave us pause fer thought. Not shore how much hit changed ar attitude or ar behavior.

Mommy alla's said she loved us all equally. She and Daddy may have actually believed hit. Or even they might have loved us all equally but hit shore didn't peer that way ta most of us wen we wuz growin' up. Cosetta, the oldest, wuz naturally favored. But then she had so much responsibility. She wuz like a little mother ta us most of the time. She wuz often left alone ta care fer a bunch of us while she wuz still jest a child herself, as fer back as I can 'member.

Cosetta had no childhood; she wuz robbed of hit ta take care of us young'uns and ta help with all the household duties. Mommy wuz always pregnant or so hit seemed durin' Mommy and Daddy's first fifteen years of marriage. I know Mommy couldn't 'ave managed without her. Every eighteen months or so, Mommy wuz shootin' out another baby 'cept twice she had a miscarriage: once between Mary Jane and me and once between Everett and Barbra Ann. Cosetta wuz pulled from school after the fifth grade ta help Mommy at home 'til Daddy found her a live-in housekeepin'/babysittin' job 'bout the time she turned 15 wen she left home, never ta return agin. She got married wen she wuz 17.

Next, thar wuz Fern, who had polio wen she wuz two and had ben in and out of hospitals and rehabilitation centers ever since. When Fern got polio, thar wuz such a scare about polio that no one wanted ta be near anybody who might have the sickness (virus) or even anybody who wuz even round somebody who had polio. Everybody wuz too skeered. When Fern got sick and the symptoms pointed ta what Mommy and Daddy had heard might be polio (Fern wuz losin' control of her muscles; she could no longer walk or even stand on her own), everybody avoided ar family (what thar wuz of hit at that time) like the plague.

Daddy could not get anybody ta take him and Fern ta Booneville ta see the doctor, so he had ta walk and carry Fern all eleven miles.

When the doctor saw Fern and examined her, he wuz purty shore she did have the onset of polio and instructed Daddy ta take her ta Lexington ta the Polio Center fer further evaluation. Daddy wuz able ta catch the Greyhound Bus ta Lexington, whar he and Fern war isolated in the back until they arrived in Lexington. Upon thar arrival at the Polio Center, Fern wuz evaluated and diagnosed and immediately put inta an iron lung, whar she survived fer a long time.

Wen they first started lettin' her out of the lung, they fitted her with complete lag braces on both lags, and she had ta start walkin' with crutches. Her left side had almost withered away (atrophied). As she got older, some muscular coordination did come back, and as she advanced inta adulthood, she wuz able ta give up the crutches and modify the braces so that she only had ta wear a short brace (below the knee) on her right lag and a full lag brace on her left lag. Even though she wuz able ta give up her crutches, she sometimes needed a body ta lean on in difficult situations or challengin' terrains—steps, steep hills, rough terrain, etc.

Fern wuz a special case. Because of her hospital stays and rehabilitation therapies, she had had all these experiences and had met all these different people. I wuz always fascinated by Fern. She could sass and get away with hit—usually. Her sense of humor wuz exceptional, and did she ever have a mouth on her; Lord, did she ever! She wuz ever ready ta get personal inta everyone's business. She never minded askin' the most intimate details 'bout a person's goin's ons. She almost never knew when ta keep her trap shut.

However, she managed ta get her share of whuppins, too. She had ta wear some kind of brace(s) most of her life and used crutches when she wuz younger, as I jest mentioned. She had ta have support wen she traversed ta the outhouse and then back agin, and often, that wuz me. She wuz smart as a new whip, and Mommy hoped she would finish school and make somethin' of herself. Cause of her handicap, she wuz bussed ta the Booneville schools and interacted with other kids and seemed ta know what wuz goin' on in the world. I 'member her larnin' me the songs "*In the Streets of Laredo*" and "*God Bless America*," and she had lots of interestin' stories ta share. However, she dropped out of school after finishin' the eighth grade and got married wen she was 16 ta Robert James (Jim) Smith, who wuz Mommy's age, twenty years older 'en Fern. Jim wuz a story into himself.

Jim, Fern's husband, had been in WWII and wuz wounded at Normandy; he wuz shot in the lag and suffered from what is now called PTSD. I don't recall the why, but he took me ta visit his family up in Clay County without Fern. I 'member hit wuz atter dark wen we got ta the turnoff from the gravel road onta the dirt road that ran back up in the holler whar his ma lived in a little cabin. So, at the turnoff, we stopped at Metcalf's little country store and Jim bought us a hunk of baloney and some crackers fer supper and an orange pop. Seems like I 'member his ma and one of Jim's sisters living in that little cabin. The next mornin', his ma made us some breakfast, and atterwards, we drove ta visit 'nother one of his sisters and stopped at her house. I wuz surprised ta larn that she and her husband had had twenty-two children, fourteen of which lived ta adulthood—quite a brood.

Next in line wuz William David, third oldest and the eldest son. We all thought our parents believed the sun rose and set by him. Ta be fair, though, he did have a lot of responsibilities (like Cosetta). Atter Daddy left fer work in Cincinnati, he wuz the man of the house. But even afore Daddy left fer Cincinnati, we all felt he carried a certain preference. Daily, he went ta school early and started the fire in the big pot-bellied stove in ar one-room schoolhouse so the temperature would be tolerable when school picked up (started). He did the milking and fed the livestock. He wuz the hunter with (or without) Daddy killin' squirrels, rabbits, raccoons, and possums (I don't really 'member any possums) ta supplement ar meager larder.

Mary Jane, who wuz next older than me, well, she kinda got stuck with the scullery work, chief cleaner, and bottle washer. While tendin' ta her clean-up duties at night she would become a songstress, sangin' at the top of her lungs, much ta the annoyance of the rest of the clan who war attemptin' ta listen ta some program on the battery-powered radio such as "*The Shadow*" or "*The Lone Ranger.*" Many of the words of her diatribe made little rhyme nor reason—otherwise fabricated. However, mind ya, I don't 'member any of the rest of us volunteerin' ta assist her. Agin like Cosetta, she wuz pulled from school atter the fifth grade, and wen we moved ta Cincinnati, found employment at the Old Mill Cafeteria wen she wuz 16 and got married afore she turned 17. Wen we first moved ta Cincinnati, Mary Jane, Thelma Jean, and I chummed round a lot together. We called arselves Huey, Dewey, and Louie. Wen the Elvis Presley movie, "*Love Me Tender*" first came out she took me to the mid-night showing. Then Mary Jane got all interested in boys and that was that.

Following me wuz Henry, the more aggressive one, the hunter, and the skirt chaser. When we war littluns, Henry, Everett, and I war almost the same age; there wuz a thirty-four-month span from mah birth to Everett's with Henry 'tween us. We played together some and fought each other—a lot—like tomcats and got more than a few whuppins together. Of course, hit wuz always one of the other ones' fault. I sorta pulled away wen I stayed with Grandma and Grandpa Bishop wen I wuz four, and then every summer wen school wuz out and a lot of weekends as well. I missed (thankfully) havin' ta share in the hand-me-down shuffle in clothes that Henry and Everett had ta endure. Grandma alla's bought me mah school clothes, so they tended ta be a little nicer. That wuz 'cause they usually came from Sears & Roebuck or Montgomery Wards. Do I sound a little uppity? Maybe, I suppose.

Wen we war very little, Henry, Everett, and I tended ta be competitive—that is, very, *very* competitive. Daddy brought home this wee beagle hound pup and tol me hit wuz mine. Now I never had anythang that wuz jest mine, mine by mahself that I didn't have ta share. I had always lived in a world of sharin' 'cept when I wuz at mah grandma's. Hit wuz no wonder I loved stayin' with her and Grandpa so much. She could wind me round her little fanger and I would jest eat hit up.

Now Daddy knowed the beagle hound pup wuz still goin' ta be his 'en an' that the hound wuz goin' ta really be fer the whole family. Daddy also knowed he could trust me ta care fer the pup an' make shore hit got fed and watered if'n I bought in ta the thought that I had any part of ownership of the pup, and that's why he tol me the pup wuz mine. I did take good care of 'em, 'cause I wuz gullible, lonely, an' really wanted somethin' ta belong ta me and most of all 'cause I really loved mah pup, Buster. Buster wuz a darlin' puppy, and I poured all the pint-up love I owned inta that little dog. He wuz mostly light brown but had a little black saddle and the tip of his muzzle wuz covered with white. His head wuz brown all over. 'cept in the center of his forehead, he had a white star. I called hit, the Star of Buster. His chest wuz also white and all four feet war white, too. His tail wuz light brown like most of the rest of 'em, 'cept the very tip of his tail wuz a russet red. His big floppy ears hung below his chin and swung like pendulums wenever he wuz excited, which happened a lot. He had the brightest eyes, and wen he wuz happy, they sparkled, but wen he wuz sad, they war pitiful and would stare at me, and he would look like he wuz goin' ta cry every time I had ta leave him alone, by his-self.

Wenever I would come ta fetch 'em atter school fer our little walks, he would yap at me and then he'd be all over me, jumpin' and lickin' me like everythang. He had the wickedest tongue and wuz so squirmy I couldn't hold him still. But atter ar walks and playin' awhile, he would be content ta lay in mah lap and let me pet 'em and I could almost hear 'em purr. As he would start ta doze off, I would start in scratchin' behind his ear and his little hind lag would start in scratchin' and kickin', and if'n I started scratchin' faster, his lag would start going faster too. If'n I would go real fast, his little lag would be goin' forty miles a minute. Then I'd stop real quick, and he'd look up at me with those wistful, beautiful eyes and if'n I stayed still, he'd poke me with his nose, and if'n I still 'nored 'em, he'd jump up and start licking mah face with his sloppy tongue all the while waggin' his tail so fast I wuz a feared hit wuz goin' ta fall off. Then I'd have ta pull 'em off me.

Hit wuz obvious Daddy had played me, but I didn't mind. As a matter of fact, I liked hit. Anyway, I wuz never a big eater, so I would save a little of whatever I wuz havin' ta eat fer the pup, be hit a piece of cornpone, or a biscuit, or a part of mah gravy, or whatever, and I made shore Buster had water and wuz secure in the smokehouse whar I kept him most of the time wen I warn't thar. Ever day atter school, I would come home and let Buster out of the smokehouse ta play and we both got ar exercise, together. So, Buster really wuz mine 'til the school term ended no matter what anybody else said.

Then, as in years past, I wuz off ta stay with Grandma and Grandpa. Buster wuz more than half grown by that time and I really would have liked ta have taken 'em with me, but that wuz a no-go. Atter I had packed mah thangs in a poke and told everybody I wuz leavin', I still had ta say good-bye ta Buster.

Buster wuz waitin' fer me at the door with his tail goin' sixty miles a minute trying ta jump all over me. He thought I wuz goin' ta take 'em fer a walk. I did reach down and picked 'em up and hugged 'em and let 'em nuzzle mah neck. He started in lickin' mah face, which tickled, so I had ta let 'em down. I let 'em foller me ta the gate, and I patted his head one last time. Then, I quickly squeezed thru the gate and shut hit tight behind me and latched hit. Buster rared up on the gate with his tail still jest ah waggin' and his ears ah floppin'. But as I walked away, he started in ah whinin' with a few intermittent barks and even a growl or two, and he wuz scratchin' at the gate jest baggin' me ta take 'em with me.

As I started out on mah way ta Grandma's house, I could see thar war dark clouds gatherin' overhead, and then thar wuz a light drizzle of rain that started ta fall. Afore I hurried off, I glanced back at 'em and I swear I could see tears well up in his little eyes—mine too. Hit wuz really hard fer me ta leave 'em thar. Worse yet, I didn't realize hit, but that would be the last time I would ever see mah little dog. Fer, while I wuz gone that summer, Henry took Buster huntin' with a pack of other dogs, and I wuz told he sicced the other dogs on Buster and they wound up killin' mah poor little Buster pup, the first livin' thang that I thought that wuz actually mine. I jest laid claim ta 'em fer awhile and took care of 'em and had a chance to give 'em mah love fer a short while. I, of course, wuz very hurt and saddened by what Henry had done, and I grieved a lot. I'll never ferget what Henry supposedly did. I long ago fergave Henry's indiscretion, but I guess I'll alla's have trouble letting hit go.

While I wuz away at Grandma and Grandpa's durin' school summer vacation, Henry, mah brother eighteen months younger than me, wuz attemptin' ta become the third hunter in the family post-Daddy and William David. Henry later did become an honest ta goodness, genuine, successful hunter.

But ta the event ta which I am relatin'... Henry had set out a couple of traps and wuz in the process of checkin' his traps. Wen he approached his first trap he was disappointed that thar wuz nothin' in hit. Empty. The trap wuz jest like he'd left hit. The second trap wuz located over a small embankment, and the sight wuz partially blocked by a big fallen log and hidden by a group of hazelnut bushes but had been set nearby some varmint's den. Wen Henry hoisted himself over the fallen log and parted the hazelnut bushes he quickly spotted movement in his trap. He thought ta his self, *by golly, I've caught mahself a fox!* but be wuz too far away ta be fer shore, so he cautiously approached his trap, hardly daring to breathe, almost on his tippy toes.

Now normally, a trapped varmint will rise on hits haunches and face forward barin' hits teeth, growlin', threatenin', showin' that hit's ready ta pounce and defend hit's self. Not so with this critter. Hit turned hits self round as if hit wuz goin' ta run away in spite of hits lag bein' caught in the trap and what must have been agonizin' pain, lowered hits head, kinda scrunched up hits body and raised hits black-and-white-feathered tail skyward.

As soon as Henry wuz in close enough range, the varmint let loose with a nauseous, sickly, all-encompassin' fine spray that covered Henry from head ta foot. His exposed skin, his face and hands, and 'specially his eyes began ta burn and stang like he wuz on fire. In spite of his self, tears started flowin' freely, runnin' down his face, and he started ta gag somethin' awful. He felt like he couldn't breathe. His lungs war protestin' as the vile vapors engulfed 'em and tween the gaggin' he began ta cough.

Hit warn't a fox a'tall. Hit wuz a polecat (a black and white skunk), and the polecat had dranched Henry good and proper in payment fer trappin' 'em in that dern trap. He backed away while holdin' his hand ta his mouth and doin' his best ta breathe. He turned round quickly and ran as fast as he could, lickety-split, pushin' his self wildly through the bushes, runnin' and jumpin' helter-skelter down the mountainside. He tussled through a briar patch with the thorns grabbin' 'em ever which ah way almost rippin' his clothes, scratchin' his skin causin 'em ta bleed but stoppin' him not. He hardly felt the pain, and what pain he did feal he 'nored .

He bounded cross the couple of hollers that twisted in his way 'til he wuz out of breath. He finally reached the creek and, as quick as he could, jumped inta the creek, clothes and all. He soaked his self in the creek fer hours, lettin' the water cover all of him as much as he possible, even dunking his whole head under the water, but then jest keepin' his face exposed so he could breathe, 'til his skin wuz gettin' all wrinkly. Though no matter how much soakin' he did, thar wuz no gettin' rid of the polecat's retaliation, and fer all of his efforts, he earned himself a berth sleepin' in the barn loft 'til the polecat's perfume wore off. Atter some several nights. Phew!!!

Now Everett wuz next in line. Everett held the record fer bein' the baby in the family fer the longest time 'til the end of the baby-producin' years—three years and five months in all. He had a hard time givin' up his title when Barbra Ann wuz born 'cause he still wanted ta be the baby. As the baby he got preferential treatment, and he knew hit. However, the truth wuz he had ta give up the title of bein' the baby of the family and settle on that he wuz still the baby boy, albeit temporarily. Everett wuz also the good lookin' one, alla's. Fortunately, we had few mirrors round fer Everett wuz hard-pressed ta pass a mirror without admirin' the feller grinnin' back at 'em.

As teenagers, Henry, Everett, and I would go scourin' round ta the local churches; hit wuz a good way ta meet girls. Interestingly, as the church services would near thar closin' sessions and thar call fer the prayer rail went out, I would go up along with Henry and Everett, but no matter how reverently I concentrated and prayed, I could never get the blessin' and zeal they seemed ta get, so atter awhile I held back and no longer joined 'em at the prayer rail.

Barbra Ann. Sweet, angelical Barbra Ann. I wuz first notified bout Barbra Ann's arrival wen Daddy came over ta Grandma's ta do some plowin' and told me I had a new baby sister. Imagine that. Mah first real interaction with her wuz atter returnin' home afore school took up. I had ta take her dirty diapers down ta the creek and warsh out the poop. However, she wuz such a cute baby and I had ta nuss (hold) her, rock her, and give her her bottle. I enjoyed that. The rest I jest took in stride.

Babies ar so innocent. She wuz such an intelligent toddler, too. She has always ben smart and entertainin'. Wen she wuz jest a wee thing (maybe 5), and we war all in the main bedroom whar Jim, Fern's husband, wuz shaving, Barbra Ann announced, all innocent-like ta all of us, that she shaved too; she jest shaved with the butcher knife! We never larned why Barbra Ann thought she felt the need ta shave at her young age. She wuz alla's the stubborn one, stubborn as an ornery mule, more stubborn than me (I thank), and wen she had her mind made up, nothin' could change hit come hell or high water! Because of that, she wuz often bullied and/or beaten unmercifully not only by Daddy but by her older brothers as well.

Wen I left for the Air Force, she warn't quite twelve, and wen I returned, she wuz almost fifteen but had turned into a ravishing beauty. While I wuz home on furlough, I took Barbra Ann on kinda a brother/sister date to the Shubert Theater ta see *The Merry Widow*.

Barbra Ann left school when she wuz 15 and married this dashing young soldier (Senor) who hailed from *"South of the Border down Mexico Way."*

Bonnie Lou wuz the oldest twin (by fifteen minutes), and ya know how cruel kids can sometimes be. Well, we (I do hope I wuzn't included) ribbed her unkindly sometimes, tellin' her that they (the hospital staff) got her mixed up at the hospital, implyin' that she warn't one of us. That wuz jest cruel. Thar wuz at least one incident whar Mommy had been brought the wrong set of twins while she wuz at the Onedia Hospital fer thar birth. Hit seemed like a second set of twins war born jest 'bout the same time as Bonnie Lou and Bobbie Jean.

Anyway, Bonnie Lou always tended ta be a bit sullen. As a baby and even wen she wuz younger, she wuz in constant motion. She rocked all the time. Hit wuz a good thang she and Bobbie Jean war at the end of the line. Hit appeared Bonnie Lou wuz goin' ta rock the baby crib off hits joints 'til hit disintegrated. Hit's like in a litter the runt gets picked on. Well, that's kinda like hit wuz with Bonnie Lou. She got more than her fair share of teasing or taunting. On the other hand, she wuz a lot like Daddy. She had (has) a heart of gold, and hit's always ben very difficult fer her to say no. Tharfore I thank many people took advantage of her good heart. Mommy alla's kept Bonnie Lou's (and Barbara Ann's as well) hair combed and braided inta two plaits hangin' down her back, her two pig tails we called 'em.

Hit wuz different, though, for Bobbie Jean. So much fer thar not bein' favorites. From the moment he got squeezed out into the hospital's artificial light, he became the apple of Mommy's and Daddy's eyes (particularly Mommy's), their little darling. I don't believe thar wuz any envy thar; hit wuz jest the way hit wuz. I thank the youngest, like the oldest, particularly in a large family, alla's have a special rapport with thar parents. And I thank this wuz born out in ar family. I thank too he wuz the favorite of his older siblings as well.

Back ta Mommy. As I mentioned earlier, I tended ta be the sickly one. I recall throwin' up and bein' very hot and feelin' sick all over and Mommy makin' a pallet fer me on the porch whar she wuz bathin' mah forehead with cold rags. She wound up gettin' Hardin Hensley (cousin) ta drive us to Booneville ta see the doctor whar I got a penicillin shot in mah behind. I 'member hit hurt purty bad. This wuz the first episode (that I recall) of many bouts of tonsillitis and penicillin. I tended ta be plagued with tonsillitis throughout most of mah childhood and early adulthood. The penicillin alla's worked wonders, fer within an hour or so I would go inta the "sweats," and the symptoms would disappear, and I would feel as good as new.

Mommy wuz a very devout and religious person. She believed all thangs war possible through prayer. She would sometimes go fer days fastin' and prayin', somethin' we kids did not alla's understand. She could get ta the point whar she could work herself inta a state of frenzy and hit wuz almost like she wuz havin' an out-of-body experience. I would remind ya that she and Daddy belonged to the Church of God, the Pentecostal Branch, better known as Holy Rollers. Their members often spoke in tongues, shouted praises ta God at the top of thar lungs, shook in a frenzy, jumped, ran, and yes, rolled on the floor and did all kinds of emotin' with tears sometimes streamin' down thar faces.

I recall once when Daddy wuz away workin' in Cincinnati, and Mommy had been fastin' fer some days, we kids had gone ta bed fer we war scheduled fer school the followin' mornin' wen we war awakened in the middle of the night by Mommy's loud praisin' of the Lord, shoutin' and clappin' her hands, with tears streamin' down her face while at the same time her countenance wuz jest beamin'. She wuz in a highly agitated state and wuz pacin' through the house, first through one room and then the other, praisin' the Lord with each step she took, at the top of her voice seeming to shake the whole house, piercin' the darkness and shatterin' the surrounin' solitude. She wuz makin' a circuit through the house, in and out, and round and about jest ah prayin' and ah shoutin'.

I woke up not shore if'n Mommy wuz havin' a fit or if'n she wuz losin' her mind (her sister had been in and out of a mental institution twice by that time), but very frightened 'cause I warn't shore what wuz happenin'. Mary Jane came flyin' into ar room scared ta death and jumped inta bed with me and William David. Mommy came tearin' inta the room right behind her, praisin' the Lord and thankin' Jesus. As Mommy came in rite behind her, Mary Jane hopped from ar bed and jumped clear over inta the bed with Henry and Everett and screamed, "Oh, don't let the devil get me!" and then sought refuge in the loft by quickly climbin' up through an openin' over Henry's and Everett's bed. However, Mary Jane skinned her right shin in the process of makin' her escape as she shimmed up the wall and hid in the darkened loft, and we didn't hear a peep from her atter that.

I ducked my head under the bed covers and flattened mahself down behind William David as best as I could, hopin' the turmoil would soon pass and somehow I would not git caught up in whatever wuz goin' on. Not shore how long all that emotin' lasted, but the twins, Bobbie Jean and Bonnie Lou, woke up and started cryin', then howlin', addin' ta the bedlam. Perhaps Barbara Ann added her voice to the din as well, but if'n she did, I don't 'member hearin' her with everythang else goin' on. Anyway, the babies' cries and screams seemed ta brang Mommy back ta a somewhat normal stage as she needed ta tend ta 'em, and thangs soon quieted down, and I thank in spite of hit all I soon drifted back ta sleep.

Mommy wuz stalwart, hardworkin', and I believe she alla's tried ta be the best mother she knew how with what God had given her ta work with. She managed the family's resources, whatever they happened ta be. Fer almost every day of her life, that I can recall, she would get up afore any of us and make breakfast, usually biscuits and gravy. She would make us dinner (lunch), and what wuz left over, we would have fer our evenin' meal, supper, usually cornpone and milk. Weekly she did the family warshin' and ironin'.

When we first moved back ta Kentucky, we had no electricity, so Mommy would take her warshtub down ta the creek and set it up with her scrub board and do the family warsh; hit wuz an all-day affair. She had this big black iron kettle fer bilin' out the dirtiest grit, grease, and stains, most alla's the whites. Later, Mommy and Daddy war able ta afford a secondhand gasoline washer that wuz tethered on the porch. I say tethered cause wen hit wuz runnin' hit sounded like an airplane that wuz being amped up fer takeoff and shook and rattled the entire house. Hit badly needed a muffler. Bein' round the warshin' machine, a body should have had earplugs, even though I don't thank we knowed what earplugs war in those days. In addition ta this work, Mommy wuz mostly responsible fer raisin' the garden and cannin' the fruits and vegetables fer the winter months and doin' the shoppin' and whatever else a mother and wife wuz responsible fer.

Mom, in later years, would always lament that her biggest regret in all her life was that she didn't have more to give us kids growing up! But in retrospect, all of us turned out pretty well. I think Mom and Dad did alright with the resources they had—the best they could! Not sure I could've done as well had I been in their shoes.

FAMILY PHOTO

Left to Right, Back Row: Henry, Cosetta, Barbra, Mary Jane, Wiley, Fern, Everett, William David. Middle Row: Mom & Dad. Front Row: Bobby & Bonnie.

5. LIVING WITH GRANDMA AND GRANDPA

Mary Elizabeth Reed (7/12/1888-10/9/1966): David C Bishop (7/4/1885-5/15/1968) Married 3/21/1907); Photo taken 9/1961

Grandpa and Grandma's house wuz mah second home. No, I take that back. Hit wuz more than mah second home. I wuz left with 'em when I wuz two. Uncle Wiley took me with 'em when he wuz on a furlough visit from the Army and left me with 'em. I'm not shore of the mechanics or the thought process that went on that caused that particular event. I have discussed hit ta a degree somewhar else. However, I did start stayin' with Grandpa and Grandma Bishop in earnest wen I wuz 4. This happened atter Aunt Cassie wuz hospitalized at the Richmond Mental Hospital in Richmond, Kentucky, atter she suffered a nervous breakdown. Aunt Cassie wuz 23 at the time. That wuz the second time Aunt Cassie had been hospitalized fer a nervous condition. The first time she had been hospitalized wuz in Lexington, Kentucky. I don't know the rationale fer mah goin' ta live with mah grandparents. I suppose hit wuz 'cause they war lonely without Aunt Cassie, 'specially Grandma. And Grandma just thought I wuz the cat's meow and a purty special little boy!

Grandma doted on me—spoiled me rotten, she did. I would have done anythang ta please her; Grandpa too, fer that matter. I would foller 'em round like a little puppy. They alla's had time fer me. They war never too busy and would let me help 'em share in whatever they war doin'. They seemed ta like showin' me thangs and helpin' me ta help them do little tricks. They had patience with me and that counted fer a lot with me. Grandma nussed (to hold and/or comfort usually on one's lap) me on her lap 'til I jest got too big. I 'member sittin' on her lap 'til my bare feet would be touchin' the floor. I loved huggin' mah Grandma, and she'd alla's hug me right back, clutched me to her ample bosoms, and patted mah head, callin' me her sweet, little boy or Little Wiley. She would sometimes rock me in her arms and nuzzle mah neck even though I thought I wuz gettin' too big fer that. I still liked hit, even though I pretended I didn't.

She alla's called me Little Wiley as long as she lived. They both had the patience of Job wen hit came ta me; jest seemed ta dote on me and I on them. Grandpa could neither read nor write, but I believed he knowed every song that wuz ever written (of course he didn't) 'cause he loved ta sang and he sang all of the time, and usually at the top of his voice. I could hear 'em while he wuz workin' in the barn, tendin' ta the animals, hoein' in the garden, or jest totin' on down the road. He wuz a great mimic, too. He could sound jest like almost any kind of bird and most kinds of animals. He could alla's fool me. Hit wuz jest like he wuz talkin' ta the animals. He wuz ferever in good spirits and alla's had the time and patience fer me. I don't 'member him ever sayin' an unkind word ta nobody. He knowed all these wonderful stories 'bout Daniel Boone and the Injuns and many other neat stories as well.

I 'member the one he told me 'bout when Daniel Boone had been captured by the Injuns wen he wuz explorin' and huntin' over in Ohio. He wuz in the process of helpin' 'em split this huge log and had hammered a wedge inta the partially split-open log. Then he lined up his new Injun Comrades on both sides of the partially split-open log and showed 'em how with their bare hands, they could help him ta finish pullin' open the log the rest of the way. Daniel Boone wuz at the head of the log whar he had inserted the wedge and wuz actin' as thar cheerleader urgin' the Injuns ta start pullin' and ta kep on pullin' and as they pulled, he told 'em ta widen thar lags and set thar feet fur ah part and breathe deep. "Take a real big breath, dig in yer feet and pull real hard," he yelled, and he suddenly jumped up and with a quick swing of his ax knocked out that wedge causin' the partial split log to snap back together, entrappin' all of the Injuns' hands. This allowed Daniel Boone ta escape back across the Ohio River into his beloved Kentucky afore the Injuns could get themselves free. Later, I would read the same story (perhaps a little different version) in a biography 'bout Daniel Boone. Booneville, the Owsley County Seat whar we lived, wuz named fer

Daniel Boone fer he had camped on that site durin' one of his many explorations inta the innards of what wuz ta become Kentucky.

Sometimes Grandpa would tell me 'bout wen he lived on the Kentucky River whar he wuz born and growed up. That wuz afore he met Grandma. He talked 'bout going ta an all-night Irish jig with dancin' and music with bangers (drummers) and fiddlers and all kinds of carryin's on (his description). Hit wuz hard fer me ta imagine mah Grandpa in such settin's. Even though he spent all that time on the river and really enjoyed fishin', he never larned ta swim. He often quoted me this little sayin', but not wen Grandma wuz round, *"A fisherman's luck is a wet ass and a hongry gut."* More seriously though, he often talked 'bout his mother, Cat (Catherine) Bishop. Hit seemed they war very close.

One such event stands out in mah mind. He wuz away from the family doin' some work and wuz in his bed one night, and jest as he wuz driftin' off ta sleep, somethin' roused him, causin' him ta look upwards. Wen he looked up, he saw his mother hoverin' over 'em, like she wuz floatin in the air, with this beatific smile and a heavenly glow emittin' from her whole bein'. She gently descended towards him with both arms outstretched and kissed Grandpa on his forehead, then rose up agin over 'em, and then quickly jest disappeared, kinda blinked out, leavin' complete darkness behind her. That wuz the night he wuz ta larn she passed from this earth.

Grandpa wuz very savvy about so many thangs. He knowed a lot about nature, such as the names of all the trees and plants—those that would bear fruit or nuts and wen they would be spected ta be ready ta eat. He even knowed wen they would blossom in the sprangtime. He knowed thar would be cold spells followin' the times wen the dogwoods shed thar blossoms (Dogwood Winter) and wen the blackberries shed thar blossoms (Blackberry Winter, less severe). He knew wen hit wuz alright fer me ta start goin' barefoot on the first day of May 'cause then hit would have been the time fer old Jack Frost ta have ben on his way back up north. Wenever thar would be a storm rollin' in, Grandpa and me would alla's have ta take shelter wharever we would happen ta be. As the storm would make hits way towards us and the thunder rumblin's would be gettin' louder (storm getting closer), Grandpa would nod his head at me, kinda wink and smile, and tell me that wuz the sound of God rollin' in the tater wagons. Atter the storms would pass and the earth wuz coolin', and the fogs war bilin' up all over and round the mountains (hence the Great Smoky Mountains), Grandpa's wisdom wuz that hit wuz the groundhogs all comin' outta thar dens ta bile up thar coffee.

Grandpa's father (John Bishop) wuz a soldier in the Civil War. He enlisted into Company D, 47th Kentucky, 11 Aug 1863, and received a pension fer his service. Grandpa's maternal Grandpa, Charles Cole, wuz shot and killed in Manchester, Kentucky July 24, 1858. I've never ben able ta find out the reason why he wuz shot (accident, ambush, fight, or what). Atter Charles Cole wuz killed, his whole family got split up, and Lucy Catherine Cole, one of Charles Cole's daughters, came ta live with our great-great-grandparents Abraham (Abel) and Nancy (Robinson) Bishop (Grandpa's mom and dad) in the area whar they war livin' which is now known as Bishops' Bend. Accordin' ta records Lucy Catherine (Cat) Cole and John Bishop war married on March 6, 1869, a few years atter he finished his stint with the Civil War.

Grandpa growed up with one brother (Robert Grant [Bob] Bishop), who got married at the age of 16, and one sister (Mary Jane Bishop). Mary Jane married her first cousin, Charles Alexander (Alex) Bishop. Both his brother and sister had sixteen children each. Thar are records ta indicate thar have been ancestral Bishops (Fourth Great-Grandpa Samuel Bishop) livin' in Bishop's Bend since 1786. Tharfore ar roots in that area run deep.

Hit's hard ta imagine what old people looked like and how they war wen they war young. Grandma and Grandpa Bishop war married on March 21, 1907. Grandma wuz 18 and Grandpa wuz 21. Uncle Floyd wuz born a little over a year later. While Grandma wuz pregnant with Uncle Floyd and Grandpa wuz away fer some reason or 'nother, Grandma found a pint jar of Grandpa's moonshine and drank the whole thang. I don't know the immediate effect the moonshine had on Grandma but hit caused her ta have a lifelong regret throughout the rest of her life, fer she carried a heavy load of guilt fer doin' that and believed that wuz the reason that Uncle Floyd grew up ta be so wild and why he acquired such a taste fer alcohol.

Aunt Lydia's birth follered Uncle Floyd's by 'bout sixteen months. Atter Aunt Lydia's birth, Grandma contracted child-bed fever (Puerperal Fever) and almost died. As soon as Grandma had recovered from the child-bed fever, her mother, Lydia Reed, became terminally sick, so Grandma took Uncle Floyd and Aunt Lydia and went ta stay with her mother and father and cared fer her mother 'til she passed in 1911. Even atter her mother passed, Grandma still stayed with her dad and continued ta cook and keep house fer 'em. She wuz never very clear 'bout what that wuz all 'bout.

Finally, in January 1914, Grandpa took the sheriff with 'em and told Grandma he wuz thar fer his children. Floyd and Lydia war comin' with 'em. Grandma could stay with Great-Grandpa Wiley Reed, or she could go with him and the children. This occurred accordin' to Grandma cause Grandpa's ma kept aiggin' Grandpa on ta go brang his children home. I alla's like ta thank hit wuz love that caused Grandpa to seek out his sweetheart and young'uns, and that wuz the reason he wanted 'em ta be together. Grandma did elect ta go with Grandpa and the children. Uncle Wiley wuz born ten months later, follered by Mom, Aunt Etta, Aunt Cassie, and finally, Aunt Naomi. Lydia unfortunately passed wen she wuz 9, and then Naomi passed wen she wuz 5.

Grandma had some of their belongin's she kept in a wooden box under her bed; some clothes, shoes, some pretties, etc., and a lock of each of the girls' hair. On occasion she would pull out the box and smell the items and rub 'em against her face and just cry and cry, real quite like. And she would take me up the mountain and round the ridge ta the Bishop Graveyard whar her two little girls war buried alongside her mom and dad. We would jest sit thar and she would stare at the grave sites fer the longest times. She would kinda moan and I would see tears steadily and quietly spillin' down her face while she sat thar grievin', lettin' long-ago memories flow across her psyche. She would be in a trancelike state, dreamin' 'bout what might have or could have ben fer her two precious little girls who war snatched from her at such tender ages. I could see Grandma lost and fixated in her memories and even though I felt saddened fer her I wuz left out fer they warn't mah memories. Made me feel bad though, but I didn't know what ta do but ta give her mah bestest BIG hug.

If we had 'em or could find 'em, we would take flowers and leave 'em at the grave sites. As an aside, sometime atter Great-Grandma Lydia passed, Great-Grandpa Wiley remarried and sired two boys, and other than hearin' Grandma talk 'bout 'em, I don't know much else 'bout Grandma's half-brothers.

The house whar I first stayed with Grandma and Grandpa wuz a most interestin' one. Hit no longer exists. Hit burned down some years ago, a long time now. Hit wuz actually two log cabins connected by a covered closed breezeway. The breezeway sarved as a kitchen and dinin' room. The lower log cabin had a stone chimney with a double grate; that is, the grate opened ta both the main bedroom and sittin' room as well as the kitchen. Both grates had iron stakes driven into the walls of the chimneys whar Grandma would hang her black stew pot during the times wen thar wuz a fire going in either of the fireplaces. White clay filled the voids between the logs, and thar war old newspapers pasted on the walls, which may have helped a little with insulation but did little ta enhance the decoration of the room. I do 'member some of the newspapers had pictures, but most of 'em jest had words, and I couldn't read then, so I don't know what they said.

Thar wuz one small winder on the east end of the room that ya could look out and see the garden, and a door ta the south that went out ta the porch. From that door, thar war three steps that led down ta the porch level. One of Grandma's bantam hens had made her nest behind the porch steps, and when I stayed with Grandma and Grandpa, they would let me gather her aggs fer 'em, but I had ta be real careful so I didn't break 'em. The porch opened up into the yard which had no fence. At the end of thar yard wuz the public

trail that led down ta the beginnin's of Upper Wolf
Creek and if'en ya follered hit upwards hit wuz called
Black House Holler and went ta the ridge that circled
the mountains all round. On the right side of the yard
wuz thar garden that wuz fenced in with palin fencin.
On the other side of the trail the earth fell away rather
steeply but they did have a good-sized corn crib and
thar wuz an open (not fenced-in) garden patch round
and below the corn crib.

Back inside the main room Grandma had two beds,
both had iron bedsteads. I thank the beds ar worth
special mention here. Grandma had shuck and feather
beds. Each bed had regular coil springs overlaid by a
shuck bed, overlaid by a feather bed on the top of hit.
The shuck bed wuz like a large pillow-like apparatus

that covered the springs, most entirely enclosed with a slit whar the corn shucks war inserted and whar wen the beds war made daily, the corn shucks war fluffed ta maximize comfort before being respread out on the springs. The corn shucks war changed out each fall as new corn wuz harvested and new shucks war available. The old shucks war provided ta the livestock either as bedding or as feed. Atter the shuck bed wuz fluffed the featherbed wuz piled on over the top of the shuck bed. The feather bed wuz a large pillow-like apparatus stuffed with chicken and/or duck down feathers and then sewed closed. Sheets and quilts war then layered over the featherbed. How many quilts war layered depended upon how cold the weather wuz going ta be. Only one quilt wuz used in the summertime, and on real hot stuffy night that one quilt wuz hardly needed a'tall, either. Instead of pillows, Grandma used bolsters.

Over the bed whar Grandma and grandpa slept thar wuz a large, framed photograph of Great-Grandpa and Grandma Bishop.

The second door wuz located on the northwest corner goin' inta the kitchen. In addition, ta the two beds in this room thar war four or five chairs lined up round the fireplace. The room wuz usually purty dark 'specially if hit wuz cloudy, and at night thar would be light from the fireplace if hit wuz lit or from a coal oil (kerosene) lamp. Wen the lampshade would get sooty hit would be mah job ta clean hit 'cause

mah small hand could reach inside and I could get all the soot out. The upper room also had two beds and a fireplace with a chimney located at the west end of the building. Thar wuz a large, framed photograph of Great-Grandpa and Grandma Reed hanging over one of the beds. Thar wuz a door ta the south with large stone steps leading ta the yard out front.

The breezeway kitchen and dinin' room had a rectangular table with a bench fer the young'uns seatin' that ran long one side, and a kitchen cupboard, in addition ta the fireplace already mentioned. Thar war nails or hooks on the wall over and round the fireplace fer hangin' pots and pans and fer dryin' fruits and vegetables. Seatin' fer the grown-ups wuz the chairs from the lower bedroom and they would have ta be carried back and forth with each meal. Thar wuz a small bench with a bucket of water which contained a communal dipper, and an upside-down fifty-pound lard can on which sat a pan fer warshin' up with a communal towel fer dryin'.

They had no plumbing nor electricity. They didn't even have a well. They war able ta get thar water from a sprang on the other side of the stream past the barn, hog lot, and corn crib. I recall Grandpa carryin' water in a galvanized peck bucket from the sprang. Near the sprang also wuz whar Grandma would set up and do her warsh, one day a week. She had a warsh tub and a warsh board. Grandpa would carry a small table from the kitchen to set the warsh tub on. He would set hit under an ole willer tree, and the willer tree branches would almost cover Grandma while she wuz warshin'. Any small breeze would set the willer leaves ta twirlin' and flickerin' and if'n the wind picked up the leaves and the whole tree would start inta sashayin', flippin' and dancin' round, but so would all the other trees and bushes in the area. I could imagine watchin' the trees and bushes wavin' in the wind gusts it would be a little like watching the ocean tides rollin' in. And dependin' on the strength of the wind gusts the swayin branches made noises and I would pretend they war tryin' ta talk ta me.

In mah mind, I can see Grandma with her sunbonnet over her brow all bent over that warsh tub going ta town rubbin' those clothes on the warsh board with the water and soap suds lappin' and slappin' on the sides lickety-split. Wen Grandma got goin' on her warsh board, hit would be talkin' back like it was set to hit's on rhythm—*rub, rub, rubba dub; rub, rub, rubba dub*—and the sweat would be jest rollin' off'en her forehead. Her laundry soap wuz lye soap she had made herself. She made hit out of hog fat she would render wen the hogs war butchered, and lye in her ole black kettle she normally used fer bilin' clothes on warsh day. The sprang wuz below thar big cornfield that had several large rock piles scattered 'bout. In earlier years, the cornfield had so many rocks that the rocks had to be culled and piled inta those big piles scattered 'bout. Grandma alla's told me ta be real careful round the rock piles fer snakes like ta make thar dens in 'em. 'Tween the cornfield and the stream thar war three large tulip poplars that provided some extra shade over the sprang while Grandma did her warshin'. They stood like three guardin' sentinels. I called 'em the three sisters. In the sprang time the tress had these beautiful yaller tulip like blossoms burstin' out all over. Made a purty site.

Dental hygiene at that time and place wuz not great. Both Grandpa and Grandma lost their natural teeth early, long before I knowed 'em fer I don't recall ever seein' 'em with thar natural teeth. The nearest dentist wuz located in Beattyville, Kentucky, some twenty-plus miles from whar they lived. They both had all their teeth removed at one time and, like many (most) mountain people, war forced (larned) ta gum their food. Grandma found a way around the circumstance by gettin' her false teeth by mail order. Needless ta say, fittin' wuz a problem. Tharfore, the only time Grandma would wear her choppers, as she called 'em, wuz wen she wuz going ta go inta town or wen she wuz going ta be out in public, which war rare events.

Grandpa, on the other hand, had his dentures made and fitted by a real live dentist (Uncle Wiley had paid fer 'em), but he had the darnedest time adaptin' ta 'em. Grandma insisted he wear 'em ta the post office and ta the store a distance of about a mile and a half one way over the mountains, cross the ridge, and down the Indian Creek gravel highway. Told 'em he needed ta git use ta warin' 'em 'cause Uncle Wiley had paid a lot of money fer 'em ta 'ave 'em, and hit jest made no sense fer Grandpa not ta ware 'em.

On the way back from one of his ventures, Grandpa felt the call of nature and meandered off into the woods through some bushes and attempted ta do his business, but in spite of tryin' his best efforts—no luck. (He had a chronic problem with constipation.) Hit wuz those darn dentures! So, like any thankin' man, Grandpa jest removed the offendin' appliances and laid 'em on a rock beside a nearby huckleberry bush. After he completed his business, he stripped off a few tulip poplar tree leaves, cleaned his self, pulled up his overalls, fastened his galluses, picked up his packages and groceries, and headed back fer home, minus his dentures—which he had fergotten.

By that time hit wuz getting' purty dark. When Grandpa got home, Grandma noticed his dentures war missing. "Dave, whar ar ya teeth?" I'm shore Grandpa wuz like the startled deer caught in the car's headlights. Grandma said he seemed dazed, like he didn't know what she wuz talkin' 'bout, and then hit struck him he had taken his false teeth out in the woods ta do his business and had plumb fergotten 'bout 'em. The next mornin' wen he went back ta search fer the dentures, he couldn't find 'em. Thar wuz absolutely no sign of 'em. Probably some varmint had found his false teeth in the night and had absconded with 'em. Anyway, that wuz the end of any effort of gettin' Grandpa ta wear dentures. He "gummed hit" fer the rest of his life.

Even though Uncle Floyd (Grandma and Grandpa's oldest son) wuz primarily responsible fer Grandma and Grandpa losin' their farm on Bee Branch, he wuz also the one responsible fer savin' Grandpa's life later. I'm not shore of the timeframe, but I believe this event occurred in the late 1920s or early 1930s. Anyway, time is not the most relevant factor. Typhoid fever wuz rampant in that area round the time ta which I'm referrin'.

Drinking from communal dippers or cups wuz common practice and also so wuz drinkin' from the mountain streams. This practice wuz still in effect while I wuz growin' up in the mountains. Unfortunately, Grandpa came down with a case of typhoid fever, and in spite of the best efforts of home nursin' care and home remedies, he wuz gettin' worse by the hour and fadin' fast. Accordin' ta Grandma, he wuz jest bout knockin' on death's door.

They sent fer the doctor, but he refused ta drive all the way from Booneville (ten miles and then walk another mile down the holler) unless they could pay 'em fer his services. Grandma had no money and no way of gettin' any money. 'Nor did she have anything of value with which she could offer the doctor fer payment.

It wuz Uncle Floyd ta the rescue. He went ta the doctor and told 'em he would have his money (hard cash) waitin' fer 'em by the time he got ta the house, swear ta God (a great big lie!). The doctor did show up and gave Grandpa some medicines that saved his life, Grandma wuz shore. Of course, Uncle Floyd did not show up with any money or payment of any kind. The doctor wuz as mad as an old wet hen but finally settled on taking three of Grandma's best Red Hampshire pullets (young hens). He parted with a lot more than three naughty expletives aimed at the absent Uncle Floyd.

I wuz entertained with lots of interestin' stories of Grandma's and Grandpa's lives wen they war growin' up and tales handed down to 'em. Wen Grandma wuz a young girl, her mother sent her with a pie plantin' (rhubarb) cobbler pie ta share with a neighbor widder lady who lived down the holler. When Grandma arrived, Mrs. Yonkers, the widder, wuz all pleased ta see Grandma and have her visit 'cause visitors war kinda rare and alla's welcomed. Plus, she had a real sweet tooth, and really loved pie plantin' pie.

She invited Grandma in ta sit down a spell, offered her a glass of buttermilk, and said, "Sit yerself up by the hearth and warm yer cockles, child." Mrs. Yonkers had a good-sized fire goin' in the fireplace with her stew pot hangin' out over the glowin' coals. Atter some visitin' chitchat and gettin' caught up with goin's on, Mrs. Yonkers turned ta Grandma with this puzzled look on her face and shared, "Ya know, wen I went ta the store the other day I bought some of those new-fangled coffee beans and I have had them bilin' over the fire all day and they have ben cookin' 'em fer hours and they jest don't seem ta be getttin' tender a'tall. I keep testin' 'em but thar jest stayin' as tough as rawhide." At that time coffee beans war jest bein' introduced inta the Great Smoky Mountains. Unfortunately, Mrs. Yonkers didn't understand coffee beans war unlike the beans she tended in her garden that she dried out and saved fer making soup beans. They war never going ta get tender. No one had told her that first they needed ta be ground up and brewed to make a concoction fer drinkin', not beans few eatin'. In spite of her best efforts, she would not be havin' soup coffee beans fer her dinner.

Then, thar wuz a young lady called Martha, who wuz spectin' her beau, Randy, ta come a-courtin'. They had been sparkin' fer some time now and she wuz hopin' Randy would ask her ta get hitched soon, but he shore 'nuff wuz takin' his time. Now Martha lived with her ma and pa in a small cabin (some would even call hit a shack) with ten brothers and sisters, so the only place for any privacy wuz in the loft.

Anyhow, Martha takes herself a pan of water ta the loft fer a spit bath and a set of clean clothes. She had been out workin' in the fields all day hoein' corn and wanted ta do a little sprucin' up afore Randy got thar. However, time wuz slippin' away from her.

Martha hurried up with her fixin's, finished her bath, and wuz 'bout ready ta put on her fresh clothes wen she happened ta 'member hearin' the neighbors talkin' bout that if'n a person could get their lag round thar neck, that person could marry whoever they pleased. Martha wuz purty gullible and kinda desperate. I mean, she wuz tard of bein' an old maid at the ripe old age of 16 and needed ta get away from all those kinfolks. No sooner said than done. Well, done with a lot of effort.

First, she tried stickin' her neck under her lag but hit wouldn't go. She bent down as fer as she could but only managed ta git the top of her head ta the center of her knee. She next scooted down and braced her left foot against an upright 2 x 4 and her right foot against an overhead brace, and with her body feelin' like hit wuz almost bein' torn in two with a lot of contortions and stretchin' and more contortions, she hunched her back and bowed her head 'neath her kneecap and wuz able to butt her head under her lag. She felt her lag stuck at the top of her head, but with a lot of patience and a little more effort, the lag gradually slipped over her head until hit firmly rested around her neck.

She had done hit! She got that ole lag right round her neck! She took a deep breath and closed her eyes. "Oh

God," she fervently prayed, "make Randy want ta marry me and make 'em ax me soon." She took her lag from round her neck. But there wuz a problem! No, I misspoke. She tried ta take her lag from round her neck but hit wuz stuck! She tugged and pulled, and flopped and pulled, and moaned and cursed, and flopped and jumped, and prayed. And jest as she thought she wuz doomed, and her back wuz goin ta break rite in two, she gave one mighty pull and one last lunge and felt her lag come free, at last.

However, at the same time her lag slipped free from round her neck, she felt the loft floorboards give way underneath her from all her floppin' and thrashin' round. As the earth—I mean the loft floorboards— gave way, she felt her life flashin' right afore her very eyes. She landed with a spee—lunk relatively unscathed, beautifully unadorned in her birthday suit, right beside Randy, who had jest come inta the house seconds afore, jest in time ta hear some of the commotion overhead up in the loft. She barely missed landin' rite on top of 'em. Afore the fall, he had been wonderin' what in the world wuz going on up thar, rite over his head. The moral of the story is getting' yer lag round yer neck fer gainin' a betrothal worked, 'cause Randy and Martha war married shortly atterwards. Hit worked, at least in this case.

Many of mah grandparents' stories centered round courtin'. This wuz a short one. Church often played a central role. In that time and place, social functions war few and fur between. Thar war no movies, restaurants, coffee shops, and leisure time wuz extremely limited. Hit wuz on jest such a Sunday mornin' that James R had ridden over ta Sara Ann's house some three miles' distance on his trusty old horse, Bullet, ta escort the fair Sara Ann ta Sunday Services.

Ah, hit wuz a glorious sprang mornin'. The hillsides war covered with the early flowerin' trees and the buds war burstin' out in a fresh yaller green. The birds war flittin' 'bout and serenadin' the earth. Ya could see spikes of sunlight filterin' through the trees overhangin' the dirt road. The earth wuz fresh and pregnant with ah new beginnin', and that evidence wuz sprangin' up all round, everywhar. An occasional breeze managed ta slip through all the overgrowth, but overhead thar wuz a slight swishin' of the tree and saplin' branches as they swayed backards and forwards in concert with the wind. Thar freshly borne leaves hungrily soaked up the sun's rays as a lazy cloud slowly crawled across the sky, casting an ominous shader as hit paraded cross the sky.

Somewhar overhead, a hawk spiraled over the tree tops searchin' fer food, and in the not-too-fur distance, a couple of crows could be heard cawin' or cursin' in the woods. Thar war splotches of color scattered everywhar from the emergin' spring flowers. James R wuz in high spirits as he neared Sara Ann's house. This wuz truly a day God had made.

Sara Ann wuz a ravishin' beauty with flamin' red hair that hung all the way down her back. She had sparklin' blue eyes that could pierce inta tomorrow, a smile that could melt the coldest of hearts, and she stood only five feet and one inch tall.

Now James R was a brawny hunk, muscles from here ta thar and back agin from workin' in the fields all day. He stood six feet and three inches tall, but wuz quite shy. He wuz the eldest of a brood of seven and wuz already 23, so his folks war anxious fer 'em to find a decent God-fearing young lady to tie the knot and have 'em some more grandchildren. Two of his younger sisters collective already had four grandchildren. A third sister wuz already engaged to tie the knot.

Oh, almost forgot to mention that James R's daddy wuz the preacher fer the congregation that met on Sundays to hold prayer services at the Upper Wolf Creek Schoolhouse.

James R and Sara Ann had already been courtin' fer over six months and hit wuz just a matter of time afore he popped the big question. Everybody wuz 'spectin' hit. Wen James R arrived at Sara Ann's house, she met 'em dressed in her best Sunday go-to-meeting finery: a beautiful handmade blue gingham full-skirted dress with puffed sleeves. Ta James R she wuz purty as a picture. Atter he said his howdy-do's ta Sara Ann's family, the blissful couple saddled up and rode off up the mountain headin' fer church.

I should mention that Sara Ann's pa had saddled up their old mare for her ta ride alongside her beau, and as wuz the custom, he had strapped on the mare's back a sidesaddle that ladies mostly rode in those days.

Wen they arrived at the church (schoolhouse), the gallant James R quickly dismounted from ole Bullet and stepped over ta Sara Ann ta assist her in dismountin'. He held up his arms fer the petit Sara Ann ta slide off of the sidesaddle in order ta get off her mare. Sara Ann released the mare's bridle reins, scooted down inta James R's outstretched waitin' arms. Unfortunately, Sara Ann's beautiful gingham skirt caught on the sidesaddle's horn, which left the lower portion of Sara Ann's body completely exposed.

Even more unfortunately, ar poor heroine Sara Ann wuz wearin' no underclothes underneath—none a'tall—so she in all her glory wuz on exhibition fer all the world ta take a gander at.

James R wuz frantic but wuz struck with a bright idea: "Gentlemen, pass me yer hats! Pass me yer hats quickly, now, please!" Fortunately, in those days, all the men round did wear hats and hastily came ta James R's assistance ta share. Hats provided cover until Sara Ann's skirt could be unhooked and restored round her beautiful figure and 'til the situation and calm war manageable agin. Problem temporarily solved. This wuz recalled ta me as an event that actually occurred and had been witnessed by folks known ta mah grandparents.

Wen Grandma wuz jest a youngster, she lived with her family on Cow Creek. They had neighbors who lived a couple of miles further up Cow Creek on a wide plateau on the right-hand fork called Buzzard's Roost. Whar the right-hand fork split off thar wuz a grove of pine trees on the right-hand side and a stand of chestnut trees on the left-hand side. This wuz a few years afore the chestnut blight hit Kentucky and killed off all the chestnut trees.

The neighbors war an older couple. Actually, they war later middle age, Felix and Piney Hacker. Felix and Piney war faithful Christians who had worked hard all their lives, but the years had not been kind ta either of 'em. Felix wuz a few years older than Piney, and his hair wuz thinning, and what was left wuz turning gray. He wuz beginnin' ta become stooped in the shoulders and didn't get about as well as he used ta. His skin was weathered, roughly tanned, and hardened from all the years of outside work and exposure ta the elements. Each year seemed ta add a few more wrinkles and additional aches and pains. His joint didn't work as well anymore but did complain a lot more. Age wuz slowin' both of 'em down a rite smart. The years war slowin' 'em down.

Piney, in spite of all of her toilin', wuz a little more rotund, and her complexion wuz ruddy, but the lines on her face ran deep and made her 'peer older than she actually wuz. She wuz strong-willed and had been a real go-getter all her life. Necessity kept her goin'. She wuz God-fearin' and every day thankful fer her many blessin's and didn't have time nor the inclination to waller in self-pity, or dwell on minor incapacities.

They lived in an austere cabin: bedroom, kitchen/dinin', and a sort of a lean-to at the end of the kitchen fer their milk cow and old nag. Thar furnishin's war minimal but sufficient. Piney had an extensive garden out front, and Felix had a large cornfield on the right side of the cabin. On the left, they had an orchard with a dozen or so apple trees, nine peach trees, four cherry trees, and three pear trees. In the back of the cabin, they grew alfalfa and hay fer feedin' thar stock. Wen the hay and alfalfa got ripe the Hackers would harvest hit, and store what they could in thar lean-to. The rest they'd rake up in haystacks ta tide the animals over fer the winter months.

The Hackers had very much wanted a family and prayed and prayed ta God ta give 'em children, but in thar almost thirty years of married life, thar had been none. Thar war rumors that Piney had lost (miscarried) several. The clock wuz tickin', and wen hit seemed time wuz runnin' out, Piney miraculously discovered she wuz with child, agin. She and Felix war overjoyed. They had wanted this baby so much, fer so long. They planned on doin' everythang possible ta ensure **that this time** they got themselves a baby. Each night afore going ta bed, they got down on their knees and prayed ta God, givin' Him thanks fer what seemed like thar final chance ta have themselves a baby.

So hit progressed. Piney's belly bump continued ta swell and got bigger and bigger with each passin' day. Felix discovered a new sprang had come back ta his step as he reveled in the glory of becomin' a father at long last. As Piney's due date neared, Felix sought out the best midwife in the county, Heather Wilds, ta come stay with 'em durin' the final days leadin' up ta the blessed event. Unfortunately, Heather had only ben thar a few days wen she wuz called away ta assist with a breech delivery clear cross the county several miles away. Heather felt bad 'bout leavin' the Hackers, but she had been helpin' care fer this other family and now the mother wuz deliverin' early and wuz in trouble with an expected breach birth. She needed ta get thar as soon as possible. She wuz purty shore the Hackers would be alright and hopefully she'd be back afore the Hackers' baby came a knockin'.

A couple of days atter Heather left the Hackers' house, a terrible storm came blowin' in with hurricane-force winds with lots of thunder and lightnin' and rain, torrents of rain. The thunderin' wuz so bad that hit shook the whole cabin, and the lightnin' flashes war so bright and frequent hit made everythang very light outside even though hit wuz heavily overcast making everythang all most peer like hit wuz dark. In all this turmoil, Piney's water broke, and the birthin' contractions and pains started in. "Oh, Lord." She gasped as she drew in a deep, ragged breath. "Honey, ya got ta go atter Heather and git her back 'ere quick as ya can. Cause I know I'm goin' ta need her help. Ya knows I ain't done this afore. And I'm a little feared. I shore don't know how long I ken stand doin' this by mahself."

Felix quickly grabbed his coat and hat, gave Piney a big hug and a kiss, and said, "I love y'all. And I'll be back real soon!" He made a mad dash fer the other end of the cabin ta whar he kept their nag penned up jest in case this happened. Piney could hear his brogans thumpin' through the kitchen as he made his way out onta the lean-to. She could hear ever step he took as he went on his way out the cabin.

The storm, instead of peterin' out and passin' through, seemed ta be pickin' up strength and intensity. The thunderin' wuz crashin' overhead almost constantly, and the lightnin' wuz lightin' up the whole room. Piney could see out thar winder that the rain wuz comin' down in sheets and buckets. Piney had started in prayin' as soon as Felix left her room: "Oh, let mah ole man be alright, Lord. Let him get through this awful storm, Lord. I know he's gettin' his self-soaked cause I ken hear and see the rain pourin' down. Keep 'em from catchin' his death of cold or pneumonia. Watch over him and protect him, Lord, fer he's all I got in this whole world! Oh Lord, please have mercy on us all. Please, Dear Lord, don't let nuttin' happen to 'em. Keep 'em on the straight and narrow and bring 'em back ta me as soon as ya can, Lord." And this continued on and on. The worry and prayers seemed ta keep Piney's mind off of the pain and contractions. As the storm continued, the appeals ta God became louder, and louder, and more intense with every passin' moment.

When thar was a pause in the thunderin', a reassurin' rather strong but still fairly faint voice could be heard calling' from the other end of the house—from the lean-to, "Now, Piney, quit yer worryin' an' frettin', 'cause I ain't gone nowhar yet, and yer worryin' ain't doin' the baby no good, no how, so jest stop hit!"

Shivareein' wuz a custom often played on newlyweds on thar weddin' nights. Well-meaning friends, neighbors and family members would gather round 'til the signal wuz given the newlyweds war 'bout ready fer bed and everybody would start in makin' the durnest racket beatin' on pots and pans, rangin' cowbells, and effen they had horns or whistles they would blow 'em as loud as they could, others would yell, scream and holler and march 'round the cabin 'fore bargin' in and snatchin' the bride and stuffin' her inta a warsh tub. Then, they'd attack the groom and hoist him onta a rail. Then hoist both of 'em on some of the stronger men's shoulders and parade the poor couple 'round the cabin several times with all the merriment and noise continuin' all the while bangin' on the warsh tub with sticks. Effen, they war really mischievous they'd sprinkle salt in thar sheets, as well. All in good fun, as a way of welcomin' them into thar new status of matrimony.

As I already mentioned, Grandma had lots of stories. She told of a circuit rider preacher who would wait ta do his rounds 'til he would be shore his visits coincided with the season when the blackberries war in season so he would alla's be able ta find ripe berries ta eat. Also, 'bout another circuit rider preacher who stayed with thar family and wuz helpin' his self ta the lion's share of supper. As with all mountain folks, the hosts alla's tried ta put their best foot (food) forward.

This particular event occurred in the fall of the year. A hog had been butchered, so pork chops war on the menu. Hit wuz already dark by dinnertime. All the family wuz crowded round the table, includin' the preacher. The kitchen wuz dimly lit with a coal oil (kerosene) lamp. The blessin' (grace) wuz said, and supper wuz progressin' along wen the preacher reached fer his third and the last helpin' of pork chops. Jim, Grandma's older brother, supposedly unintentionally, also reached out with his fork and, instead of stabbing the pork chop, stabbed the preacher's hand. He pretended he hadn't seed the preacher reachin' for the last pork chop, 'cept everybody thought Jim did hit on purpose.

Accordin' ta Grandma, the preacher yelled like he had jest been gutted and thar wuz blood spurtin' out of his hand like no body's business. Great-Grandma Reed wuz not pleased a'tall fer her son, Jim's behavior. Grandma also told 'bout peddlers with pack horses brangin' goods ta the mountains. 'Bout one complainin' mightily when Great-Grandma Lydia tore a little piece of cloth ta test hits strength and durability. The peddler wuz not pleased 'bout Great-Grandma testin' his merchandise. She told Grandma she warn't in the habit of buyin' no pig in a poke. (Great-Grandma Lydia smoked a corncob pipe most of her life.)

When Grandma and Grandpa war still newlyweds, Grandpa went out in the woods and picked up a whole bunch of chestnuts, took them ta the store, and traded 'em in for a cut glass pitcher as a gift fer his new bride, Grandma. That pitcher is now one of mah most prized possessions. It's the story behind its purchase that makes it so valuable to me. Wen I stayed with 'em the pitcher sat in the middle of thar kitchen table and held some spoons and forks.

Most all the clothes Grandma wore war handmade from feed or flour sacks and sewn by Mommy. Ar family struggled as we war growin' up, but so did Mommy and her family. When Mommy wuz small (probably preteen), Grandma would climb up the mountain and cross the ridge and traverse down the other side of the mountain barefoot ta warsh clothes by hand on an ole warshboard fer twelve hours a day or more fer a mere ten cents!

Life improved fer Grandpa and Grandma wen Uncle Wiley joined the Army on January 13, 1942 (one year and one month afore I wuz born) shortly atter the bombin' of Pearl Harbor by the Japanese. He wuz able ta claim Grandma and Grandpa as his dependents. Even though thar allotment wuz not a lot, hit wuz significantly more than they had before. By allotment rules, a portion of Uncle Wiley's pay wuz diverted ta Grandma and Grandpa, and the rest wuz supplemented by Uncle Sam. Grandma tried very earnestly ta keep thar expenditures within those amounts allotted by Uncle Sam and ta bank that portion from Uncle Wiley's pay fer him.

I 'member she and I takin' the "Blue Goose" inta town ta do her bankin' (cash her check--US government check) and deposit that portion of Uncle Wiley's pay inta his account) and fer her ta buy a few tricks. The Blue Goose wuz a bus that ran on the gravel highway. Hit went inta town and back twice a day. I don't recall if hit ran only on certain days or not. The service wuz long ago discontinued. Hit wuz a mile or more hike from Grandma's house up over the steep mountain trail and round the ridge ta even catch the bus, and, of course, the same distance ta retrace the route goin' back home after our adventures in the Booneville metropolis (population round 100).

But hit wuz alla's worth hit—a real break fer us. We had a plate lunch at the restaurant on the corner (hit is no longer thar) and visited the courthouse (hit burned down some years ago). Grandma took me ta the Barber Shop fer a haircut. Didn't like gettin' mah hair cut then. Still don't. Bunch of old guys war thar jest talkin' up a storm, jest talkin' and talkin' and not sayin' much of anythang. Ole Henry Slick wuz thar (he wuz one of the few black men that lived somewhar round). I do recall one of the ole codgers asking Henry, "Henry, jest what do ya reckon?"

"Well, Suh," Henry replied," if'n I's tells ya what's I knows, then y'all will know what ya knows an what I's knows, too." *That's right real true,* I thought ta myself. Better jest ta listen and keep mah mouth shut and mah thoughts to mahself. That would get me in a lot less trouble. That Henry Slick wuz one real smart feller, I figured.

The only thang 'bout buyin' tricks at the town stores wuz that Grandma and I had to pack 'em some mile or more round the ridge and down the holler. After a day out with Grandma, hit could get purty tarin' even though we did stop and rest ever now and agin. Ya knows, when ya start packin' a load, hit don't seem that heavy at first, but atter ya goes a fur pace, hit will jest get heavier and heavier. And fer a four-year-old, hit don't take very fur.

Ya know Grandma most never disciplined me. All she had ta do was raise her voice or look at me cross-eyed or give me the ole evil eye. I wuz her pet, her precious little one, and I really did want ta please her most all of the time. 'Cept this one morning and hit still pains me to tell ya 'bout that little incident.

The day started off not a lot different from most of the other'ens. Grandma roused me from bed and told me breakfast wuz ready. Hit wuz still dark outside. I slept in mah long-handles but quickly put on mah woolen shirt, bibbed overhalls, socks, and brogans. Grandpa had the fire goin' in the grate, but the room wuz still cold. I could hear Grandpa warshin' up in the kitchen. He had already fed and milked the cows as well as fed the horse, hogs, and ole Wolf, the dog. Wen we all sot down fer breakfast, Grandma first said the blessin', thankin' God fer the food fer the nourishment of ar bodies, and fer all the rest. She sometimes could go on quite a bit, 'specially wen I wuz really hongry, she alla's seemed ta take longer. Breakfast wuz fried aigs, fatback, cooked apples, biscuits, butter, and jelly with milk fer me and coffee fer Grandma and Grandpa. Afore they drank thar coffee, they would pore hit on their saucer fer hit ta cool first. Guess they didn't like thar coffee real hot.

Atter breakfast, Grandpa got ready and left fer the store and post office. Up at the chicken house, the roosters war making a heck of a racket. I thank they war tryin' ta see who could crow the loudest ta get us to brang 'em some breakfast (corn). We did. Grandma and I bundled up and took a bucket of corn which Grandpa had shelled the night afore, up ta the chicken house, unlatched the door ta let the chickens out, and scattered the corn round.

The chickens could hardly contain themselves as they competed ta get their share, runnin' here and thar and peckin' like crazy 'til all the corn wuz gone and cluckin ta beat the band, and then lookin' fer more. In the winter, the hens didn't give Grandma a lot of aigs— hardly enough fer her ta use. In the sprang and the rest of the year, thar would be more aigs than she could use. Grandpa would take those that war more than she needed ta the store ta sell fer a little extra money. Also, in the sprang, some of the hens would want ta go settin'. Meant they'd have a whole nest full of aigs and set on 'em 'til they hatched fer 'bout ah month. Grandma would feed the new chicklets raw oatmeal. In addition ta the hatched chicklets, Grandma would mail-order fer more chicklets. Wen they war due ta arrive, Grandpa would have ta go ta the post office ever day so's he'd be thar wen they came in. In spite of that, though, thar would alla's be a couple of dead'ens.

Atter the chicken feedin', we come back ta the house and Grandma cleaned up the kitchen and swept the floors. I held the dustpan fer her ta sweep up in. She made the bed and put some shuck beans in her stew pot on the hook by the grate to cook fer most of the day, so they'd be ready fer ar supper. Then, she got her ironin' out, started ironin', and warn't paying me much mind. I had a couple of empty thread spools I was rollin' cross the hearth but that got old and borin' purty quick.

Now hit wuz a cold, blustery, overcast day, the clouds war hangin' low, and hit wuz kinda spitin' snow, and so Grandma wouldn't let me go outside ta play. Grandma kept on ironin' and fer once didn't have a lot of time fer me, or so hit seemed and of course Grandpa wuz gone. I wuz jest plain ole bored and gettin' really ornery and contrary. I tried several times and several thangs to get her attention, but ta no avail. Nothin' wuz workin'.

I wuz gettin' more and more aggravated and disgruntled by the lack of attention, and the more I wuz bein' 'nored the more disgruntled and contrary I wuz gettin' ta be. Now, at that time, mah maiden Aunt Cassie wuz confined at the Richmond Hospital 'cause she had had a nervous reality reaction (nervous breakdown) and wuz thar fer treatment ta help her ta get better. I knowed that Grandma wuz worried 'bout Aunt Cassie and wuz hopin' ta get word that she would get ta come home real soon. She talked 'bout her a lot. And ever night in her prayers, she would go on, and on, asking God ta make Aunt Cassie well and ta let her come home. At least on those nights wen I wuz still awake, I would hear her sayin' so in her prayers.

Well, agin I hate ta tell ya this, but the Devil had really got the better of mah soul and good senses, if'n I had had any. I stood hit as long as I could, but I hate bein' 'nored and Grandma wuz actin' like I warn't even thar. So, I goes up ta mah Grandma ta whar she wuz ironin'. I gets real close ta her and I looks right up at her and I sez, "I hope Aunt Cassie doesn't get ta come home a'tall." Whoooo, that got her 'tention, and did I ever get a dirty look, a *real* dirty look, but Grandma didn't say a word. She jest kept on ironin', like mindin' her own business, then as if'n she hadn't heard me or if'n I warn't even thar.

Now that really got mah goat, so, then I drapped my lower lip and stared right up at her real hard tryin' to give her mah evil eye cause she warn't payin' me no mind, and I sez in mah really loud, and mean and nasty voice, "I hope Aunt Cassie dies in that hospital thar, and never gits ta come home!"

Wham! Smack! right on the side of mah face! That wuz the only time in mah life that mah grandma ever struck me. I'm shore if'n someone could've heard me they would've thought Grandma had killed me. The shriek that came out of me wuz torn from mah inner bein', straight outa mah heart! I had only ben trying ta git Grandma's attention, and I had wanted a reaction, but not like that one. How could she? I wuz wounded ta the very depths of mah soul. I wuz more than killed.

I mean that wuz nothin' compared ta the beatin's I wuz used ta gettin' back at home, but then again hit wuz so much more than that. Ya would ah thought I'd ah ben toughened up by that time. I should ah ben use ta a little physical abuse. But this wuz a different ballgame; different player.

I mean, lookin' back, I knowed I more than axed fer hit, but hit absolutely broke mah heart. I wuz besotted, mad, confused—and 'member, I had been 'ccused of being a little devil. I mean, anyone else in the world could beat me up, abuse me, hurt me, even call me names, but fer mah grandma ta strike me no matter what I might have done wuz unthankable. The smack hurt, but the bigger hurt was to my soul, my heart. Hit peered mah whole world wuz shattered in two.

Now, I only had on mah inside clothes, but I struck out fer the door and made a mad dash cross the porch, through the yard, past the garden, and in a blue flash, I wuz away. I had ta git out of thar. The snow wuz comin' down pretty steady by that time, and I wuz leavin' tracks in the snow. I knowed the path Grandpa took out of the holler wuz up Coon's Point, a steep embankment that wuz a shortcut up ta the ridge, the one that Grandma had trouble climbin'. The longer one up Black House Holler wuz not nearly so steep and wuz easier fer Grandma ta climb, so I didn't thank Grandma could foller me if'n I went up Coon's Point, the steep one.

I wuz goin' atter Grandpa ta make 'em take me home ta mah mommy and daddy's house. And I knowed he would do hit, too. He alla's told me I wuz his little buddy. Alla's called me his bed buddy. I would show Grandma she couldn't treat me like that. How could she 'ave ben so mean ta me? I climbed clear ta the top of the steep mountain and turned left onta the ridge. The exertion alone kept me almost warm even though the wind seemed ta be pickin' up and mah exposed hands and face war feelin' icy, but I kept on goin'.

All round me, the trees stood like skeletons havin' long ago lost thar clothin'. The foliage wuz brown and shriveled or bare too, 'cept fer some scattered evergreens (ferns), and too, thar was a couple of pine trees scattered round the mountain side. Unfortunately, thar wuz nothin' ta hold back the bitin' wind or the chillin', icy snow and sleet pellets. Mah fangers war beginnin' ta lose thar feelin's and mah face wuz becomin' numb. My breath wuz comin' out like the fog in the Smoky Mountains and hit wuz gittin' harder ta breathe all ah the time.

I started inta thankin', *how will Grandma git alone without me?* She needed me ta help her feed the chickens and look fer aigs. And who wuz goin' rub her ackin' back wen hit got ta hurtin' her so mighty bad? Grandpa couldn't do hit nearly so good as me, Grandma alla's said. Too, how would I git alone without mah grandma? Who would tell me stories and read me books? Who would be thar to love up on me? Ta nuss me and hug me and call me thar little boy? Nobody at home would do that. They war alla's too busy doin' other thangs ta fool with me.

At Mommy and Daddy's house, thangs shore would be a lot different. And I started in ta feel even more sorry fer mahself. Then the snowfall began ta get even worse. The snow wuz fallin' faster and heavier, and the wind wuz makin' the snowfall look like billowin' sheets. If'n I had been dressed warm enough and the situation had been different, I might have even enjoyed bein' out in the snowstorm, and if'n thangs hadn't happened like they did. Hit wuz kinda like lookin' inta one of those snow globes like Aunt Etta had, but worse cause this'en wuz real, and I wuz cold, freezin' even!

I trudged ahead, round the ridge I went, past the cliff overhang whar I alla's thought wuz whar the haunts hid away, but they only came out at night, I figgered, so I should be OK, I thought. Now that I wuz on a somewhat leveler plain and wuz not endurin' the extreme exertion of climbin' almost straight up, I wuz gettin' colder and colder and colder. What if'n I just fell asleep and froze ta death like the little Match Girl in the story Grandma read me 'bout? I began ta worry and mah steps started ta get slower and slower. And the road peered to look longer and longer. Thar wuz a couple of tears slowly rollin' down mah cheeks, and I wuz fraid they might freeze. Also, the lump in mah throat seemed ta be gittin' bigger and breathin' wuz comin' even harder.

Mah plans ta meet up with Grandpa didn't seem nearly so good the colder I got. No. I might not have thought this'en out so well. So, when I came ta the next hill on the ridge, hit looked awfully steep, and right there and then, I decided ta go back home ta Grandma. And, about halfway back on the ridge, I met Grandma carryin' mah overcoat and overshoes. I ran into her arms and hugged her tightly, and we war both cryin', and I told her. "Grandma, I didn't mean hit. I didn't mean hit a'tall."

"I know, honey." She soothed me by huggin' me tight and helpin' me put on my overcoat and overshoes. I already felt warm all over even if'n my skin was still cold and I wuz shiverin' somethin' mightily. All wuz right agin with me and the world, and with mah grandma.

Once, in the middle of the night (hit seemed), Grandma woke me up and helped me ta get dressed. If'n I'm 'memberin' correctly, hit wuz still wintertime. We bundled up in ar winter clothes and struck out with Grandma holdin' mah hand. Grandma had gotten word that Aunt Cassie wuz ready ta come home. Hit wuz still pitch dark, but Grandma had a coal oil lantern ta help us see ar way. We climbed up Black House Holler and then meandered round the ridge, finally ta the gravel road where Hobert Wilder picked us up and drove us ta the hospital at Richmond, Kentucky, ta brang Aunt Cassie back home.

Everybody wuz glad ta see Aunt Cassie come home, but logistics changed a bit. Now, instead of me sleepin' with Grandpa and Grandma, Aunt Cassie got ta sleep with Grandma and I wuz regulated ta sleepin' with jest Grandpa. I warn't shore I wuz real happy fer that change but eventually, like most thangs, I got use ta hit.

Having Aunt Cassie round wuz much like havin' another child round. She wuz very childlike in many ways. She alla's called Grandpa and Grandma pappy and mammy. I never really understood that, fer I never heard anyone else call their daddy and mommy pappy and mammy. She had only gone ta the second grade in school but could write her name and could figger numbers in her head like nobody's business. I wuz told she had gotten brain fever from workin' out in the sun all day and gettin' too hot, which wuz the cause of her nervous condition.

Aunt Cassie told me 'bout havin' a vision while in the hospital. In hit, she had a visit from her grandma (Lydia Reed, who she had never met) and her two deceased sisters, Lydia (who she also had never met) and Naomi, her baby sister. All of 'em had passed and war livin' in Heaven. They all sat round her bed and told her she wuz gettin' out of that place (Richmond Hospital) and she would never be in a place like that again fer the rest of her life.

Hit wuz only a few days later wen Grandma and I came to pick her up and brought her back home. I wuz very impressed by her story, and she retold it many times over the ensuin' years. I earnestly believed what she had encountered wuz a miraculous vision and really hoped and wanted hit ta be true. Unfortunately, Aunt Cassie wuz incarcerated twice more in a mental capacity afore she passed in 1983.

In 1947, Uncle Wiley came home on furlough and decided the farm that wuz adjacent ta the one he already owned down the holler would be a more suitable place fer Grandma and Grandpa and Aunt Cassie ta live versus the ole dual log cabins whar I had been livin' with 'em. So, he bought hit from Fred Taylor. Despite sharin' a last name with us, Fred Taylor wuz no kin ta us, but his wife Nancy wuz, fer she wuz born a Hensley, tharfore she wuz a first cousin ta Daddy. Grandma Taylor's maiden name wuz Hensley.

The new house wuz quite different from the dual log cabins. Hit wuz a four-room structure—three bedrooms and a kitchen. Thar wuz a dual chimney fer the two main bedrooms and durin' the move-in process, the two other rooms war modified so that the kitchen/dinin'/storage room wuz stretched ta about two-thirds the length of the house and the remainin' third wuz converted inta a porch. The house required a new roof, and Daddy wuz hired ta do that.

Thar wuz a fairly good-sized smokehouse jest outside the kitchen door, a spacious chicken house by the chip yard, and hit also had about ten chicken coops fer raisin' chicklets, and a pig pen at the fur end of the chip yard fer fattenin' hogs fer slaughter. On the north side across the creek wuz the barnyard. Within the barnyard wuz a corn crib on posts and a two-story barn. The top story wuz a loft fer hay and some storage fer vegetables or miscellaneous stuff. Thar wuz a hog lot directly 'cross from the house on the other side of the holler and an outhouse about fifty yards from the main house. A palin' fence bleached to a light gray by many years of exposure ta the sun encircled the yard and garden, and thar wuz also a separatin' palin' fence 'tween the garden and the yard.

The two main rooms faced north, and there wuz a passageway 'tween 'em with an entry/exit key lockable door in the center of the passageway. The lower bedroom wuz kinda like the guest bedroom and had two double beds loaded down with ah whole bunch of extra homemade quilts. Thar wuz a winder between the two beds. At the foot of the far bed, Grandma kept her mother's ornate family rocker, and on the side wall, a picture of Grandma's mommy and daddy, Lydia Mason and Wiley Reed. On the near side of the room wuz a handle wind-up phonograph. Aunt Cassie would let me play some old 78 RPM records as a special treat. Thar wuz a small table at the end of the near bed that had an assortment of purties; one wuz a hen with two chicklets and another wuz a hollered-out glass fish that could hold candy. Thar wuz another winder on the north side of the room close ta the foot of the near bed. Near the fireplace in the corner wuz an antique dresser and mirror. The door ta this room wuz normally kept closed.

The main bedroom had two double beds at the far end of the room. Both heads of the beds war at the east end. Between the beds wuz Grandma's Singer sewing machine. The inner bed wuz Grandma's and Aunt Cassie's. Aunt Cassie slept on the outer side by the wall, Grandma on the inner side. The farthest bed was Grandpa's (and mine when I stayed with 'em). I already mentioned I had the far side. Thar wuz a winder right above the sewing machine. At the foot of Grandpa's bed, two Army-issue trunks war stacked.

Much ta Grandma's chagrin, an assortment of miscellaneous paraphernalia usually wound up on top. Hangin' over Grandpa's bed wuz a picture of his mommy and daddy, Catherine Cole and John Bishop. At the end of the trunks wuz a small chest with their battery-powered radio on top, used for listenin' ta Grandma's preachers, WLW's 700 Club, fer news but mainly weather out of Cincinnati, Ohio, and on Saturday nights the Grand Ole Opry. My favorites on the Grand Ole Opry war June Carter, Earnest Tubb, Little Jimmy Dickens, Minnie Pearl, Grandpa Jones, Roy Acuff, Eddie Arnold, Hank Snow, and Walt Whitman. Listenin' ta the sangin, the music, the stories, the dancin' (dos-a-dos), the laughin', and clappin' wuz alla's the high point of mah week. Grandma would alla's jest shake her head and mutter somethin' like, "Sech carryin's on!" But I knowed she liked hit too, even though she said she mostly liked hit fer the gospel songs. Truth be told thar warn't a whole lot of gospel songs. But I liked hit all. I liked everythang 'bout the Grand Ole Opry.

A second winder wuz on the wall jest behind the radio. On the wall jest afore goin' inta the passageway separatin' the two bedrooms wuz Grandma's chifforobe. Thar wuz a large pantry in the corner on the right side of the fireplace whar Grandma kept her canned goods. One day wen I everbody else wuz outside and I came inta the room a big black snake came crawlin' out of the pantry, and nearly scared the poop out of me. Scared the snake too. I started in hollerin fer Grandpa who came ta mah rescue and killed the snake.

In front of the pantry, thar wuz a large dresser. Also, thar war removable planks in front of the fireplace fer storin' items that needed ta be kept from freezin' in the winter. Thar war five homemade straight-backed chairs with bark seats that Grandpa redid as necessary with hickory bark strips. Grandpa had one. Aunt Cassie had one. Grandma had one. And thar wuz another one for company, and I had one. Fer mealtime, chairs had ta be carried ta the kitchen fer the adults and then returned round the fireplace atter everyone wuz finished eatin'. I alla's toted Grandma's chair fer her. I, on the other hand, sat on the bench, which was pretty much stationary on the south kitchen wall.

Unlike at home, I actually got ta sit and eat jest like everybody else. Thar wuz a winder above the bench but hit wuz alla's ta my back when I wuz eatin', but then agin I didn't need ta pay attention ta much else wen I wuz eatin'.

In the middle of the south wall of the bedroom at the foot of Grandma's bed, thar wuz a door leadin' inta the kitchen. The eatin' table pretty much sat in the middle of the east end of the kitchen. At the extreme east end of the kitchen wuz a door ta the outside, which had no lock but could be kept closed with a latch. Thar wuz an outside screen door ta help keep the flies out. In the summertime flies could be a real menace. Grandma would buy fly paper and strang hit from the ceilin' ta catch those flies that got inside in spite of the screen door. Jest outside the door on the left side of the steps goin' out wuz the slop bucket used for collectin' dishwater (no detergents used) and fer whatever leftovers not eaten that war saved ta be taken ta the hogs. I would sometime supplement the hogs' diet by pullin' horse weeds and pig weeds, and then I would carry 'em and throw 'em over the hog lot fence. That seemed ta be a real treat fer the hogs 'cause they would grunt and shove and war real piggish 'bout who got the lion's share of the greenery.

Comin' in the door from the outside thar wuz a wood-fired kitchen stove on the right side fer all meal preparations. Behind the stove wuz an array of nails fer hangin' beans, apples, pumpkins, squash, or whatever Grandma might want to preserve by dryin' 'em out (dehydrating). Hit wuz also used fer storin' pots and pans. Ta the left side of the room wuz an upturned fifty-pound lard can with a warshbasin on top. Above that wuz a shelf with a two-and-a-half-gallon bucket of water with one communal dipper. A communal dryin' towel could be found hangin' on the door goin' inta the bedroom along with Grandma's and Aunt Cassie's sunbonnets.

Continuin' past the door on the left would be where bulk lard, flour, and cornmeal war stored, and jest past that would be Grandma's china cabinet, which at one time wuz painted green but wuz at that time a very faded green with net wired front doors. Grandma's plates and cups and saucers war muchly faded from all the use they had endured over the years. Cutlery of what thar wuz sat in a pitcher on the table. A goodly portion of hit wuz US issue (borrowed, I 'spect, from the US Army; Uncle Wiley wuz an Army cook, atter all). Past the china cabinet wuz another large piece of furniture, and fer the life of me I don't 'member what hit wuz called 'cept hit really wuz a good piece. The remainder of the room wuz used fer storage on both sides, but thar wuz a path kept in the middle fer gettin' ta the porch.

The porch wuz mainly bare 'cept for a primitive rocker that wuz a sawed-off portion of a tree trunk fer hits seat and hit wuz painted red. Hit wuz too heavy ta tote about. If'n folks wanted ta rest up out on the porch, they'd have ta carry chairs out from the bedroom. In the warmer months Aunt Cassie would have her houseplants hangin' all along the south side of the porch, along with growin' mornin' glories strung up alongside all the posts.

Hit wuz gettin' ta be late spring in 1948 and I'd been stayin' with   Grandma and Grandpa most of a year by this time. We'd all settled in at the new place. Sprang plantin' had been done and we'd all ben out hoein' in the garden. I mentioned the smokehouse afore. Well, the smokehouse entrance door wuz from the yard and wuz flush with the earth but going inta the garden thar wuz a little drop away so that the fur end of the smokehouse wuz on log pillars in order ta keep hit level.

Now Grandpa had an ole dog named Wolf, who wuz not very friendly and he could be downright cantankerous. Wolf wuz chained ta one of the log pillars so's he could be in the shade wen the sun wuz out, and also out of the weather, in case hit rained. That wuz whar he wuz fed and had his waterin' dish. He wuz not allowed to roam free 'cause he wuz so vicious and had ben known to kill Grandma's chickens—a big no-no! I wuz determined I wuz goin' ta be best friends with Wolf. I wuz goin' ta show everybody I could tame 'em and make him mah buddy. Alla's I had ta do wuz ta talk kindly ta 'em and pat his head and scratch behind his ears and make shore he had enough water ta drank.

Now, both Grandma and Grandpa, as well as Aunt Cassie, had warned me ta stay away from that dog. But would I listen? Fer the last couple of days, I had been sneakin' by wen nobody wuz lookin' and pettin' Wolf on the head and tellin' him what a good dog he wuz, and he seemed ta like that. I wuz shore I could tame 'em, couldn't I? I mean, I already said so. I wuz shore we war well on ar way ta becoming best chums.

Well, on that day, wen everybody wuz in the garden hoein' tatters, I would show 'em jest what I could do. All the tatter hoers war jest ah little ways away from the end of the smokehouse wen I told Grandma I needed a drank. I laid down mah small hoe and purposefully strode over ta Wolf fer his ritual pettin'. However, that mornin' Ole Wolf must 'ave gotten up on the wrong side of the bed, or maybe his breakfast jest hadn't agreed with 'em, fer wen I reached out ta pet 'em, he grabbed mah arm with his fangs along with a menacin' growl, and almost bit mah arm in two, causin' me to fall on mah face in the dirt. And with that, he wuz all over me slashin' and gnashin' and tearin' me somethin' fierce. I thought I wuz ah goner fer shore, that he wuz goin' ta eat me all up.

I wuz lucky Grandma and Grandpa war so close by, otherwise I probably wouldn't be here ta tell ya this tale. Of course, Grandma bandaged me up and took care of me real good, but I had lots of bites, gnashes, and open sores. All thoughts of taming ole Wolf and makin' him mah best buddy war quickly fergotten, and atter that I warn't so keen on stayin' with Grandma and Grandpa any longer. I missed mah Mommy and Daddy and all mah brothers and sisters.

I had ta admit ta mahself I had been lonely livin' with jest Grandma, Grandpa, and Aunt Cassie. I guess I sorta missed all the kickin' and screamin' and arguin' and, yes, the fightin' at mah home.

I wanted ta go home. So, when Daddy came ta do some work fer Grandma and Grandpa, home I went, ridin' up behind Daddy on ole Bessie. I 'specially felt bad leavin' Grandma, fer she hugged me real close, and I could tell she didn't want me ta go 'cause she was cryin' real hard all the while.

Atter mah extended stay with Grandma and Grandpa had come ta an end, I made many short visits back ta their home in the holler, and I did stay with 'em on all the breaks between school grades 'til I graduated from high school. I wuz makin' one such visit along with Cosetta and Mary Jane one winter day. Not shore how old I wuz at the time but I wuz still a purty little one. Also, I don't 'member 'xactly what month hit wuz but hit wuz mighty cold. I do 'member that. The wind made hit feel even colder. Wen hit wuz blowing in our faces we couldn't hardly breathe and hit made walkin' real hard, almost pushing us backards.

We got Jim Baker, who lived close ta the river, ta set us cross the Kentucky River in his boat. By that time I think I wuz already half-frozen. The problem wuz gettin' cross the river wuz only halfway to Grandma's house and hit wuz gettin' colder by the minute. I had on my ole winter coat that I had 'bout outgrown. The lower parts of mah arms and hands war stickin' way out. I didn't have no gloves neither. My shoes war for all purposes 'bout worn out; didn't matter, though, fer we could only afford one pair a year. Thank goodness I did have on mah overshoes, which did help some.

Anyway, by the time we finally got to Grandma's house, I had no feelin's left in mah face or in mah feet, and mah hands war completely numb and frozen as stiff as boards. I couldn't even bend mah fangers. When Grandma saw us, she burst into tears. 'Peered I wuz the worst of the lot. She sot me down near the fireplace, pulled my shirt and coat sleeves back out of the way, fetched a pan of cold water from the bucket in the kitchen, and held mah hands in the water ta thaw 'em out.

At first I didn't feel nuttin' fer a good while, but then mah hands started in tinglin' and then hit wuz like thar wuz all these needles explodin' underneath the skin and hit hurt mighty bad. Hit was like mah hands war on fire. In spite of mah best big-boy efforts, these big tears started rollin' down mah cheeks, and Grandma wuz cryin' rite along with me. As mah hands thawed and feelin's begin ta return, Grandma started in rubbin' 'em and blowin' on 'em ta help the blood ta recirculate. After the three of us had somewhat recovered, Grandma made us some hot cocoa. We all three seemed ta suffer no untoward consequences, 'cept I have all mah life had difficulty with cold hands. Don't know if this little incident had anything ta do with hit or not.

I first came into Grandma's and Grandpa's and Aunt Cassie's lives when I was born, and they were in their mid-to-late fifties; Aunt Cassie was approaching 19. Grandma lived to be 78, and Grandpa lived to be 83. Aunt Cassie had a much shorter lifespan, living to be only 59.

I have an early memory of Grandma when I was left there by Uncle Wiley, but not sure I remember Grandpa much from that episode. I have a vague memory of Aunt Cassie when she and Grandma came to visit us on Clay Street in Cincinnati but a much better picture when Grandma and I retrieved her from the Richmond, Kentucky, hospital after her second nervous breakdown.

Grandma was the first to pass just a few months before Sue's and my wedding. It was very hard fer me, for Grandma was the first person who was really close to me who died. I didn't do well at her funeral, and it was everythang I could do not to lose it when I witnessed them lowering' her casket into the ground in the area by her mother and father and her two little girls she had lost all those many years ago. The hardest thing was knowing that I would never be able to see Grandma, the person I had loved so much in this life, again.

From this point of her burial, all that I would have left would be memories. I did console myself with the fact she was no longer in pain—she had suffered so much in her declining years. Mostly, I remember Grandma as a strong woman, maybe not so much in her later years as her health began to fail her, but she was the one who kept that household on track and running. And I always knew she loved me, for me. I always felt in her eyes I could do no wrong, so I always tried to maintain her faith in me.

Grandma made an imposing figure: big-boned and a good 5 feet 10 inches tall, stout, and heavyset (some might even say overweight) as Grandma tipped the scales at over 250 pounds in her heyday. She was light-complected and often had rosy cheeks especially if she had been out in the sun despite always wearing her sunbonnet. I always thought she was a beautiful, warm, and generous person, and whatever she said or wanted me to do, it was in my mind, the right thing to do.

She had this long, slightly auburn hair, and when she combed it out, it reached down past her waist. Though she normally wore it twisted up in a bun that stretched across her head from ear to ear. By putting her hair up in a bun, it pulled it away from her face and gave her an angelic appearance. I always thought that God's grown-up angels would look somewhat like Grandma. Later, though, in her seventies, her hair began to lose some of its color and was streaked with white but retained some of that color until her death.

In her later years, she suffered from her legs and feet swelling something awful. You couldn't tell she had ankles. She had high blood pressure, an enlarged heart, and congestive heart failure. At night she complained of stomach pains causing her to clutch at her chest and emit low moans. She would chew on dried ginseng for relief. In retrospect, I believe she was experiencing acid reflux.

When I was smaller, she liked to nuss me on her lap, but as I got older, she was content to just rub my cheeks, my head, my back, or even my hands. It seemed to comfort her just to touch me, which in turn always pleased me. Her hands were always a little rough from all of her work, and in the winter, they would be chapped and cracked from the cold.

Grandpa was about the same height as Grandma but was as skinny as a rail and had a much darker complexion. Said it was from his Irish side. I believe somewhere back in hie genes there was a bit of Native American blood, which may have also influenced his coloration. Grandma often said he ate like a horse, but for the life of her, she couldn't put any meat on his bones. She couldn't fatten him up. He was always going, much like the Ever-Ready Bunny. His face was weathered from all the years of working out in the elements. He had two deep furrows running across his brow, always looking like they were trying to frown, but on top was a smaller, shorter one that was uplifted like it was trying to smile. I've mentioned before he had no teeth, so when he smiled it was a toothless one.

His uniform, without fail, was bibbed overalls, a long-sleeved shirt (never saw him wearin' a short-sleeved one), and an old floppy hat. Often, on his bibbed overalls, there would be patches on his knees and sometimes on his backside over his rump area, and there might even be patches on top of patches. He, too, was never outside without his head covering. To complete his ensemble, he always wore a pair of brogans. In wintertime he would add an old coat, overshoes over his brogans, and change his floppy hat for a cap with earmuffs or ear flaps and maybe a pair of gloves complemented his ensemble, and underneath he would be wearing a pair of long handles.

He had a big bald spot on the back of his head and was also balding somewhat in the front. What hair he had left was as black as coal. Even when he got older, his hair retained most of the black color; however, it did become streaked with some gray before he died. He loved to sing, as I've already mentioned, usually at the top of his lungs. He seemed to know hundreds of songs; in retrospect, some I think he embellished. However, his favorites were "*Rock of Ages*" and "*Amazing Grace.*"

He never met a stranger and didn't mind sharing items about his personal life with anyone, including when he started drawing his old age pension checks when he turned 65, even how much money he had. He was so proud that he had a little money now, for most of his life had been such a struggle with very little, or no money.

Anyway, he used to embarrass me to no end with his forthrightness in sharing the smallest details of his personal life. Grandpa had had no formal schooling. I guess there were no schools close to Bishop's Bend on the Kentucky River where he was born and growed up. Anyway, he could neither read nor write, and anything requiring a signature, he would mark down using his familiar X.

Grandpa did know a lot about nature and farming. He knew the names of the trees in the woods and most of the plants growing around. He was fascinated by the hatch marks on the trees that indicated the surveyed boundaries that delineated parcels of property. Grandpa worked hard, and in hot weather, he sweated a lot and often would come home with his shirt soaked. After drying out, especially as the week progressed, you could see the white salty residue on the back of his shirt and underneath his armpits because his clothes were changed only once a week. To boot it all, I never knew Grandpa to take a bath— not even a spit bath.

He did shave, though—once a week, with a straight-edged razor. I would watch him pull out the old strap and he'd whip the razor up and down on both sides to make sure it wuz adequately sharpened; I mean sharpened real good. Before he started to shave, he'd check it by first testing a few hairs on his arm. Before he started his shaving procedure, he would heat water in the teakettle on the kitchen stove, usually while dinner was being prepared. He would pour a goodly amount into the washbasin, where he would wet and rinse his razor as he shaved.

As Grandpa's years added up, one of his peculiarities was that well within five seconds or so, upon him sitting down, you would see his chin slowly dropping on his chest, and in another instant, he would be fast asleep; he may have suffered from a form of narcolepsy. Not sure about that. Grandpa always called me his bed buddy, as I always slept with Grandpa whenever I stayed at their house, always on the far side of him, next to the wall.

6. FAMILY DIET GROWING UP

Food—the essence of life! Feeding themselves and ten kids had to have been a struggle for our parents, but somehow, they did it and we all survived. Breakfast for all those years was pretty rote—biscuits and gravy and a glass of milk when ole Bessie (our cow) was giving milk. Sometimes there was not enough to go around, and we had to save it for supper, which would normally consist of a glass of milk and cornbread (hereafter referred to as cornpone).

Cornpone, or Southern cornbread, is made only with cornmeal, buttermilk, salt, eggs, and lard. Our glasses often consisted of jars from bought peanut butter, commercial jelly, or fruit jars. Dinner, or what most folks call lunch, would normally have been pinto beans or fried potatoes or sometimes baked or infrequently fried sweet potatoes with cornpone. This was the big meal of the day. Leftover cornpone was kept for supper as well as any other item not consumed for dinner.

During the school year, we kids ran home during the dinner (lunch) recess, where Mommy would always have whatever food was available waiting for us. We would gulp it down and then run back to school, a distance of about three-fourths of a mile each way. Of course, the garden did supplement our food supply. First, in early spring, leaf lettuce. Had to be picked by hand and thoroughly washed and dried, then scalded with hot bacon grease or lard, mostly because bacon was rarely available.

With my grandparents, I learned to go "wilding," which was searching the woods, pastures, and meadows for edible plants that were cooked as greens—there were numerous ones that were tasty when they were just emerging in the spring. I will attempt to list some of the more common ones: purslane, wild garlic, wild onions, nettles (but only after cooking), ground elder, shoney, garlic mustard, wild mustard, cow parsley, purple dean-nettle, common daisy, dandelion, chickweed, lamb's quarter, dock, mallow, plantain, watercress, chicory, miner's lettuce, violet leaves, wild leeks, henbit, etc. One of the more notorious ones was poke, more widely known as "poke salad." Even after the poke plant began to mature, the stalks could be cubed and fried and tasted much like Okra, at least to me.

Our grandmother told the story about an older, widowed lady who lived up the holler from them when Grandma was a youngster. Obviously, this widowed lady lived close to the earth. She was very poor and struggled to survive and make ends meet. She did have a cow that she and her husband owned before he passed. Early in the spring, when the trees were just beginning to leaf out, the earth was becoming all fresh, and new plants were sprouting everywhere, the widow lady would take her cow out to pasture and follow the cow around and watch her carefully and note every plant the cow grazed on. For every plant the cow consumed, the old lady would also pick that kind of plant for herself and take it home and cook it for a "mess of greens." Her reasoning was that if it was good enough for her cow, it was good enough for herself. The proof was in the pudding, for she never poisoned herself.

Getting back to the garden supplements we grew and harvested. There were mustard greens, peas, and green beans, and if the green beans got overly ripened before they were picked, they could be further dried and reserved for soup beans, beets, carrots, cucumbers, radishes, green peppers, hot peppers, onions, tomatoes, corn for corn-on-the-cob, Irish potatoes, sweet potatoes, squash, pumpkins, apples, and peaches. We had a pear tree, but I don't remember it producing' very much.

In addition to all those things we grew ourselves, there was a plethora of edibles to be gathered seasonably growing in the wild. We picked blackberries, which were available in abundance; raspberries; wild strawberries; huckleberries (blueberries); gooseberries; and dewberries. Occasionally, there were vendors coming by in trucks selling melons and peaches, and if Mommy happened to have the cash, she would buy a couple of bushels of peaches for canning and even bake us a cobbler peach pie if we were lucky. In the fall there were elderberries, black walnuts, English walnuts, hickory nuts, and hazelnuts. I'm sure I've left some out. Mommy canned a lot of the fruits and vegetables when they were in season to supplement our meager offerings during the lean times. From our apples Mommy made apple butter, and from the peach peelings and berries she would make a lot of jams and jellies.

Meat was not an everyday item on our daily menus. Whenever we had company, we would either have fried chicken (one piece each) or chicken and dumplings. We had pork in the fall when it got cold enough to butcher the hog—or hogs, whichever the case might have been. Hunters in the family (Dad and William David mostly—never me) did help supplement the meager meat offerings with squirrels, an occasional rabbit, and I even seem to remember a raccoon or two and maybe even a groundhog or so?

I don't recall us having popcorn even though Grandma raised some and Aunt Cassie would "cap" (their term for popping the popcorn) with a popcorn shaker over the fireplace, which we would share without salt or butter or any other kind of flavoring (pretty bland come to think of it but as we had never had it any other way it was quite acceptable). At our home, we would shell field corn and parch it in a skillet on the stovetop, and that is about the only after-mealtime treat I remember growing up with. We never had cookies or candies or any other kinds of sweets that I remember.

Desserts, on the other hand, were rare treats! On occasion Mommy would bake a fruit cobbler, usually when we had company or when Daddy came home from Cincinnati on weekends. Sometimes she made vanilla cookie pudding or, in the fall, pumpkin pies. Once Cosetta, my oldest sister, had a beau visit (sparking, as it was called then), and we had pie for dessert. The following episode involved Everett, my younger brother.

Now, I have to set the scene. We had a large round table where only the grown-ups got to sit while we young-uns stood up to eat. I would probably have been about 8, and Everett would have been about 5. Anyway, we were standing around the table with only the few adults seated in their chairs. Daddy was in Cincinnati and Mommy had the honor of saying the blessing. As soon as Mommy had finished the blessing and the amens were rendered, Everett started jumping up and down, adamantly yelling, "Pass the pie! Pass the pie, please! Pass the pie, pass the pie, please! Pass the pie!" The only thing was the pie was sitting right by his plate! Everett, I guess, has always had a sweet tooth and, at that time, wanted to make sure he wasn't left out and was putting his dibs in up front to get a piece of the pie before it was all gone, and he was left out. He has never lived that incident down to this day.

Ice cream (vanilla only) was a real rarity. I think (not sure) we got a quart (might have been even a half gallon) for the whole family. Anyway, my portion was about a tablespoonful. You have to consider we had no electricity until I was about 8, and it was eleven miles into town (the only place ice cream was available to purchase), so by the time ice cream got home, it was getting pretty soft—melting fast, particularly if the day was warm. Neither Mommy nor Daddy drove any sort of vehicle, so they had to depend on someone else for transportation.

I don't remember us ever having any big holiday meals, not Easter, not Thanksgiving, not even Christmas! Birthdays, too, were not celebrated—just another day to survive. We were fortunate to have enough food for any given day, and some days, I doubt if there was enough to go around.

7. SEEKING AN EDUCATION

One starts gettin' educated the day they're born. However, mah entry into the formal process began with that horrendous dog bite from Ole Wolf and mah return to the family fold in the spring of 1948.
At the start of the school year, all mah older siblings headed off ta Brookside Elementary School (except fer Fern 'cause of her handicap due to polio; she went ta the county school in Booneville, Kentucky. A yaller school bus would pick her up jest cross the gravel road by ar house and atter school would brang her back in the afternoon.) Brookside wuz a one-room schoolhouse that catered ta all eight elementary grades. Hit usually started with twenty-somethin' students at the beginnin' of the school year. A few would move away, or jest drop out afore the school year wuz completed. Hit wuz the same schoolhouse whar ar Daddy completed his eight years of schoolin' despite himself.

The schoolhouse had no electricity or plumbin'! Hit had been painted white with a black tar-shingled roof. Both ends of the buildin' had no winders. The winders along both sides war the only source of light 'cept in pleasant weather wen the single door could be kept open. The north end of the buildin' faced the gravel road, and the south end faced the Right Fork of Island Creek and wuz located forty or fifty yards from the creek. From the gravel road, the right side of the buildin' (west) had five large winders, the left (east) had four winders, and the door wuz close to the north end, which wuz the entryway.

On the inside, the north end of the buildin' had a large blackboard on the wall. In front of the blackboard to the left wuz the teacher's desk, and to the right wuz an area fer class recitation. Thar wuz a bullet hole in the upper left-hand corner of the blackboard. I never knowed the source or what the reason wuz fer hit bein' thar. Each class would be called ta the front fer recitation, dependin' on the subject and the time.

In front of the teacher's desk and facin' hit, thar war two parallel rows of twelve double student desks. That still left room in the back of the buildin' for a recreation (play) area on those inclement weather days wen students could not go outside. Thar wuz also a closet on the left side fer storage and hooks along the wall fer hangin' winter clothin'. Underneath the last winder on the left side wuz a table that held a two-and-one-half-gallon bucket fer water. Hit wuz freshly filled from the neighbor's well each mornin' at the beginnin' of the school day.

Drinkin' water wuz replenished as necessary, maybe once or twice durin' the day. This chore wuz assigned to some of the older boys. Thar wuz one community dipper available fer all of the students. A large pot-bellied coal-fired stove wuz located in the center of the room and wuz used to heat the schoolhouse in cold weather. Thar wuz an outdoor privy located not fur from the front of the school fer the girls. The boys' outdoor toilet wuz located 'cross the field in the back of the school. Fer the boys, no loiterin; wen one had to go! Toilet necessities war at the generosity of someone brangin' an outdated Sears Roebuck or Montgomery Ward catalog. I'm not shore I ever heard of toilet paper wen I wuz growin' up. Leaves, weeds, corn cobs, or whatever wuz handy could be used if thar war no catalogs available! Knew them intimately. Yep!

In mah beginnin' year, the teacher, Miss Miller, wuz young, fresh right out of Teachers College. Hit jest so happened thar wuz only one student enterin' the first grade, Teddy Dean, that year. Miss Miller didn't like the idea of Teddy bein' all by his self in the first grade, so she consulted with all the other students, 'specially Cosetta, mah oldest sister, ta see if thar might be anyone else eligible ta attend the first grade.

Hit came down ta *me*. Miss Miller asked Cosetta if she thought her (ar) mom would consider allowin' me ta enter school early so Teddy wouldn't be alone in the first grade. Wen Mom wuz consulted, hit wuz like, "Hallelujah! Whar do I sign up? Can't wait ta get that young'un out from underfoot and let someone else be aggravated by 'em! Maybe they can keep 'em straight, and good luck with that!" An answer ta her prayers. God had been listenin', atter all.

So, I started first grade a little early, at 5 years old, shortly atter mah fifth birthday. And I found I really enjoyed hit. I wuz in mah element. Ta mah 5-year-old eyes, the schoolhouse seemed enormous. However, on the second day I wanted ta ask Miss Miller a question but she wuz havin' recitation fer a different grade, so she told me ta go back ta mah seat and sit down and wait mah turn.

The way hit worked wuz the students war separated by grades. The first graders war in front on the right side and hit progressed ta the back with the bigger kids—or I should say the senior grades—in the rear of the school. The teacher would call the students by grade ta the front of the room by her desk fer recitation fer different subjects. At the point in question, she had the fourth grade doin' thar thang, which included mah big brother William David.

I had finished drawin' all the numbers she had told me ta do and wuz a little lost as ta what ta do next. I didn't want ta jest sit thar, and Teddy wuz still busy with his drawin's so I couldn't ax him. I needed somethin' ta do. Anyhow, we had ben told we war not permitted ta talk with each other wen school wuz goin' on. So that wuz why I went up ta inquire of Miss Peters 'bout what I needed ta do next, and I didn't understand why I couldn't ask her a question if she wuz jest talkin' ta William David. I felt I wuz jest as important as 'em. So, wen she told me ta go back ta mah desk and sit down, I didn't like what she told me, and I didn't like her tone of voice neither. Hit jest didn't make sense ta me. So, instead of returnin' ta mah seat and sittin' down like she said, I turned round and acted like I wuz headed fer mah desk, but wen I got near the front I made a quick detour and a mad dash out the door and headed fer home jest as fast as mah legs would carry me. I didn't like bein' told thangs I didn't like ta hear. I wuz jest goin' ta go back home ta Mommy and Daddy, nuff of this nonsense. I would show her a thang or two.

I didn't get very fur, though. Miss Miller saw what wuz happenin' and guessed mah intentions. She immediately stopped her recitation with William David's class, and ran right atter me, and boy she could run fast, 'specially fer a grown-up, faster than me, as hit turned out. She caught me afore I got much past the corner of the schoolhouse, grabbed me up, and gave me a big bear hug. Surprised the heck outta me.

"Whar do you thank you're goin', ya little bugger?" she queried with a small, breathless chuckle. Even though I wuz mad at her. I mean, she had jest hurt mah feelin's, hadn't she? She wuz laughin' at me, but her huggin' me made me feel better, and though I wuz 'bout ta cry, I told her I thought I needed ta go see mah daddy, 'cause I missed 'em, and I wuz shore he needed ta see me. "I thank he needs me," I said, snifflin'. She said hit wuz OK, but that goin' home ta see mah daddy needed ta wait 'til atter school wuz over 'cause she needed me ta stay with all the other children and with her. She gave me 'nother big bear hug, drapped me down, took me by mah hand, and led me back inta the schoolhouse. I didn't 'ave no other choice so atter havin' a few dry sobs and wipin' mah nose on the back of mah hand, I settled right down and hit turned out I wuz alright.

I did well in school and caught on ta readin' quickly 'cause I liked hit. Our first book wuz 'bout Dick and Jane. I soon discovered I enjoyed readin' the stories in the older kids' books as well. Grandma had taught me most of mah ABCs and mah numbers so that I could count up to 100. Hit didn't make sense ta me ta say 100 and somethin', but wen hit finally got splan'd ta me, so I understood hit, then I got along jest fine.

A big highlight of that first year wuz practicin' fer the County Fair. Miss Miller would line us all up along the gravel road in pairs fer "practicin' pradin'." Teddy and I war in front cause we war the littlest, and we got ta lead the parade. However, Miss Miller would walk in front of us, showin' us whar we war supposed ta go. She, me, Teddy, and two other students carryin' our school banner which announced that we war the Brookside School.

Several of the students war goin' ta compete in different events at the Fair. The events war divided inta athletics (runnin', jumpin', chin-ups, etc.) and scholastics (readin', handwritin', etc.) I wuz goin' ta do a verse that mah grandma had larnt me. I knew hit by heart (from memory). "Little Boy Blue" by Eugene Field:

> The little toy dog is covered with dust,
> But sturdy and staunch he stands;
> And the little toy soldier is red with rust,
> And his musket molds in his hands.
> Time was when the little toy dog was new,
> And the soldier was passing fair;
> And that was the time when our Little Boy Blue.
> Kissed them and put them there.
> "Now, don't you go 'til I come," he said,
> "And don't you make any noise!"
> So, toddling off to his trundle bed,
> He dreamt of the pretty toys;
> And as he was dreaming, an angel song
> Awakened our Little Boy Blue
> Oh! The years are many, the years are long,
> But the little toy friends are true!
> Ay, faithful to Little Boy Blue they stand,
> Each in the same old place
> Awaiting the touch of a little hand,
> The smile of a little face;
> And they wonder, as waiting the long years through
> In the dust of the little chair,
> What has become of our Little Boy Blue,
> Since he kissed and put them there.

The mornin' of the County Fair, the yaller school bus picked us up, and hit seemed hit drove us ferever

(eleven miles). Finally, hit drapped us off in front of the county jail, whar we all waited fer the parade ta start. We had ta wait a long time afore we got ta parade, and thar warn't no place ta even set down, and I shore got tired of jest standin' round doin' nothin'
.

However, the parade finally started, and we follered some other schools down the road, round the courthouse, down 'nother road, cross the bridge—the bridge that Daddy had helped build—and then inta the County School Grounds whar we had ta stand agin 'til everybody else got thar. Then everybody had ta sang "The Star-Spangled Banner" and a preacher man said a prayer, and some man said a bunch of somethin' which I didn't understand 'cause I wuz jest interested in getting on with thangs 'cause I wanted ta do my recitin' and see the fair. I had never seed a fair afore. I wuz excited ta see what wuz goin' on.

Atter the parade and the holdup, Miss Miller told me ta wait in place for her ta come and collect me fer mah verse recitin' 'cause hit wuz one of the first thangs goin' on atter the parade. Cosetta waited with me. I wuz purty excited. Thar war all kinds of thangs goin' on at the Fair. Thar wuz a Ferris wheel and a merry-go-round and swangs that went round in circles, and other apparatuses which I didn't know the names of, and music playin' and people rushin' round like crazy, everywhar. Sorta 'minded me of watchin' a bunch of ants swarmin' round an anthill.

Hit warn't long afore Miss Miller came back and took me off ta the high school buildin', whar we had ta wait in the hallway 'til they called mah name ta go inside ta recite mah verse. Wen they did get round ta callin' me,

I wuz hopin' they would hurry up so I could go and see what wuz goin' on at the Fair.

I went in and stood in front of the judge (another grown-up lady, a teacher from the Booneville school, I wuz later told). The lady wuz all dressed up in a bright red dress and she looked like she had had too many moon pies. Her face wuz as broad as hit wuz long and wuz real rosy too, and her neck sorta plunged down inta her chest and bosom, which she had plenty of. Grandpa woulda said she wuz purty fleshy (overweight). She wuz friendly 'nough ta me, though, and smiled at me and asked me mah name. I told her. She asked me what I had prepared fer her. I told her "Little Boy Blue" by Eugene Field jest like Miss Miller and I had gone over hit and over hit. She told me ta go ahead, and I did. I shore wuz glad to recite mah verse and ta get out of thar. I think I did purty good. I didn't forget nuttin'.

However, I found out later in the day when prizes war announced I didn't win any ribbons. Ribbons war awarded fer first, second, and third places. Miss Miller seemed more disappointed than me. I hadn't expected anythang, so hit didn't really matter that much. Not ta me anyhow. I wuz jest glad ta do hit and get hit over with. Miss Miller said she wuz still really proud of me even if I didn't get no ribbon. That made me feel real good.

Anyway, I really did enjoy mah first fair. I met up with mah friend and fellow classmate, Teddy, and we had the bestest time. We rode the merry-go-round, the swangs, and the Ferris wheel. We even saw a black bear. Gosh, did he ever stank! I don't thank he musta ever had a bath, and his toilet offerings had been left right thar fer everybody to see and smell. Shore didn't smell like no cow or horse poop. Stunk even worse than the hog lot. I had ta panch my nose 'til we got outta thar. I shore did keep mah distance, though, 'cause I don't mind tellin' ya I wuz mighty skeered of 'em.

I suppose every little boy falls in love with their first teacher if'n they're as nice and purty and smelt as good as Miss Miller did. Nor wuz I the only one. Everybody in the whole school liked Miss Miller—I mean *really* liked Miss Miller. And ya know what? She really liked us too. But ya know, half ways through the school year, she played a really dirty trick on us and got married and quit teachin' school at Brookside. I wuz jest heartbroken. How could she do this ta me? They had ta close Brookside School 'cause they didn't have ah 'nother teacher ta teach us!

Most of the kids, includin' mah older brother and sisters, war hauled off by bus to the Island City School way up the road. Not me, though. They said I wuz too young. That wuz jest not fair. I wuz later ta find out that thar would be many times I would find life not ta be fair. Perhaps this wuz not the first time, but fer shore, hit would not be the last! Fortunately, the school board did find a teacher fer Brookside fer the next school year, and I wuz passed on ta the second grade along with mah friend, Teddy.

Games at School
Curiously, we didn't have a baseball, a football, a soccer ball, or a basketball, so we didn't play any of those games. No one owned a ball or other paraphernalia needed fer those sports. Sometimes, one of our classmates would come up with a rubber

ball and we would use a stick fer a bat and play a simplified version of baseball if we had enough players ta make up two teams. Rocks were plentiful, so they war used ta mark the bases. We had two fifteen-minute recesses—one in the mornin' and one in the afternoon—plus a one-hour lunch (dinner) break. Most kids went (ran) home for the midday break. So, games had to be time limited. Games normally included tag, hide and seek, kick-the-can, London Bridge is fallin' down, Mother/Father may I, jump rope, jacks, blind man's bluff, etc. Before the fair, we did get some time out ta practice fer events, includin' readin', penmanship, poetry, racin', jumpin', chin-ups, etc.

Thar wuz a large flat field right by the school below the gravel road that wuz an ideal place ta run and play in (tag, racin', hide and seek). I don't 'member what year hit happened, but that particular year, the local farmer decided ta plant backer (tobacco) in ar playfield.

By the time the school year started, the backer (tobacco) plants war shoulder-high ta many of us and taller than some. We kids war somewhat befuddled that someone would have the audacity ta trespass on what we felt wuz rightly ar playground, without a how-do-you-do or nuttin'. Well, on the other hand, the backer field, even with the half-grown backer, still made a great place fer tag, hide-and-seek, racein', etc., as I jest mentioned, 'cause hit wuz easier ta escape or hide. However, we war mindless of the damage we war doin' ta the backer plants, tearin' off many, if not most, of the lower leaves (the cash portion of the crop). Wen the local farmer happened ta inspect his backer crop, he discovered what wuz happenin' and reported hit ta our teacher, Mrs. Burnsides.

Behind her back, we called her Mrs. Polly Pig Tail (or even worse, Mrs. Polly Pig Turd—some did; I didn't, or at least I'm not ownin' up ta hit). I don't recall why we called her that, 'cept she never seemed ta have a hair out of place and some of us thought she wore a wig. Plus, she wuz a purty strict and demandin' teacher. Some even called her mean. She didn't put up with no nonsense from any of us. Wen she first came ta teach at Brookside, she wuz Mrs. Clemmons, but then she got married and became Mrs. Burnsides. 'Cept, she didn't stop teachin' atter gettin' married like Miss Miller did.

Wen she wuz Mrs. Clemmons, she drove a Model T car, but wen she came back atter marryin' Mr. Burnsides, she drove ah 'nother kind of car, I thank hit wuz called a Nash. We guessed her new husband musta had a lot of money. She and her husband lived up on Do Creek (pronounced Doe creek) near whar mah Aunt Rachel, Uncle Eli, and cousins lived. Now ta the matter at hand. Wen our teacher, Mrs. Burnsides, larned what the whole school had been up ta, she told us what a bad thang we had ben doin'—we war absolutely not allowed ta destroy other people's property—and that we must not set foot in the farmer's tobacco field (we knew she meant the backer field) ever again. She wuz very disappointed in us, and she expected better from her students.

Fer the damage we had caused, every one of us wuz goin' ta be punished. She ordered us ta line up one by one and come and lean over her desk. Then she took out her dreaded paddle and gave each of us a healthy swat! Out of the whole school, only two cried—mah brother Henry and Landon Day. I guess I felt sorry fer Landon. He didn't have a mother or father. He wuz kept by (lived with) his grandma in a house on the hill cross Island Creek on the other side of the Brookside School. The kids at school whispered behind his back that he wuz a bastard. I didn't know what a bastard wuz, but the other kids made hit sound like hit wuzn't somethin' very good. I played with 'em anyway 'cause I didn't thank hit wuz catchin', and I liked 'em. I even stayed all night with 'em one night. He slept with his grandma, and I slept on the couch that night and didn't catch hit; at least, I didn't thank I did.

Atter finishing first grade and school wuz out, Grandma wanted me ta come back and stay with 'em at least 'til school started agin, and I wanted ta. But this time, I shore wuz goin' ta stay away from Ole Wolf and keep mah distance from 'em. Grandma would buy me mah school clothes and a few tricks and even give me some pocket change if'n I would come and stay with her and Grandpa and Aunt Cassie. Mommy and Daddy agreed that I could spend the time 'tween school, so off I went. Plus, I really liked stayin' with 'em 'cause they all treated me like I wuz really special. Grandma certainly did. I could do no wrong in her eyes. She wuz alla's tryin' ta fatten me up, though. When I wuz a little'en' I never had much of an appetite, but Grandma would alla's try urgin' me on by tellin' me "Little Wiley, ya gotta eat so's hit keep ya from gittin' hongry." But despite her concentrated efforts hit didn't seem ta work real well, and she'd say, "You're jest skinny as a rail and ya ain't got no rump a'tall." She loved ta tell and laugh 'bout the one warsh day when she wuz very late getting' us dinner (lunch) wen I had stopped playin' and musta ben hoverin' 'bout her whar she was tending ta her warshin' and she raised her head up and looked over at me and axed me effen I wuz gittin' hongry. I told her I wuz so hongry I wuz 'bout ready ta get down on ma all fours and ta start grazin' on the grass and weeds like Aunt Cassie's cows effin I didn't git a bite ta eat soon, 'cause ma innards war 'bout ta jump outa ma mouth I's so hongry. She thought that wuz jest the funniest thang. She did pause her warshin' and fixed us some vittles. Can't member what they whar, now. Jest member they filled me rite up.

I larned ta hoe and weed in the garden and helped Aunt Cassie feed the chickens, gather the aggs, and plant her flowers. Fer her flowerbeds, we first had ta dig 'em up good so the ground would be nice and soft. No, I take that back, I first had ta go scoop up buckets of chicken poop from the henhouse and scatter hit on the flowerbeds, and then we would till the flowerbeds mixin' in the chicken poop as we went along with ar hoes. Now the chicken poop wuz all dried out, so hit didn't really stank, or at least not too much, or at least I didn't seem ta notice hit. I jest had ta warsh real good wen we got done.

Atterwards, we would scatter lots and lots of seeds cross the prepared dirt, and on top of that, we layered some black organic dirt we had previously gathered from the woods, aka nature's compost. The flower plants didn't always emerge as intended. Thar would be bald spots in some places and in other places thar war jest clumps of young seedlin's. That would cause us ta carefully thin and transplant ta even things out ta help the plants grow better. Then, later, we would have ta watch fer weeds and painstakingly pull them out so as not ta disturb the new flower plants.

Aunt Cassie also had what seemed ta me hundreds of tuberous flowers—dahlias, lilies, gladiolas, and cannas—which war stored under the smokehouse and covered with mounds of dirt ta insulate 'em from the winter's freezing temperatures. All these had ta be retrieved and replanted all 'round the yard—no small task cause some of 'em war multiple tubers and required really big holes ta plant 'em in. I guess hit wuz from Aunt Cassie I larned ta love and appreciate flowers.

On days I wuzn't otherwise occupied, I roamed the woods and fields round, lookin' fer wildflower bouquets fer Grandma and Aunt Cassie. Thar war and still ar, I believe, a lot of wildflowers in that area—too numerous ta enumerate here but I will list a few of the ones that I most fondly 'member: wild phlox, butterfly weed, daisies, poppies, clover, rhododendron, goldenrod (state flower of Kentucky), trillium, American tiger lilies, ironweed, milkweed, wild aster, shepherd's purse, henbit, Queen Anne's lace, winter cress, bloodroot, spiderwort, azaleas, catch fly, prairie rose, thistle, morning glories, coreopsis, bachelor buttons, passionflower, black-eyed Susans, etc. This is certainly a truncated list and not all the wildflowers mentioned ar adapted to bein' cut flowers fer bouquets.

On mah wanderin's, I would occasionally see rabbits and I would whistle (as Grandpa had taught me) at 'em, and usually they would stop and seem ta listen and turn thar heads first this a way and then that a way with thar ears stickin' straight up. Wen I would try ta sneak up closer, they would hop away faster than I could say Jack Rabbit. I saw squirrels and possums rarely, for this area wuz well hunted. Even rarer, I would catch a glimpse of a fox.

Fortunately, very rarely did I ever catch a glimpse of a polecat, but whenever I did, I wuz sure ta take off in the opposite direction. I encountered their scent often and hit would immediately put me on mah guard. I always tried ta make sure I gave 'em lots of room, fer I did not care ta encounter one up close.

Grandpa did trap and catch groundhogs, which Grandma would cook atter Grandpa had skinned, gutted, and cut them up inta pieces. I never larned ta acquire much of a taste fer groundhog meat. Daddy and William David hunted raccoons, but I never encountered one in the wild, not ever. I did encounter snakes—lots of snakes—and I wuz deathly afraid of 'em no matter what kind they war. Thar war too many scary snake stories from Grandma and Grandpa. I thank most war nonpoisonous, but I wuz always unwilling ta take a chance.

We had lots of toads, frogs, and tortoises round. Hit wuz a challenge trying ta catch bullfrogs. We never did catch any and eat their lags like I later larned folks in France did. They could jump faster than lickety-split and further than me, too. Tortoises could be found all round and made interesting temporary pets. Of course, the larger animals, once native ta Kentucky, had long been hunted ta extinction or had sought refuge elsewhere, such as bison, elk, deer, black bear, mountain lion, bobcat, and wildcat. Some still said thar war wildcats roamin' the hills, but in retrospect, they war probably jest abandoned house cats.

One of my most memorable memories wuz the solitude of the mountains and valleys surroundin' Grandma and Grandpa's place. Perhaps not the solitude a'tall but the multitude of the varied birdsongs that echoed from the woods and meadows back and forth both night and day. Hit wuz difficult to differentiate one from another, but wen they war in sight, some war easily recognized, others less so. On top of the list wuz the cardinal, the Kentucky state bird with their distinctive call: *Wet chew! Wet Chew! Wet chew!* The male alla's dressed in his scarlet uniform, and the female outfitted not quite so brilliantly.

Next wuz the robin redbreast, whose first appearance early in the year wuz shore ta announce spring's impending arrival. Thar wuz the lonely-sounding, plaintive, haunting call of the mourning doves. Whenever they war particularly vociferous, Grandma would say they war calling fer rain or that rain wuz on hits way.

Some of the more brightly plumaged birds war the blue jays—which had harsh, scolding screeches and war mean bullying birds—goldfinches, chickadees, indigo buntings, bluebirds, woodpeckers with their loud shrill call, and loud drummin' or rappin' on trees as they sought out grubs or insects burrowed within the barks of trees—always soundin' ta me as if they war knockin' on the tree trunk askin' if'n they couldn't come in.

If ya happened ta be close enough ta hummingbirds, ya could hear the rhythmic flutterin' of their wangs as they beat 'em by the millisecond. Perhaps with less distinctive plumage, I would classify blackbirds, crackles, cowbirds, barn swallows, meadowlarks with their flute-like whistle, bobwhites with their distinctive bobwhite call, tufted titmouse, crows with their throaty, course call—like they war tryin' to clear their throats.

Grandma alla's told me ta watch out fer the hawks, fer they would steal her chickens. Owls' hoots and screeches could be heard all through the night. Buzzards and turkey vultures (never could tell them apart 'cause they war usually too high up in the sky). If'n, they war on the ground feedin' on some varmint, I always gave 'em a wide berth 'cause I wuz downright skeered of 'em, and the varmints of which they would be feedin' would usually be rottin' and stankin' ta high heavens.

Special mention goes ta the whip-poor-will. Native Americans called 'em Soul Catchers and purported that atter death, they carried souls ta the other side. Grandma insisted that should a whip-poor-will alight on somebody's roof and call out inta the night, someone in that household wuz bound ta die soon.

Now, these war jest a few of the Kentucky birds that I wuz most familiar with cause thar are more than 350 bird species that call Kentucky home.

I also got ta help plant and cultivate the cornfields, a somewhat arduous task fer a 6-year-old. But with each passin' year, I grew inta the task. Of course, afore we started plantin', the fields would already have ben plowed and furrows laid every three ta four feet apart. Our first job wuz to dig a small hill (hole) every three feet or so and then we would deposit four grains of corn and two runner bean seeds (usually Kentucky half-runners) if this wuz an area whar we would be tendin' beans as well. If we war combinin' squash or pumpkins also, we would add five pumpkin/squash seeds every fifth hill and skip three rows, then repeat the process fer squash/pumpkins.

Atter the seeds war in place, they would be covered with a small amount of earth, and a large spoon of chemical fertilizer would be added on top of the earth, and in turn, more earth would be added ta cover the fertilizer. The next task, wen the corn would be four ta six inches tall, would be the hoein' and thinnin'. Each hill would be thinned ta only two cornstalks, and if thar war squash/pumpkins, they would also be thinned ta two. All encroachin' weeds in and round the corn rows would be eliminated either by usin' a hoe or usin' one's fangers ta actually pull out the offendin' weeds. Then a small amount of earth would be heaped round the roots of the corn/bean/pumpkin plants fer insulation and ta help retain moisture. In three ta four weeks the hoein' would be repeated. Hit wuz a lot of hot, dirty work. We always took a bucket of water with us fer breaks we took atter every few rows, and we would quench ar thirst, which kept us hydrated. Of course, wen I wuz younger, I couldn't keep up with the adults, but as I grew older and matured, I not only could keep up, but could even outpace Grandpa.

Atter breakfast every mornin', I wuz in the habit of standin' out on the kitchen stoop and checkin' the weather. Or, more correctly, I should say checkin' the daily weather forecast. Thar wuz a group of silver maples linin' the holler that ran outside the garden palin'. The silver maples war tall 'nough ta obscure the lower portion of the hog lot that covered the butt of the opposite mountainside. Of course, if hit wuz already rainin', that wuz that. But wuz hit goin' ta be an all-day affair or only a shower?

By closely observin' the silver maple leaves, a prediction could be made. If the leaves war steady, had no movement, and drooped significantly below thar branches, hit wuz a purty good indication we war in fer a rainy day. On the other hand, if the leaves stood upright and thar war some waverin' with their white undersides showin', hit wuz probably a shower passin' through. Should the mornin' be clear and the sun already peepin' over the mountaintop, and the air be heavy with the bitin' stench from the hog lot and the silver maple leaves be barely stirrin', hit wuz goin' ta be a hot and humid day. If the leaves war intermittently rustlin', then calm with their directions facin' eastward, a thunderstorm would be expected by afternoon and maybe inta the night. If the leaves war intermittently rustlin' but the branches dancin' unnaturally up and down, then prolonged calm with their directions facin' westward, these war the worst storms and would be expected within a few hours. These storms, fortunately, war rare events. The reason I so delighted in the rainy weather wuz 'cause I got a reprieve from workin' in the fields in addition to the Sunday off day.

I 'member durin' our breaks, atter rehydratin' and lyin' in the grass/weeds in the shade with mah straw hat somewhat over mah eyes, gazin' up at the heavens and watchin' the clouds lazily crawlin' cross the vastness of the sky as fur as I could see in any direction. Wanderin' whar the clouds war goin' and whar they had ben. What would be the final destination of these clouds I wuz watchin'? Would I ever get thar? The clouds took on all sorts of shapes and sizes. Gazin' at them, I could visualize all kinds of animals, people, thangs, and places. Did they keep their same shapes atter they glided out of mah sight? And as I got older, I felt a yearnin' ta follow the clouds over the horizons, fer I knew another world (life) awaited me sometime, somewhar out thar. Thar had ta be a whole new entity waitin' fer me. Where would hit lead? Wen would my adventure begin? Sometimes, I felt I could hardly wait.

Now, from mah ramblin's, you'd thank with all mah chores and workin', I'd had little time to mahself. Well, that'd be a little misleadin' 'cause on Sundays, we didn't do much of anythang since hit wuz the Lord's Day, and we had ta keep hit holy by restin'. Thar war no churches or Sunday meetings nearby fer us ta attend. We jest listened ta the preachers on the radio. Also, thar war other times I would be left ta mah own devices ta go explorin', like Columbus or Lewis and Clark, Magellan, Vasco Da Gamma, Daniel Boone, or David Crockett 'cause thar war lots of woods round and animal trails ta follow and all the creeks and hollers and their tributaries ta plunder. And inquirin' minds needed ta know. I might've even 'ave discovered gold or silver somewhar, or perhaps somethin' even more important. Unfortunately, I never did!

Of course, I used the time ta play, but hit always had ta be by mahself as thar war no other young'uns round fer what seemed like miles.

Looking back, hit really wuz purty much a lonely existence. But I had ta make do. Hit wuz an opportunity ta learn self-reliance. However, with a big stick ta drag 'tween mah legs ta act as mah charger, I could be Red Ryder, Roy Rogers, Gene Audrey, Tex Ritter, the Lone Ranger (comic book heroes), or any kind of make belief cowboy, and I would be off ta save some damsel in distress. Sometimes I would take Boone, Aunt Cassie's black and white dog, along with me ta pretend ta be mah sidekick Gabby Hayes or Tonto, 'cept he warn't a real steady companion fer the slightest scent of a varmint; the sight of a rabbit or the skittle of a squirrel overhead in the woody canopy and he would be off like a bullet or inta a barkin' frenzy. Hit would be me who would be chasin' atter him. Fer if'n I didn't bring Boone back to Aunt Cassie, hit would be heck ta pay, and I'd never hear the end of hit.

Sometimes I would use an old rag Grandma had given me fer a cape, and I would become Superman, flyin' through the air faster than a speedin' bullet, faster than the speed of sound affected by jumpin' off of a fallen log or some large rock; a wonder I didn't break a lag or somethin' else. Or I could even be Hercules, the strongest man in the world, or Thor, the Norse God of Thunder.

I had a piece of cast-off palin' that made a plausible machine gun/military rifle that I would take ta war, huntin' down ta kill me a mess of Japs or Nazis jest like mah Uncle Wiley. Or I would stick a chicken feather in mah hair and paint mah face with water paints and would be ready ta go on the warpath with mah trusty bow I had fashioned out of a stout Hickory branch and strung with a thick piece of twine. I would use dried-up weed sticks fer arrows. These war supplemented by long, dried-up ironweed stalks fer spears and a sturdy root I had found fer a tomahawk. I would be ready ta go on the warpath and scalp me some palefaces. Mah imagination had no limits, fed by comics, historical readin's, and the wonderful world of fiction and make belief. I guess I must of ben some quirky kid.

Afore I go further, I must tell ya about ar summer evenings. Atter a hot summer day workin' in the cornfields, Aunt Cassie and I would carry ar chairs outside ta the east end of the house ta set 'tween the house and the garden palin's by the pretty-by-nights (four o'clocks) flowerbed whar thar would be some shade and hopefully a little breeze. Jest on the other side of the garden palin's hollyhocks and sunflowers peeked through the slats at us fortified by a slew of red horseradish blooms. At the west end of the flowerbed wuz an old fashion rose bush and at the other end was one of the numerous bunches of Aunt Cassie's dahlias. As the sun would quickly dive behind the mountaintops, hit always seemed the evenin' breeze would pick up ta dry some of our sweaty clothes and cool us off a bit while we found a bit of comfort in the shade.

But the best part wuz the evenin' chorus kickin' in jest as and atter the sun went down. Hit would be barely audible at first, but as the evenings would slowly lower her skirts of darkness, hit would reach a crescendo ta hits steady state reverberatin' throughout the area—cicadas, crickets, hummin' moths suckin' nectar from the pretty-by-nights and horseradish blooms, bullfrogs croakin' fer mates and other frogs callin' from the creek, whip-poor-wills joinin' in, and thar would be the screech of a nearby screech owl and the hoot (or hoots) of a further-away hoot owl and many other sounds jinin' the chorus that I couldn't recognize or don't 'member.

Throughout the darkness, in all directions, thousands of lightin' bugs would create a palette of natural unreproducible beauty seemingly stretchin' ta infinity with the on again, and off again, and on again, and off again, changin' the image much like a kaleidoscope afore one's eyes, every second. Magic!

But ta cap hit all off, on particularly cloudless nights, we would have a canopy of billions of stars jest overhead; almost as if we stood on ar tippy toes, we could reach 'em. 'Course, we couldn't. If'n ya looked at the tops of the mountains, ya could see the starry canvas restin' on jest the tops of the trees, and from thar, the whole mess of stars reached upward, kinda like lookin' up from the inside of an umbrella. Sometimes, thar would be so much starlight hit would be like a somber sunlight. Ya could see purty much whar ya wuz walkin' as long as ya warn't in the woods, 'specially if'en thar wuz a good bright moon out as well.

The year 1950 wuz a year of change—I lost mah front teeth, the twins war born, and Daddy left us...or so hit seemed. Atter the twins war born, thangs war gettin' purty dire financially. Thar wuz no work fer Daddy in ar neck of the woods. Coal mines had shut down, the loggin' companies had gone elsewhere, and hit wuz wintertime, so thar wuz no one needin' farm help. Ar bills on credit war almost insurmountable. Mommy wuz frantic. Hit's mah belief that Mommy prevailed on Daddy ta return ta Cincinnati while the family stayed behind and continued life in Kentucky while Daddy searched fer work in Ohio. Thar war other men round whose families lived in ar neck of the world in Kentucky and they worked in Ohio and commuted back and forth on weekends.

So, in November 1950, Daddy set off ta seek his fortune fer us in Cincinnati, near the same place we had departed in 1947. The night atter Daddy left fer Cincinnati, our teenage cousins who lived cross the creek, tryin' to prank us war stealin' round the house in the darkness, makin' what they thought wuz a funny commotion thankin' they would skeer us. William David grabbed his shotgun and fired a couple of volleys in the direction of the commotion, and that wuz the last we heard of that! So, who got skeered? We later larned our cousins took off like a bunch of banshees war atter 'em. That wuz the end of thar attempts at tryin' ta prank us.

Hit wuz hard gettin' used ta Daddy not bein' round in spite of everythang. Cosetta and William David kinda stepped inta the role of bein' Mommy's secondhand bosses. That didn't go over real big with me, though. I kept tellin' them they warn't the bosses of me.

Hit wuz getting' on ta Christmas wen we had this massive snowstorm, four or five feet on the ground. Hit wuz white everywhar and the glare from the snow made hit so I could hardly see. If the sun happened ta come out, the glare on the snow wuz so fierce, I really had ta squint ta see anythang a'tall, all the time holdin' mah hand up over mah eyes fer shade. Then hit warmed up jest a little, so the snow began ta start ta melt, and fore it melted very much we had a light rain and then a real cold Northern hit us dead center. Hit got so bone-chillin' cold—temperatures dropped below zero. Everythang turned ta ice. Thar war mammoth icicles hangin' everywhar. Thar wuz an ice pack on top of the snow and hit wuz slicker than snot and a body couldn't hardly walk without bustin' thar butt, and none of us had skates. What a mess it wuz! Hit woulda ben a good time ta go sleddin' but hit war jest too dog gone cold. Effen ya even stuck yer head outside yer breath would come bilin' out of ya in a great big fog and the wind would cut through ya like a knife. So, we only went outdoors effen we jest had ta.

Roads war nigh impassable lessen your vehicle had chains and sometimes not even then. School wuz on hold. William David wuz still able ta tend ta the livestock, so we war still gettin' milk, but our coal supply had dwindled down ta nothin'. Thank goodness we had wood fer cookin' and taters and beans and Mommy's cannin' and other essentials, and the animals had corn and hay stored by. We had ta keep a fire burnin' in the grate else we woulda froze fer shore, and all of Mommy's cannin' would have froze and busted, and then whar would we've ben? Hit wuz jest too cold ta sleep in the upper room no matter how many covers we used, so all ten of us crowded inta the two beds whar thar wuz a grate and we could keep a fire goin'. We all slept foot ta head and head ta foot—twins and everyone included—and somehow we managed not ta freeze ta death. Our coal shortage wuz getting' critical, fast, so Mommy used her last bit of money ta send William David ta our cousin, Hardin Hensley, ta secure a load of coal. Afore Hardin could brang the load of coal, our neighbors, somehow being aware of our plight, had pitched in and bought a load of coal fer us and hit wuz delivered afore Hardin got back with his 'en.

I thank I've mentioned afore that birthdays and holidays war not celebrated with any particular fanfare or special acknowledgment, but that year, Cosetta attempted ta make us chocolate fudge fer Christmas. Unfortunately, she didn't bring hit ta the correct temperature, so we ended up with a purty thick chocolate soup or puddin'. Didn't matter ta us, though. We ate hit anyway as if hit war the best thang we ever had, ever since fried chicken and apple pie, and we war more than thankful ta get hit.

The best thang yet, shortly atter Christmas, one of our neighbors, who also worked in Cincinnati and sometimes came home on weekends, stopped by our house with a letter from Daddy. Daddy had gotten a job at a sheet metal company and had sent Mommy some money. He wuz goin' ta be able ta come home fer the weekend in a couple of weeks. Atter that, he wuz able ta come home on weekends purty regularly. I know hit is difficult ta imagine what that meant ta us. Think of throwing a rope to a drownin' man. Well, hit wuz sorta like that with us at that time.

On mah visits to Grandma's, she would alla's give me a little spare change, and instead of buying treats I would spend the money on secondhand comics, which I could buy fer a nickel each. Then I would hide the lion's share of the comics under this cave-like rock at Grandma's. I did keep a few in Grandma's house. But Grandma didn't fancy that I would spend all mah money on comics, and that wuz the reason I felt I needed ta hide most of mah comics.

Thar wuz a stand of pines a few hundred feet on a knoll above Grandma's house. Underneath the shelter of the pine trees, pine nettles made a lush ground cover. Hit wuz thar on a wallowed-out bed I would steal away atter rescuing mah comics from thar hiding spot. I could read ta mah heart's content while Grandma assumed I wuz off playin' or explorin'. As I read through the comics, I would imagine mahself takin' on the roles of the heroes, and in mah mind, I encountered all kinds of adventures. As I read, (or reread) the wind in the pines would fan over me and sang a melodic song, sometimes jest above a whisper. Wen the wind increased hits speed, the sounds of the pines swayin' would, too. Thar war all kinds of birds flittin' from branch to branch, callin' and chatterin' away. My little hideaway in the pines always kept me company.

Wen I wuz in the fourth grade, a miraculous event occurred. A bookmobile started makin' routine visits every two weeks ta our school. We could check out library books ta read ta our heart's content. The wonderful world of fiction had jest been introduced ta me in a magnanimous way. Heretofore, I had only ben able ta borrow other kids' readers and whatever comics I could get mah hands on, plus the Bible, which I had read cover ta cover. Now, I must admit in the Bible thar war a lot of words I didn't understand (guessed at thar meanings; had no dictionary) and couldn't even begin ta pronounce, so I jest skipped 'em. With the bookmobile, a whole new world opened up. I would completely immerse mahself in a book and lose mahself ta the world. Mah problem wuz that I would get so caught up in mah readin' I would neglect other thangs like chores and schoolwork. However, if left ta mah own devices, I would 'ave spent mah days and nights readin'.

Afore hit wuz time fer me ta begin the sixth grade, 'nother calamity struck. The Board of Education couldn't find a teacher fer little ole Brookside School agin. The solution wuz ta bus us to Island City School, jest like what happened wen I wuz in the first grade, 'cept this time I wuz ta be included. Island City is a little bit of a misnomer. Hit is hardly more than a wide place in the road. Hit is located very near the Owsley and Clay Counties line.

In addition, ta the schoolhouse, thar wuz a combined general store and post office and a few scattered houses round. We had a few of our cousins living nearby—all Hensleys and some of their kids war enrolled at the Island City School with us. The Island City School wuz a duplex schoolhouse in that hit still serviced all eight elementary grades but wuz split in half with <u>two</u> teachers. One room housed grades one through four, and the other room housed grades five through eight. So, Henry and Everett war in the grades one-through-four room, and Mary Jane and I war in the five-through-eight room. Mr. Callahan wuz the teacher for grades five through eight. He had a daughter, Joyce, and a son, Rodney, who war both in my class. Joyce wuz more competitive scholastically, plus she wuz really good-looking.

Not a lot stands out 'bout Island City School, 'cept I recall eatin' a lot of peanut butter and cracker sandwiches and moon pies fer lunch, which included tomatoes wen they war in season, and sometimes we got bologna sandwiches instead of the peanut butter ones. I distinctly 'member February 17, 1954. Hit wuz mornin' recess. I wuz standin' outside the schoolhouse. The sky wuz overcast and hit wuz drizzlin' a fine mist, and I wuz cold. I had a sore throat and could feel a bout of tonsillitis comin' on. No one had bothered ta even mention hit but hit wuz mah birthday—mah eleventh birthday. Hit was just another day, though!

Thar is one other event that stands out from that year. The older boys (not me) from Island Creek School war able ta form up a baseball team ta play at a school over in Clay County nearby. I don't 'member of hearin' or knowin' much about real baseball and hadn't the foggiest idea beyond the simplified, modified version we had played with a rubber ball and a stick fer a bat. And in that case, we played fer three outs and then changed sides, and we played 'til we got tired or 'til most of us had ta leave and go do chores.

At the Clay County School game, I kept hearin' 'em talkin' 'bout playin' Indians. What Indians? I couldn't and didn't understand, and I wuz too bashful ta ask anyone. Thar war no Indians thar, so maybe this wuz completely different from what we had tried ta play whar we lived? And wuz this, atter all, a game they had larned from the Indians? Hit wuz rumored that all the Indians from ar neck of the woods had ben rounded up, herded away, and war now isolated in Oklahoma or somewhar fur West. I had heard that Grandma Taylor use ta write ta a couple of 'em.

The whole school went ta watch the game with the Clay County team—me included, of course. Hit appeared to be a purty even match, as best as I could determine. You hit the ball or not, and if you hit hit and the hit warn't caught, you ran round the bases—three rocks scattered around the field with a fourth one whar the guy would be standin' tryin' ta hit the ball. If I looked at the pattern of the four rocks splayed out in the field, hit almost made some kind of square. Hit wuz sorta like what we had been playin', 'cept they had a real baseball bat and a real baseball. I wuz still a little confused, so finally I picked up mah nerve and ventured ta ask one of mah classmates which Indians they war playin'. He laughed and loudly announced, "Indians? Not Indians, dummy! *Innings*. They are in the sixth *inning*." On the way back to ar schoolhouse, everybody knew 'bout mah faux pas. Boy, wuz my face red. Took me the rest of the year ta live that one down.

Wonder of wonders! The school board found a teacher for Brookside school for the 1954–55 term—mah seventh-grade term. The school year passed much too quickly. One highlight of the year: I won a blue ribbon (first place) fer reading and a yaller ribbon (third place) fer the high jump at the County Fair. Unfortunately, this school year wuz the finale fer Brookside School, fer at the end of the school year, the Owsley County Board of Education decided ta consolidate many of the schools throughout the county—the end of an era. This included closin' Brookside School. So fer the 1955–56 term, mah eighth grade year, I wuz bussed to Booneville High School, whar I rejoined the Callahan siblin's, Joyce and Rodney. Also, Mr. Callahan wuz thar as our math teacher.

Booneville High School wuz really different. We met in the mornings in the Home Room whar attendance wuz taken, then went ta a different room fer each subject. We also had a period fer physical training (PT) in a separate building (gymnasium)—mah first effort at gym—and I quickly discovered I wuz not the most athletic boy at Booneville High School. Not even the most athletic boy in thar eighth grade—fur from hit. They even had a basketball team! Fer lunch thar wuz a cafeteria whar meals cost fifteen cents per day, and they war purty good. I found hit all bewildering' at first, but I caught on purty quick, and at the end of the year, I had my first graduation from school and even have the diploma ta prove hit.

Along life's journey, 'specially wen you're younger, thar ar a number of thoughts and ideas 'bout what directions you would like yer life ta take—what pursuits you would like ta foller, how you would make yer mark in this world. Thar wuz one incident that occurred in the eighth grade that caused me ta thank I wanted ta be a writer. Mrs. Miller (a different teacher than I had in the first grade), ar English teacher, gave ar class an assignment ta write a Christmas story. I chose ta retell the original' *Christmas Story* but through the eyes of the donkey stabled beside the manger whar the baby Jesus wuz born. Of course, even at that point I did go on a bit. I later larned that Mrs. Miller wuz so enthralled with mah little effort she read mah prose ta every one of her classes. She gave me an A+. I wuz overjoyed by the attention and wuz so thrilled by the compliment that I could almost feel mah buttons popping. I thought shore from Mrs. Miller's high praise, I wuz destined ta be the next Mark Twain.

Just a quick summary here. I attended the 1956–57 school year at
Cutter Junior High School in Cincinnati Ohio, and then graduated again. This time from junior high school. I spent three years at Robert A. Taft High School, where I earned my high school diploma. I started college courses at the University of Cincinnati (1960), followed by the University of Maryland,

University of Dayton, the Ohio State University, and Wright State Univer and finally wound up getting my Bachelor of Science Degree in Civil Engineering from the University of Arizona in February 1972. Then, I received my Master of Science   Degree in Industrial Hygiene from the University of Cincinnati Medical School (1977), the university where I had first started taking college courses way back in 1960, a total period of seventeen years. I also took numerous technical and professional courses during my Air Force career. (Air War College, Air Command & Staff, Officer Training School, etc.)

Figure 1 Wiley's Senior Photo

Today, being able to get an education is pretty much taken for granted. However, it was not always so, for it was not too far in the distant past that many poor people in this country found education a luxury. Here, I can only speak for the people I grew up with.

In Appalachia, around the area where I grew up, it was considered sufficient for most girls to receive basic reading, writing, and some arithmetic. It was significantly more important that girls learn to keep house, sew, cook, and take care of their husbands and family. God had already given them the facilities for having babies. Girls were not expected to be after scholarly pursuits but rather setting their sights on catching a suitable husband. After four or five years of primary schooling, many young girls were pulled from school to help with the basic housekeeping chores until they were married off.

Boys, on the other hand, needed to hone their educational endeavors sufficiently to enable them to provide for their families. An eighth-grade education was considered plenty sufficient by most farm families. After that amount of education, boys were expected to help with farming and contribute to the family's income in whatever manner was required until the time they struck out and started a family on their own. What else was there for them to do?

8. GROWING UP

[After departing the Kentucky hills, I quickly attempted to abandon my hillbilly drawl as fast as I could. In those days I pretty much kept to myself, didn't talk a lot, and I was a fairly good mimic. So, picking up the local dialect was not too difficult. At my tender age of thirteen I did not need anything further to make me stand out from my peers. So, for the remainder of this memoir I will attempt to leave out the Appalachian vernacular, even though a word or phrase may still creep in.]

It all started on a Wednesday evening in the middle of May 1957. I was living with Mom and Dad and five other siblings on Pearl Street in Cincinnati, Ohio. There were eight of us living in a four-room apartment. By most standards, it would have been judged pretty small and fairly primitive.

Upon entering the apartment, there was a small kitchen with two large windows looking out into the building's interior hallway. There was a gas range and sink on the right, a doorway to the left leading to the dining room with a table and chairs, and a bed, which I shared with my next younger brother, Henry. There was also a window in the dining room that looked out across the alley and onto the next building.

Leading off from the kitchen was the great room, even though it was not that big. That was Mom and Dad's bedroom but also coupled as our living room because our only couch was in that room, too. Windows looked out onto Pearl Street, and directly across from us was a big discount furniture store.

Leading off to the left of Mom and Dad's room was the fourth room, which held two more beds, one for Barbra Ann and Bonnie Lou and the second one for Everett and Bobbie Jean. Mary Jane had also shared this room until her recent marriage on April 24, 1957. We had *no* bathroom. There was a toilet (commode only) in the crook of the stairway, one for each apartment.

There were four apartments on each floor. Our apartment was on the third floor. Most of the area around our building had been demolished in anticipation of the freeway system that exists there today. Our building was one of the last left standing on the entire block. It was owned by an attorney whose office was located in the Carew Tower Building, the tallest skyscraper in Cincinnati at that time. I sometimes took the monthly rent money to his very elaborate office on some umpteenth floor. We had been living there for just about nine months at this referenced time.

We moved from the hills of Kentucky, Appalachia, Owsley County, on the Left Fork of Island Creek near where Dad's mother's relatives had settled in their migration from the Eastern Kentucky and West Virginia area. We had left the family homestead, the place where my dad's parents lived, when they came to this area when Dad was 7 years old (1921). The homestead house originally was built as two rooms with a stone chimney between them with a grate fireplace opening to each room. There was a mantle above each fireplace. The floor was set on hewed sandstone blocks. Sometime after the original two rooms were built, two additional rooms were added. All were covered by a tin roof, which made for a melodic symphony during a rainstorm or just a rainy day, good sleeping times.

The two original rooms were Mom and Dad's room plus the kitchen/dining room. Mom and Dad's room had their double bed, a baby crib, an additional double bed, plus Mommy's Singer sewing machine. It was located between the two beds placed below the window that looked out onto the porch that extended along the whole end of the house. Plus, there was a pantry-like room by the fireplace where Mom kept her canning.

The adjacent kitchen had a large round table in the center. Mom said you could always find a place for another person at the round table. Chairs were only for adults and were shared between the two rooms. Mom and Dad's room doubled as the living room, particularly so in winter because there was a fire in the fireplace, so everyone hovered close by to try and keep warm. Therefore, chairs were aligned around the hearth.

The bedroom acted as our living room, but there weren't enough chairs fer everyone, so some of us wound up either sitting' on the floor or on one of the beds. Sometimes the older ones nussed some of the young'uns or we just stood warming' first one side then the other. Fer mealtimes the chairs needed to be toted to the kitchen for the adults, and once meals were finished, toted back to the hearth. Kids always stood to eat.

There was a cabinet for holding our rotating supply of dishware; we suffered from a fairly large inventory of breakage—a cook stove, a washbasin, a drinking bucket, and a dipper. Yes, everyone drank from the same dipper. After electricity came to the area, Mom and Dad purchased a refrigerator.

The two additional rooms (served mainly as bedrooms) were called the upper and lower rooms. The upper room was for the boys, Bobby Jean not included. The lower room was for the girls and sort of the formal living room, almost solely used for company, which was a rare event, indeed. Sometime later, Mom and Dad added a potbelly stove and a couch, even though I don't remember them being used a lot.

It is my understanding that when the house was built, there was a hand-dug well carved out near the western upper corner of the house. Not sure how deep it was, but with dry spells, it was probably apt to go dry. Sometime prior to my history of living there, a well was mechanically drilled down into the hard water table! The water stunk something atrocious and discolored almost everything it touched into a dark copperish brown. The sulfur and iron content must have been sky-high, but you know, once you got used to it, you barely noticed the rotten egg smell and taste. The best thing was none of us had hardly any cavities growing up and even into our young adulthood! Great for our teeth; I reckon it added to the fact that we almost never had any sweets.

Toilet facilities? Across the yard, past the coal pile, the woodpile, and through the barnyard to the outhouse.

In the summer heat, the smell and flies were a nuisance, but in the winter, when the temperatures were around zero and below, you can bet your bottom dollar you kept your visits to the outhouse to the shortest time possible. There was no fancy squeeze the Charmin fluffy white cottony rolls of plush white toilet tissue hanging around in the outhouse to complete one's business. No siree! You were lucky if there were any remnants of the Sears & Roebucks Catalogs left and hoped to heck it wasn't just the glossy, slick color pages, for that never helped finish the business at hand very well.

After our move back to Cincinnati, I tried comparing environments; it was all relative. My big stumbling block was fitting in socially. I was probably asocial, to begin with. I was terribly shy and skinny as a rail. At 13, I was nearly as tall as I am now (5'10"), and I doubt if I weighed 100 pounds. If you looked at me, you would have thought I was anorexic, and I probably was. My brogue was so thick you could cut it with a knife. I think a lot of people may have had a difficult time understanding me, what, with my brogue.

Additionally, I had no front teeth, so if I thought I might laugh or even smile, I would cover my mouth with my hand. As everyone knows, kids are not necessarily kind, so I heard lots of the terms: hillbilly, ridge runner, briar hopper, cracker, red Necker, white trash, etc. However, the name-calling wasn't all that bad, for many of my classmates' families hailed from the hills of Tennessee, Kentucky, and West Virginia. The black families mostly migrated from the Deep South for various reasons but mainly to try and make a better life for themselves, same as the rest of us. A large percentage had been in Cincinnati for some time and were pretty well acclimatized, certainly much more than me. Most of these folks had left austere situations (like us), looking to try to better their lot in life.

Mom gave me twenty-five cents each school day for lunch money, but I was too bashful to eat in front of the other kids with my missing teeth. I would save up my money and go to the movies, which only cost thirty-five or fifty cents depending upon which theater I went to—and these were double features. In addition, I also smoked, I am a little embarrassed to admit, so a good portion of my lunch money went for cigarettes. I knew nothing about the city, about city life, or what was expected, and I had no friends. The other kids at school may have been somewhat like me, but I was just way too introverted to try to get to know them. We lived in a very depressed area of Cincinnati (otherwise known as the slums). But I digress.

Back to the Wednesday in May 1957. My social life was church, church, and more church. I felt like I had church coming out of my ears. There had to be more to life than just church. Mom and Dad were very religious, especially Mom. Our family was attending a Church of God (Pentecostal-like/Holy Rollers) on the corner of Second and Broadway. The church room had previously served as a saloon but had been transformed into a church pastored by the Reverend and Mrs. Stewart (this was the same area where Roy Rogers was born).
The church was having a revival all week, and we had been going to church almost every night. I had had my fill of church. I was looking for any excuse for not going with the family that Wednesday night, and I

remembered Mom had promised me a dime to wash the windows in front of the apartment. Now, there were two windows, so I calculated that would earn me twenty cents, still a paltry amount. I bargained with Mom that I would wash the windows rather than going to church, and she countered that I could wash the windows on Saturday. I told her I had promised to mind Cosetta's two little girls, Cassie and Charlotte. She worked and lived a few blocks away from us on Baum Street on Saturday. Mom after some debate did relent, and I did get to skip church, but in all fairness, I really did a yeoman's job on those windows.

Any job worth doing was worth doing well, worth doing to the best of your ability. That's what my grandma always told me. I was very proud of the job I had done on the windows and was anxious to show it off to Mom when she got home. It appeared church had gone on longer than usual, but that was what happened in those revivals when everybody got in the spirit and really got to praising the Lord, and one excited enthusiasm fed off of another and then another, and so it would go. Therefore, for whatever reason(s), it was pretty late when the family dragged themselves home. If I had had any sense, I would have gone ahead to bed and not broached the subject until the next day.

However, you don't know me. I could not wait to show Mom the great job I had done and to proudly show her the sparkling windows. Why the windows were so clear ya could hardly tell there was glass even there except for the wooden frames. Mom barely looked at the windows, much to my disappointment, and said, "They look good, Wiley," and opened her purse and handed me a dime. The whole attitude was just wrong! It was like OK, but more like a dismissal

I had worked so hard, and for a dime. I had understood it was a dime for each window. I felt I was getting half of what I had been promised. I felt cheated! Somehow, we had had a breakdown in communication. Mom just couldn't do this to me. I should have just kept quiet, but recall, I had just turned 14 a couple of months before, I'd been being bullied at school, and it seemed I was nearly invisible at home. I think my teenage hormones must have been kicking in, so I did something completely out of character, even for me, something I will always regret. I started yelling at Mom that it just was not fair. I was being cheated, and I'm sure I went on and on.

Unfortunately, this triggered my exhausted dad, who was already in bed by this time. He came running into the dining room in his boxer shorts and T-shirt, with his face all red and his blood vessels already engorged with his belt out, folded in his hand, at the ready. I should have seen the writing on the wall and taken quick notes. Now Dad had had a long day already hauling sheet metal and then had spent hours at the Holy Ghost Revival, so he had to have been dead tired; bad luck for me! Dad started giving me the beating of my life. In an attempt to lessen the brunt of the beating, after a few wallops of the belt across my front side, I cowered across the bed on my abdomen, offering my backside, but it did little to lessen the bite of the belt. Dad may have had a hard day and been tired, but he was still strong and still had a lot of strength left. I was feeling it. I don't know if he may have even had a bad day but for whatever reason he seemed to be taking all his frustrations and angst out on me and my backside.

I bit down on my tongue so that I wouldn't cry out and stole away to a little corner in my head where I could shut out the world. Dad was soon in one of his frenzies and I lost count of all the wallops. When I felt Dad was nearing exhaustion, I told him if he was nearly finished, I was going to get the heck out of there and he would never see me again.

Well, that was not the right thing to say, for it just invigorated Dad, and the beating resumed anew, but in a renewed furor. After forever, it seemed, Mom finally pulled Dad off me. However, true to my word, I staggered off the bed and limped outside, for I was badly bruised and seeping blood in a few places and ran down the stairs into the cool night air, even though I hurt all over. Fortunately, it was a balmy night for the middle of May.

For all my bravado, what in the world was I going to do? I certainly was not going back there to spend another night under the same roof with that man. (Even though, in retrospect, I brought it upon myself, but perhaps not to that severity). I was on the path to becoming homeless and possible ruin ("*Streets of Laredo*" was brought to mind). I didn't even have a jacket on. I walked (limped) downtown, circled Fountain Square a few times, wandered the streets for a while, and then hiked myself up to Eden Park, where I curled up beneath some pine trees and slept fitfully, shivering with the cold off and on until it was daylight.

I waited until midmorning when I knew Dad would have gone to work and my siblings would have left for school and Mom would be pretty much alone in the apartment. I telephoned her with the dime she had paid me from a public phone booth and told her I would like to come and pick up some of my clothes and that I had some friends who were going to take me to Indiana. (The friends were figments of my imagination.) Mom was crying and begged me to come back home. I told her I was coming to pick up my clothes and hung up the phone. We left it at that. I was in a real pickle. I didn't know what I was going to do, but I did feel I could not go back and live under the same roof with my dad after surviving the shellacking of my life,

When I got to the apartment, Mary Jane, who had recently gotten married, was there with Mom. Mary Jane told me I didn't need to go anywhere (Mom was still crying) and that I could come live with her and Doug, her husband (newlyweds for a month). I saw a way out, so I agreed and moved in with Mary Jane and Doug. Silly me.

They lived in a one-room apartment around the corner on Pike Street. Their apartment was furnished and was very sparse. I slept on the floor wrapped in a quilt and used a rolled-up towel for a pillow. It was very intrusive on my part. I was often sent to the hallway to read while they had their lovemaking sessions, which happened pretty frequently. They both had day jobs. However, I didn't stay with them very long, for as soon as school was finished for the year (maybe three weeks), Mary Jane and Doug took me down to live with Grandma and Grandpa for the summer. But, while living with Mary Jane and Doug, I learned to iron and even learned some basic cooking skills, not a bad trade-off. I usually tried to prepare some kind of meal for us by the time they got home from work.

At the end of the summer, just before school started, I returned to live with Mom and Dad. That was my last physical altercation with my dad, and I forgave him for the beating, but I have never been able to forget it. It just happened to be one of life's lessons forever imbedded in my mind.

9. MY FIRST BOSS

It was early March 1960, and I was sitting in Study Hall, last period of the day, reading some Western fiction, which I was and am still really partial to. My homework was completed, had there been any, when a runner from Mr. Williams's office summoned me. Mr. Williams was the vice principal, a tall, thin black man who I had rarely seen in my three years at Robert A. Taft High School. He was often called the "Shadow" behind his back, of course, after the popular radio program.
I was a senior approaching graduation in early June. Mr. Williams was known as the disciplinarian; couldn't imagine what I had done to be called down to his office. Long story short, management at Photo Suppliers Inc. was seeking an office person (boy) part-time, maybe to go full-time after graduation. He had to be white (our school was almost all colored—called African Americans now).

Anyway, I got the job. The firm was owned by a Jewish family with headquarters in New York City and had branches in Atlanta, Georgia, and Cincinnati, Ohio. The Cincinnati office was composed of ten people. There was Levi Shem, the office manager (one of the headquarters' partners). He actually hired me, and I guess you could say he was my big boss.

Benjamin Mikal was the second partner for our branch. Both men were salespeople and traveled a lot. They were the lifeblood for the survival of our branch. The office staff consisted of three ladies: the office manager, Judy King, a single mother who was probably in her late thirties; Rachel Mikal, an older lady and part of the Photo Jewish family; and Ima Tottington, also an older lady who lived in a hotel. She was a rabid Republican and was not bashful about letting me know it.

I had always felt a special empathy for Ima. She was pretty much a loner, somewhat like me, I thought. I was intrigued that she lived by herself in the Plaza Hotel. She kinda reminded me a little bit of the Auntie Mame character I had recently seen in the movie of the same name. I don't think she had any family and I never heard her speak of any friends. She seemed to communicate only with us folks in the office. I always tried to be nice to her, but then I was friendly to everyone. Ima was probably in her late fifties or perhaps even in her sixties. She was about five and a half feet tall. Wasn't skinny, nor was she fat. Wasn't particularly pretty, nor was she ugly, just plain, plain.

She did have lots of wrinkles, though, and seemed ancient to me. She had really black hair, except sometimes, towards the weekend, her roots would start showing and I could see the gray peeping through her scalp. She had false teeth that didn't fit really well, for on the rare occasion when she would really laugh out loud, really guffaw, her uppers would slip a bit—not that I would ever have said anything to her about it. I would always pause to say hello to her whenever I would pass through the office. If she wasn't busy or on break, I would linger for a little chat and inquire about her day and what she had been up to. Of all the people who worked there, she seemed to be so lonely, and I felt a little sorry for her. I mean, I knew what it was to be lonely.

We had a congenial repertoire going until one day we were in the office alone because everyone else was having their lunch. I had finished mine earlier and

Ima was sitting at her desk munching on hers. We were chatting away all friendly-like when I made the mistake of jokingly telling her that if she voted for Nixon, she would just be wasting her vote, throwing it away. I thought she was going to explode on the spot. I should mention here this was right after the Nixon/Kennedy debate on TV. For a moment there was complete silence. I could see Ima becoming really rigid-like with her face turning red, and she had just taken a bite of her sandwich. It occurred to me she might choke on it or, even worse, spit it out all over me. Her jaws began to clinch, and I swear the hairs on her head started to stand up. I hoped her hair clips held; if not, I wasn't sure what was going to happen. The look she gave me is hard to describe now. Her eyes kinda quenched then seemed to roll around in her head a little, and it was like there was fire flying right towards me. It was a little bit frightening to be truthful.

Instead of exploding, she really gave me a piece of her mind and what for. She did her best to put me in my place by asking me, "What kind of a young upstart are you to be advising your elders about voting? Everybody has their right to vote for whomever they want to. It's their own mind to make up. Do you want the Pope to be running this country and telling you how to worship? Are you some kind of communist freak?" Jeese! And she didn't stop there but kept on going on and on, and on, and yelling, almost at the top of her voice. I half expected the guys who were taking their lunch in the far back to come running in to see what the heck was the matter. She looked like she might be going to have a fit or some kind of an attack. God, I shore hoped not, for I wouldn't know what in the world to do with everyone gone out to lunch.

What had I done? What had I let myself in for? How was I going to get out of this one? I hadn't really been telling Ima how she should vote but was only trying to make the point that I thought Kennedy was the better choice for president and if she went ahead and voted for Nixon, she would just be wasting her vote. Bad timing and bad move on my part. Fortunately, Judy King came strolling back, chewing on her apple, looking first at Ima and then at me as if to say, "What in the world is going on with you two?" I was so relieved to see Judy. I could have kissed her for her timely intrusion, for I hadn't known how I was going to get away from Ima. Making my escape, I slunk to the back of the warehouse with my tail between my legs, way out of Ima's influence and way out of her sight. I never, ever spoke about any type of politics to or with Ima again, as long as I worked there. Truth be told, I pretty much kept my distance from Ima after that episode.

The physical portion of the staff was made up of four men supervised by Randy Crochet, a hillbilly from the hills of Kentucky, just like me. He was my first direct boss; more about him later. The two other men, Jim Hudson and Robert Burns, were middle-aged packers, even though they seemed pretty old to me at the time. They were responsible for packing up all the orders Mr. Shem and Mr. Mikal had secured and getting them ready for shipment or local delivery. I was the fourth member.

Probably the most interesting person on the staff was a gentleman who worked by himself, Special Projects. He spoke no English and was the uncle of one of the owners, Levi Mikal. He was so thin he almost looked emaciated, just skin and bones, and had the most haunting look about his eyes. He hardly spoke to anyone. He had the most gaunt, forlorn look about him like he could see right through a person, or he was reliving some deep personal trauma, which could well have been true as he had been a prisoner at one of the Nazis' concentration camps during WWII. I don't remember which camp. I was fascinated by the numbers that he showed me, which were tattooed by the Nazis on his left arm.

One of the chores I was responsible for was to commandeer kosher lunches for the Jewish staff and anyone else who desired them. I usually brought a kosher lunch to Levi, and he would nod at me in acceptance and mutter to me something in some language that I took to be thanks. I never knew what language he was attempting, if it was Yiddish, Polish, German, or something else. When he looked at me, it was as if he was looking right through me with this haunted, blind stare. Of course, at the time, I was completely unaware of the conditions, tortures, and unbearable stress he must have encountered during his incarceration. I could never have imagined the anguish and losses he endured during his life as a prisoner in a concentration camp.

Now, for Randy Crochet. Randy was a short person, probably about 5'4", with a bit of a short-person complex—shall we say Napoleonic complex? He had attended Robert A. Taft High School, the same as me, graduating a few years ahead of me. He was probably in his late twenties, was married, and had a little boy who I think was 3 or 4 at the time. He lived in Newport, Kentucky, same as me, and offered to let me ride with him to and from work, except I had to walk five blocks to his house in the morning and five blocks from his house after work to my parents' house. He charged me two dollars a week for the privilege. Doesn't sound like a lot, but my pay was one dollar an hour or forty dollars per week, ten of which I shared with Mom. After these deductions I was left with less than $28 a week. I was able to save most of that so that I could pay for tuition when I started evening classes at the University of Cincinnati in the fall term. Randy was a bit of a bully, and as he was my direct boss, I didn't know how to get my own back. Also, I felt he was a person who was really stuck on himself and enjoyed patting himself on the back, which reminded me of my grandpa's saying that self-bragging don't amount to a hill of beans!

My job at Photo Suppliers was really as a gopher—go for whatever any of the staff wanted. I did whatever I was told to do. I did a lot of the local deliveries around the city, mostly to Camera Shops using a handcart, accepted deliveries, and then did restocking. I helped to conduct inventories and assisted Randy, whose other main responsibility other than being warehouse supervisor was to fill orders from stock and sort them for packing, and I also helped anybody in any way I could.

10. OFF TO THE WILD BLUE YONDER

February 17, 1961 (my 18th birthday), I enlisted in the United States Air Force. After I graduated from high school, I continued to work at Photo Suppliers Inc., where I started working part-time while I was still a senior in high school at Robert A. Taft. My title was stock boy; I was really a gopher—ran errands and did anything that everyone else needed. The pay was paltry—$1.00 per hour, and of that, I gave Mom $10.00 per week.

I had been attending night classes at the local University of Cincinnati. At first, I enrolled in four courses but soon found the course load was too demanding, so I dropped one course. Up until Christmas, business was so brisk at work that I was required to work a lot of overtime, sometimes up to twelve hours a day. As Christmas approached, business began to slack off. It slacked off so much that my big boss called me into his office the week before Christmas and told me that after Christmas, I would be furloughed. And so, I was furloughed after Christmas 1960.

Mom and Dad never had much to say about my efforts in pursuing a college education. Therefore, I didn't know how they really felt about it. Was I trying to get above my rasin? I had the feeling that, in their own way, they were accepting of my educational pursuits and proud of my efforts.

After I lost my job and tried unsuccessfully to find a new one, I went to the Air Force recruiter and was conditionally accepted for military service. Mom offered that she and Dad would borrow the money for me to continue to pursue my college education. I was completely flabbergasted, touched, and proud of their offer. But I couldn't let them do that. It wouldn't have been fair to the rest of my brothers and sisters.

As I already mentioned, my job search had been very disheartening! I also had signed up for unemployment. After a couple of weeks of making the rounds of different employment offices, my enthusiasm began to wane quickly. It was then I decided to pay my local Air Force Recruiter's Office a visit. I considered all the branches of service but remembered discussions with my high school buddies that the Air Force was the best service to see the world, learn a trade, and also pursue an education. Anyway, I preferred their blue uniforms!

The Air Force recruiter was most friendly and extremely positive. He ran me through a battery of tests, which I passed with flying colors, except for the mechanical portion. No worries. With my scores, I could have my choice of careers, he bragged. He had me fill out all this paperwork and then discovered a roadblock. I was only 17. Would my parents sign for me to join the Air Force? No way. Mom and Dad said it was my choice if I wanted to join the Air Force, but it would be my doing, not theirs. If something were to happen to me, Mom said she wouldn't be able to live with herself.

A few days before my eighteenth birthday I went ahead, did my physical, and passed, except I was thirteen pounds under the minimum weight standard for my height. The Air Force had to request and obtain a waiver for me. Taking the actual physical examination was strange for me, but no exception for the thousands of men who had done it before me nor for the hordes that would follow in my wake. I peed in a bottle, had a needle stuck in my arm for what felt like having half my blood withdrawn, had my temperature taken, and weight and height measured. I was then passed down the line for a chest X-ray, an eye test, a peek at my head, and a visual check of my eyes and ears. Then I had to stick out my tongue and say "Ahhh" and then again for a look-see at my oral cavity. However, the most dreaded part of the physical examination was still to come.

About twenty-five or so of us men, ranging from 17 to 30-something, discarded all our clothes except for our undershorts. We lined up almost shoulder to shoulder and stood there waiting for the doctors, one in front and one in back. Once we were all lined up and ready, we were given the orders to drop our drawers. I would have never imagined the variety of drawers ranging from tiny briefs to almost G-strings, regular briefs, boxer shorts, and some boxer shorts that were knee length and almost looked like skirts. And the colors? Some of the colors I didn't know even existed. First down the line was the doctor at our back and the order was given: "Bend over and spread yer cheeks!" I hoped I hadn't gone since I had taken a bath that morning, but all of a sudden, for the life of me, I couldn't remember. Gosh darn it, if not, I shore hoped I had wiped well back there. Anyway, I felt that this must be what livestock felt like when they were being assessed at the market for sale or, worse yet, getting ready for slaughter, except they couldn't and weren't required to pull apart their cheeks, and hopefully we weren't going to be slaughtered.

But the worst part was the doctor getting *physical* in front. His instructions were, "Okay, men, straighten back up." This was followed by the good doctor marching down the line and grabbing each one of us by the testicles, squeezing them, and barking at us to turn yer head and cough. Thank goodness, I was braced in a good, steady stance when the doctor got to me. I thought I was prepared, even so it was a complete shock when he grabbed me **there** and told me to cough. Whoaaaaa! I felt myself getting weak in the knees, my eyes beginning to bug and tear, my heart was starting to stammer, and I could feel my hair trying to stand on end. It was one of those moments when time just stood still. I know it didn't take that long, but I don't know if I was holding my breath or what, but it seemed like it took forever. I mean. I am sensitive. **There!** Oh Lord, I surely hoped this was not an omen of what it was going to be like to be in military service. But it too, did pass.

After my physical examination ordeal was over, I finished the rest of my paperwork and waited for my eighteenth birthday to take the oath of enlistment. It took place in the Recruiting Office in Cincinnati on February 17, 1961. It was heavily overcast that day. There was a light drizzle, and it was spitting snow with a bone-piercing wind. After all of the new recruits had finished taking their Oath of Enlistment, the swearing-in officer congratulated us on our having taken the Oath of Enlistment, welcomed us into the United States Military Forces, wished us the best of luck in our future military careers, and then released us with instructions that we could return home for the rest of the day and night. The seven Air Force recruits were instructed to meet our escort at 0900 (9 a.m.) the next morning at the Cincinnati Airport to fly to

Lackland Air Force Base, San Antonio, Texas, to start basic training.

Of the twenty-five plus brave hearts who had attended and participated in the Oath Ceremony, there were only seven of us who met at the Cincinnati Airport that early Saturday morning along with several members of my family to send me off on this amazing adventure that was going to change my life forever. I don't remember all of my family who were there, but there was my mother and my Aunt Etta; my sisters, Cosetta, Fern, and Mary Jane; Mary Jane's husband, Doug; and several nieces and nephews. I was later teased by some of my fellow inductees that I had been sent off by my tribe. None of the other recruits had anyone there to send them off. I guess I did feel pretty special after all—and I was.

While this was not the first time anyone in our family had been in an airplane, it was certainly my first time. Coasting down the runway and getting ready for takeoff was nothing extraordinary—much like riding in a car or bus, except we were tilted up and the noise was a lot louder. I was seated by a window and geared up with high expectations for all the adventures that would be unfolding.

We sat at the end of the runway waiting for, I didn't know what, engines running, sounding like we were really going places, but we were just sitting there; strange. Unknown to me were the dynamics and the protocol of flying an aircraft. After some time, we were given the clearance to take off. With what seemed like just a little burst of speed, the plane tilted up and up and up, and the earth started to fade away. Almost before you could say, "Jack be quick," we were going higher up through the clouds, and the farmhouses and barns I had been watching seconds before were fading quickly away as we were flying through a foggy soup of low-hanging clouds. A voice over the intercom reminded us to keep our seat belts fastened until the captain turned off the *Fasten Seat Belt* signs.

It wasn't long before the sun was shining, and we were above the clouds. There were oceans of puffy, fluffy, white clouds below stretching across the horizon. It was like looking at a bunch of cotton candy strewn out as a blanket covering the world beneath us. It was all so new and exciting, and at first, I expected something different to happen soon. Nothing did. Just the endless clouds and the constant drone of the four-engine props. The newness and excitement soon began to wane and even began to get a little boring. I had been so keyed up the night before with such heightened anticipation I could hardly sleep. It wasn't long before some of that delayed weariness kicked in and I felt myself dozing off. I would briefly wake up and gaze out my window, hoping for a change; same old, same old.

We arrived at Dallas Airport sometime in midafternoon. The only problem was our flight to San Antonio was not scheduled to leave until 8:30 p.m. I'm not the most patient person for waiting. I didn't even have a book to read. Just killing time!

Upon arrival at San Antonio, we were shepherded to the Military Reception Area (waiting room) to await transportation via the Blue Goose—an Air Force bus used to haul the troops to Lackland Air Force Base (AFB).

Upon arrival at the base, we were taken directly to this enormous dining facility, cafeteria-style. By that time, I was dog-tired. Whatever appetite I had had long deserted me. I was more nervous in anticipation than anything else, plus I really didn't know what to expect or what to do. I tried to watch what everyone else was doing and follow their lead. I did get through the meal and was then herded into this large Military Reception Center.

There were rows and rows of chairs, and by the time I was funneled in, I was sitting midway on the right-hand side of this cavernous room (center) about the twelfth row from the front, a fairly inconspicuous spot, or so I thought. The Center continued to fill with multicolored-dressed young men in much the same predicament as me. I later learned at this stage, we were all called rainbows because of our multicolored and varied dress.

Basic Training, Lackland AFB, Texas

We were all seated, and there was a little buzz to the room when this little, five-foot-five-inch, buzz cut, red-haired, smart-alecky-appearing uniformed guy strode to the front of the room and yelled, "Attention!" I guess most of us had had some drill instructions; some had even had ROTC training. Or we got the gist of what action was required.

Anyway, most of us stood up and the rest seemed to follow in some kind of dazed fashion. "OK, I see we need to try that again. Sit down!" and sit we did. After a small pause: "Attention!" Again, we arose. "Damnnn! You dipshits, are really slow! Don't you understand English?" The uniformed guy with the stripes may have been short, but there was nothing small about his voice. His voice was booming loud and really had a barking bite to it. It was obvious he had done this before, and he appeared used to being the boss! There would be no messing around with this guy.

Anyway, could he ever yell! Not only could one hear him all the way to the back of the auditorium, but one could also hear him a couple of blocks away, I thought. "Well, that didn't seem to work very well. Did it? So, let's try to make it a little more simple. I'm going to say, 'Sit down!' and I want to see all—every one of your f***ers' asses—hit those chairs immediately and at the same time! Do you understand? Do you get it?"

We responded, "Yes, sir!"

"First," he barked, "let me repeat that. I'm going to say, 'Sit down!' and I want to see all—every one of your f***ers' asses hit those chairs immediately and at the same time! Now, you got it?"

And again, we responded, this time with a little more gusto, "Yes, sir!"

Again, the sergeant (Sgt), as I later learned was his correct title, called for our response.

This time, in a much louder and robust response, "Yes, sir!"

"And then I'm going to say, 'Stand up!' and there had better be no hesitating nor lollygagging' on anyone's part! Ya got that? You bunch of mommies' boys!"

We responded with our best hearty, "Yes, sir!"

"Stand up!"

"Sit down!

"Stand up!"

"Sit down!"

"Stand up!"

"Sit down!"

"Stand up!"

"Sit down!"

This went on for so many iterations that it seemed endless, and I think the sergeant was beginning to get hoarse. I know I was already tired, and I was getting more tired. I hoped I didn't get a cramp. It was getting ridiculous and silly, I thought at that point. Good Lord! I thought to myself, *what in heaven's name is wrong with this man? What in the world is he trying to prove? What **is** his problem?*

This was not like the game 'Father, may I,' was it? Like we used to play in grade school? Was this what being in the Air Force was going to be all about? The sergeant was beginning to sound a little looney to me by that time. Remember, it had been a long, tiring day since Mom made us breakfast and I bid the family farewell at Cincinnati Airport and flew in an airplane all day. I was grimy, dirty, sweaty, a bit out of sorts, weary, tired, and I just wanted this little squirt of a man to get on with it. I was beat and my eyelids were wanting to droop and, better yet, to close outright.

I also already mentioned I was kinda in the middle of the pack, hidden away, or so I thought. The whole thing was getting to me, and I must have smiled a little at the shenanigans—a little smirk, maybe even wrinkled my nose, and perhaps I might have raised an eyebrow. I don't know. I don't recall. This was getting to the point of being beyond ridiculous. But before you could say Jack Sprat, that sergeant was right there in my face, nose to nose with me, with his hot breath scorching my chin and smelling of garlic. I don't know how in the world he could have possibly seen me where I had been partially hidden amongst the throng of nondescript humanity hidden away, with none of us particularly standing out from each other.

I had felt somewhat safe in the middle of the crowd even though I had been bone tired, and I knew my brain must have been somewhat muddled. When I had heard the pause in the sergeant's cadence of commands and the room had become deathly quiet, there was a coldness that settled over my being, and I had felt an icy grip beginning to squeeze at my heart as I had glanced at the sergeant and saw he was looking straight at me with this maleficent stare and an evil no-nonsense grin.

He Instantly left his podium, hurriedly strode down the central aisle until he came to my row, took a brisk left-face maneuver, and was then right in front of me, toe to toe. I felt my heart sinking to the bottom of my shoes.

"Ya thinks it's funny, dipshit? Huh? Just what's so funny bout it? Please tell me and share the joke with all the other f***ers here, so we can get on with it! Let us all have a laugh, huh!"

Complete silence on my part. I neither knew what to say, or what to do, so I just stood there looking stupid, wondering what in the world was happening and what I was going to do. I had to clamp my teeth together, otherwise I knew my mouth would fly open. We certainly couldn't have that happen.

"Well, ya don't have yer mommy here to coddle ya and to wipe yer ass fer ya! Do ya? Yer goin have ta learn to take care of yourself and be a man fer the first time in yer little no-good-fer-nothing life. You hear me, dipshit?" He spit out at me in a loud enough rant for everyone in the center to hear. I felt his spittle spattering my face, but just stood there, keeping my peace.

How in the world had this little runt singled me out and got to me so quickly? And why? There must be a reason.

I had never been attacked like this before. He wasn't all that hoarse yet, either. I was shaking all over, perhaps not externally but certainly internally (well, maybe a little externally, too), and I was sure the blood was going to drain right out of me. I prayed under my breath, "Please, God, don't let me faint in front of this arrogant squirt and all these other people." By then, I would certainly have been shaking in my boots, except I wasn't wearing any. I also prayed I wouldn't piss myself and was thankful I had emptied my bladder before coming into the Reception Center; otherwise, Lord help me, I don't know what might have happened.

My throat was dry 'cause all my spit had deserted me, so I could barely squeak out a "Yes, sir." All that time, I was staring straight ahead, not daring to look at that little man straight on. I could see out of the corner of my left eye there was a streak of what looked like mustard on the right portion of his upper lip. Normally, I would have just politely pointed this out to the person, but not right then. No siree! Not on anyone's life.

"When I say "Sit Down, dipshit, your skinny little ass had better be the very first one to hit that chair. You understand that dipshit? Ya hear me? Ya got it?" he hawked out right in my ear.

And with the help of the Almighty, I was able to squeak out another "Yes, sir." The sergeant strode back to his podium with his boots striking the concrete floor like each footfall was a warning meant just for me. He turned his head in my direction and gave me a menacing glance and an evil stare. My already-pounding heart went into overdrive, and I think I might have been close to having a heart attack.

But under my breath, I muttered, "Ready, set..." and when the sergeant said, "Sit down!" I do believe my skinny little ass was the first one to hit the bottom of their chair!

I did survive the Reception Center, and as luck would have it, that little runt of a bellowing sergeant was assigned to be my training instructor (TI). But it wasn't all bad.

The recruits (now called troops) I had traveled with from Cincinnati were all reservists. By some luck of the draw, I, along with a few other regulars, would be training with them. This meant I would be assigned to a newly constructed dormitory with four troops to a room instead of the open bay barracks where the rest of the regular recruits would be housed. In addition, our billets would be adjacent to the Women in the Air Force (WAF) training area. According to my later cohorts' consultations, training was much easier; not sure about that one.

In spite of arriving for basic training late Saturday evening, there were to be no sleep-ins Sunday morning! I was finally able to get to bed and was so exhausted that I fell into an almost immediate deep sleep. We were awakened at O Dark Thirty before Reveille, with each door down the hallway progressively being bludgeoned open by our new TI and his assistant TI with their batons along with their yelling, "Get your lazy assholes out of bed, now!" as they made their way up the hallway towards our room!

"The day is wasting! We have work to do! You can't sleep your life away! Y'all are wasting yer time rotting in yer bunks now! If there is anyone left in their bunks after five minutes, we will come in and drag yer asses out of those bunks by the hair of yer head..."

We had minutes to quickly dress, fall out and assemble in some kind of superfluous order of four sections (lines). I became awake immediately and was on point. I dived into my clothes. Don't recall ever having gotten dressed that quickly before. Then it was a mad dash outside in front of the barracks where we started to mill around, but that didn't last long.

"Line up in four equal lines." Slight pause while we hurriedly attempted to obey. "If you are taller than the man in front of you, move forward!" Then the TI yelled, "Left face!" Most of us had no idea what that meant. "Alright, alright, dipshits, what I want you to do is turn and face me."

That, most of us understood, so we complied and turned and faced him. Giving up on military commands, he instructed us to extend our right arm and push away from our nearest neighbor as far away as we could, and that was the formation in which we took roll call that first morning. We were then quasi-marched to the chow hall for breakfast, then back to our barracks (not dormitory) to make our beds and ready our rooms for inspection.

That first morning was a gift. The making of beds and readying the rooms for inspection would be completed before fallout in the future. My attempt at bed-making was rather futile. I had done a little bed-making before, but not much. I attempted to mimic what my roommates were doing but surmised no one in this room would be taking home a blue ribbon for bed-making. No accolades for our room and from all the shouting and moaning from the nearby rooms it appeared most everyone else was suffering a similar fate.

The inspection commenced with the inspectors coming up the hall and inspecting each room as they progressed. I wasn't sure what to expect but was sure it wasn't going to be good. I could hear a lot of noise as they approached our room, and it did not sound good. The assistant TI came staggering into our room and started laughing. "You call that bed made?" He chuckled. "Looks more like a pile of shit! My cat wouldn't even take a dump on the likes of that!"

He then tore off my blanket, followed by the sheets, and then threw the pillow and mattress on the floor, appearing to aim them at me, but they fell at my feet.

"Dipshit, you are simply hopeless! I'll bet they don't even sleep on beds where you come from. Or do they even have beds? I'll bet you've never even slept on a bed before. Shore doesn't look like it. Let's see if you can sort all this shit out and then start over!"

Next, he started on the rest of the troops in the room. They didn't fare much better, if any. Turned out we spent the next couple of hours learning how to make a military bed with hospital corners. Always forty-five degrees, no more, no less. When the bed was made, all tucked neat and tight, the real test was if we could bounce a quarter in the middle of it. I still make a wicked military bed, and you can always stick a pencil through my hospital corners, but it's difficult to bounce a quarter on these queen- and king-sized beds anymore.

Next, I had my baptism in mass—personal hygiene! We were given forty-five minutes to completely shower, shave, brush our teeth, and tend to the calls of Mother Nature. Modesty had fled the premises and was nowhere to be found forever after. There was one large latrine (washroom) with multiple showers and urinals and toilets for each floor. The melee of men (young boys, some of whom barely needed to shave) smashed together in an enclosed space, all who were nearly naked except for their underwear, which consisted of a variety of colors (I was just used to white), sizes, and shapes (I only had worn Jockeys and a couple of my brothers wore boxers).

The troops ranged in age from those barely 17 to some of the reservists hoping to avoid the draft to the Army, in their late twenties or even early thirties. Skin tones ranged from ebony to almost albino. Shapes ranged from mine, which looked emaciated, to others who had to get a waiver or at least go on a strenuous diet in order to be below the maximum weight standards. Heights ranged from a little over five feet to well over six feet. Some body shapes were almost comical looking.

What was the most alarming was to stand side by side along the urinals, to take out your jewels and do your business or listen (or even see—there were no doors) men doing and even smelling them doing their other business. There were often calls to the cubicle, "Man, you're rotten—what the H ya been eating?" or "For everyone's sake, you gotta change your diet." If I had had the opportunity I would've been mortified, but it appeared everyone else was taking all this in stride. Wow, this was a completely new world to me.

The rest of the day, except for breaks, was used for practicing marching maneuvers and commands: Forward march! Left turn! Right turn! To the rear, march! About face! Attention! Troops, halt! Dress right dress! Dress left dress! These were considered the basic commands and more would follow later. At this point I was just majorly confused and wondering what in the world I had signed up for. Was I cut out for all this? How long was I going to be able to last in this outfit? There was mass confusion going on in my head. Everything was just running together.

Monday morning started out with a bang! First, Reveille and basic housekeeping and personal hygiene, and then we were marched to the barbershop. I had been warned about the haircut long before I signed on the dotted line, but I had hoped to lessen the severity of the impact by a trip to my barber a couple of days before my induction. I had him cut away a large portion of my hair. In those days, I had a full head of hair, which I kept in control of with more than a little dab of Brylcreem.

I stood in line with all the other victims, awaiting my turn. The barber seemed to take a special glee in shearing away my (our) locks. It was worse than a flat top or a burr; I was a skinhead just like everyone else by the time the barber was finished. So much for my pre-barbering back home; waste of time and money. I guess I should've known.

After the barbershop, we were marched to Clothing Issue to receive class A blues, a garrison hat with insignia, a flight cap, a fatigue cap, neckties, blue shirts, fatigues, boxer shorts, socks, undershirts, belts, dress shoes, and boots—with a duffel bag to carry everything. All that stuff was heavy, and we were required to carry it while we were marching (or should I say attempting to march—more like staggering bake—at least me) back to our barracks. By the time I dumped the duffel bag on the floor, my shoulders were rubbed raw. We were instructed to discard our civilian paraphernalia and pack it up, and it would be locked up during our tenure in basic training. Then we were to don our new military gear, making sure we first removed all tags and buttoned everything that had buttons before we stowed them away. Once we were uniformed up, we were no longer considered rainbows but airmen!

Basic training was five weeks long, and it went by quickly, even though, at the time, the days seemed to drag by as I wasn't sure I was going to make it through to the end. Many troops washed out (couldn't hack it) for a variety of reasons, both physical and mental. Others were sent back to repeat an extra five weeks of Basic training (RETREADS).

We had lots of inspections to make sure we were maintaining our rooms according to standards—shoes brilliantly shined and aligned at the foot of our cots in descending order, spit-polished, soles as well as tops, underclothes folded or rolled in precise order, clothes without any tags all facing the windows, shirts and coats buttoned, and there should never be dust discovered on any crevices or under cots or in corners during a white-glove inspection. (No dust bunnies, Heaven forbid!) I learned that spit-shining shoes didn't necessarily mean using spit but that water, along with the polish and a lot of time, effort and muscle grease, worked just as well. However, it was laborious and very time-consuming.

All free time was either spent studying, cleaning up, or shoe shining. There was no time for leisure reading, but then, who had books? Reading material consisted of the handouts we were given in class that we would be tested on. We spent a lot of time being tested. That was an attempt to make the best fit for the trainee and the needs of the Air Force (the emphasis here was on the needs of the Air Force). With my aptitude tests, I was listed for nine different career categories. Basic training consisted of taking classes (military history, military rank structure, when and where to salute), rifle range, target practice marksmanship qualification, and gas mask training (when we had the gas mask training, it consisted of putting on and fitting the gas mask). All this was a new ballgame to me.

Unfortunately, when we assembled for the gas mask/gas chamber training and physical exercise (exposure), the inspector discovered my gas mask bag was defective and I had to go back to the Issue Station to get a new one. While I was gone, the training for the preparation and conduct to maneuver through the gas chamber continued without me. There was no waiting for me. By the time I returned I had missed a good portion of the lecture.

So, when I was lined up to enter the gas chamber, the attending sergeant discovered I had not re-buttoned my gas mask bag—an absolute strict requirement. I had missed the part of the lecture where, before entering the gas chamber, everyone was to make sure their gas mask bag was securely closed and buttoned. Therefore, as punishment for my negligence (no fault of mine and no opportunity to explain the reason that my bag was left unbuttoned because I had missed that portion of the class because I had a defective bag to begin with). I had to go through the gas chamber without a gas mask; that is, I carried my mask in my hand. Even though it was only tear gas, it was still pretty awful. By the time I was able to exit the gas chamber, copious tears were streaming down my face, the tear gas was stinging my throat and lungs and made it hard to breathe so my best efforts at breathing were shorts gasps. I couldn't take a deep breath because it was too painful, and I was getting lightheaded before I could get through the chamber. Worse yet, I felt the top of my fatigue shirt was sopping wet so everyone could see my predicament; however, this was considered my faux pas and it garnered me no sympathy whatsoever. I felt miserable from the tear gas and knew I looked even more so. There was even some finger-pointing and snickering at my predicament from some of the other recruits which did not help my already sagging libido.

We spent a lot of time marching, always marching and practicing marching for the graduation parade. We had housekeeping and latrine duties, as well as dormitory guard duties. The final week, we had the obstacle course. It was really kinda fun, except it was pretty hot that day. We had to jump, crawl, run, climb, scale a twelve-foot wall, climb up a rope net, jump and grab a hanging rope, and swing on the rope over a small lake. If a troop didn't make it, they would get dunked in the lake and would get sopping wet, which would add extra weight for continuing the rest of the course. It was much like swinging on a grapevine back in the Kentucky mountains. I had done a lot of swinging on grapevines for recreation with my buddies back in the mountains, so I found this part to be a piece of cake.

Then we had to crawl on our stomachs, knees, and elbows under what seemed like eighteen inches of barbed wire with bombs (grenades) going off on both sides with blanks being fired overhead. The final obstacle was to cross Leon Creek on a rope slung over it by locking ankles and pulling our bodies hand over fist to the other side. I was doing pretty well until I got midway and found the rope was wet and slippery, and my hold gave out. I wound up losing my grip, falling, and getting dunked in Leon Creek and even lost my glasses in the melee. Fortunately, this was the last obstacle on the course.

Basic Training Obstacle Course, Lackland AFB, Texas

As it turned out, the runty, mean-appearing TI wasn't really so bad. Everyone got picked on and got stressed. That was just part of the program to see how a person could perform under stress and humiliation. The story was going around that they put saltpeter in our food to keep our libido down. I think most of us were just too stressed and scared to think about sex too much. But then maybe I'm just speaking for me.

Every one of us had to pull a shift of guard duty periodically during our training. On one such evening, when I had been assigned guard duty, I was surprised when our TI casually stopped by, seemingly to chat. He made me nervous and uncomfortable. I mean I didn't know what to talk to him about and at that time, almost any authority figure invading my personal space was enough to give me the heebie-jeebies. To say I was intimidated by him was an understatement. Guess that came somewhat from my interactions with my dad. I was (and still am) a pretty shy and very private person.

I felt sure this would not have a happy ending, but to my surprise, after some inane chit chat, the TI mentioned that he had observed my records, he had been watching my progress in basic training, and that I had some very good scores on the Air Force Qualifying Exam (I had done OK except I could have done better on the mechanical portion). He remarked that he thought I would do well in the Air Force. Then he left. Boy, that was unexpected and came out of left field. Maybe I would make it through after all. In the fourth week of training, our senior TI (the little sergeant) had some kind of heart condition and was hospitalized, so our final week of training got somewhat curtailed. The assistant TI was left to run the show by himself, and he did the best he could. The silver lining of all this was we got to skip the final mandatory parade. I was not terribly disappointed. Marching had not been my forte.

After basic training, it was off to Basic Medical Specialist Training (BMST), which was in late March 1961. I still remained at Lackland Air Force Base and had been selected to be trained as a medic, which meant getting moved to another barracks across the base. Not a very long trip. Of the nine career specialties I had qualified for, the needs of the Air Force boiled down to me becoming a medic. I was a little disappointed at first, but I thought, *What the heck, whatever will be will be,* and I would just have to make the best of it. My thought was we'll just have to wait and see how this turns out.

Because the Medical Specialist Training had recently been cut from eight weeks to five, my class got to spend a few extra weeks in Personnel Awaiting Training Status (PATS), which was a kind way of saying we were gophers or free labor for whoever needed extra help. This meant I got to be really experienced at kitchen patrol (KP) (lots of duty on pots and pans working at the chow hall and arising a O' dark thirty to assume said duties), yard work—mowing, trimming, planting, whatever—even some garbage details. I would like to say it was fun. It wasn't! It was March, then April, and the Texas sun was heating up; it got to be downright hot! I found the warmer temperatures to my liking, not the really hot ones, though—those in the 90-degree-plus range, hotter than I was used to.

Unfortunately, our barracks were not air conditioned and became hot and stuffy, and made sleeping at night a challenge. However, when you're bone tired finding your sleeping niche was not that hard in spite of the uncomfortable temperatures. Unlike my basic training modern barracks, which had four men to a room, we were now housed in open bay barracks (thirty to forty men to a bay). This meant even less privacy. Double bunks. Bunks lined up from one end of the bay to the other. Lots of snoring at night. Whatever modesty four men to a room permitted before was now a thing of the past. Though there was no change in our housing status, it was a relief when classes actually started. To our surprise, there were five Women Air Force (WAFs) in our class. That was still a time when the military was made up almost entirely of men except for nurses and medical specialists.

The BMST course passed quickly. Major event! At my eight-week point in the Air Force, I was promoted. I received my first stripe. I was now an Airman Third Class. I was somebody. I had arrived and was a part of the real Air Force. I was no longer a slick-sleaver, somebody to be looked down on. After these past eight weeks it was a really big deal to me. I wasn't always sure I would make it to that point, but by golly, there I was. I graduated near the top of my class, and then, I, along with most of my class, were off to Gunter Air Force Base, Alabama, for the succeeding Medical Technician's Course (MTC) (early June 1961).

11. TOUR OF THE DEEP SOUTH 1961

I was allowed to go home for a couple of weeks after completing Basic Medical Operations Training. I flew home. When I got home it seemed like everything had changed, but it also seemed like nothing had changed. I tried to reconcile my recent experiences with my surroundings and the people I knew and held dear. I realized things would never be quite the same again. No matter how much I tried to explain and share my experiences and what was being laid out before me, I innately knew these experiences were going to be uniquely mine, and no matter how much I attempted to share them, they would always be just mine.

After my visit home, I was off to Gunter Air Force Base, Alabama, just a hop and a skip from the infamous Montgomery, Alabama. The city where Rosa Parks had taken her historical bus ride in 1955. More recently, a white mob had brutally attacked a whole group of Freedom Riders who were touring the South, challenging the inhumane segregation laws—the laws that allowed bias and inhumane treatment of one segment of society against another. They attacked them with baseball bats, hammers, and pipes at the Greyhound Bus Station on May 20, 1961. The police force idly stood by observing the brutal beatings as if that was a Saturday afternoon exhibition being put on for their viewing pleasures. Several people were seriously injured. The whole city was in an uproar. June 1961 was probably not the best time to be assigned to Alabama, but orders were orders, and I was on my way, regardless. I'm not sure I understood all of the historical ramifications that had transpired and were transpiring in and around the vicinity of where I would be stationed for the next few months.

From Mom and Dad's house, I traveled to Montgomery by Trailways Bus, a competitor of Greyhound. As we drove further south, I kept my eyes riveted to my window and watched as the familiar lush green deciduous trees, and corn, tobacco, and soybean fields gave way to the stark evergreens and cotton fields. Patches of uniquely colored bare earth were now part of the landscape. Instead of the dark loam or sometimes light clay color, I was used to seeing, the earth was now a rosy reddish color. Traversing through Georgia and through Alabama, I saw fields and fields of what I assumed was cotton. It was still green, so I couldn't tell, but these fields certainly weren't the tobacco, corn, or soybean fields that I was used to seeing in Kentucky and Ohio.

As we pulled into some of the small towns (and even cities), I was amazed to see the signs posted WHITES ONLY or COLORED. These were on drinking fountains, toilets, and certain areas of eating establishments. I guess I had heard of this. I did know this kind of atmosphere existed in the Jim Crow South. But to actually see it with my own eyes, it added a whole new perspective to my experience and thinking. I noticed that the further south we went, the humidity got worse, along with the racism. Did one have something to do with the other?

Most of my classmates were the same ones I had at Lackland AFB from my Basic Medical Operations Course. They had transferred to Gunter along with me. There were two black students in my class. Interestingly, one shared a last name with me—Taylor—and the other's last name was similar enough,

Traylor. Not sure what that was supposed to mean. Perhaps the Almighty was trying to tell me that we are all brothers under our skins, or at least closely related.

Because of the racial situation in the Jim Crow South and especially around the Montgomery area, off-base liberty was very limited. In normal times, in technical (tech) school, students would be allowed more liberal passes to the local community. My friends Taylor and Traylor were not even allowed off base. Period! Because of the ongoing local turmoil. However, because almost everything was now off-limits downtown, it was hardly worth the effort to even try to visit the big city. There was a movie theater on base and an airman's club where we could purchase 2% beer. I tried the beer just to keep up with the guys but honestly never did develop much of a taste for it. My more experienced comrades complained that it took a lot of 2% to get a good buzz going. I certainly would not have known. We were limited in ways we could spend our off-duty time. I spent most of those hours studying and learning new card games—Spades, Hearts, Clubs, and Pinochle—and discovered I got to be quite competitive at most of the card games.

Medical Technician's School was a whole new ballgame. Biology, anatomy and physiology, psychology, mental health, field training, trauma, bandaging and splinting, nursing care, etc., etc., and etc. I was training to be a real-life medic and found it fascinating. I took my studies seriously and was at the head of the class. We were told that when the assignments came down, our standing in the class determined the order in which we would be able to select them.

I had my heart set on going to England, so I just hoped there would be at least one assignment there. Somewhere in the back of my mind, I was under the impression that most of our ancestors were from somewhere in the United Kingdom. I seemed to recall my grandma telling me that one of her grandmothers had come from England as a missionary. Also, most of the literature I read was set in England, so I was interested in seeing where the action had taken place that I had read about, perhaps even Sherwood Forest and especially London Town.

Towards the end of the two months, I got my practical assignment (hands-on experience to start putting into practice the things I had learned) to the Maxwell Air Force Base Hospital Intensive Care Ward. I was assigned three patients to provide intensive special care for during my eight-hour shifts, plus some gopher-type duties, which were merely the normal rites of passage.

One patient stands out in my memory—one whom I shall never forget: David Schimmel, a second lieutenant (2nd Lt) who was maybe a couple of years older than me, and had been in an awful motorcycle accident, and was paralyzed from the neck down; a quadriplegic. 2Lt Schimmel could easily have been the model for Michelangelo's David, who stands proudly in Florence, Italy, if one just added some hair. Or he could have been a model for any of the bodybuilder magazines, except for the fact that he was in a coma. His head was shaved and was as smooth as a baby's bottom. He, according to his chart, was six feet one inch tall, one hundred ninety-one pounds, would normally have had blond hair and blue eyes, and he had an enviable muscular development.

I was dumbfounded when I first saw him lying immobile in the Stryker Frame, moving not a muscle, looking almost like a mummy, with his chest barely moving up and down, and even then, only with mechanical assistance. There was a hole drilled into his skull and a band inserted into the hole attached to the Stryker Frame. His legs and feet extended at the other end of the frame by weights. It was like he was almost suspended within the Stryker Frame. He was attached to a feeding tube. A respirator was breathing for him slowly, causing his chest to rise up and then releasing it back down. He had an IV in his right arm and a urine bag dangling on the side of the bed, the other end attached to his catheter. He couldn't say a word or make a sound on his own. I felt I had to be very quiet around him, that I shouldn't make a sound. The nurse in charge felt no such compunction as she went about her duties and instructions to me in showing me what I needed to do.

He had casts on both legs and another on his left arm. I was struck by how strikingly good-looking he was. I could imagine him being his high school star quarterback, homecoming king, Guy Most Likely to Succeed, etc. Once, he had the world waiting to grovel at his feet, but on a dark, rainy night, with his motorbike going a little too fast, he had skidded on a lonely stretch of highway. He had tried to correct the skid but lost control and crashed headfirst directly into a mammoth old hickory tree, severing his cervical vertebrae forever, dashing all of his dreams and an unimaginable lucrative future. The head nurse told me the prognosis for the lieutenant was not good and, in all probability, he would remain a quadriplegic for the rest of his life for however long he might live. His prognosis was grave and probably extremely limited.

My care for 2nd Lt David Schimmel was to monitor his vital signs (pulse, blood pressure, respiration, and temperature) every twenty minutes and to assist with his turning as necessary (prn). We had no automatic machine that did vitals for us in those days, so my care included checking for cyanosis in toenails and fingernails, applying eye drops, moistening his lips with Chapstick, keeping track of his IV and feeding tube, emptying and changing urine bags, and changing his diaper (I needed assistance with that one). Also, I had to bathe and shave him.

To say I was a little apprehensive and somewhat nervous about caring for someone in this serious of a condition in my first undertaking would have been a gross understatement. Taking care of him was considerably different than taking care of trial patients (plastic mannequins) at the class lab we had been training on or even caring for my infant nieces and nephews. His skin was real, warm to the touch, and there was a beating pulse. LIFE. There were real muscles and bones, a beating heart, and a breathing being, though abetted with a respirator.

I said the word *life,* but when I lifted his eyelids to administer his eye drops and looked into his pupils, it was like looking into a bottomless pit—a vacant stare. How much life was there? I couldn't tell. Was the soul still lurking somewhere in there? This was anatomy in the flesh and getting personal, but where was the soul? That was a strange experience, but I reckoned I could do most anything if I had to. I had bathed nieces and nephews, but it wasn't quite the same thing here. I mean, they kicked and squirmed and laughed and cried, screamed even, and I always got all kinds of feedback, be it good or bad. Not so with the lieutenant.

As I washed him, he was no help at all. His limbs were completely flaccid and lifeless. I had to hold on with one hand while I washed with the other and, at the same time, did my best to avoid casts and bandages to make sure I didn't get them wet. And it didn't end there. After changing his diaper, I had to wash his bum just like one does with an infant. At the end of the bath, the most squeamish part was handling his most private parts and using special care with the catheter.

When I returned on Thursday, the charge nurse told me the lieutenant had been shipped out to California to be close to his parents. I would never see him again, but I would never forget him either, the young man who appeared to have had the world dangling on a string and suddenly he lost it all. He had his life as he knew it cut short by a most egregious and unfortunate motorcycle accident. This was my first encounter with a motorcycle accident, but it would not be my last. As a medic, I would be involved with many more motorcycle accidents, some not so severe, several quite severe, and some ending up in loss of life, a couple involving kids out of the barracks where I lived. My phobia against motorcycles only increased with my experiences with all of the recoveries from injuries involving motorcycle accidents. When I became a father and grandfather, I did my best to steer our offspring away from these, in my mind, death traps.

Caring for Lt Schimmel was mentally traumatic for me, for it was my first time experiencing up close the precarious facets that hold one's life forces in balance. Even though this was not a battlefield incident the result would be similar or could even be thought to be parallel. This was an example of a young, healthy individual with what appeared to be a bright future ahead, and suddenly it wasn't.

Back at Gunter, as our class neared its end, excitement was mounting. I had managed to maintain my standing in class. I was able to maintain the highest-grade point average. I had my fingers crossed that there would be at least one assignment for England. That morning, the assignment locations were to be announced, and we would be granted the opportunity to select our first permanent assignment after completing all required training. The whole class was in a tizzy. I could hardly wolf down my breakfast in anticipation.

The class training instructor (TI) got up in front of the class with the assignment list and announced he was going to read off all of the assignments first, and he started with, "And we have eleven slots for Jolly Ole England!" I could hardly believe what I had just heard. I took a quick breath, and I knew my eyes must have widened. Why had I studied so hard—so diligently—for eleven slots??? Then the TI continued with the allotted numbers as he enumerated each of the England assignments.

The TI kept on going down the list until he had completed all thirty-seven assignments. There were several stateside assignments and some others overseas, including *one* to Chateauroux Air Force Station, France. When he finished, he called out, "Airman Taylor? Airman Wiley Taylor? (Remember, there were two Airmen Taylors) What is your choice?"

My response, out of the blue, surprising myself even, was, "Sir, I'll take Chateauroux, France, please." After all, there was only one assignment to France, and I had taken two years of French in high school. Now I would get a chance to use what I had learned, put my French into practice, I thought. When I got to France, I would be very humbled that I had learned so very little and had retained even less of my French lessons. But I was confident I would get by somehow. More to follow.

12. O'ER THE OCEAN

Looking back, February 17th through October 9th had passed in a blur. After finishing technical training for the Medical Technician Course at Gunter Air Force Base, Alabama, I was allowed my second leave to go back home to Kentucky. It would be the last time I would see my family for three whole years.

During my leave, I took Mom down to visit with my grandparents and Aunt Cassie on Upper Wolf Creek. That would be my last visit with them on Wolf Creek, for after I went to France, they would leave Wolf Creek and move over to Hobert Gabbard's old place on the highway (Indian Creek Road). Our trip was the first part of October, and it was almost as if the mountains were ablaze with color. The gold and reds spread across the mountainside as far as I could see. It was as if Mother Nature had donned her most fancy dress to honor my impending departure.

Upon completion of my leave, I took a Greyhound Bus to Philadelphia, the city of Brotherly Love, and then had to wait several hours for a military bus to Fort Dix, New Jersey, to board my military contract aircraft flight to Paris, France. While all this was very exciting, it was like a whirlwind—too much, more than I could easily take in at one time. I would have liked to disembark in Philadelphia and have a quick look-see at the Liberty Bell and Independence Hall but there wasn't time.

At Fort Dix, I, along with other military troops (including all branches of service, some with family members), were herded into the contract plane, and when the plane was fully loaded, we took off late in the evening. We flew across the great Atlantic Ocean during the night. My vision was completely obscured. I could see nothing. I did manage to doze off fitfully several times during the flight but got little real rest.

It was late morning by the time we landed at Orly Field outside Paris. There would be no sightseeing in Gay Paree either. There was a US military attaché office where we had to check in, which was all the processing required for me to enter France as part of the US military. There was no passport required. Military orders were all that was needed. Then I had to wait for a military aircraft to finalize my journey to Chateauroux Air Station.

By the time I landed at Deols (Chateauroux's Airport), I felt like a zombie with my limbs barely ambulatory and like my brain had been fried. I wasn't even sure which end was even up. Whatever emotions I might have had departed sometime during the flight over the ocean.

When the plane landed in Chateauroux and I was finally let off, I was met by my sponsor in a field ambulance, A1C Roy Zuker, the senior occupational therapy technician for the hospital. He drove us to the medical barracks. The medics had a whole building to themselves. Then we marched (actually walked) upstairs. There were four open bay rooms—each would accommodate twenty men—beds, lockers, and wardrobes.

Chateauroux-Deols Air Base, France

When I arrived in France, Châteauroux-Déols Air Base was one of three of the United States Air Force bases located in that country. It was located in the Indre department of France, about three miles northeast of Châteauroux and about one mile northeast of Déols in Central France. At that time (during the Cold War), Châteauroux-Déols was a front-line base for the United States Air Forces in Europe. The USAF base at Châteauroux-Déols actually consisted of two separate facilities about five miles apart, Châteauroux-Déols Air Depot (CHAD) and La Martinerie Airdrome. The base was home to some 8,000 Americans between 1951 and 1967, where the USAF Hospital was located, where most of the troops were housed, and where most of the facilities were located. The site later became home to the Châteauroux-Déols "Marcel Dassault" Airport. The base while I was stationed there was under the command of the Air Force Logistics Command headquartered at Wright-Patterson Air Force Base in Ohio.

Communal latrines and showers were located in the middle of the building. It was going to be back to that again. I was disappointed but I was used to living without privacy by that time. All the newbies were housed upstairs. Only senior personnel got to move downstairs into the three- and four-men rooms. Oh well, it could have been worse. On the plus side, my bed was already made up by my sponsor, with a spare blanket lying on top of my trunk. Perhaps that was a good omen. At least all of the bunks were singles. No double bunking.

I signed in at the Orderly Room and met the first sergeant and squadron commander, who after a brief interview going over some basics referred me to the medical superintendent, Senior Master Sergeant (SMSGT) Deveraux. After my meeting with the superintendent, he assigned me to work in the Emergency Room—my first real job in the Air Force: 24 hours on and 48 hours off. Once I got settled into my work routine and with my supervisor's (Master Sergeant [MSgt] Bennet) permission, I enrolled in the University of Maryland base's extension program to work on some college classes as soon as the first enrolment at the University of Maryland's Extension course became available.

While working in the emergency room, I had a great mentor, SSgt Lendowski, originally from Latvia, who seemed to be an expert at everything medical. After quickly learning the ropes, I found I was in

Chateauroux AFB Hospital, France

my element. All the doctors assigned to the hospital rotated through the Emergency Room, so I soon got to meet all of them. Part of my job was assisting the Emergency Room doctors in whatever procedures they were involved with. I also got to hone up my skills in administering shots and bandaging and was even taught to suture. After a trial basis, I was sent with the ambulance on emergency runs.

Some of the accident sites were pretty awful. Alcohol often was a big factor. It appeared that with many young men on their first extended venture away from home they were motivated to try their hands at excessive imbibing in alcoholic beverages. Also there seemed to be a plethora of chronic imbibers in both the enlisted and officer career cadres. Alcohol was the source of many of my ambulance runs. Motorcycle accidents were usually the worst, but sometimes drunken drivers crashing their cars could be just as bad. The blood and gore didn't seem to bother me. I felt I was doing my part and was being useful; I was doing what I had been trained to do.

I took my five-level examination and passed with a 90 percentile, the highest in the hospital. My enrollment at the University of Maryland started with French and English Literature. My high school French didn't cut it. Even with the addition of college-level French, it was still a bit of a struggle to communicate with the locals. My Kentucky drawl did not seem to mesh well with my attempts to mimic the French accent. At first, I got a lot of blank stares and a few giggles and snickers. Conversational French was more of a necessity because I had to communicate with most of the hospital's French staff, who spoke little or no English. However, I did get more assistance from the natives because I did speak a little French and made an effort to have conversations in French. My French speaking attempts did seem to earn me some favor and encouragement.

After a few months of working in the Emergency Room, I was assigned to assist Airman Second Class (A2C) Tom Green in the Immunization and Allergy Clinic, where I learned to process the troops through their immunizations and how to do a battery of allergy tests. One almost seven-footer, 200-pounder-plus contract employee came through the line and shared with me, "I faint when I get shots." "Sure," I responded. I was always getting wise crackers like this. I was sure he was joking. However, I gave him his shots, and yep, he fainted. I tried to catch him as he fell; despite his girth, I was able to just sorta ease him to the floor as he almost took me down with him. I had smelling salts on hand, and smartly grabbed them from my tray and revived him quickly. I let him sit on the floor for a few minutes until I felt he was going to be alright. When I thought he was about as good as new and could be on his way with just a minor interruption to the immunization line. I referred him to our attending physician to exam him and make sure he was OK before releasing him back to duty.

After another couple of months, I was assigned to be the Airman in Charge (AIC) of the Immunization and Allergy Clinic; quite an honor, I was told. In this position, I was responsible for managing and administering all immunizations as well as all allergy testing. This was in the days before we had disposable needles and syringes, and therefore, all our needles and syringes had to be sterilized. For allergy testing, I received concentrated serums and had to dilute them to the strength prescribed by the allergist before administering them. Also, the hospital management decided to start an Airman of the Month Program. My boss (my non-commissioned officer in charge, or NCOIC), MSgt Bennet, submitted me to meet the board, and I was thrilled to be selected to be the hospital's first Airman of the Month. (Before I left Chateauroux, I was again selected as Airman of the Month, and as it turned out, I was the last one before the base was permanently closed. General De Gaulle had pulled France out of NATO, and subsequently, the United States had to close all of its military installations within France.

As much as I enjoyed my time in the Emergency Room and Allergy/Immunology Clinic, it was not to last. The powers in authority felt I needed more diverse experiences and on-site training, so I was rotated to the Medical/Surgical Ward, then to the Dependent's Ward; finally, I was named ward master of the combined Dependent & Medical/Surgical Wards as downsizing continued at our hospital after the construction had been completed at the new hospital at Evreux Air Force Base and the Air Force

Hospital Center for France had been moved from Chateauroux to Evreux.

After a budget cut that deleted the grounds manager's position, I took on the additional position as the airman in charge of the hospital grounds and responsibility for the same. Two reasons I volunteered for this additional duty: (1) I enjoyed working outside, and my experience with Aunt Cassie and my work on the farm came in handy, and (2) I was relieved from the barracks clean-up duty, which came around every third week and included cleaning the bathrooms, toilets, showers, basins, scrubbing the floors and everything to do with making sure the bathrooms were spotless. Some of our medical airmen (youngsters) would go to the club and drink themselves silly. They just couldn't hold their liquor and would come back to the barracks and spew (vomit) all over the bathroom. There would be vomitus everywhere; not very pleasant to clean up.

Additionally, we would have to clean, sweep, mop, wax, and buff the hallways. I gladly took on the grounds manager position for the hospital and gave up the barrack's clean-up duties. Also, I was given two troops to help me, but I was the one who did almost all the work. I was still having a little trouble delegating. On the positive side, I was the one who got most of the credit when the hospital grounds got rave reviews from almost everyone, including the base commander and the general (two-star) in charge of the whole Chateauroux facility.

13. WARD DUTY

The medical superintendent decided I needed to broaden my experience, so he assigned me to the twenty-five-bed Medical/Surgical Ward. I had been promoted to A2C; I had two stripes now! I missed the Emergency Room and the Clinic but soon adapted to ward duty.

Patients were often on the ward for days at a time for many reasons: psychiatric, alcoholism, appendicitis, hemorrhoids, broken bones, car accidents, cancer, pneumonia, ulcers, etc. You name it. I started on days, but because the ward operated on a 24-hour basis and there were three shifts, I was soon on shift rotation. I quickly discovered I didn't like the midnight shift (11-7) but preferred the evening (3–11) shift because if I scurried around and got all my required duties done, I would have time to visit and play games with the patients. I enjoyed playing games, and it gave me an opportunity to interact with patients on a more personal level and get to know them. So, I asked for and was permanently assigned to the 3–11 shift. Plus, I got to sleep in every morning.

I found I liked helping and interacting with the patients. I tried to treat each person as I thought they would like to be treated. For most of the patients, that went well. For a few, though, it was a real challenge. Ulcer patients seemed to be the most difficult to interact with, were demanding, and very little seemed to please them. Their glasses were not even half full; their next days were going to be worse than their past ones, and they worried constantly so I could easily understand why they had ulcers. I did try to be sympathetic with them and their numerous complaints anyway.

One young, very fit thirty-three-year-old pilot was brought in from the flight line after a fly-in from the States by ambulance with excruciating abdominal pains, which was thought to be appendicitis. Turned out he had had a severe heart attack. Before he could be air-evacuated to a definitive treatment center, he passed away. A real and unexpected tragedy!

We had a padded cell for acute, disturbed psychiatric patients. It was used mainly for suicide attempts or patients who, simply put, had nervous meltdowns. I was always a little leery of these patients, mainly because I didn't understand them, and I had heard so many "crazy" stories about them. I suppose my experience with my Aunt Cassie caused me to have somewhat of an innate trepidation whenever I had to work closely with any of them. However, with experience, I soon learned that they mostly suffered from a different kind of illness, and generally, they were pretty harmless. Depression played a big role. We had one grossly overweight (600 pounds-plus) civilian employee who was hospitalized to lose weight. Things were going well until I happened to walk into his room unexpectedly and discovered a huge bowl of spaghetti and meat sauce he was devouring (wolfing it down) that his wife had sneaked in. So much for keeping him on his strictly regulated weight-loss diet!

One Friday evening (Saturday morning, actually), I had just hit the rack (bunk) after completing my rigorous 3–11 shift when I was rudely awakened by one of the guys. Tom Sprester from down the hall who was still up partying and who had answered the hall telephone. He was roughly shaking my shoulder and yelling, "Wake up, Wiley! Wake up! There has been a bad traffic accident! They need you over on the ward pronto!"

It was now Saturday morning, sometime after 1 a.m., going on 2 a.m. I was sure I had barely closed my eyes and didn't think I had even gotten to sleep yet. I hurriedly scrambled into my wrinkled, discarded uniform, hurried to the latrine, splashed cold water on my face, and ran to the hospital as fast as I could. Two ambulances were already at the Emergency Room with their emergency lights rotating, as well as a couple of security police cars. I scurried down to the ward in order to help get things prepared for arriving patients. It seemed seven base airmen had been out partying and drinking and had last visited Joe From Maine (local GI bar hangout) and were out cruising (speeding, I'm sure). All seven had been crammed into a small Volkswagen Bug somewhere on the outskirts of Chateauroux when their driver lost control and ran head-on into a large oak tree. Three of the occupants were killed outright and one died in the ambulance on the way to the hospital. The remaining three were being brought to the ward for critical nursing care after first receiving life-sustaining and stabilizing care in the emergency room.

The next twelve hours would be the most critical—that would be my job along with the assigned supervising nurse who had responsibility for both the Medical/ Surgical and Dependents Wards. The regularly assigned corpsman made sure I had plenty of coffee, but I was able to keep going on adrenalin alone, almost. All three airmen were heavily sedated, so much of my duties were monitoring and taking vitals.

We had no automation in those days, so it was strictly rote mechanical.

They each had IVs going. IVs had to be kept clear, running, free of air bubbles and changed as needed. In spite of the situation, things were going fairly well as I rotated between the patients, checking vitals, assisting physicians when they came in as needed, changing bandages, etc., until around 10 a.m., when it appeared Airman Jose Martinez was becoming alert. I quickly went over to his side. He was an aircraft mechanic, 20 years old, and had been on Chateauroux all of three months. He was of Mexican descent, had a muscular build, dark close-cropped hair, and smelled like a keg of beer. He had a big bruise on his forehead, a gash on his right cheek with six stitches, a broken left humerus, a crushed right foot, and multiple bruises all over his chest and abdomen.

He kinda waved his right arm in front of his face, and I thought he was indicating he wanted to sit up. "You OK, Airman?" I queried. He sorta nodded or shook his head, so I put my left hand behind his back and my right hand under his right arm between his elbow and shoulder and gingerly pulled him forward and upward. About halfway up, he quickly turned his face toward me and vomited all over the front of my uniform. It consisted of alcohol, Joe From Maine's partially digested chili, with stomach fluids. They were all streaming down the front of me, saturating my white smock and permeating my inner soul.

Now, normally, I have pretty much an iron stomach, but that does not include vomitus. This was a yucky mess: partially digested chili mixed with Lord knows what kind of alcohol and stomach secretions, and it stank to the high heavens. It quickly saturated my uniform, and I could feel the hot gooey muck scorching my chest as it started to pool southward, and the stench of the alcohol and partially digested whatever's mixed with all the stomach secretions created this noxious cloud that set my head to spinning. Almost instantaneously, I helped Airman Martinez back to recline in his bed, held my breath as best as I could, gritted my teeth, clamped my mouth shut, and made sure his airway remained clear.

While battling my own reverse osmosis urges, I fled to the latrine. I could no longer control my reverse osmosis and had my own bout of upchucking. Because of my rigorous tasking, there had been little time for grabbing a quick bite, so it was mostly just coffee there for me to upchuck. Fortunately, there were more clean smocks on the ward, so I ditched my soiled, smelly one and hurriedly changed it for a clean one, after quickly washing most of the awful reside off myself and I was back on duty as quick as a wink. All three airmen were cared for and survived until they could be evacuated by the next special air evacuation for definitive medical and surgical care at our large European medical center. The last feedback we got was that their prognosis was great. And hopefully all three survived.

Eiffel Tower, Champs-De-Mar Park by Il Vagabiondo on Unsplash

I continued to take classes at the University of Maryland whenever they melded with my shift. I became distracted a little by the environment as well. I was able to get off one weekend a month and almost every free weekend I spent in Paris. I got to know the city of Paris well, so well that I was often asked to be a guide for some of the newcomers—especially the nurses. It was a simple excursion to take the bus to the Chateauroux Gare (train station), buy second-class tickets, and then go to the dining car, order a bottle of wine with soupe potage or soupe onion and une baguette and we would be in Paris in no time at all. Quick Metro ride to the Left Bank, Saint-Germaine du Pres, where we found a hotel for about $5.00 a night for two, and almost across the street, we could have five-course meal for little over a dollar.

Our hotel was near La Sorbonne University with loads of students and Notre Dame and Sainte-Chapelle (Christ's Crown of Thorns), all contained on Ile de Cite, which was just a stone's throw away. I attended my first mass inside the Notre Dame Cathedral with hordes of others. It was all in Latin, so I didn't understand a word but enjoyed the ritual and ambiance. Other fascinating highlights of the City of Lights: The Louvre, Arc de Triomphe, Hotel des Invalides (Tomb of Napoleon), Hotel de Ville, Musee d'Orsay, Le Champs Élysées, Place de la Concorde, Tuileries Gardens, Le Opera, Bastille, the Eiffel Tower, Elysees Palace, Moulin Rouge, Le Lido, Sacre Coeur, Montmartre, and Rodin's Museum—to name some of my favorites. The French Metro was a quick study and made getting around in Paris a breeze. There were never-ending things and people to keep an inquiring and inquisitive mind alert, exploring, and sampling the extraordinary numerous facets life had to offer that were so different from my roots growing up in the isolated hills of Appalachia's Eastern Kentucky. I was like a sponge absorbing whatever, whenever, and wherever I could. Life was shore different there for this ole Kentuckian who had grown up mostly barefooted in the Appalachian Mountains.

From the AF base, I had the opportunity to explore France and a lot of Europe. Orleans, the city of Joan of Arc, was nearby, and so was Limoges of the renowned china factory where many of the officers' wives went to supplement or restock their hordes of fine china. Mont Blanc was practically in our backyard. Also within a day's outing were Rouen (where Joan of Arc was burned at the stake) and Mont St Michel, the island city. It was just a long day to the Normandy Beaches and back. I was able to go a few times to Mont Blanc with friends with vehicles. Several of the troops living in the barracks did have cars, so I was happy to be invited to tag along on whatever excursions were being planned, depending upon my schedule.

Mt Blanc: Photo by Grillot edouard on Unsplash

Mont Blanc was my first encounter with really tall mountains with high elevations. It was a treat to leave the base in the summertime to don winter apparel and have a snowball fight with friends near the peak of the mountain. Mont Blanc is the highest mountain in the Alps and Western Europe, rising 15,777 feet above sea level. It is the second highest and second-most prominent mountain in Europe, after Mount Elbrus, and it was the eleventh most prominent mountain summit in the world.

There were an interesting couple of phenomena we encountered as we drove throughout the French countryside. We would drive for miles in what appeared to be very near poverty-stricken areas with dwellings that were mere hovels and centered in these areas would be a small village with a few, maybe a dozen or two, dwellings, but then there in their midst would arise this huge Gothic Catholic cathedral—amazing! The second phenomenon I found peculiar was while driving around the countryside; we would see cars pulled off along the side of the road and folks answering the call of nature without a "How do you do?" Sometimes, a monsieur, a madame, or a whole family would be involved. There were no rest facilities along the highways, so I guess they just made do with their necessaries. I guess when you gotta go, you gotta go! And they did go in front of God and everybody without batting an eyelash.

14. EXPLORING EUROPE 1961-1964

There was a lot to do and see in the vicinity around Chateauroux Air Force Base, and almost all of France was within a day's journey. I had all of my accrued vacation time to go exploring. But first, it's time I introduce my best friend, Ralph Gochenour. Ralph was a surgery technician and had arrived at Chateauroux about a month after I did. Actually, we had gone through basic training and basic medical fundamentals at nearly the same time. We also had been stationed together at Gunter AFB—he for the medical surgery technician course and I for the medical technician course.

We didn't know each other, nor had we even met. I had heard about this airman who drove a red MG Midget and who had driven down to New Orleans. He just happened to be Ralph. He was assigned to the same open bay as I was in Chateauroux, and we became good friends. I learned he liked jazz, played the trumpet, and wanted to travel. Ralph's trumpet practice did not endear him to many of the troops in our bay, for he was clearly no Dizzy Gillespie or Al Hirt.

Ralph was a big guy, always having a problem with his weight; most of his Air Force career was spent on the weight control program and dieting, off and on. Ralph joined the medics' football team and then took a part-time job as a bartender at the Airmen's Club. He bought a lime-green Volkswagen Bug. We became fast friends, traveling companions, and later roommates.

After Ralph got out of the Air Force, I was the best man at his wedding, and the year after that, Ralph was the best man at my wedding. We have remained friends to this day.

Mont Saint-Michel was about a three-and-a-half-hour drive from the base, and we timed our visit there so the tide would be out; the only way to enter the island was when the tide was out, so the road (entryway) was accessible. Also, the exit was accessible only at low tide, so of course, we had to wait until the tide was out again to leave Mont Saint-Michel. It is a tidal island and mainland commune in Normandy, France. The island lays a little more than half a mile off the country's northwestern coast, at the mouth of the Couesnon River near Avranches, and is somewhat less than twenty acres in area. As of

Mont St Michel, France: By joel protasio on Upsplash

2017, the island had a population of thirty. The commune's position made it accessible at low tide to the many pilgrims to its abbey. Incoming tides would strand, drive off, or drown invaders, which made the island highly defensible. A small garrison fended off a full attack by the English in 1433. Louis XI recognized the reverse benefits of its natural defense and turned it into a prison. Mont Saint-Michel and its bay are on the UNESCO list of World Heritage Sites. It is visited by more than three million people each year. Over sixty buildings within the commune are protected in France as monuments.

The base theater had just shown *The Longest Day*, the movie that recreated D-Day, the invasion of Europe by the Allied Forces that was the beginning of the end of the Nazi regime. Most of us were toddlers or babes in arms when that occurred, but there were several of us medics who were anxious to see where these events had taken place, especially after just having seen the movie.

The Normandy Beaches were approximately a four-and-a-half-hour drive from the base. There were five of us who planned on taking the trip: Al Brooke from Medical Supply, Bob Crane and Joe Alexander from the Dental Clinic, Dick Johnson from Administration, Steve Howard from the Hospital Chow Hall, and myself. Steve Howard, like me, hailed from Kentucky somewhere around the Louisville area. Steve was able to scrounge some rations from the chow hall for us to take on our excursion—it was going to be a long day (not the longest)—a gallon of peanut butter, two loaves of bread, a gallon of milk, two large jars of jelly, and a half gallon of pickles. One of the other airmen brought six large bottles of Coca-Cola. We left early in the morning, around quarter to five, because of the long trip. We wanted to see the beaches and the American Veteran's Cemetery.

D-Day Omaha Beach Landing, Normandy, France

Omaha Beach was the second beach from the west among the five landing areas of the Normandy Invasion of World War II. The assault began on June 6, 1944 (D-Day), by units of the U.S. 29th and 1st infantry divisions on the beach. Many of those soldiers drowned during the approach from ships offshore or were killed by the defending fire from the German troops placed on heights surrounding the beach.

It was towards noon when my buddies and I arrived at Omaha Beach. After taking a quick survey of the deserted beach and the lapping tongues of the Atlantic Ocean lazily rolling in and then falling back on themselves, we chowed down on the rations of peanut butter and jelly sandwiches. When we had finished our quick lunch, I did a walkabout and gazed around me. The eerie silence was almost deafening. I had recently finished the book *The Third Reich* and was filled with righteous indignation and damnation for what Hitler's Third Reich had accomplished in their quest to establish the Aryan Race—for the millions murdered and slaughtered, and the beat was still going on at the time of the Allied invasion.

That date and time in history was the turning point. I looked around me at the blood-soaked sand (not visible at the time of our visit, of course) of the thousands of young men who were wounded and slaughtered there. (My brother-in-law, Jim Smith, was wounded there). Time and the natural elements had erased all traces of that suffering and their demise. It wasn't only the Allied youngsters who met their fate, but many of those waving the Nazi flag had gasped their last breaths as well. These young men, many of whom were mere boys, were our age, some even younger.

The Nazi troops were often conscripted soldiers commandeered from countries conquered by Hitler's Third Reich. If I listened carefully, there was just the sound of the waves breaking on the shore, but over and above this silence and the constant ocean breeze, I could almost hear the cannons, the machine gun fire going off overhead, grenades exploding, gunfire everywhere, and the screams of the wounded and the groans of the anguished; of those that lay wounded and dying—youngsters going to meet their maker before they even had a chance to live. The lucky ones were killed outright; those less lucky lay bleeding out as their life forces slowly ebbed away as they called out for a medic or to their comrades or loved ones far away, or mournfully prayed to their God until their last breaths escaped them and their life-forces forsake them. Their bodies would later be hauled away by the clean-up/scavenger teams. Some may have even been pulled out to sea. Then there were those who would lose limbs and/or would carry scars for the rest of their lives; scars that would not just be physical but mental as well—terrifying nightmares. What a dreadful waste of humanity!

There was war rubble still standing as a monument to that awful and glorious eventful day—a rusted-out tank, blown-out bunkers, landing apparatus still offshore—all made an inglorious, unforgettable image of the destruction that mankind could levy upon itself in the name of what?

Later in the day, we were off to visit the American Veteran's Cemetery. Talk about being somber. There was row after row, after row, after row, after row of those who had given their all—their lives. Rows and rows, and rows of those whose lives were taken from them. They were somebody's son, somebody's brother, somebody's husband, somebody's lover, somebody who wanted a chance, somebody who

Normandy American Veterans Cemetery, France

dreamed of a future. Somebody who walked the earth no more, now they lay in the cold, dark, and dank earth decaying, already returned to dust, absolving themselves back to the earth, to nothing. Mostly a memory. Too soon, would they no longer be that?

The Normandy American Veterans Cemetery and Memorial is a World War II cemetery and memorial near Colleville-sur-Mer, Normandy. It honors American troops who died in Europe during World War II. It is located on the site of the former temporary battlefield cemetery of Saint Laurent, covers over 170 acres, and contains more than 9,000 burials. A memorial near the cemetery includes maps and details of the Normandy landings and many of the military operations that ensued. A bronze statue, the Spirit of American Youth Rising from the Waves, stands guard at the center of the memorial. The cemetery also includes two flag poles where, at specified times, people gather to watch the American flags being solemnly lowered and folded. The cemetery, which was dedicated in 1956, is reported to be the most visited cemetery run by the American Battle Monuments Commission (ABMC), with one million, or more visitors a year.

Ralph and I off to Spain
I took my first vacation with my good friend, my good buddy Ralph Gochenour, in his lime-green Volkswagen Bug. We had a little over one hundred dollars each to spend on our two-week expedition to sunny Spain. However, we had been able to purchase gas coupons through the AAFES program, so buying gas was already taken care of.

Ralph was a seasoned traveler; he knew what he was about, what he wanted to see, and how to get there. Ralph was and is one smart cookie. Me? I was a complete novice. I learned a lot from Ralph. He was the driver, and I was to be the navigator except I didn't know how to read a map! However, under

Ralph's tutelage, I quickly learned. He suffered no fools, me included.

We started out from Chateauroux and stayed near the western boundary of France through Bordeaux and made our first stop at the seaside resort town of Biarritz. We stayed at a modest but impressive hotel that included the evening meal. It was like a family meal; whatever was served was what you got. There was no menu to order from. We had duck with all the trimmings. It was delicious. The French people really know how to cook.

We spent the next day on the beach. The weather was superb. It was my first experience with the ocean, but this happened to be the Atlantic Ocean. I thought the waves were fierce. They probably were not, but they seemed so to me. Ralph really liked the water and swimming. When I first got in the water, the waves seemed to be trying to push me back out, and as I retreated, they tried to pull me further in (Ying-Yang). Strange sensation. I had taken swimming in school, so I was fairly proficient. It was great fun once I got used to it. I did manage to get a smashing sunburn, though; I looked like an overdone lobster. Before the trip was over, the sun had bleached my hair until I looked like a towhead again. When we returned to the base, some of the troops accused me of using Clorox to bleach my hair because it had turned so blond.

From Biarritz, we were off to Madrid across the barren and desolate mountains and plains of Spain. We drove for miles and miles without seeing a soul or a living creature of any kind. Just nothing and nothing. High up in the hills on the way, we could see what looked like cave-like dwellings dug out in the hillsides. Fortunately, we had a tank full of gas and had a hearty breakfast because it was poor getting's until we got to Madrid. In Madrid, we were able to obtain lodgings in the Visiting Airmen's Quarters at the Torrejon Air Force Base, and through the base, we were able to get tickets to a bullfight!

Our tickets to the bullfights were a surprise and a little unfortunate, for our seats were on the sunny side (the reason they were so affordable), and it seemed hotter than H, and it didn't take long before I was drenched through and through with sweat. I don't think I had a dry stitch left on my body. My clothes felt like I had jumped into the swimming pool with them on, except it was so hot they were not steaming. Fortunately, the humidity was low, so as soon as I got out of the sun, evaporation dried me off, but I couldn't get rid of my body stench. You know it is bad when you can smell your own body odor. No matter how uncomfortable I was, I was still much better off than the bull(s). One matador was bestowed with both ears and the tail, which I presumed was a great honor. The bull, on the other hand, was dragged out of the arena to be served up for dinner that night. *Ah bien* (oh well), as they say in French.

It was a treat for our little immersion in a new culture. Come midday, it was siesta time. Everything and everybody paused, closed shop, and stopped whatever they were doing for a couple of hours. But the evening lasted until midnight and sometimes beyond. We tried to visit as many of the sights as we could cram into the time we had. We saw flamenco dancers (bravo!), the Prado Museum, the Crystal Palace and Buen Retiro Park, the Royal Palace, the Heart of the City, the Fuente de Cibeles, and the Temple of Debod. We ate lots of seafood, including octopus. Too soon, we were off to Toledo.

Toledo was the home of one of my very favorite artists, El Greco. Along the way, we stopped to view some of the remnants of the Roman Aqueducts. When we arrived at the entryway to the city, Ralph and I stopped to have a beer. Ralph loved beer. A youngish Spanish gentleman overheard and recognized our accents and came over and struck up a conservation with us. We were a little leery at first. But, after visiting for a while, we learned he was a local, born and raised in Toledo and was quite proud of his hometown. He was working in London, England, and was home on vacation. It appeared he wanted an opportunity to practice his English on us and was intrigued by our Yankee accents. He insisted on treating us to more beers and boiled crayfish. (My first boiled crayfish—not bad!) Then he wanted to show us his city and insisted on giving us a guided tour. Turned out to be a fortuitous and happy event.

Toledo is an ancient city set on a hill above the plains of Castilla-La Mancha in Central Spain. The capital of the region was known for the medieval Arab, Jewish, and Christian monuments in its walled old city. It was also the former home of the Mannerist painter El Greco, as I already mentioned. The Moorish Bisagra Gate and the Sol Gate, in Mudéjar style, opened into the old quarter, where the Plaza de Zocodover was a lively meeting place.

After Toledo, we headed south through Cordoba to Seville. Seville is the capital and largest city of the Spanish autonomous community of Andalusia and the province of Seville. It is situated on the lower reaches of the river Guadalquivir, in the southwest of the Iberian Peninsula. It was originally founded as a Roman city and is home to three UNESCO World Heritage Sites. Seville was bursting with antique charm. The Alcazar palace complex was a stunning collage of architectural styles, and the Cathedral is famed for its beauty and its status as the burial site of Christopher Columbus. The Metropol Parasol was the world's largest wooden structure, a massive mix of grids and swirls that contained a market and a terrace observatory.

We stopped and did some swimming and sunbathing along the Mediterranean. I had begun to tan a little, but not very much. Tanning is just not in my blood. Sunscreen helped a lot. Waves on the Mediterranean Sea were not nearly as impressive as those on the Atlantic, but the views were nothing to sneeze at (especially the two-legged ones with curvy figures and topless bathing were not uncommon). We stopped off at British-owned Gibraltar and viewed some of the monkeys that inhabited the Rock, and then we were off to Granada and the Alhambra.

Granada is a city in southern Spain's Andalusia region, in the foothills of the Sierra Nevada mountains. It was known for grand examples of medieval architecture dating to the Moorish occupation, especially the Alhambra. This sprawling hilltop fortress complex encompassed royal palaces, serene patios, and reflecting pools from the Nasrid

Alhambra, Spain

dynasty, as well as the fountains and orchards of the Genera life gardens. One of the memories that sticks in my mind was going up to the mountains to watch the gypsies dance and listen to their music; completely fascinating. The gypsy mothers swarmed around us with their hands out, begging for money while clutching a baby or small child sucking on their exposed breasts. Different culture, different world. Architecturally and historically, the highlight of Granada had to be the Alhambra, which revealed the influence of the Arabs, who had controlled a vast amount of Spain for many years.

The Alhambra was originally constructed as a small fortress in the later part of the ninth century on the remains of ancient Roman fortifications. It had been largely ignored until its ruins were renovated and rebuilt in the mid-13th century by the Arab Nasrid Emir Mohammed ben Al-Ahmar of the Emirate of Granada, who built its current palace and walls. It was converted into a royal palace in 1333 by Yusuf I, Sultan of Granada. After the conclusion of the Christian Reconquista in 1492, the site became the Royal Court of Ferdinand and Isabella (where

Christopher Columbus received royal endorsement for his expedition to the New World). The palaces were partially altered in the Renaissance style. In 1526, Charles I of Spain commissioned a new Renaissance palace better befitting the Holy Roman Emperor in the revolutionary Mannerist style. It was ultimately never completed due to Morisco's rebellions in Granada.

Next, we were off to the port city of Valencia, which lies on Spain's southwestern coast, where the Turia River meets the Mediterranean Sea. It's known for its City of Arts and Sciences, with futuristic structures including a planetarium, an oceanarium, and an interactive museum. Valencia also had several beaches, including some within nearby Albufera Park, a wetlands reserve with a lake and walking trails.

Unfinished Sagrada Familia Church, Barcelona, Spain
Photo by Eber Brown on Unsplash

Following Valencia we headed for Barcelona, the second largest city in Spain and the cosmopolitan capital of Spain's Catalonia region known for its art and architecture. The fantastical Sagrada Familia Church and other modernist landmarks designed by Antoni Gaudi dot the city. Museum Picasso and Fundacio Joan Miro feature modern art by their namesakes. After Barcelona, we headed up and over

the Pyrenees back to France and Chateauroux. What
an experience! What and education!

15. EXPLORING EUROPE 1961-1964 II

Munich's Oktoberfest with Ralph in His Lime-Green Volkswagen Bug

It was a beautiful, breathtaking drive up through northern France into Germany. The leaves were putting on their fancy dress with magnificent hues, and they were spectacular, but in my heart, I must say it was not quite as awe-inspiring as the autumn foliage in Appalachia, where I grew up.

We drove up into Germany and stopped and visited an old schoolmate of Ralph's from his hometown in Indiana who was stationed at the US Army Post near Stuttgart. We spent the night with him in his barracks. A couple of his bunkmates were on leave, so he loaned us their cots for the night. It was a big open-bay affair, so we made ourselves right at home and joined in with the Army troops. Some of them were curious about how life was in the Air Force, but they were more curious about the French Mademoiselles. *C'est la vie!*

The next morning, we were off to Munich, where we stayed at a USO Guest House. I'm a little fuzzy about what all we did in Munich, but I do remember we drank a lot of beer, Ralph way more than me! I can still see in my mind the Frauleins carting the half dozen or more beer steins in each hand to the tables at the Hofbräuhaus Beer Hall. I can also hear the rowdy songs emanating from all around the beer hall. I didn't know German, but I could tell they all seemed to be having a great time. And I do remember the fog that covered the city for most of   our visit there.

From Munich, we visited the Dachau Concentration Camp. Dachau was a Nazi concentration camp opened on 22 March 1933, which was initially intended to hold political prisoners. It was located on the grounds of an abandoned munitions factory northeast of the medieval town of Dachau, about ten miles northwest of Munich in the state of Bavaria, in southern Germany. It was eerily quiet as we entered the Camp entrance. There were hardly any other visitors besides Ralph and me.

The original ovens used to cremate the corpses. Dachau Concentration Camp, Germany

The day was heavily overcast, and a cold wind was blowing, which somehow seemed appropriate. There was a chill running up my back the whole time we were there and goose bumps all along my arms and neck, and it wasn't due to the weather. I couldn't stop shivering. It was almost like I could feel all the poor souls who had passed through there, physically never to leave. Only their souls departed after a torturous and inhumane experience that no human should ever have to have been exposed to or manhandled by another human being the way they were. Did their ghosts still lurk around?

It was estimated there were over 200,000 souls who entered the Dachau Concentration Camp. Less than 70,000 were liberated by the Allied Forces (Americans) in April 1945. And those that were liberated were in a gross condition; most were "Walking Corpses." Some of the freed prisoners fell down dead even as the liberators arrived, sick, starving, malnourished, walking skeletons with skin sagging from their bones. Can we at least take some comfort that these poor souls' last earthly breaths were taken in the glorious relief that their worldly torture, pain, and grief were finally over, and it was freedom, the liberating freedom air they would be taking into eternity with them! So, we could take some solace with them that their last thought on this earth was perhaps, "FREE AT LONG LAST!"

The atrocities committed there by the Nazi regime against other human beings were brutal, cruel, inhumane, illegal, and beyond fathomable to the normal human psyche. Worst, I think, was looking at the ovens built for cremation and the mounds outside where the ashes were disposed; pansies were in colorful bloom—an absolutely beautiful array. What a dichotomy! If there could have been a saving grace, the gas chambers that were to have been connected to the ovens were never completed because of sabotage, according to the literature. The Dachau Concentration Camp was far from being the worst camp in the Nazi network of concentration camps, we were to learn. As we tramped through the camp, I hardly felt how that could have been possible. Little did I know. After

Dachau we returned to Chateauroux in a far more somber mood with a lot to consider. What would make one group of humans treat another with such inhumanity and such disregard? To me this seemed beyond savagery. After all wasn't the hue and cry extolled by the Nazi's to make Germany great again?

Our next excursion was to Scandinavia with Ralph and another buddy. Denny Neilander, a dental technician. This was to be a three-week, mostly camping excursion. We each had about $150 to grubstake the trip. We borrowed a tent from Family Services and bought non-perishable food from the commissary. We also borrowed sleeping bags and other camping necessities as well. Ralph's Bug didn't have a big trunk, so we loaded a big carry-on, also borrowed from Family Services, on top of the Bug and set off.

Figure 3 Ralph putting on the final touches for our trip

I was going to be our camp cook. Oh, joy! My one incident of attempting to recreate my mother's mackerel patties went over like a lead balloon. I guess both my camping comrades were used to salmon patties and had never heard of mackerel patties. So much for my attempt to challenge their palates.

Denny felt he had to roll up the tent sides in order to air it out. I don't know where, but he came up with some incense, which he burned and put me into a coughing frenzy. I hadn't minded the mackerel smell all that much, anyhow. From Chateauroux, we set off through Northern France to Belgium. After sixty years, my brain is a little foggy, so I may not get these in exact order, and some I may even disremember. The two cities that stand out in Belgium in my mind are Antwerp and Brussels. One thing I distinctly remember is the fountain in Brussels was a statue of a little boy taking a wee. In Antwerp, it was the ravages of war that linger in my mind. It looked like a giant tornado had blasted its way through and leveled almost the entire city, but everywhere I looked, they were in the process of busily rebuilding. It reminded me of watching all the bees hovering and mingling around my dad's beehives

From Belgium, we drove to the Netherlands. We visited the Keukenhof Gardens, where the tulips were in full bloom. The garden was laid out like a multicolored patchwork quilt, mostly composed of tulips, hyacinths, lakes and fountains, and green spaces. Then we were off to Utrecht (the Rijisky Museum), the Hague (home to the U.N.'s International Court of Justice, headquartered in the Peace Palace, and the International Criminal Court), Gouda (cheese), Delft (china), Amsterdam (Anne Frank), and Rotterdam (a lot of WWII devastation and rebuilding were in evidence there as well).

Photo by Farah Almazouni on Unsplash

From the Netherlands, we drove on to Germany through Hanover and Hamburg and took a ferry into Denmark. Our next stop was Copenhagen (Little Mermaid), the land of Hans Christen Andersen. Somewhere in this, we passed an island castle that we were told was supposed to have been the model for Shakespeare's Hamlet.

From Denmark, we drove to Sweden, where, like England, they drove on the wrong (left) side of the road; so, did Ralph, thankfully. It felt really, really strange to me. I kept wanting to duck away from oncoming traffic for they appeared to be coming in our lane of traffic, right at us. Fortunately, it was not me driving. Didn't seem to bother Ralph though.

We stayed in Stockholm. You know, I don't really remember much about Sweden except there were a lot of trees and it was cold. It was May, and at the campgrounds, most of the showers only had cold water, so when we took showers, and as you can imagine they were BRIEF!

From Sweden, we drove to the Kingdom of Norway, back to the right side of the road. Norway is a Scandinavian country encompassing mountainous topography. Oslo, the capital of Norway, sat on the country's southern coast at the head of the Oslofjord. It was known for its green spaces, glaciers, deep coastal fjords, and museums. Many of these were on the Bygdøy Peninsula, including the waterside Norwegian Maritime Museum and the Viking Ship Museum, with Viking ships dating back to the 9th century.

Bergen, with colorful wooden houses, was the starting point for cruises to the dramatic Sognefjord. We did not partake of any of the available cruises—limited time and limited finances. Norway is also known for fishing, hiking, and skiing, notably at Lillehammer's Olympic resort. The scenic views were spectacular.

I didn't know why I felt so drawn to this land, but years later, I discovered that some 17 percent of my DNA is Scandinavian. So, however it happened, somewhere in the far recesses of my heritage, there lurked great-great-great-great grandfathers and/or grandmothers who hailed from this region of the world. Most likely, it occurred on one or more of the Viking raids where they plundered, pillaged, raped, and wreaked mayhem on the United Kingdom. The people of Scandinavia were very friendly, and most spoke English well. I was particularly impressed by Frogner Park (Vigeland's) there. It is the world's largest sculpture park made by a single artist. It represents the relationship of people with people. Its statues depict people engaging in various typically human pursuits, such as running, wrestling, dancing, hugging, holding hands, and so forth.

Frogner Park (Vigeland), Oslo, Norway

After Oslo, we retraced our route back to Belgium, and our last countries visited were Luxembourg (the Queen's Palace) and Lichtenstein. By that time, we were practically broke, scraping the bottom of the barrel. We pooled our money as we had just a couple of bucks between us. Just enough to buy one large Jambon, a small hunk of cheese, a baguette, and a bottle of wine to share until we got back to Chateauroux.

16. AU REVOIR CHATEAUROUX

Towards the end of my assignment in France, a surprising incident occurred. February 17, 1964, I was still stationed at Chateauroux Air Station, France, in the USAF Hospital as a corpsman. I still worked the 3–11 shift with eight months left on my European tour. This was my day off.

My friends Bill and Marilyn Bobo had invited me to their apartment for dinner. Bill was a laboratory technician, and Marilyn was a schoolteacher. They were recent newlyweds. Marilyn's sister was a captain nurse who had worked in the OB/GYN ward. I already knew her because she helped me during my stint in managing Allergy/ Immunizations. Over the past summer, Marilyn came over to spend her summer break with her sister, Eleanor (Captain Florence). I introduced Bill and Marilyn on a foursome bike ride we took to explore the nearby French countryside. Mother Nature took it from there. A few months later, they were married. Marilyn joined Bill at the air base and was able to get a job at the local dependent school. Eleanor had subsequently PCS'd (permanent change of station; been transferred) back to the States to Andrews AFB.

As it neared quitting time, I meandered over to the medical laboratory where Bill was cleaning up, preparing to turn over laboratory duties to the evening person (the lab was staffed twenty-four hours per day), and then we went by the dependents' school to pick up Marilyn. Marilyn prepared an English roast with potatoes and carrots for dinner, and SURPRISE!! Marilyn had baked me a birthday cake. MY FIRST BIRTHDAY CAKE EVER!!! For my twenty-first birthday celebration.

In our family, birthdays weren't a big thing to celebrate. Can you imagine?? Marilyn couldn't believe I had never, ever had a birthday cake to celebrate my birthday, so she had baked me one. What good friends they were. And what, with ten kids? Almost one birthday a month, sometimes two. Birthday cakes just weren't on the menu—matter of fact, birthdays were hardly ever mentioned at our house as I was growing up. We were just lucky to have enough food on the table to go around. Desserts of any kind were a rarity. After dinner and celebrating with my first birthday cake ever, and after helping to clean up the kitchen, we topped off the evening with a nice game of Hearts and a couple of bottles of wine. Of course, I won. How could I ever forget that day? It's unforgettable.

It was nearing the middle of September, and my three years in France were almost up. I still had heard nothing about my impending reassignment. It dawned on me that I needed to take my future into my own hands, so I marched myself across the base to our local Consolidated Base Personnel Office (CBPO) to see if I could discern what was going on. The young (my age) airman scrutinized my records and detected no impending relocation assignments for me. When I reminded him my three years in Europe were fast approaching in just a couple of weeks, that caused him to put a call in to the Headquarters United States Air Forces in Europe's CBPO. It appeared my data had gotten lost (misplaced) in the shuffle. I was to be offered a plum assignment in Germany if I so desired. I didn't so desire! I hadn't seen my family in three years. I just wanted to go home and see my folks; even though I had long ago outgrown my homesickness, perhaps some vestiges of it still lingered. My family was still most important. I wanted to go someplace where I could be near my folks. Then I was offered an assignment to the USAF Hospital at Wright Patterson Air Force Base (WPAFB), Ohio, which would be pretty darn close to Mom and Dad. I accepted it, orders were issued, published, and would be waiting for pickup by the next day.

Captain Strum, our charge nurse, insisted on having a farewell party for her departing ward master, me. The party was held in the closed Medical/Surgical dayroom, and a gaggle of hospital personnel attended, including our chief nurse, Major Turnrose, my former boss, NCOIC Hospital Services TSgt MacGee, almost all of the ward staff, including our cleaning lady, Madame Berson, and one special patient, 8-year-old Duane Reynolds who had been in and out of the hospital for the past several months.

Duane had some kind of blood immune disorder and was due to be air-evacuated to Wiesbaden, the main hospital in Europe, for definitive evaluation and possible treatment the following week. During Duane's numerous stays in the hospital, he and I had built a special rapport. We had sorta adopted each other. Duane was more like another younger brother to me, as we had a special bond. Duane, on the other hand, had no siblings, so I was his stand-in older brother. He was very envious of the time I had to be away from him. I always tried to find time for us to play checkers or cards or just talk. We had become close. Even on my days off, if I was in the area, I would try and find a couple of hours to visit him. So, he had implored his mother to let him attend my farewell. Now, there he was in a wheelchair with his mother.

We had cake and ice cream, and there were a few speeches. The whole staff gave me a beautiful leather attaché case to set me on the way for my college career. Everyone knew about my off-duty college courses and my dream to pursue a college education. Madame Berson came up and gave me a hug and presented me with a beautiful handwoven neck scarf with tears streaming down her face. I was touched by her genuine emotion. She had taken the place of my dearly absent grandmother in that she was always looking out for me. Madame Berson was probably about seventy years old and spoke no English and was one of my favorites. She hastily wiped her tears as she turned away, and I, in turn, almost lost it too because I was very fond of her and knew I would miss her.

The last to present was my little buddy, Duane. His mom rolled him up in his wheelchair, and he reached up to me, gave me a hug, and then took this package out of his lap and handed it to me. "Go ahead and unwrap it," he smirked at me. He had this s..t-eating grin on his face and seemed he could hardly contain himself as he waited for me to undo the package. From his attitude I figured he was up to no good but couldn't imagine what in the world he had brought me. I did unwrap it, and lo and behold, what I was holding in my hand was a small chrome/silver cap pistol. My first thought was that I was a little old for cap guns or to be playing cops and robbers. I certainly was surprised and must have looked more than somewhat quizzical at Duane, for he then giggled at me and said, "It's for keeping all those girls off of ya when they're swarming around ya and the going gets rough and tough." He was grinning from ear to ear.

He thought it was the funniest thing in the world. Little smart aleck! I often wondered what happened to our little Duane, but I do hope that all is well with his soul wherever he might be. I still have the little pistol among my favorite keepsakes and whenever I see it, it always brings a smile to my face.

There were a few more intimate fare-the-wells before I boarded the bus for Paris, then back to the US, but I will spare you all of the boring details. More appropriately, I left Chateauroux with mixed feelings. I was three years older and hopefully more mature and wiser. I learned so much and made so many friends. I learned I could do things; a lot more than I thought I could. I was an Airman First Class (three stripes) with my five-level. I had traveled over most of Europe and seen more than I ever thought I would. I had added to my education resume both with college and military courses.

There was still a sense of loss. Most of the people I had known I would probably never see again, and this time in my life would soon fade into a hazy memory. And I have learned over time that one can never really go back to what once was. It was with a bit of sadness and loss that I knew—I had to let go and look forward and embrace whatever the future might hold for me.

17. BACK IN THE USA

After spending my leave at home and getting reacquainted with my family, it soon became time to start my new assignment at the USAF Hospital Wright Patterson Air Force Base (WPAFB), Ohio. Clearing-in was the first order of business, and the main item on the checklist was a visit to the NCOIC of Professional Services, Chief Master Sergeant Pickens. I was confident that because I had done so well as assistant ward master and then as ward master at Chateauroux, I would be assigned to one of the numerous patient wards. Not so. I was assigned to Master Sergeant (MSGT) Bletchly, NCOIC Emergency Room. Of course, the WPAFB Hospital was much larger than the one at Chateauroux: 500 beds versus 50 beds. Living quarters: I was assigned to a three-man dorm room where I was the ranking airman. One Airman Second Class (A2C) was a corpsman like me who worked on one of the wards, and the other was an Airman Third Clas (A3C) who was administrative and worked in the Admitting and Discharge Office.

The Emergency Room was another learning experience, an education in itself. I renewed my suturing skills and became proficient. You could say I learned to sew a fine seam, and I was usually chosen to sew the more definitive wounds. I did casting, bandaging, shots—lots of shots and cleaning—and all other chores assigned. Some of my encounters in the Emergency Room were gruesome, others harrowing, some sad to the point of devastation, some comical, and a few even X-rated, but I shan't bore you with all the details.

I had been at the WPAFB Hospital for a couple of months and was checking patients in at the start of the morning when MSGT Bletchly came sauntering back from having breakfast with his cronies (other senior sergeants) from our dining room downstairs (daily routine). His office was just inside the main portion of the Emergency Room, along with a row of telephones. I could hear one of the telephones ring from where I was processing patients. I heard one ring, and then I heard a call for MSgt Bletchly.

"Yes, MSgt Bletchly here!" I heard him shout into the phone. He rarely used a regular voice when talking on the phone or when barking orders. Then, a pause with a few seconds of silence. Then, a bellowing, "Airman Taylor, get in here, now!"

Good Lord, what have I done? I thought to myself.

Thoughts were running through my head a mile a minute. I quickly tried running through events of the past hour, then the past day, days—what could I have done? What could have happened? Nothing popped right up in my head. I motioned for Airman Sikes, who was helping me, to take over for me. I then went wide-eyed and shaking in my boots (except I had on my regular military issues) and scurried into MSgt Bletchley's office.

"Y-Yes, s-sir?" I stammered.

While still holding the phone to his ear with his left hand, he said, "You're sure 'bout this?" And then he reached out his right hand to me and said, "Congratulations, Staff Sergeant (SSgt) Taylor."

I thought he must be kidding or maybe playing a joke. But no, he insisted the promotion came from Chateauroux Air Station, France. I had been promoted to SSgt with less than four years in the service. This was after the Korean War, when there had been a massive military drawdown, and promotions had become stagnant or almost nonexistent. It was not uncommon for A1Cs (my current grade) to retire after twenty years of service with that grade.

To stir the pot even further, there were two other A1Cs promoted to SSgt along with me; one had fifteen years of service, and the other had sixteen years. Both were administrative types. Rumors flew rampant. There was a search through military regulations to see if my promotion was even legal. It was. Then it was rumored that I had gotten my promotion because of a liaison or liaisons with the chief nurse at Chateauroux (or with some of the other officer nurses)—not true! People sure can have wild and vivid imaginations, can't they?

After my promotion, I was permanently assigned to the night shift, which was great because it allowed me to enroll at the University of Dayton to take a class in chemistry. Working the night shift was a trip in itself. My main coworkers were two very experienced SSgts who were nearing their twenty years of retirement. They seemed to know everything about running the Emergency Room. I was fortunate to have them tutor and guide me.

They both had aged beyond their years. I suspect this was because of too much overindulgence in spirits, even though it never seemed to influence their performances. I knew after our shifts they would end up at the local bar where they could really put away the booze. They loved Boiler Makers and, on a few occasions, induced me to imbibe with them. I, on the other hand, could not hold my liquor that well, and after a couple of shots followed by gulping some beer,

I would stagger back to our barracks to my room to sleep it off, and suffer the consequences later when I would wake up.

They were both small men, about five feet six inches, and thin, almost frail. They appeared to be close friends. They were roommates and slept just across the hall from my room. The third member of our team was Tillie the toiler, an energetic, seemingly very experienced middle-aged, rotund single African American lady who was a workaholic and was a hoot a minute. She had no teeth, but that didn't stop her from talking a mile a minute whenever we had a break together. To hear Tillie tell it, she had been around the block a time or two or maybe three or four. I did consider Tillie a worldly, wise sage who abounded with loads of experience. Why, she even had been acquainted with Nat King Cole before he became famous. And boy, did she have some stories to tell! She would keep me in stitches for hours on end whenever we had a bit of time to ourselves.

My favorite of her stories was set during WWII when everything was rationed, including rubber and elastic. This particular incident occurred one day when she was shopping at the very crowded Rike's, the local upper-class department store similar to Macy's. They were having their big semi-annul sale. Tillie had just been paid, and her newly acquired cash was burning a hole in her pocket (pocketbook). She needed a titillating frock to impress a new beau who had invited her to the local jazz mixer where Rex Fallon and the Hot Wires were performing.

In addition to her new beau, she had a thing for Rex as well. She felt with the right accouterments, she would impress her new fellow, and who knew where the action might take her from there. As I already mentioned, the store was very crowded, shoulder to shoulder, which made it difficult to maneuver about.

Tillie was able to maneuver herself close up this big sales bin and she happened to stretch across the bin to reach for this frilly dress that some fancy dressed lady had been carefully examining, and with a great deal of hesitation then the lady had slowly discarded it back in the bin. This might be just the one Tillie had been searching for. Tillie had taken a hankering for the frilly dress, so she immediately started to make her move. But, as she stretched across the bin, she suddenly felt the cheap imitation elastic band that had been holding up her step ins (underpants) give way, and they began to slowly slither down her thighs. "Oh Lord, what could she do?" She thought to herself. Her heart started racing and she was about to hit her panic button.

She clamped her mouth shut quickly, felt she dare not breathe, stood stock still, trying to stand very rigid, and quickly grasped the offending underpants against her left thigh, and to reinforce the situation further, she slowly extended her legs as wide apart as she could to help relieve the situation. She hastily looked around for the nearest ladies' room and thought that if she could hold on for dear life and duckwalk through the boisterous crowd, she could somehow manage to get out of the situation with a prayer and a little luck. First though, she quickly glanced around somewhat embarrassedly to see if anyone had noticed what was going on. Thank goodness everyone was too engrossed in trying to do their own thing to pay much attention to anyone else or anything else. They were too engrossed in helping themselves to the sales items.

As she quickly looked over by the elevator, she beheld this dapper stock boy with his overloaded cart, giving her his best effort of his come-hither gaze with a cocked eyebrow and a shit-eating grin as he casually swiped a forelock over his right eyebrow and gave her a slight nod; his best effort as a come hither. He thought Tillie was giving him the "come on". Tillie sensed the idiot's presumptive interest and muttered to herself, "Oh Lord, preserve me!" under her breath, and at that very moment...*WHAM!* Some idiot trying to push into the sales table abruptly bumped into her and elbowed her out of the way, causing her to stumble and nearly lose her balance. Worse yet, she felt her underpants taking on a life of their own as they slid further down her thighs, slipping down her legs, and they landed with a plop without a by-your-leave around her ankles right on top of her shoes in spite of what she thought was her splayed legs. Because when she got the nasty unwelcome bump in order to save her balance, she had to sharply bring her legs quickly together dislodging her hold on her broken underwear that resulted in them being displayed around her feet.

She was in shock—just froze. Then it came to her what to do. She calmly dropped her purse and, at the same time, stepped out of the offending underpants. Then quickly stooped down, grabbed her purse, and at the same time, while pretending to examine its contents, scooped up the underwear, scrunched them inside the purse, snapped it shut, and nonchalantly, without batting an eyelash, beat a hasty retreat right out of that department store. Her last panicky thought as she neared the exit was, what if she was picked up by the store's detective for shoplifting her own underpants? Thankfully, she wasn't. She wasn't even stopped. I thought that it took quick thinking and guts to pull it off. Hearing Tillie tell the story and envisioning her antics as the story unfolded, I laughed so hard I was practically crying before she got to the end.

There were a lot of ambulance runs, and I even delivered a baby. Well, in all honesty, I was there to catch the baby when he popped out, made sure he was breathing, cleaned him up a bit, and placed him on his Mommy's tummy. I covered both of them with a blanket. Then we loaded them on a stretcher and high-tailed it to the hospital. Didn't even cut the cord. Fortunately, they lived only a few minutes from the hospital.

The worst accidents seemed to happen during the wee hours of the morning, and we had some most interesting cases during my shifts. Perhaps one of the saddest, most touching incidents involved a young A3C dental technician who lived a couple of doors down the hall from me. He was barely eighteen and had been at the hospital only a couple of months. I didn't know him well, but we had shared a couple of meals at the Dining Hall. He hailed from Minnesota. He owned a motorcycle, which he was very proud of, and on this particular night, he took it out for a ride, which resulted in him having an accident and a broken neck. He was still alive and barely conscious when we picked him up but in very, very bad shape. He kept muttering, "Sorry, sorry, sorry..." I never determined what he was trying to tell us he was sorry about.

We started an IV, patched him up as best we could, alerted the neurosurgeon on call, and notified the

Surgical Suite. The Surgery Staff retrieved him, and that was the last time I saw him. We learned he died the next day. What a waste! He was not the only victim I encountered who was maimed or lost their life in a motorcycle accident. In my mind, motorcycles are dangerous, and I am no fan of them.

My four-year commitment was about to end, and I was in a quandary as to whether to commit to another four-year stint or to get out of the Air Force. If I got out, I would need to get a job and try to continue my education part-time on my own. When I was offered the early promotion to SSgt, it helped me make up my mind. I was going to reenlist. And re-enlist I did—on my birthday in 1965 (I was 22). I also got a tidy reenlistment bonus and got to sell my accrued leave that I hadn't used up to that date.

For the first time in my life, I decided I was going to own an automobile. But what car did I want to buy? That was a big question. I mean, I didn't know a lot about automobiles. TSgt Olsen, our assistant NCOIC, had just bought a newly released Ford Mustang (their first year to be manufactured), and according to him, it was the greatest thing to come on the market since sliced bread. He took me for a ride, and I was impressed. I decided from his recommendation and my one little ride that was the car for me.

A1C Billy Wilson, who lived next door, was a good friend and owned a car. He drove me to the Fairborn Ford Dealership, but they didn't have the Mustang I was looking for. No worries, the salesman assured me he would get me whatever car my heart desired. Well, first, I had always dreamed of having a convertible, and I thought that red would be attractive for catching the eyes of the opposite sex, especially if it was matched with a black leather interior. I thought that would make a winning combination. "No sooner said than done," the salesman was quick to respond as he hastily started the paperwork. After the preliminary paperwork and an earnest down payment, I left the dealership with an order for my first car: a new model 1965 red convertible Mustang.

My 1965 Ford Mustang Convertible (Nellie)

There was one slight hitch, though: I didn't have a driver's license. I did have a learner's permit. I had taken driver's training in high school some five years earlier, so I did remember the basics, and I would have three to four weeks before my new car was delivered. I had to rely on friends and coworkers for practicing driver's training.

Fortunately, my new dream car arrived in just over a couple of weeks. Unfortunately, I had not been able to secure the driver's license, so my brand-new Mustang convertible sat very lonely without me at the dealership.

I was ready to take my driver's test, but there was a problem with scheduling the appointment because appointment reservations were backed up for weeks. Finally, after what seemed like forever, I was able to take my driver's test, and thank goodness I passed on my first try. Then, I was off to the dealership to pick up my very own little red Mustang convertible; in some ways, this was one of the more memorable moments of my life.

I had been at the hospital about nine months when Chief Pickens, the NCOIC of Professional Services, left a message for MSgt Bletchly that he and I were to meet him first thing in the morning in his office. Of course, I did as I was told and stayed around after my 11–7 Emergency Room shift was over. More trepidation.

After the normal pleasantries and How-do-you-do's and us taking our seats, Chief Pickens looked directly at me with his beady little eyes and said, "MSgt Bletchly and I have a favor we want to propose to you."

They were asking me for a favor? It must really be bad. What was I going to do? Could I refuse? I mean, I was just getting into the swing of things in the Emergency Room and thought I was really making progress and doing well. Everyone seemed satisfied with my performance. Plus, I had been enrolled at the University of Dayton and felt I was making real progress all the way around.

He continued, "The Commander at Newark Air Force Station (AFS) wants a superior, top-notch medical corpsman to assist the station's civilian nurse with managing the medical program for the station, and

MSgt Bletchly and I feel you are the best man for the job."

My face was red, and my ears were burning. Chief Pickens was really laying it on thick! That usually did not bode well, I had learned. What would I be getting myself into? Where in the heck was Newark AFS? The only Newark I was familiar with was Newark, New Jersey?

He continued, "Newark AFS is the Inertial Guidance and Calibration Center for the Air Force. The work there is mostly done by 3,000-plus civilians; however, it is managed by an Air Force Colonel commander and an Air Force Colonel vice commander with about thirty-five or so other military personnel. Your primary duties would be to look after the military personnel, do public health inspections and emergency care, and assist Nurse Turner, the civilian nurse, in other duties. If you agree, MSgt Bletchly and I would like to take you on a day trip to meet and greet the folks at Newark AFS sometime in the next few days."

If I agreed??? How could I say no? Little did I know, this meeting and that decision (was it my decision?) would change my life forever!

18. NERK, OHIO

As it turned out, Newark Air Force Station (NAFS), Ohio, was not so terribly far from Wright Patterson Air Force Base (WPAFB), a little over 100 miles. I enjoyed the drive over with my two supervisors, Chief Pickens and MSgt Bletchly, but I was more than just a little bit intimidated by the two of them. They didn't pay me much mind, though joking and reminiscing as we drove along. They rode in front, and I rode in back. I occasionally responded to a direct question, otherwise I remained lost in my own little world, watching the scenery whizz by. It was mostly cornfields, alfalfa, or soybean fields. Some of the old barns were of particular interest. Both my supervisors liked hearing the sound of their own voices, for there was hardly a quiet moment on the way over to Newark or on the way back, either. I was quite content to let them monopolize the conversation. Too soon, we arrived at Newark AFS.

Our first encounter was to meet with the station commander, Colonel (Col) Larson; however, he was not there, so we met with Col Fox, the vice commander. I did my best to keep my confident face on and expect the best. It was a happy coincidence to learn that Col Fox had been the base commander at Chateauroux AFS when I had been stationed there. I had never had any interaction with him in France. A good omen?

Next, we met with Major Shellberger, the administrative chief, who was responsible for the Dispensary and who would act as liaison between me and Chief Pickens at the W-P Hospital.

Lastly, we met Nurse Turner, the NAFS chief nurse (the only nurse). She was a delight, and I knew immediately we would get along fabulously well. And we did most of the time as long as I agreed with her and followed her lead in most of her decisions.

Nurse Turner was of Germanic origins, robust, very outright, and somewhat boisterous, a real extrovert. Was a bit overweight and was a platinum blonde. Perhaps the blonde was aided by chemicals. Nurse Turned gave us a quick guided tour of the dispensary. She saved the best for last. She showed me my very own office with a desk and supplies and a door that closed for privacy. Wow! This would be a real come-uppance in the world for me, and not only that, but I would also get my very own RESERVED parking spot. Can you imagine! Everyone seemed pleased that I had been chosen, and I was willing to give it a try. So, it was a go! Before our visit ended, a tour of the facility was also planned and executed.

Newark AFS was constructed in the early 1950s to house and support aluminum presses in the manufacture of aircraft wings, but this program was curtailed in 1953, and it was never used for that purpose. From 1953 to 1959, it was used to store industrial equipment and was designated as Air Force Industrial Plant Number 48. In 1959, it became the Heath Maintenance Annex of the Dayton Depot. The Dayton Air Force Depot personnel associated with the Air Force calibration program began their moves to the Heath Maintenance Annex in April 1962, and by June, most had been relocated to Heath, Ohio. In June, the name was also changed to the 2802nd Inertial Guidance and Calibration Group under HQ Air Force Logistics Command. By July 1962, the Metrology function was fully staffed. By the end of

1962, the primary calibration labs and the Air Force Measurement Standards Laboratories were completed. In November 1962, the facility was named Newark Air Force Station. It was renamed Newark Air Force Base in June 1987 (long after I had any official interaction with the facility).

I met a lot of people on our visit that day, but except for the people already mentioned, most remain a blur in my mind. Our main tour was Building 4 (Bldg. 4), which was really the guts of the operation of Newark AFS and where almost all of the critical work was performed. All of the other buildings were maintained to support the operation going on within Bldg. 4. One of our first stops on our tour was to greet Commander Lewis, who was with the Navy Corps of Engineers overseeing a major renovation project for the Air Force within Bldg. 4.

However, what really caught my eye was this beautiful, attractive, redheaded young lady sitting at a desk behind Commander Lewis. When I first saw her, she absolutely took my breath away, and I know I must have just stared at her. I could feel the blood rushing to my face, and I'm sure I was so intrigued I probably had my mouth open. (Hopefully my tongue wasn't hanging out.) She was so immaculate. Not a thread or a hair was out of place. To break the spell, I pretended I needed to tie my shoe so I would be able to break my stare and perhaps regain a bit of my composure.

Figure 4 Sue in her office as she looked when we first met

Bldg. 4 was a manufacturing factory. Two places stood out that day. The Beryllium Room was a clean room under negative pressure and required us to don gowns like we were going into surgery. Beryllium is highly toxic and requires close monitoring to prevent employee exposure. Bldg. 4 had several floors underground. On one of those floors, there was an acoustic chamber. When we were inside the acoustic chamber with the door closed, there was no ambient noise. I could hear my neighbors breathing and hear my own heart pounding in my chest, and even the blood gushing through my ears which made a sloshing sound. What a neat experience. What an experience!

The day drew to a close almost too quickly, and my mind was filled with all this new information. This was going to be a completely new ballgame for me. Both Chief Pickens and MSgt Bletchly assured me on the way back to the hospital that I was the right choice for the job and that I would excel. I was in the back seat, kinda zoning out, when I heard Chief Pickens say to MSgt Bennett, "Did you get a good gander at that Navy commander's good-looking secretary? She sure is a beaut!" I felt my heart do a flip-flop. I couldn't have agreed more. I didn't say anything. I just kept very quiet all the way back to Wright-Patterson AFB, lost in my own thoughts and visions of the Navy Commander's secretary.

19. NEWARK AFS DISPENSARY TIME

For the last four and a half years, I had lived under the fairly regimented auspices of the Air Force military, with men and a few women sharing a similar fate. Here, I was about to be cast asunder into a brand-new element with which I was unfamiliar and knew little about. To say I was apprehensive is an understatement. It was like being on a roller coaster, taking the ride for the very first time. I didn't fully comprehend what I was getting myself into. Here, the consequences would be more permanent and potentially life-altering. This was not going to be a two-week vacation but an assignment that did not have a termination point in sight. I needed to hunker down and plan for the long haul.

For the first time in my life, I would be responsible for finding my own lodging and my own nourishment, that is, food to eat. No more relying on Mom's or Grandma's cooking or chowing down at the Mess (Chow) Hall. I was to be given a separate allowance for food and lodging. I was really going to have to watch my budget with some real concentration, minding my own Ps and Qs. There would be no buddies around to lend a couple of bucks until payday, even though I had always been loath to participate in this practice, ever. I was going to have to learn to live on my own! Time to Manny up.

So, with mixed emotions, I bid my comrades adieu at the W-P Hospital after partying the night before. I realized this would probably be the last time I would lay eyes on most of them. My tenure with them was now history. I was finding life in the Air Force much like a revolving door; constantly, people were coming into my life, and other people were leaving.

I arrived in Heath, Ohio, late on a Sunday afternoon and checked into the Heath Motel, which was near Newark AFS. Next morning, I drove to the Newark AFS and parked in my very own parking slot: RESERVED for me. I could still hardly believe that I earned my very own parking spot! Once parked, I greeted Nurse Turner and began the process of checking in.

Secret clearance was required for entrance into Bldg. 4, which I had already obtained before leaving Wright-Patterson AFB, but I also would be requiring a special badge to enter Bldg. 4. I was enamored of my new office. Nurse Turner advised me I could purchase an economical breakfast and lunch at the Station Cafeteria. One major problem was solved, at least during the week. Now, my next problem was finding lodging, which turned out to be more of a problem.

On Nurse Turner's advice, I moved from the Heath Motel to the Newark Hotel, which was less expensive but was still beyond my budget for any extended period. I looked at a small trailer for rent—real squalor, a roach haven—and then a couple of places that took in boarders, but I couldn't imagine competing with half a dozen other men for the bathroom in the mornings. Lack of privacy, like in the barrack, I hoped to keep in my rearview mirror. This could be even worse. It was getting to be discouraging.

After coming back from one such visit, I know I must have been looking down and despondent. I know my dogs were dragging, and it must have shown. Mrs. Turner took me into her office and said, "I may have something for you. I know the director of the Newark Red Cross, and she has a big house in downtown Newark. She told me that if I ever came across an honest young person looking for a room to rent, she would be interested in meeting with them. She gets home a little after five o'clock. I could call her if you are interested. What do you say?"

At this point, I was tired and confused and a little desperate but still somewhat leery. But what did I have to lose?

"Sure, go ahead and give her a call," I replied to Nurse Turner, and she did. I met Mrs. Martin, the local Red Cross Director, after dinner at her home on Church Street which was a short walk from downtown Newark. The house was a three-story structure with a parlor, dining room, and kitchen on the first floor with a stairway leading up to the second floor. The second floor had three bedrooms and a bath with a stairway leading up to the third floor, where Mrs. Martin had her bedroom and private bath. I met and chatted with Mrs. Martin in her parlor. She had a lot of questions about me, but we seemed to have an instant rapport. I liked her immediately.

She was small in stature, thin, but very nimble and quick on her feet, smart and quick of wit. She had a quick, friendly, infectious smile, with completely white permed hair and the kindest eyes. What was there not to like? She was probably in her late sixties or early seventies.

She gave me a tour of the house, pointing out that my bedroom would be the back one overlooking the yard next to the bathroom on the second floor. It had a regular full-sized bed, one dresser, and a closet. Suited me fine. The rent would be $10 a week. That I could afford—was in my new budget. I moved in the next day and stayed there until I left Newark. My lodging was taken care of. Mrs. Martin and I proved to be a good fit for each other.

Her husband had died young, leaving her to raise two daughters by herself. One lived in Mansfield, Ohio, and had three children. I only saw her family a couple of times, but I do remember their Siamese cat. Once, while Mrs. Martin was in Mansfield visiting her, I drove Miss Long, Mrs. Martin's sister, to her house, where we saw her daughter in the play *My Fair Lady*.

The other daughter, Ginny, lived nearby and visited her frequently. Ginny had a 9-year-old son named Jimmy, who loved to play games, and I was frequently invited to participate and was often included for dinner (no extra charge) with them as well, even though that was not part of our rental agreement.

Miss Long, Mrs. Martin's maiden sister, lived by herself a few blocks away in the old family home. She was retired and seemed fairly well off. She was usually there for dinner as well. Mrs. Martin's brother and his wife lived nearby, and he had been one of Newark's previous mayors.

While living there, I tried to make myself useful. I helped with chores, did yard duties, and acted as chauffeur whenever Mrs. Martin needed to go somewhere. Also not included in our rental agreement. She didn't have a vehicle, nor did she drive. She normally walked from her house to her office downtown. I think Mrs. Martin felt I was the son she never had. She did have a couple of beaus visit her while I lived there, but they amounted to naught.

Work at the Air Force Station was not demanding nor overtaxing. Primary duties consisted of helping Nurse Turner even though, theoretically, I was assigned to take care of the military folks. Mostly, I took temperatures and blood pressure and performed first aid. Occasionally, I took ambulance runs or assisted patients to our contract physician whenever they had an injury beyond our scope.

The most significant ambulance run was a call I received from Bldg. 4. The call stated that an elderly gentleman had passed out and needed help. Even though I ran to Bldg. 4 as fast as I could, I found the patient completely unresponsive. No pulse! Not breathing! I started CPR immediately. The ambulance crew arrived monetarily and loaded the patient, and we were off to the local Newark Hospital. I continued CPR with no apparent effect all the way to the hospital. The patient was probably in his late sixties, tall—exceeding six feet and grossly overweight—I'm guessing over 300 pounds. After we turned the patient over to the emergency crew at the hospital, we waited around to see if there was anything else we could or needed to do. After some time, the physician in charge came out and told us that, in spite of our attempted rescue efforts, there was nothing we could have done. The patient had had a massive heart attack. Also, he had had a long history of cardiac complications.

Other work was more mundane. I helped schedule and monitor physical examination appointments. I took prescriptions for our military and their dependents as well as military retirees (a lot of our civilian employees were also retired military) to Lockbourne AFB to have them filled. While at the base, I picked up supplies to restock the Dispensary. Prior to flu season, I set up outside Bldg. 4 and gave flu shots to everyone I could badger into getting one. I even attempted to accost the Navy's secretary (remember the good-looking red headed girl?), imploring her to get her vaccination against the flu. I rattled on a bit, attempting to use every bit of silvery-tongued salesmanship I knew, but she turned me down flat—my first turn down by the perky, gorgeous, cute redhead who I found so entrancing. That was not going to be the end of it, as you will later learn. I would not be put off that easily.

My new duties to me were in the areas of public and occupational health. Before being assigned to Newark, I had to have special on-the-job training in bioenvironmental engineering and veterinary medicine in the areas of public and occupational health. I conducted sanitation inspections of all public facilities, including bathrooms and break areas, as well as the cafeteria. I checked food items for correct temperatures and expiration dates. I monitored the collection of Beryllium samples taken from the Clean Room to make sure that they remained within the Occupational Health and Safety Standards, checked safety procedures and safety gear, and provided safety equipment as necessary. Of course, everything had to be documented and signed. Precise record-keeping was paramount!

Even with all that, I enrolled in the Ohio State University Newark Extension Campus for a couple of courses after work. When I wasn't actually performing duties, I had time to do some homework and study at work. Mrs. Turner encouraged that. And too, I was delighted to run into the pretty little redhead, the Navy commander's secretary, at Ohio State Extension College, where we were both enrolled part-time.

There was something about her! Every time I saw her, I realized I was becoming more smitten and could feel my heart begin to beat a little faster just at the sight of her. For some unknown reason, I just couldn't get her out of my mind. I was hesitant and too shy to do anything about it—yet.

My office had a window that provided a direct line of sight to the entryway to Bldg. 4, and I knew that Sue (I found out her name was Sue Rauch) came over to our building to collect and send out mail a couple of times a day. It was almost like I was glued to the window when I knew it was time for Sue to be doing her mail run, hoping to get a glimpse of her. To add fuel to the fire, Commander Lewis, the Navy commander who was Sue's boss, would come over to see Nurse Turner and would casually drop by my office and just chat. Somehow, the conversation would always turn to Sue. I knew he could detect my interest in Sue because, in those days, I blushed very, very easily. Even though I tried to remain calm and hide my emotions, they were there in plain sight. I was very shy, and I suppose backwards. One day, Commander Lewis stopped by for his little chat and hinted that I should ask Sue out, out like on a date. And I responded, "Sir, I think Sue already has a boyfriend." I had been able to surmise that information from some casual chats during breaks at the university campus. I mean I had been trying to size up the situation already, on my own.

To which he said, "Yeah, but I don't think that's going very well—or anywhere, for that matter. Not now, anyway." Then he changed the subject. "You know Sue is having a little trouble with her math course. I think you would be a good person to give her a helping hand." And without stopping to take a breath, he continued, "I'm going to send her over for you to help her. You don't seem to be that busy right now." Without giving me time to respond and without further comment, he left.

My heart was beating a mile a minute, my palms were getting all sweaty, and my face was flushed as if I had a fever. Was this really happening? Did he really mean it? Was he really going to send Sue over to my office for me to help her with her math? What was I going to do?

I need to set the stage here for the ensuing episode. The military contingent, with some civilian volunteers, had been working on weekends to build a clubhouse under the leadership and tutelage of Major Knight, our civil engineer. I had been helping with the construction, and the grand opening was set for the following weekend with entertainment (a live dance band). This was to be quite the event for the employees of Newark Air Force Station. I had been busy with schoolwork and even though I had been a willing participant in helping to build the club house I hadn't given much thought to attending the grand opening.

Sue arrived with her math textbook and homework, and we were engrossed in the finite calculations, solving the homework equations. We were making real progress, I thought, when Nurse Turner stuck her head in my office door and, after making some small talk about some projects I had been working on, she said to me, "Wiley, you need to invite Sue to the grand opening of the clubhouse this weekend!"

Oh God. My heart stopped. I felt the air rushing right out of my lungs, the blood gushing to my face and I could feel it turning beet red. I had a hard time finding my breath. I couldn't believe Nurse Turner had the gall to stick her nose in and say that! I glanced over at Sue. She was looking down at her book, avoiding looking either at me or Nurse Turner. I could plainly see the beautiful freckles that spread across her cheeks, and I had this bizarre impulse to reach over and touch her cheek to make sure they were real. Instead, I did nothing. I froze. I didn't know what to say. What could I say? What should I say?

I peered at Sue and forced my tongue from the roof of my mouth where it was stuck and stammered out, "Would you like to go with me to the grand opening of th-th-th-th the Club, Sue?" And to my utter amazement and delight, she said yes, or maybe she just said OK.

I felt like celebrating, pumping my fist in the air and yelling, "Thank you, Jesus!" but managed to keep my cool and mumble, "All right to pick you up at about seven, Sue?" I already knew where she lived even though I pretended I didn't. Didn't want her to think I was a stalker. Sue agreed and gave me directions to her house. I guess I needed all the help I could get, and so with the help of Commander Lewis and Nurse Turner, my stars were beginning to align. I really liked Sue, but up to this point, I felt she was way too far out of my league. That was why I had been hesitant about making my feelings known...except for maybe some small flirting from time to time.

So, it began.

20. SPRING & LOVE IN THE AIR

What a night! Our first date was heavenly. I tried very hard to be the perfect gentleman and ooze a lot more confidence than I felt or even possessed. I rang the doorbell for Sue. Sue answered and was immaculately dressed, appearing poised and self-assured. She looked like one of the debutantes that you see posing in a fashion magazine. I was absolutely smitten. After all this time fantasizing about the little redheaded Navy secretary, was this actually happening? *I could be a goner. Maybe she could find it in her heart to develop feelings for me,* I thought. Perhaps this was presumptuous at this very early stage.

Figure 5 Sue's Graduation Photo

The evening went well. The music was loud and necessitated sitting fairly close (my advantage), and we began trying to get to know each other. Sue was a little hesitant about sharing her background. She did share that she was a homegrown girl, had one sibling, a brother named Bob, five years older, who lived and worked in Chicago, and she still lived with her mother and father. Her father was a lifelong employee of the local Owens Corning Manufacturing Company. Her mother was a stay-at-home homemaker. She was close to her Aunt Sissy, half-sister to her mother, and she had an Uncle Willard who lived nearby.

Her father was the oldest of ten children, and all of his siblings and their families lived in and around the local area. His mother was still alive and lived in Newark. I attempted to impress Sue with my exploits in France working in the hospital at Chateauroux and my extensive travels throughout Europe. I did share that I was from a large family, with ten kids like her dad, but I didn't go into a lot of details.

We danced, even though I was far from being the world's best dancer. There are those who would go as far as to say I was grossly lacking in that department. However, I did manage not to step on Sue's feet, at least not too much, but I seriously doubted if she was impressed with my dancing skills. Sue, on the other hand, was a very good, graceful dancer. I found out that Sue enjoyed dancing. I was enthralled to be holding her close to me during the slow tunes. We chatted some more and listened to music. All in all, I felt it was a wonderful evening.

I escorted Sue to her door and hesitantly gave her a quick goodnight kiss even though I desired much more and would have liked for the evening to have gone on. On Monday morning, Nurse Turner wanted to know all the details. Busybody! I was mum and as noncommittal as I could be. My response was, "She is really a nice girl, and I really like her." Other than that, there was naught that I was willing to share.

"Well, you better strike while the iron is hot, and don't let her get away," was Nurse Turner's advice. Like I needed that. I had been on pins and needles since Saturday night, thinking about Sue and our date. Had she thought about me at all? If so, what did she think? Had I made any kind of impression on her? I was in a bit of a mess. And I was anxiously waiting for enough time to pass so I could call her. I didn't want to appear overbearing or overeager or for her to think I was stalking her, so I waited until about 10 a.m. to call her. When she answered, I was tongue-tied, so at first, there was silence. I had to think fast. "Good morning, Sue. This is Wiley over at the Dispensary, and I was wondering if you still needed help with your math?" (Was I talking too fast? Did I sound overeager? I do that sometimes when I'm anxious or nervous.)

"No, Wiley, we did all the problems for the homework and there is nothing more to do until class on Wednesday," she answered.

Then my words came tumbling out. "Sue, I really enjoyed our evening together. I liked being with you and enjoyed your company. And, well, I was hoping you would consider letting me take you out to dinner and maybe a movie?"

"When were you thinking about?" she asked.

"How about Friday after work? Say I pick you up at around six?"

And our dating began.

A couple of weeks into our dating, I was invited to have dinner with Sue and her folks, which included her uncle Willard and his significant other. I brought flowers from Pounds Nursery, as Mrs. Martin had suggested was the best place to get the freshest flowers in town. I was left alone for a few minutes with Niggy, the ebony-black cat, while Sue was helping her mother with dinner. Everyone else was on the back porch.

While I was sitting on the sofa, I surveyed the room, and the warmest feeling came over me. It was like a voice inside my head spoke to me, "You belong here." I had never in my life had such a premonition before, and I've never, *ever* shared this with anyone until now. Sue's Mom's spaghetti dinner sealed the deal—it was the best spaghetti I had ever tasted in my life, and I loved spaghetti (still do). I smiled to myself as we enjoyed the scrumptious pasta. It was absolutely preordained that this was to be the woman that was meant to be in my life. It was fate—ordained—no discussion!

Did I mention that Sue also owned a 1965 convertible, a blue Corvair? Life appeared good! I was in love, and it appeared that love just might be reciprocated (or there was a chance it could be).

Sue's 1965 Corvair Convertible

Work was on an even keel, and college courses were piling up with fairly impressive grades. I was 23, older than all my siblings were when they had tied the knot, so in truth, my thoughts were turning to marriage. I was confident, without a doubt, that I had found my soulmate, the person with whom I wanted to spend the rest of my life, to raise a family with, and to grow old together.

Our courtship advanced rather smoothly. As we got to know each other better, we learned that our cultural backgrounds were miles apart. We talked about a possible future together. However, it was time for Sue to meet my family. I had reservations because there was such a lot of difference in our backgrounds; because there were so many in my family, I was afraid Sue would be overpowered by the sheer numbers.

Our backgrounds were so different. For many generations, my family had lived in Appalachia with limited exposure to education and the developing world. Their lives had centered around eking out a living from Mother Nature for generations. My family, for the most part, was on the lower end of the poverty line, mostly minimally educated and Pentecostals.

Sue's family was fairly typical, somewhat conservative middle-class Methodists, much more cosmopolitan. Her family had lived near metropolitan life for some generations. As it turned out, there was nothing to be concerned about. Sue appeared to be her calm, sweet, confident, and gracious self and seemed to take everything in stride. My family absolutely loved her.

I was now committed to the Air Force until February 1968. Would I get out of the Air Force and go to college and get a degree and do what? I really liked medicine. My dream of dreams would have been to become a physician, but being a nurse would not be a bad choice either. There were other options. Or should I seek out the Air Force as a career? I felt I had more potential than the career path that I was on in the Air Force, hence I was pursuing all the evening college courses that were available to me.

And what about Sue? She had a good-paying job as a secretary and was bright and intelligent. She, too, was pursuing college courses.

And what about kids? I'd always wanted kids. As long as I could remember, I'd dreamed of being a dad! And the more kids, the merrier. I had done a lot of babysitting with nieces and nephews, helped with younger siblings, and taken care of small children in the hospital under a number of stressful situations. I felt I had a real knack with kids and thought I would make a good dad. I felt I was ready! It was just a matter of finding the right partner whom I loved and who shared the same dreams. I thought I had found that person in Sue.

Sue, on the other hand, was a little more hesitant about children. She wasn't sure she could be a good mom. Her relationship with her mother was not always ideal and had somewhat soured her motherhood prospects. To me, Sue's hesitancy on this point was a minor stumbling block, and I felt with time, it would take care of itself. I loved Sue and wanted to share my life with her, to build a family with her, and to grow old with her, as I already said. I had had some infatuations before, but I never felt this kind of love for anyone.

I bought rings. Should I have consulted Sue first? Perhaps. My knowledge about this sort of thing was pretty limited. I went to the jeweler's a couple of times before I finally settled on what I felt was the best choice within my budget. The jeweler was an older gentleman, and you could tell he had been doing this for a long time. He was somewhat overweight, balding, and wore spectacles. He advised me, "Son, I'm going to tell ya, this will probably be the best bargain or the worst purchase you will make in your whole life." Obviously, it has turned out to be the best one.

I planned my proposal. I made dinner reservations at the fanciest restaurant in town, ordered a dozen roses from Pounds Nursery, and left my room with time to spare. Picked up the roses and was about a mile away from greeting and picking up my sweetheart to propose we set in motion the plans for a life together when the right front tire of my Mustang had a flat. Not only was the air going out of that tire, but it was also going out of my evening as well. I felt my planned evening deflating just as fast. I could have thought, *well, we can just do this another day,* but you know, when you work so hard and have plans, you want to make things happen. Plus, I'm an action person—goal oriented.

Strike one! I knew next to nothing about cars or changing tires for that matter. I knew how to drive, put gas in them, and on a good day, I could check the oil and tire pressure. Mom and Dad had never had a motor vehicle of any kind. Mechanics was far from being my thing. I certainly knew nothing about changing tires!

Strike two? Was this some kind of omen? We had no mobile phones in those days, but fortunately for me, there was a farmhouse just a little way back from the graveyard where the tire had gone flat. Oh, did I tell you I had the flat tire on the road just beside the graveyard? Good thing I wasn't particularly superstitious.

Anyway, I walked back to the farmhouse, knocked on the door, and fortunately, they were home. I explained the situation and asked to use their phone. They invited me in and offered me the use of their phone. I called Sue's house and her brother, Bob, answered the phone. I told Bob that I had had a flat and embarrassedly told him I didn't know how to change it. I was going to have to call the garage or roadside assistance to come out to put the spare on. Would he tell Sue I was going to be somewhat late? Bob kinda chuckled. He said he could help me change the tire, and in no time at all he and Sue arrived at my car and Bob actually changed the tire for me. Within a few minutes, Sue and I were on our way. No Strike three, thank goodness!

We had a wonderful dinner. We even had wine with dinner, and Sue actually sipped some of her wine, maybe half of it. We had discussed a life together before and I believed we both knew how we felt about each other. We just hadn't formalized it.

I didn't want my proposal to be the typical down-on-one knee brandishing the ring in Sue's face. So, while we were waiting for dessert to be delivered, I asked for Sue's left hand underneath the table. We were seated opposite. I slipped the engagement ring on her ring finger while I sat transfixed on her beautiful visage, staring into her gorgeous eyes. You know, I don't remember her actually saying YES, but she also didn't say NO. But it was a yes, and undoubtedly, I was the luckiest and happiest man alive.

That's how it happened, and we were engaged.

21. WEDDING BELLS

Sue and I had planned our wedding for April 16th. That way, our anniversary would always fall one day after payday, so we would have a little money to celebrate our anniversaries. In the interim, a sad event occurred in my life. My grandmother Bishop passed away on October 9, 1966. It hit me hard. My grandmother had been a special person in my life. She had always been my champion. We had a special bond. I had felt our closeness slipping away after our family moved to Cincinnati in 1956. I continued to spend my summers with her, Grandpa, and Aunt Cassie until I completed high school. She was the first person in my immediate family to pass on. She left a void in my life, and I felt very saddened and depressed about her passing.

Military career-wise, I was stagnant. I was eligible to be promoted to E-6 (technical sergeant), but before my records could meet the promotion board, I needed to complete an in-house four-month technical course for the award of the 7-level proficiency. My military powers (superiors) chose to send me to technical training at Sheppard Air Force Base, Texas, on the first of December 1966. Remember our wedding was planned for the middle of April 1967? This meant that I would finish training just a couple of weeks before the wedding, and I would miss Christmas entirely. Oh, woe was me! However, I didn't have much choice in the matter.

Nellie, my red Mustang, and I struck out for Texas, and our first stop along Highway 70 was in the boonies of Missouri at a $3-a-night motel. I needed to really start pinching pennies with the wedding a little over four months away. I would be living on Sheppard Air Force Base for the next four months and would have only my basic pay as my separate rations (housing and food allowance) would be withdrawn as long as I was attending school.

The following four months turned out to be a pretty dismal and lonely existence. Sue and I did keep in touch with a constant flow of letters, but there was certainly no access to social media or cell phones like there is today. Long-distance telephone calls would have been exorbitantly expensive and not on our budget. However, I kept busy with all-day classes, homework, and studies.

There were about forty medical NCOs in the class, all vying for our 7-level certification required to be eligible to be promoted to E-6. There were two NCOs in a room. My roommate was an older SSgt Williams who hailed from New Zealand, a most interesting chap. He was really into classical music and had numerous tales about growing up in New Zealand and Australia. He had relatives who lived in both countries. He talked a lot about one brother who lived in Australia. I suppose after he retired from the Air Force, he would return to that area as he had no family in the United States that I was aware of.

After being in school for a few weeks, there was a common chant that went around our barracks from most of the married men. It went something like, "I'm going to be a new daddy again (or for a few, perhaps for the first time). Do you want to know when? Just nine months after I get home." They were a bawdy lot and were getting hornier as the days progressed. I know they missed their families. But not as much as I missed my Sue, I was sure.

Sue was on my mind constantly. I missed her so much. I would hurry after classes to the mailroom to check for letters, but it was hardly enough. I missed being with her, just her presence, the feel of her hand in mine, her skin touching mine, the feel of her lips, her smile, the sound of her voice, just knowing that she was nearby or that I would be seeing her soon.

The nights were no better. I would be enthralled in a blissful romantic encounter with my dearest Sue where we would be closely embracing and pouring out our love to each other, clasped in each other's arms with our hearts beating rhythmically, her calming breath soothing my feverish soul. I was filled with so much love for Sue that my heart felt like it was almost to the point of bursting. Then I would suddenly awaken to find myself cold and alone and grossly disappointed that I had just been dreaming and I could hear my roommate softly snoring in the cot underneath. It was going to be a long four months, but I placated myself with the thought that at the end of this trek, I would be joining my darling as man and wife, and we would have a whole lifetime together.

When I could keep my mind on things and concentrate, I studied hard. I wound up graduating as an honor graduate. One milestone event occurred while I was a student at Sheppard AFB. I gave up smoking! I had been smoking since I was twelve. Sue was bothered by cigarette smoke and was even allergic. I should have given up smoking for her before then, but I was addicted. When I told my bit of a smart-aleck roommate my desire to give up smoking for my prospective bride, he told me he was the only person he ever knew who quit smoking. Everyone else just stopped for a while. I then told him, "Buster, if you can quit smoking, I can too." I gave what cigarettes I had on hand to one of the NCOs across the hall, and I have never smoked another cigarette to this day. Even though cigarettes weren't particularly expensive in 1967, it still helped me to save a few extra pennies.

First of April, and graduation did happen. I hurriedly packed up and loaded Mustang Nellie and, with a tailwind at our backs, retraced our trail back to Newark and my Love. Sue had done a yeoman's job of getting things ready and sorted out for our wedding. Her family had been a great support. There were still a bunch of things Sue and I needed to do before our wedding.

Mrs. Martin, my landlady who was now a sorority house mother at Muskingum (Coshocton Community College), had invited me to stay in my old room at her house and, in addition, had invited my mom and dad to stay in the spare room for the wedding. Ralph Gochenour, my buddy from Chateauroux, France, was going to be my best man. I had been his best man the previous year when he and Mary were married. I invited William David to be one of my groomsmen, but William David and Martha Lou didn't make an appearance, so I asked Everett if he would substitute for William David. He did. Everett's wife, Donna, was also at the wedding. My other groomsman was Bob, Sue's brother. Barbara, Agustin, and Chris were there. Barbara was one of Sue's bridesmaids. Bonnie Lou came and stayed at Sue's parents' house. Bobbie Jean was there too.

April 16, 1967, I became a husband, married to my beautiful, wonderful, redheaded wife, the former Sue Ann Rauch. My wedding day has always been the highlight of my life. I, who had grown up with nothing almost all of my life, now had my very own darling companion with whom I could curl up on dark, stormy nights. We could chase butterflies, dreams, and rainbows to our hearts' content and work on building our future together. Life was grand! I felt as if I had just won the grand jackpot.

All my life, I had felt there was something in my life that was missing. Now, for the very first time, I felt complete. It was like my major goal in life had been obtained, and I felt so much love for Sue I could hardly believe she felt the same for me. It was like I was almost caught up in this long-encompassing dream and was afraid that someone was going to wake me up or burst my bubble and tell me it just wasn't so.

However, the wedding was dreamlike, and the reception was great, but it seemed the day was getting to be long. I was anxious to get on the road and have Sue to myself. Know that sounds somewhat selfish. I had hoped to take Sue to New York for our honeymoon; however, a small thing like finances precluded that endeavor. We settled on taking our honeymoon in the Great Smoky Mountains. The only pall that befell our wedding day was that a good friend (George) of Sue's aunt and uncle, Sissy and Shep, passed on from a prolonged illness that very day. But in spite of the unfortunate timing of the death, there would be no stopping us now.

22. THE GREAT SMOKY MOUNTAINS

It seemed like it took us forever to get away from the reception and all the well-wishers. I was grateful for the good wishes and for the friends and relatives who attended our little event. I just really wanted to get my sweetie alone by ourselves. Honestly, I don't remember where we stopped for the evening. I didn't want to overthink the situation. I wanted us to have a memorable first dinner together as husband and wife and then get a good night's rest to start out on our honeymoon, out on our life together. I don't think either of us had an appetite for a lot of dinner. We probably did too much snacking at the reception. It had been a glorious day for us, and the best was yet to come, a whole life stretching out before us.

The Great Smoky Mountains, Photo by Byron Johnson on Unsplash

We drove to the Great Smoky Mountains by way of the Blue Ridge Parkway. It was a breathtakingly scenic excursion, but it would have been even more so if the trees had been greened out and the weather a bit warmer. When we got to the Smokies, we nestled right in. It was not as commercialized in those days. It was delightful to explore and discover and rediscover each other. We talked and shared. I thought that this was what life was all about. It was good! We also became real tourists and explored some of the Great Smoky Mountains National Park and its environs. Too soon, our idyllic days reached their termination point and we needed to start finding our way home.

We had taken the eastern route to the Smokies, so I thought we would take a more western route home, on our way back to Ohio. I wanted to show Sue some of the places I was familiar with as I was growing up and perhaps introduce her to some of my relatives, expose my roots—my raw roots—to give her a better understanding of where I came from, so to speak.

Driving back, we were still in the Smoky Mountains, just not part of the National Park. We stayed at the Booneville Motel, about eleven miles from where I mostly grew up. I admit it was rather sparse and perhaps a little primitive. But I thought nothing of it. After all this was common to me. Was what I was used to. It met my standards, though, without thinking that Sue might have a different perspective.

We drove up Cow Creek to Indian Creek on old gravel roads with their many bumps and washed-out pits with billowing dust in our wake, and we stopped at Hobert Gabbard's old place where Grandpa and Aunt Cassie were living. They had moved out of Upper Wolf Creek after Grandma had been so badly burned and were now renting Hobert Gabbard's house. Grandma had passed away just a few months earlier, as I mentioned before. Grandpa and Aunt Cassie wanted us to spend the night with them, but I knew that would never do, so I told them we had some other visits we needed to make, which was true. We visited for a short while and left.

I showed Sue the Ricetown Post Office, where I used to walk barefooted to collect mail for Grandma and then carried it over the mountain down into the head of Upper Wolf Creek, where they lived.

We then drove to Island Creek, where I was born. The old Chicken House, my birthplace, was still there, as was the old family home (homestead). It was all deserted and in much disarray. Even though the area contained lots of memories for me, I doubted if it could mean anything for Sue.

I then took Sue to see the old one-room schoolhouse where I spent most of my elementary schooling, as had my dad before me.

Before we left Owsley County, we paid a visit to my widowed Aunt Rachel, who lived on Do Creek. Aunt Rachel seemed pleased to see us. She had aged considerably since the last time I had seen her. Her flaming red hair was now streaked with gray, and her ruddy glowing cheeks had been invaded by all these wrinkles. She was anxious to be caught up on family news and shared goings-on with her side of the family. She, too, offered overnight lodging, but we again politely refused. However, she did insist on giving us a dozen eggs for a wedding present. What were we to say?

Before we left that part of Kentucky, we visited Natural Bridge State Park, and that was our final stop before getting back on the final leg of the road to Ohio.

We were starting our new lives together at Wright-Patterson Air Force Base, Ohio. This was going to be the start of something great!

23. WRIGHT-PATTERSON AFB, OHIO

We were moving in together as husband and wife. On our own. Alone. But first, we had to find a place to live. We did. On Old Dayton Yellow Springs Road in Fairborn, Ohio, just a skip and a hop from the AF Base. It was a fairly large apartment complex in their newly completed extension—first floor, one bedroom, brand new. We would be its first occupants.

Sue had a bedroom suite she had been given for graduation and some miscellaneous items, plus all of the wedding gifts we had received, which were stored at Sue's parents' house. All were picked up and delivered to our new apartment by the Air Force. We bought a sofa and an overstuffed chair along with a dining room table with six ladder-back chairs, two coffee tables, a commode table, a couple of lamps, and a twenty-five-inch color TV. We were all set to begin housekeeping on our own!

Sue was able to transfer to a similar civil servant position from Newark AFS to W-P. It was a good job in the AF Logistics Headquarters Budget Office. I, on the other hand, expected to either be assigned back to my old position in the Emergency Room or perhaps to ward master on one of the large wards. No, not to be either one! Much to my surprise, they needed me to be the non-commissioned officer in charge (NCOIC) of the Eyes, Ears, Nose, and Throat (EENT) Clinic.

It appeared there had been some turmoil within the EENT Clinic, and I was to go in and soothe the ruffled feathers between the professionals (optometrists, ophthalmologists, and otolaryngologists) and the technical, administrative staff, and volunteers. I was being handed a bucket of worms to manage. Could I say no? I could not. That was not up to me! So, with more than a little trepidation, I took on my new position.

That first morning we were due for work, Sue was up before me, and while I was in the bathroom showering, shaving, and getting ready for my new position, she was out in our very small kitchen, just working away. I had no sooner finished than she called out, "Your breakfast is ready." And what a breakfast it was. Eggs, bacon, home fries, toast, butter, jelly, milk, and coffee. Wow!

As I was finishing up, I reached for Sue's hand across the table and said, "Sweetheart, this is wonderful. Thank you." And I stood up from the table, hugged her, and gave her an appreciative kiss.

"Well, I do hope you enjoyed it, for this is the last time I'm getting up and cooking breakfast like this. If you want breakfast like your mom makes, you'll just have to do it yourself." I could see Sue was almost in tears, so I held her close in my arms and told her how much I loved her. I told her I really wasn't much of a breakfast person and that a bowl of cereal with milk was about my speed. And that I could easily fix it for myself. That all I would ever need was just her and her love. Nothing else mattered.

Then, she offered to prepare me lunch to take to work, but I explained the hospital cafeteria usually had good, inexpensive meals. I would be able to get a good hot lunch there. And I thought to myself, *Well, that's that.* And it was that and has been that ever since.

What was nice, though, was having someone to look after me or maybe for us to look after each other.

We both went to the laundry mat together, and cleaning the apartment was mostly a partnership. Sue insisted everything had its place and everything should be in its place. Should we have guests, the apartment would need a good going-over, perhaps a bit more than I would have done or even thought necessary, but I was very willing to follow Sue's lead in the matter. Sue was (and is) a wonderful wife, and I would do anything to make her happy.

Working as NCOIC of the EENT Clinic proved to be a challenge and a learning experience. My direct supervisor was Lt Col (Dr.) Angus Marshall, Otolaryngologist (ENT) and he had an assistant ENT Dr., Everett and there were also two ophthalmologists, and three optometrists (and later an actual audiologist) comprising the professional staff. My main job was to support all of them, providing all the assistance they needed and ensuring they had the equipment they required. To complete this task, I had a staff of four technicians, a secretary, and several rotating Grey Lady volunteers who assisted as receptionists for patients and helped to make clinic appointments.

Each professional area required its own dedicated assistant, plus we had another airman managing spectacle fittings, including doing some basic eye exams for physical examinations as well as ordering spectacles, calling patients when their spectacles arrived, and then making sure they had a good fit with their new eyeglasses. That technician had been a bit of a castoff (he had gotten in trouble in another section) and required some special handling, but he did a grand job for me.

In ENT, we did a lot of hearing tests as well as definitive hearing evaluations, ordered hearing aids, and made molds to fit those aids. I had to be able to cover all these tasks, so before the audiology technician finished his Air Force commitment, I was sent to be mentored by the Air Force's chief audiologist at Wilford Hall Medical Center at Lackland AFB, Texas. This training would enable me to administer comprehensive hearing evaluations.

However, my biggest challenge involved honing and executing my people skills. I learned to mediate, compromise, and do whatever it took to get the job done. I had never encountered this type of frustration before like I did working directly with the public. Part of the problem was the demand for our services exceeded our capabilities. But the major problem was within. There was a lot of rivalry between the volunteers and the secretary, then the technicians as to who got what duties and when. Even the professional staff vied for our limited resources. It was truly a balancing act, but in spite of it all, I think I thrived.

February 10, 1968

Birthdays in our family never amounted to much. I have already described the first birthday cake that my friends made for me when I turned 21. So, when Sue's birthday rolled around, I did get her a card and a gift but neglected to get her a cake. *No big deal,* I thought. Wow! What was I thinking? Obviously, I wasn't thinking. That was the first time, and the last time, and the only time, that I neglected to provide a birthday cake for my lovely wife's birthday. You see, in Sue's family, birthdays were a special day, and they have been in our family ever since. I fumbled that first one from the git-go! It wasn't that I forgot to get a birthday cake. In the family where I grew up, we just didn't have birthday cakes. I unwittingly, obviously, had made a gigantic error in judgment! I quickly learned in Sue's family, birthday cakes were mandatory, and it was now mandatory in our family as well.

I basked in my new role as husband to the sweetest woman in the world. I dearly loved my wife, and I loved my role as her husband. Sue and I enrolled at the newly established and fast-growing Wright State University, taking evening courses after work. When we first enrolled at Wright State, it was a campus of three buildings. Well, let's just say it has since grown immensely. Sue was taking business and accounting courses while I was pursuing a basic freshman/sophomore curriculum, attempting to secure enough credit hours to apply to the Air Force's Airman's Education and Commissioning Program. I actually had the hours, but certain programs required specific courses which I did not have.

I really wanted to stay within the medical career field, but the only selections being offered at the time were medical administration, nursing, and bioenvironmental engineering. I also had to take the AF Officer Qualifying Test (AFOQT) and discovered, much to my chagrin, that while the Bible extolls the virtues of the meek and foretells that they shall inherit the earth, this type of passive response on the AFOQT did not entail successful results. Hence, I had to wait another year to retake the test and, this time, respond with my active persona. By substituting the complete take-charge approach to the test and neglecting the part that I wanted to be just a team player, I passed with flying colors. The code here was to know the rules of the game. My application was sent off to the AF Institute of Technology (AFIT), and I was selected for the program, but in bioenvironmental engineering with the caveat that I successfully complete physics and college algebra first. I was assigned to the College of Civil Engineering at the University of Arizona starting in the summer session of June 1969 after all requirements had first been completed.

Another sad event occurred in my life during this period. My grandfather, David Bishop, who had always been one of my heroes, passed from this life on May 15, 1968, almost a year and a half after Grandma had passed.

Before heading off to Arizona, a few events occurred. I was promoted to Technical Sergeant (TSgt) with a nice little raise, which was announced while I was in the hospital having rhinoplasty surgery by my supervisor, who was the hospital's chief otolaryngologist and was also the officer in charge of the EENT Clinic. Sue brought me my first set of TSgt stripes while I was still recuperating in the hospital.

After living in the small one-bedroom apartment on Old Dayton Yellow Springs Road, a coworker in Sue's office told her about a new apartment complex that had just been finished in New Carlisle, Ohio. While these apartments were a bit farther from the base, they were much nicer, with two bedrooms, two stories, and even had a washer and dryer combo (also a bit more expensive). We were sold, and so we moved. The second of many moves that we would be encountering over the years.

In the apartment next door to us lived a family with a little 4-year-old boy who I was quite taken with, named Tommy. When I would come home, and

Tommy would be outside I would take a few minutes to stop and talk with him and if he had his wagon out and I had the time I would push him around in it for a little while. He was a real treat. One Saturday when I was upstairs studying the doorbell rang. Sue happened to be downstairs and answered the doorbell. It was Tommy. He asked her, "Can your boy come out and play with me, please?"

I think I already mentioned dancing was not my bag, but Sue enjoyed dancing, and I wanted to improve my dancing prowess, and I would do just about anything if I thought it would please my darling. So, when ballroom dancing classes were being offered at the Recreation Center on base, and the cost was fairly reasonable, we enrolled.

Progress was so-so. About the fourth week, my instructor did her best to tutor me and teach me step by step and instruct me about musical beat and rhythm. I recall her saying, "Just listen to the music. Feel it, let your body absorb it, and move with the music. Let it speak to you."

I tried. I really did try. I mean, I could hear the music. There was nothing wrong with my hearing. But the music just wouldn't speak my language, or at least a language I understood. What happened to my rhythm? I could feel her frustration with me building up. It was in her body language. It was like her rhythm was getting a little off when she suddenly caused us to pause in the middle of a movement, and her facial features were screwed up into a frown. In a very exasperated voice, she told me, "Sir, I'm sorry to have to tell you this, but I really do believe you are wasting your money on dancing lessons."

So much for my dancing lessons. Time to move on.

24. BACK TO SCHOOL

I had been accepted to college, to the University of Arizona (U of A), Tucson, Arizona. We were moving to the desert. Sue and I needed to unload our convertibles because we felt the heat and the convertibles would not be well suited to each other. We felt the desert was no place for our beloved convertibles. It would be just too darn hot. I know Sue hated to part with her baby Corvair, and I felt like I was selling a part of me when I sold Nellie, my Mustang. Instead, we bought a tank, an Oldsmobile '88 with air conditioning. Everyone advised us we would need air conditioning in the desert. It was a tearful, sad farewell to friends and family as we struck out for our new life-altering adventure.

We would be driving the "tank" to our new apartment in Tucson, Arizona. I had previously done a house hunting (apartment) trip on my own and had found a new apartment complex at the corner of Country Club and Lowell Avenue. It was located near a bus line that went directly to the U of A. As we would then have only one automobile, I would, in all probability, need to rely on public transportation for trips to and from the university.

Our new apartment was a one-floor, two-bedroom, air-conditioned, brand-new apartment. Just like our previous two apartments, we would be its first occupants. My apartment hunting had been an adventure. I had taken hops (hitched a ride on AF planes) to get to Davis-Monthan AFB, where I was able to find lodging in the NCO Guest Quarters while I searched for housing. I used public transportation to search for a reliable place while I was pursuing my degree. This also required a lot—and I do mean a **lot**—of walking on my part.

I was constantly thirsty and forever drinking, trying to quench my thirst. The temperatures didn't seem that bad, high eighties, but the humidity was almost nil, less than 15 percent. Even though it was reasonably warm, and I was drinking large quantities of fluids, I was sweating very little, nor did I need to go to the bathroom. I found that very strange. Had my internal apparatuses gone awry? I guess everything just evaporated without my being aware of it. Very strange, but it all worked out. That was my introduction to the Sonoran Desert.

We intended to make our trip out west into a mini vacation. We left Ohio with ample time to spare before school started. We hadn't spent any vacation time by ourselves up to this point except for our honeymoon. Off-duty time had been spent in school and in studies. Breaks always had been to visit our folks. Now we had the chance to be with each other and pamper ourselves, and maybe just take care of each other.

Our first stop was St Louis, Missouri, the Gateway to the West. We took a steamboat ride on the ole Mississippi River and visited the Gateway Arc, actually going up inside it. Then, it was off to Branson, Missouri.

In 1969, Branson in no way rivaled Las Vegas as an entertainment mecca. As a matter of fact, it was hardly more than a wide place on the road at that time. There were a couple of Country Western Honky Tonks and perhaps a couple of floor shows. I recall us attending a show there that was reminiscent of what was later to become the television *He Haw show*. We went for a boat tour on the Lake of the Ozarks, spent a day at the Silver Dollar Recreational Park, and enjoyed the outdoor theater production of *Shepherd of the Hills*.

Next stop was Meramec Caverns, which Billy the Kid and his gang supposedly used as a hideout. Afterwards, our trek westwards really started: Tulsa, Oklahoma City, and the Panhandle of Texas. There were almost no interstate highways in 1969, so we took state and little-used routes and saw out-of-the-way, uninhabited places. We would drive for miles and miles and see very little or no signs of human life. We learned to gas up whenever the gas gauge was getting below half empty and there was a gas station available. There were cattle and oil wells and little else. Lots of wide-open spaces.

From Texas, we entered New Mexico, and the world became even more sparse. We spent a night in Lordsburg, New Mexico. That was to be the last major point of civilization before crossing the Sonoran Desert. AAA had advised us to make sure we gassed up before attempting our journey across the desert. After breakfast, we stopped at the Standard Oil Gas Station to gas up. In those days, the garage attendant put in the gas, checked the oil, and checked the tires, which was standard procedure. The oil was fine, but it appeared our right rear tire was going flat. You can imagine my apprehension as I thought about us crossing the desert and getting stranded in the 100-degree-plus heat.

Of course, I wanted the tire fixed. The tire was practically new. Had General Motors put a defective tire on our new '88 Oldsmobile? Somebody was going to hear about this!

The garage technician took the tire in, smushed it around, and showed me it had lost air, and the walls were no longer firm. Took it off the rim and showed me the insides, mashed it between his hands, and told me there was damage to the wall that could not be repaired. He assured me I needed to buy a new tire and made quite a display while doing all of this.

I was absolutely furious. This was a new car driven only a couple of thousand miles. There was no way I should be needing a new tire. The technician told me I was lucky that the other tires didn't need to be replaced. I reluctantly agreed to buy the new tire but insisted on taking the "ruined" tire with us. Someone was going to reimburse me for this tire.

The rest of the trip was fairly uneventful. Despite my ire about the supposedly ruined tire, the scenery along the way was spectacular. When the dust settled and we arrived in Tucson, and I had time to get my bearings, I went down to the local tire dealer to have the tire checked out and have a confab with the manager. Thankfully, I had kept all of my paperwork and receipts. The wizened older, experienced gentleman, after hearing my story, sorta grinned and told me I was not the first person to have that scam pulled on them.

There was absolutely nothing wrong with the tire. The gas station attendant had just let the air out of the tire, making it seem like it was going flat. Any tire of that type could be squeezed. Fortunately, I had charged the new tire on my credit card, so I contacted the credit card company, and they, in turn, contacted the gas station in Lordsburg, New Mexico. The gas station manager paid for having the tire shipped back, my money was refunded, and my original tire was replaced on the car. I drove it for many more miles before I actually had to replace it.

May 30, 1969

We arrived at our apartment on Country Club Road, Tucson, Arizona. Boy was it ever hot. For the next forty days or so, the temperatures ranged over 100 degrees, and the nights were not a lot better—didn't get below 90 degrees. It was much like living in an oven for us, coming from a much cooler area. Thank goodness we had air conditioning in our apartment and in our car.

Our first priority was getting our furniture delivered and everything unpacked. We decided to invest in a sofa bed for our second bedroom. Summer school started at the university, and I enrolled in geometry and calculus for both summer terms. I met my sponsor, and there was a problem. It appeared he had flunked out of the bioenvironmental engineering curriculum (civil engineering) and was being reallocated to the administrative field.

The fact that he had flunked out of engineering was not a good start (omen?) for me. What had I let myself in for? He appeared hesitant to share his experience with me. *So be it,* I thought, and I just left him alone.

However, there was another AFIT enlisted student who, with his wife, lived near us: Dick Grandy, who was pursuing a marketing degree. Dick and his wife paid us a welcoming visit and, upon hearing about my predicament with my sponsor, took us under their wings even though he was sponsoring another new AFIT marketing student, Paul Martin. The next weekend, we went to the base theater to see *2001: A Space Odyssey*, and while we were waiting in line to buy tickets, we met Dick and his wife, who were with the couple they were sponsoring, Paul and Andrea Martin. That evening was the beginning of a lifelong friendship with Paul and Andrea and their young children, Amber, Jason, and Matthew. Matthew, the youngest, was just a toddler at the time and was still crawling around.

The first time we had the Martins over to our apartment, we allowed Matthew to crawl around and explore on his hands and knees, for there was nothing that he could hurt himself on or that he would bother. However, we forgot about Fluffy's (the kitten we had rescued from the animal shelter) cat food in our small kitchen. Matthew discovered it, and before we realized it, he was helping himself to Fluffy's cat food. As soon as we understood what he was doing, we terminated his progress, and as far as I know, he had no ill effects from eating the cat food. Both Sue and I were amazed at how well-behaved, polite, and obedient both Amber and Jason were. It was like they were just model children. Perhaps whenever Sue and I decided to have children of our own, Paul and Andrea would mentor us.

Out of necessity, I had to dive right into school and studies. Sue had more difficulty acclimating to our new environment. For the first few weeks, she was loath to even leave the apartment. Mostly, she kept to our bedroom and was somewhat uncommunicative (silent treatment). What had I gotten us into? I was concerned but didn't know what to do or how to help Sue. We were still newlyweds, just having celebrated our second anniversary. Here I was thinking we were being given this once in a lifetime opportunity to enhance our future prospects. I felt that this was a golden opportunity for us and our future, yet I was stymied by Sue's reticence and withdrawal. I didn't know how to approach the situation and help make things better for Sue. All I knew to do was to persevere and be as supportive of Sue as I could.

Sue did not like the heat and the lack of the lush green vegetation of Ohio. She complained it was like going to Hell without actually dying. I know she missed her folks and was homesick, even though we didn't talk about it that much. After about a month of this, one morning before I dashed off to school, I bent down to kiss her goodbye. She looked up at me and said, "Well, I guess I'll stay." Whoa! Where did that come from? That was a real shock. It hadn't even occurred to me that she might not stay or that she was thinking about leaving me. Had she done so, I would have been crushed, devastated! I don't know what I would have done. I'm not sure I could've made it without her. And after Sue's surprising pronouncement, things did begin to pick up. She started looking for employment, registered with manpower, and took several temporary jobs before landing a job with Colonel Arnold. a Reserve Air Force officer, who was in the process of forming/building an Aerospace Museum in Tucson. Then Sue enrolled in some classes at the university as well.

Sue's new job and our studies left little time for many recreational activities. We did take a day trip up to the top of Mount Lemmon, elevation 9,171 feet, to escape the oppressive Tucson heat. However, I was flabbergasted at the price of a cup of Coca-Cola they were requesting at the café at the top—50 cents!

Highway robbery! I absolutely refused to pay that absorbent price for a Coke. I think Sue was somewhat taken aback by my stubbornness (and stinginess). At the time, it was the principle. In retrospect, I don't know how I could have refused my sweetheart.

In spite of our schedules, we were able to do some local sightseeing in and around Tucson: Old Tucson, the San Xavier del Bas Mission, the Saguaro National Monument, the Pima Reservation, and a couple of visits to Nogales, Mexico, to get a flavor of our southern neighbor.

Perhaps our most memorable expedition was when Sue's brother Bob came for a visit, and we happened to be on school break. I made reservations for us to stay at a lodge on the North Rim of the Grand Canyon. The trip included a stop to see the Petrified Forest and the Painted Desert, both spectacular. Of course, I didn't however, allow sufficient time for all of our sightseeing, and we wound up driving across the Navajo Indian Reservation after dark with the gas tank getting lower and lower until we were almost driving on fumes with nary a gas station in sight. For that matter, the whole place seemed completely uninhabited. Finally, we came to a small town where we found a gas station and a motel where we spent the night, before continuing our travels to the Grand Canyon's North Rim.

The Grand Canyon was spectacular! One mile deep. I think the North Rim was even more impressive than the South Rim. Our cabin was somewhat rustic but certainly adequate. When I made the reservations for the Grand Canyon, I also made reservations for a mule trip from the North Rim down to the bottom of the canyon. The trail had been closed for the past couple of years because of severe storms, erosion, and rockslides. It had recently been renovated and reopened. I could tell Sue and Bob were somewhat hesitant to take that somewhat challenging adventure, but I had already paid for all three of us. I pleaded with the two of them that this would be an experience they would remember for the rest of their lives. So, after some trepidation, they reluctantly agreed to start the trip down the canyon. We mounted our mules in a single file.

There were several other tourists taking the mule train down the canyon with us. Many were in front of us. In our trio, it was Bob first, then Sue, and lastly me. The guide assured us we would be safer on the mules than if we were traversing the trail by foot. These mules had been imported from West Virginia and were trained by the very best to climb up and down mountains. Comparatively, going up on these trails on the Grand Canyon was nothing as to what it was for us going down. We hadn't gone more than quarter of a mile down into the canyon when Sue looked back and said she wanted to go back to the lodge and would wait there for us.

However, there was no place to turn around and go back. The left side of the trail was a clear drop-off, and in the far distance, if one leaned to the left of the mule, one could see the bottom of the canyon. Every now and again, one of the mules would dislodge a rock and it could be heard dropping down, bouncing and bouncing, fainter and fainter until the echoes faded away, down the side of the canyon for what seemed like a heck of a long time.

By that time, Sue was in tears and Bob was white as a ghost. There were places on the trail where it seemed the mules' hindquarters hung out over the side of the canyon wall. I chose not to look down too often.

However, the scenery was breathtaking. We even encountered a flock of wild turkeys along the trail. A few were up in the foliage; others were foraging along the forest floor. They hardly paid any attention to our passing and didn't seem to be bothered by us.

When we reached the bottom of our trail, we had a picnic-style lunch the guide had brought for us to share. The climb back up the canyon trail was not nearly so challenging or exciting. I think we all breathed a big sigh of relief when we got back to the top and had dismounted from our mules and felt very brave that we had come through the encounter alive.

We ended our vacation expedition by visiting Zion National Park in Southern Utah before turning around and heading back to Tucson.

25. TIMBO, MY LITTLE YO-YO

Monday, July 5, 1971, was to be my midterm examination for my microbiology course. I was enrolled in the summer term at the University of Arizona via the Air Force's Airman Education and Commissioning Program and was taking two courses for the summer, microbiology and advanced calculus, differential equations.

Sue's mother was staying with us to help when the baby came. The baby was overdue. The day prior, there had been major fireworks at the university. We had talked about going to see them. Sue had always enjoyed fireworks, but it was just too darn hot (102 degrees Fahrenheit) and not a great deal better inside. Our swamp cooler was not that efficient; might be cooling down to 90 inside the house. It did blow air, mostly hot air it seemed, but increased the humidity inside the house. It did help some. Without the swamp cooler it would really have been unbearable.

Sue looked miserable. Her tummy was swollen to the point she could hardly take a full breath, and it was difficult for her to bring both legs together. She had numerous blue stretch marks running across her abdomen; looked like those rivulets one sees drawn on a map. She was most uncomfortable.

Early morning, I was attempting to get in some last-minute review time for my impending exam, and Sue was taking a shower when I heard her yell out. I ran into the bathroom and found her leaning up against the shower wall. Even though she had turned the shower off, water was running off of her. She sorta sniffled at me and gasped, "It's happening!" Her eyes were wide and perhaps a little dilated. She appeared anxious, a little frightened.

I felt my heart expand to the point that I thought it would break through my rib cage. This was it. It was the time. It was really happening! I knew our baby was on its way. I took Sue in my arms, held her close, and told her the world would be all right. And it was!! I helped her dry off and get dressed, grabbed her luggage (hospital tote), and told Sue's mom we were off to the Davis-Monthan Hospital to get us a baby. And off we went. I'm not sure I remembered to feed the cat, but if I didn't, I hoped Sue's mom would. Fluffy the cat was usually pretty vociferous when she hadn't been fed.

Also, I don't remember much about the drive to the hospital—the streets, the traffic, the cacti, the houses, etc. Nothing. Time whizzed by, but I do remember that my heart was in my mouth, and I think I could hear it pounding in my ears. I was probably as nervous as I was ever going to be. I know I drove very, very carefully all the way to the hospital. "Keep it cool. Keep it cool and calm. You've got this," I kept telling myself. I kept checking on Sue to make sure she was alright, and I would pat her hand and tell her, "We've got this. We're going to get us a baby this time, for sure! You've got this!" She would either give me a weak smile or a withering glare and maybe a small moan, depending upon what was going on inside her.

We pulled up to the guard at the security gate. I quickly showed him our IDs and shared with him that we were on the way to get our baby. He smiled and yelled, "Good luck!" and smartly waved us through.

We hurried into the hospital and checked into the Obstetrics Ward. Sue's clothes were quickly taken, and she was given a hospital gown. An IV was started in her left arm after the required vital signs were taken and recorded. Nurses, doctors, and medical staff came and went. Then, nothing happened very quickly after that. It was like everything was stalled in slow motion while Sue and I were ready to put it in high gear. We were ready for and wanted action! Two more expectant mothers checked in that same morning, sometime after us. Both were delivered during the day, seemingly without much delay.

Our day seemed to be dragging on forever. Our world became a hazy blur. Nothing existed outside our little world. It was just Sue and I waiting for our baby to make his/her appearance. Contractions came and went. Contraction severity would build up, and we would get anxious, expectations would peak, and then things would fade back down somewhat. The medical staff were encouraging but stressed our need to be patient. These things couldn't be rushed, we were assured. Waiting. And waiting. And waiting as I watched over Sue. Dilations progressed ever so slowly. Baby was in no hurry to come into this world. Obviously, he/she knew when he/she was in a good, safe place and was not in a big rush to see what was waiting with us on the outside.

Sue was only allowed ice chips, so I sat by her bedside, feeding them to her, holding her hand and doing my best to comfort her. She did not want me to leave her side, and I didn't except for a few bathroom breaks. I tried my best to keep her distracted as the day wore on.

According to the doctors, our baby had been due in mid-June when Grandpa and Grandma Rauch had come down on their excursion from the Black Hills, bringing their young Scotty dog (pup—maybe half-grown) with them. We had scheduled Baby's birth when Grandpa Rauch would be there for the big event, but alas, it didn't quite work out that way. Sue's Dad only had so much vacation time and needed to get back to Newark, Ohio.

We had scheduled an inducement around what we thought was the due date. Sue was admitted to the Davis Monthan Hospital Maternity/Delivery Ward. Once in her room, she got dressed in her gown, and when she was through most of the preliminaries, they gave her labor-induced medicine via an IV. Sue did start having contractions, but Baby was having none of them. It was a no-go, or certainly a very slow go!

After she suffered through the agony of false/belabored attempted induced labor all day, the doctor said enough was enough. He told us, "Baby is just not quite ready to make its grand entrance into our world," and stopped the medication, discharged her, and we went back home and faced a couple of disappointed grandparents-to-be. A couple of days later, Grandpa and Scotty went back to Newark, Ohio, and Grandma stayed to wait out the vigil with us.

It seemed I had dreamed about being a dad as far back as I could remember. Growing up and even in young adulthood, there had been so little in my life that was really meaningful until I met Sue. Also, coming from such a large family, children were cherished, and the old adage was that when you have nothing else, you will still have your children.

Sue, on the other hand, was a little more hesitant (squeamish). Sue, being more of a perfectionist, had doubts about motherhood and raising kids. The investment, she thought, could be overwhelming. I came from a family of twelve (counting Mom and Dad) and had helped with younger siblings and babysat for seven nieces and nephews. I felt we were more than ready to start our own family. I certainly was. I was eagerly looking forward to becoming a dad. I was anxious to provide my children with those things I thought I should have had, or would have liked to have had, growing up but never had. I could hardly wait for the arrival of our baby and to have the opportunity to become a dad and to start caring for our child. I was more than ready!

Sue and I had agreed to wait to start a family until the birth would occur before or just after I graduated from the university. In September 1970, Sue perhaps somewhat reluctantly agreed to stop taking the pill and *presto!* It appeared our first efforts were rewarded. I was over the moon (ecstatic!), and I think Sue was too, except I think she still may have had some apprehensions. It was a treat anticipating what was going on with our developing little one. I anxiously watched to see when I could detect the smallest growth and then the slight abdominal protrusion.

Sue has always been the most beautiful person in the world to me, but I swear each time she became with child, she somehow became even more beautiful. There was that aura of impending motherhood that made me fall even more deeply in love with her. It's difficult to describe the thrill when Sue started feeling movement. You would have thought this was the first time this ever happened to anyone else by my reactions. Words aren't adequate to describe the feelings and emotions that flowed through me during our baby's incubation period. Sue may well have had similar experiences, but I can only speak for myself.

Looking back, I'm sure I must have appeared to be a little bit of a crazy, expectant dad. The only downside with our first one was when the baby had progressed sufficiently, Sue needed to start wearing maternity clothes, and because of that, she lost her job. Her management couldn't have a pregnant receptionist flaunting maternity clothes and out meeting clients! Management couldn't do that today, but things were much different in the early '70s.

Back to July 5, 1971, and the hospital. Was this going to be another false alarm? However, Sue's water had broken, and the doctor assured us we just needed to be patient and make Sue as comfortable as possible in the interim. It was going to be a matter of time. We were in this for the long haul. Baby was only taking its time and would make its appearance on its own schedule. It was all going to be worth it. And of course, he was right.

As the afternoon progressed, I was beat mentally, perhaps more than physically, after watching Sue go through the many hours of the pangs of the progressing childbirth. There seemed little I could do to alleviate her discomfort. If I was beat, think about my poor darling. I was just the bystander, the onlooker—well, sorta. I was the cheerleader, the hand holder, the brow wiper, the ice chip fetcher, the encourager, the atta girl, everything's gonna be alright person.

"Just breathe, Sue. Breathe. Breathe. Take big breaths and try to relax."

Sue looked wretched, like she had been through the wringer. If only I could have swapped places with her and taken on some of her discomfort and pain. When it seemed, we were about to give up hope, the attending physician came in and, after conducting another examination, announced she was fully dilated. "Baby time!" he cheerfully announced to us. Time to take her to the delivery room. Sue asked if I could go with her but was told, no; they had to do final preparations and give her medication (epidural block), but I would be allowed to come for the actual birth.

They wheeled Sue away, and then I was suited up in scrubs and a mask and entered, where I saw Sue lying in stirrups, not looking anxious at all. By that time, she had had her medication (epidural block), and I could see it had taken effect. They placed me up by Sue's left shoulder where I could hold her hand, and they placed a large mirror where I could observe the birthing process.

By this time, my heart was going a mile a minute. I was about to see my long-awaited dream come true, a real-life miracle! I was just a passive observer, yet I felt I was more than that. I was most grateful that I was allowed to participate in this blessed event by just being there to watch. I was pretty much prepared for the birthing process. After all, I had grown up on a farm and had seen a lot of puppies and kittens and a few calves being born. I knew this would be different, though, for I had never seen a baby, less on my very own baby, being born before. I knew that viewing the very natural birthing of animals was hardly comparable to childbirth, especially the birth of our child.

As the mirror came into place, I could see the top of our baby's head. It was all pinkish white but seemed to be resting, taking a pause. Nope, not ready to leave just quite yet. I could see what looked like some dark fuzz on the top of its little head. At least the baby wasn't going to be a baldy. Funny thing to think about at that particular time. Even with subsequent contractions, the baby's head just wasn't budging. It was taking a rest and wasn't going anywhere. Stubborn little coot. Or it wasn't coming out of there just yet.

Finally, the doctor elected to use a forceps-assisted delivery. That's just what he did. I watched in fascination as the doctor inserted what looked like salad tongs around the baby's head and pulled and slightly rotated the tiny little head through the birth canal. He removed the forceps, and the rest happened rather quickly.

The doctor caught the baby and held him "erect" (a very obvious him) while the nurse clipped and cut the umbilical cord. The nurse turned our baby upside down and rubbed his back, and baby Timmy gave out a heartfelt wail of protest at having been taken from his secure, isolated, climate-controlled environment and being thrust into the noisy, bright, alien, unknown world.

The doctor turned to us and said, "Mrs. and Sgt. Taylor, you have a fine, healthy, bouncy boy, and surely there is nothing wrong with his lungs!" And he gave us a hearty chuckle.

All the time, Timmy was wailing as loudly as he possibly could. The nurse deftly cleaned him off, wiped his eyes, suctioned his nostrils and mouth with a little squeezy rubber bulb thing, wrapped him in a blanket, and handed him to us.

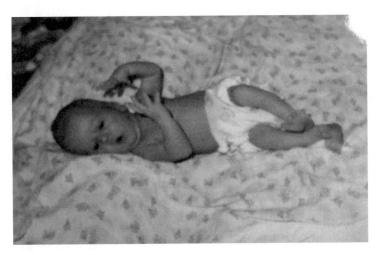

Baby Timmy

There he was, Timothy Francis! He had made it. Our little miracle. **We** had done this. I had never seen a more wonderful sight in my life. Timmy's head was kinda cone-shaped and flattened from the forceps delivery, but at that time, he was, to me certainly, the most beautiful baby ever born.

As I held the wee darling creature in my arms, time just stood still. I was filled with so much love for my beautiful wife and adorable baby; I cannot even begin to describe the pride and joy that filled my heart and my whole being. There are no words sufficient to describe the emotions I felt at that moment. It felt like my heart would burst through my rib cage any minute. I never knew that much love existed in all of the universe.

That little angel was a replica of Sue and me. Even though, at the time, I could see no resemblance to either of us. I was just fascinated. In awe. Speechless.

It was hard to fathom that I had played a major role in that tiny miracle's appearance that day. I counted all ten tiny fingers and ten tiny toes and checked out his manly little feet that were going to provide him with the foundation to find his place in this world.

Looking down at our son was like having an out-of-body experience. My feet could not have touched the floor. That was the greatest thing I had ever participated in, that I had ever done, or that had ever happened to me. It was like being handed the greatest gift I could ever have imagined. That little miracle baby was ours. He was a part of Sue and me. We had actually done this together! (Alright, Sue had been the one carrying him inside her for the last nine months!) I couldn't have been prouder!

With the help of the universe, creating another human being with the person I most loved went beyond my most fervent dreams. There was this little person so innocent and perfect who we were responsible for bringing into this world. It was then I felt the room begin to tilt and start to spin, and it seemed things were coming out of focus. Hazy. Fuzzy. That was when I realized I had been holding my breath probably ever since the baby had been placed in my arms.

When I came back to my senses, Timmy had finished his crying jag and seemed to be looking up at us even though the staff told us he really couldn't see yet. My weariness and fatigue had simply vanished. I sorta stepped back and let Sue hold the baby by herself, and I wouldn't have believed it possible but felt my love for Sue become even greater. She and the baby were the most wonderful things in my life. My world was complete!

Sue and I agreed that if we had a boy, he was going to be named Timothy Francis (Francis for her dad). Too soon, the nursing staff insisted on taking Timmy to the nursery, and Sue soon had to go back to the recovery room to get some badly needed rest. I was reminded I, too, needed to go home to get some rest as well. I needed to update Sue's mother on what had transpired.

Sue's mother! Lord, in all the excitement, I had completely zoned out and forgotten all about Sue's mother. The only thing on my mind had been Sue and the baby and their welfare.

I hesitantly left Sue and baby Timmy at the hospital and drove home with my head and senses somewhere up in the clouds. Sue's Mom was going to be SOOO happy! I was still in my partial out-of-body experience. I went inside the house, all excited to tell Sue's mom about the events of the day.

However, before I could even open my mouth, I heard, **"Well, is she dead? Did the baby die, too**? I just knew something awful had happened not to have heard from you all day, not for twelve whole hours! Nothing! I've been here all day just worrying myself sick. Felt like I was going to have a heart attack." (In other words, "You idiot, what in the world is wrong with you? Why couldn't you have called me? Did you even try to call me? Haven't you got any sense at all?")

There were some other choice words, and I could see Sue's mom was as mad as an old wet hen. I couldn't blame her. The tone was not a friendly one either, by no means, and Sue's mom looked like she was ready to do serious bodily harm to me. I felt about two feet tall and felt myself growing smaller by the minute. I was speechless when I realized how wrapped up in the situation I had been. How thoughtless it was of me not to have considered calling Sue's mother and keeping her abreast of progress (or non-progress) during the day. I thought that when Sue's water broke, we would go to the hospital and have us a baby, and that would be it. Then I would come home and tell Sue's mother all about it. Share everything.

Boy, was I wrong.

I mean, what did I know about childbirth and how long it took? Did I ever have egg on my face? I knew Sue's mother would not ever forgive me. She never really liked me that much to begin with. Now this? I tried my best to crawdaddy out of the situation by telling her about our bouncy, healthy Timothy Francis and how Sue was doing so well after her long labor once Timmy had come into the world. That Sue had had a long, laborious labor, and because of that, she had begged me not to leave her side.

Sue's Mom knew how besotted I was to Sue. I promised her as soon as visiting hours were available, I would take her to see Sue and the baby the next day. Sue was asking for her, and she really wanted to see her mom. That seemed to mollify her a little, enough for me to sneak off to bed. And true to my word, I did take her to the hospital the next day to see Sue and baby Timmy. As soon as she saw baby Timmy, everything became all right in her world, or so it seemed.

After three days of recouping in the hospital, Sue and Timmy were able to come home. We bundled him up in his little carry cradle, and as soon as we got out in the sun, he started sneezing (and he still does it—

sneezes whenever he goes out into bright sunlight). Don't know what caused it or what still causes it.

When we got home, Timmy needed a lot of holding. He was colicky and seemed to cry a lot. Maybe he just wanted attention and to be held. I needed to give him attention as much for him as for me. Whenever I was not at school, I would have Timmy with me, holding him, rocking him, or feeding him his bottle. If he was asleep, I would lay him by my side while I studied. I got the greatest pleasure of staring at our little miracle that my love and I had managed to create. I would watch the way he curled his little fingers and the way he smacked his lips when he was hungry. He had this gosh-awful frown when he was having a bad dream, and it got worse when he was awake and unhappy. He got so he could flail his arms and legs something terrible. I would sing or hum him all sorts of songs— some I knew, others I made up.

I enrolled Timmy in the payroll US Savings Bond program for $50 per month. When Timmy was ready, there would be funds available for him for college or at least to start.

Soon after I finished my studies at the University of Arizona, we sold the house on Adams Street and bundled up the car. The Air Force packed up all our belongings and trucked them away, and we headed for Ohio. Sue and Timmy languished at Sue's parents in Ohio while I was off to Texas for Office Training School for the next four months.

26. MARY BETH, MY LITTLE SWEETIE

We had planned on having a baby brother or sister for Timmy by the time he was 2. Unfortunately, Mother Nature had other plans and was not willing to cooperate with us despite all of our best efforts. But it was not for our lack of trying. I'm not sure what was going on. I mean, with Timmy, it was a home run first time up at bat, as far as I was concerned. This next one seemed to require a little extra concentration and a lot more work and effort. As my grandpa used to say, anything worth having was worth working for, *and* the work was most pleasurable and enjoyable. It was a team effort with the one person who I held most dear in this world. It was just a temporary setback, we were sure.

The days passed. Then weeks passed, followed by months. What was going on? We read up on ovulation, temperatures, enhancements on getting pregnant, and all that concerned. Almost mandatory performances? Perhaps, despite everything we were trying, it wasn't producing the desired results. There was no baby bump in sight, nor even a hint of one. However, I firmly believe that things work themselves out the way they were supposed to.

There was a lot of turmoil and stress going on in the world during that time period. Perhaps that was a factor. There was the 1973 oil crisis when lines for gasoline stretched around blocks; Watergate and the resignation of President Richard Nixon in lieu of being impeached, then replaced by Vice President

Gerald Ford; the Yon Kippur War; the end of the Vietnam War; Apollo and Soyuz for US-Soviet link-up in space; Margaret Thatcher, the first woman elected to lead the British Conservative Party; Egypt reopened the Suez Canal after eight years of being closed, and so on, and so on.

On the home front, Sue was coming into her own, learning to mother and nurture our Timbo (doing a bang-up job of it, too) and relishing her role as a typical Air Force Officer's wife. She had been content to leave the workforce and was relishing her role as a mother, wife, and homemaker. She had learned to play Mahjong and even tried her hand at Bridge. She thrived with her mates in Mahjong but not so much with Bridge, even after us having attended a few Bridge parties and even hosted one at our house. We also had little parties with other young officer couples and felt we were learning to blend in with the officer ranks and their families. We felt we had arrived. We felt it was a major accomplishment to breach the chasm from the enlisted ranks to the officer corps.

We found a wonderful babysitter via our next-door neighbor's recommendation, Mrs. Lutz, who originally hailed from France. The Lutz family lived not far from us in the surrounding neighborhood but outside the confines of the base. Mrs. Lutz seemed to dote on Timmy and would laugh about him having to take his "nuckie" (pacifier) out of his mouth to talk. Timmy could talk a lot by this time but still enjoyed the security of his nuckie.

By this time, Timmy was very verbal. His command of the language was amazing. Timmy was growing like a weed and got along well with the neighborhood kids. There were kids everywhere around us in base housing. The house next door had two kids, Sasha and

Tasha. Their dad was from Iran, an officer in the Iranian military attached to the Language School on Lackland AFB. This was before the Shah of Iran was disposed.

Both kids had Hot Wheels, and they would come riding up to our house on their Hot Wheels, asking to play with Timmy, making the most God-awful racket with their Hot Wheels. Another one of Timmy's playmates lived across the street and was older physically, but mentally, he was about Timmy's age. He and Timmy seemed to get along and played well together. His dad was in the Office of Special Investigations (OSI). On a couple of occasions, I even helped his dad with some undercover operations which I found to be enlightening.

My first job as an Air Force officer was managing the Environmental Health Program for one of the largest Air Force training bases, plus the Air Force's largest hospital. This included surveillance of all occupational and community areas and epidemiological investigations of disease outbreaks. We measured heat stress indicators to minimize heat problems with new recruits—their outdoor activities would be curtailed as the heat stressors rose and completely terminated at certain levels.

I was responsible for public health investigations, swimming pool inspections, and reporting sexually transmitted diseases. A couple of the more interesting cases to cross my desk were: a young WAF (enlisted female airman) claiming to having gotten pregnant from swimming in one of our public pools and a young male airman who contacted a venereal disease while he and his partner were taking their pleasures inside one of the base's Dempsey dumpsters.

I also advised management on engineering controls, personal protective equipment, limited stay times, and work/rest regimes for the prevention of disease or injury or degradation of human efficiency resulting from hostile work environments. Also, I did some work with the Biomedical Science Corps (BSC) and was involved with sponsoring the Pentagon-based BSC Corps Chief's biannual visit to the Wilford Hall Medical Center. I did several projects for the clinic commander and even a couple for the Wilford Hall Medical Center Major General. I learned early exposure meant a lot.

Sue and I put on our thinking caps and came up with the idea that if we could get away, away from everything, maybe we could have better luck. That is, better luck in the baby production department, plus it would be great for us to have some alone time just to enjoy each other's company. We hit upon the plan that her parents would take baby Timmy (Timmy was not quite 3 at that point) for a couple of weeks, and we could take a vacation to New Orleans by ourselves. I had always wanted to go to New Orleans, the birthplace of jazz.

Sue's dad was now retired, and Sue's mom had always just doted on our Timmy. Not sure if we shared the main goal of our proposed trip to New Orleans but rather presented it as an expedition to take a little vacation by ourselves, which was true. They graciously agreed with our plan. We all drove to the western side of Memphis and met at a Holiday Inn. Sue's parents picked up Timbo and took him with them back to Newark, and then the plan was for Sue and I to drive up to Newark and pick up Timmy at a later date sometime after our vacation.

We drove to decadent (to us) New Orleans. Our hotel was off a side street, not far from the infamous Bourbon Street, where a lot of the action took place. There was no Mardi Gras or even any parades going on while we were there, but there were a lot of other things going on. We were there in mid-to-late June, so it was warm—no, it was not just warm; it was hot and steamy, and there were all kinds of actions going on right under our noses. I could hardly curb my enthusiasm in my anticipation to get started. Sue was a little more hesitant and reserved, timid even.

But we did it. We were like little kids let loose in a candy shop, or at least I was. Sue went along more to appease me. We were tourists in the Big Easy, drinking it all up, trying to absorb everything. Beignets at the Café du Monde, dinner at Antoine's (had to borrow a jacket and tie), jazz at Preservation Hall, strolled down Bourbon Street at midnight, had some kind of drink concoction in hurricane glasses, strolled along the wharves, and reveled until we were exhausted, and our money ran out. We had taken some US bonds for just such an event.

However, when I went to the bank to cash them, the teller refused to accept them. Can you imagine me, a Lieutenant in the US military with the proper official military identification and official driver's license, and federal US Savings Bonds that specifically stated they could be cashed at any US Federal Bank with proper identification? Talk about having one's ego deflated! With my persistence and having to cajole his supervisor, the bank official agreed to cash the lousy bonds (about $100 worth). This was after they checked my credit union account via phone, which I had to pay for. Except for the bond fiasco, we had a wonderful time in New Orleans. We made a lot of unforgettable memories but left for Texas with the thought that Timbo was still going to remain our singular heir. But many thanks for a wonderful time and all the memories!

By the end of June, we were still missing our bundle of joy, the light of our lives, our little boy, Timbo, something fierce (he was still in Newark), so we headed off to pick up and bring home our favorite little rascal. It always did me good; it just melted my heart to see that little towhead again. Of course, he had all kinds of stories to tell us about all the stuff he had been doing with his grandma and grandpa. He had been helping Grandpa mow the big field in the back of the house on the John Deere riding mower and could drive the mower just as good as Grandpa— of course, while he sat in his lap the whole time with Grandpa's hands hovering over his.

Grandma had taken him up to the Ole Mill and let him feed the ducks and bought him ice cream. Both grandparents had been spoiling him rotten, but isn't that the role of grandparents? He was still glad to see his mommy and daddy, perhaps not quite as glad to see us as we were to see him, though. Time to go home to see Sasha and Tasha by way of Newport, Kentucky, to visit my folks before heading back to San Antonio.

We spent just a few days with my mom and dad. While we were there, we decided to take Timmy to Cincinnati's Zoo. This was about the first of July—an early treat for Timbo's birthday. I think Cincinnati's Zoo is one of the finest in the country. Timmy may have been a little young to have enjoyed the many aspects the zoo had to offer, but he seemed to get a charge out of the Ape House and the large animal exhibits.

To cut to the chase, the trip to New Orleans did not accomplish our objective of producing a sibling for Timmy. However, the trip bringing Timmy home seemed to do the trick. Marty Elizabeth was born on April 1, nine months later. We were overjoyed when we discovered Timmy was going to get a brother or a sister!

There was a bit of drama between the New Orleans escapade and the wonderful new miracle that was to come into our lives. Early September, again we were euphoric that Timmy would be getting a brother or sister sometime in early spring. At the same time, I was expecting a visit from one of my bioenvironmental engineering classmates from the Radiological Health Laboratory at Wright-Patterson Air Force Base, Ohio, Captain Eric Vermullen. Eric was to conduct a radiation safety evaluation on all the ionizing radiation equipment located on Lackland Air Force Base, and I was to accompany him, providing any assistance he might need.

For some reason, I was just dog tired, had no energy, and was dragging. My get-up-and-go had just got up and gone. It almost seemed like an effort to put one foot before the other. The night before I was to assist Eric with the radiation survey, I had ordered pepperoni pizza for the family, and it appeared awfully greasy to me. It made me feel nauseous. Was I having sympathetic morning sickness? Anyway, I did get to work and had a couple of cups of coffee, trying to generate some energy before my friend from Ohio arrived, which caused me to need to empty my bladder. When I went to the urinal, it was like I was passing cocoa. Had the coffee run through unfiltered and unchanged? My mind quickly flashed back to my medical technician training, and I thought to myself, *Oh, no! I'm coming down with hepatitis.*

I glanced in the mirror at the whites of my eyeballs, and sure enough, they were the color of light margarine. I hadn't noticed it before, but my exposed skin was taking on a certain Asian hue. I walked around the corner to my flight surgeon friend, waited until he was finished with his patient, and told him I felt like I was coming down with hepatitis. He did a rapid examination with blood work. Blood chemistry for hepatitis was off the charts. He arranged for me to be admitted to Wilford Hall Medical Center STAT, where I was treated and convalesced for a couple of weeks and was placed on medical leave to go home.

My recovery was slow in progressing. I did return to work but on limited duty. The blood chemistry tests for hepatitis remained high, and my fatigue problem persisted, so I was readmitted to the hospital in early January 1975 and had a liver biopsy with the subsequent diagnosis of chronic hepatitis. My prognosis was not great! The doctor told me that my experience with chronic hepatitis would hopefully be limited, but at the time could not be predicted. The prognosis with chronic hepatitis was a mixed bag. It appeared the subsequent course with the disease was too radical to make good predictions with either treatments or what I should expect. To be honest, I was told, I could live a year, or I could live two years, or I could live ten years, or I could live forty years, or I might not ever completely recover from chronic hepatitis.

What??? This was completely unexpected. All these crazy thoughts ran through my head, and it was scary. And, of course, it was only natural for me to think the worst. Have you ever been belted in the solar plexus so hard that not a molecule of air is left in your body, and you can't breathe, and you're gasping for air, and despite your best efforts, there is no air left to breathe? Well, it felt like that to me on hearing the news about the chronic hepatitis diagnosis.

Here I was, sitting on top of the world with the most beautiful wife on the planet, with the smartest and most handsome towheaded 3-year-old son, and with another baby we had been praying for and dreaming about well on the way. I was a newly commissioned officer in the United States Air Force after having served over eleven years as an enlisted troop and having received my Bachelor of Science in civil engineering, the first person in my family to have received this type of college degree. The future ahead looked bright, even exceeding all my expectations and dreams.

Now, was the bottom about to fall out of my world? I was being keenly reminded of life's fragility and my mortality! I felt the world deflating around me. Was I being told that I might not live to see my son grow up, I might not be there to help him with his homework, or be there for him and to witness him developing into a young man, and might I not even be there for the birth of our new baby? I couldn't see leaving my wonderful bride alone to take care of our babies by herself.

I felt this darkness, this self-pity, settling over me, enveloping me. It lasted a moment—seconds even. I was determined to shake it all off. *I am better than this*, I told myself. And I prayed under my breath, "Lord, let me live long enough to help Sue raise our kids and get them started in life. That's all I ask." I refused to succumb to any type of depression. I would persevere. This was all a big mistake, and I would work through it.

They started me on steroids, which I was on for over two years, with almost immediate results. I was still on light duty at work and was home for half days. Off duty, I spent time working with my NCOIC in a garden plot and on a large, rather elaborate latch hook rug that I had designed. Both were good therapy. The period which I have just described occurred over forty-nine years ago as of this writing. So, it appears somebody up there was looking out for me and my little family.

Tuesday, April 1, 1975, started off slow. Sue's mom was staying with us again, awaiting the arrival of our new baby. When asked, she had somewhat reluctantly agreed to come and help with this one, but not before reminding me what had happened with the first one (Timbo), that she'd waited all day by herself, worried sick not knowing what was going on whether Sue was going to live or die or just what had happened. I attempted to console her and promised her I would do my very best to keep her informed along the way for sure, this time. That she didn't know how much we really appreciated her. That I wouldn't ask her to come, except I had not been too well. (The chronic hepatitis thing had been ongoing for over seven months by this time.) And Sue and Timmy really wanted her to come, and that we all needed her.

That seemed to do the trick. She relented and was with us while we were in a holding pattern. Actually, Sue's mom had a big pot of soup going in the kitchen and was now coloring with Timmy in his coloring book. Timmy and I had been stacking blocks, making a fort earlier, until he'd gotten bored and wanted to help Grandma color. Sue was in the bathroom doing some cleaning, and I had returned to my hobby and was working on my latch hook rug. The time was early afternoon.

I heard Sue calling to me from the bathroom: "Wiley! Wiley! Wiley, come here, quick!"

When I rushed in to find Sue in the bathroom, she told me it was time. Her water had broken, and her contractions had started. Well, I knew from our first experience with Timmy there was no hurry. Hadn't Timmy's birth experience taken about ten hours or more?

I helped Sue to get dressed and collected all her stuff for the hospital. I put away my rug-making paraphernalia and leisurely drove us to Wilford Hall Medical Center. The hospital was less than twenty minutes away. Sue seemed to be getting a little agitated at me and was telling me the contractions were coming on pretty strong, and she thought they were coming with increased frequency. I kept telling her not to worry; we had plenty of time. Didn't she remember Timmy, and how long that took? Remember all the time we had to wait in the hospital after we got there-almost all day.

As soon as we got to the Obstetrics Ward, they checked Sue out, and they quickly told us this baby was ready to pop and immediately took Sue into the delivery room. I suited up in scrubs, just like with Timmy. I still felt pretty sure there was still plenty of time. (Me, Mr. Know It All.) I thought the hospital staff might be rushing it a little bit. Well, within thirty minutes of arriving at the hospital, I was holding Sue's hand, awaiting the arrival of our second miracle.

And indeed, the birth of our second baby was no less miraculous than the first. This baby was just a lot more eager to claim its place in the world and did not want to hold back like Timmy had. The baby was ready, like *really* ready! She (we soon discovered) appeared a little more adventurous, like in an almost rush to get out and see what was going on in the world, what she might be missing. Perhaps she was tired of living in darkness and was ready to start exploring the world. As soon as I was in place and I could see the evolving events from the strategically placed mirror, I could see the top of this tiny head covered with an abundance of what appeared to be silky black hair, and with practically no assistance, she popped out and the doctor was there to deftly catch her.

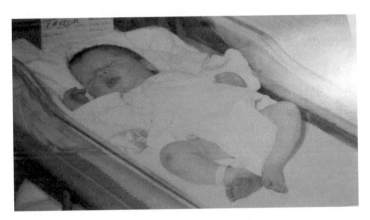

Mary Elizabeth, taken in the hospital

Birth is such an exciting and wonderful experience. After nine long months of being safely carried and coddled, fed and protected and cared for, our fragile, helpless tiny Mary Elizabeth was there for us all to love and cherish. A quick snip and she was separated from Mommy and was on her own. She was a little cyanotic but a little rubbing on the backside, and she promptly produced a healthy wail; her normal coloration soon followed.

The attending nurse cleaned her up, wrapped her in a tiny blanket, and handed her to us, saying, "Here's your beautiful daughter." And beautiful she was (and still is). She had the brightest little eyes. At that time, they looked like they were sparkling at me (like two little diamonds, appearing to bore right through me), and I would have sworn she smiled at me as if she had already recognized her Daddy. It was almost like she was saying to me here I am Daddy. Now what? This was my darling little princess, my sweetie! I had to do it, just like with our first one, Timmy. Ten tiny little fingers curled into two wee balls and ten tiny little toes. Everything was just perfect. This had to be the most perfect, most beautiful baby ever born.

Sue and I had to be the luckiest parents in the whole world. Who says lightning doesn't strike twice in the same place? I was euphoric! Over the moon. The baby was so petite, smaller than I remembered Timbo being, more fragile too, I though. I just melted again. That little thing, lying in our arms, was going to own me for the rest of my life, and my world stood still. Life couldn't get better than this, could it?

Sue, look what we have done. There are moments in one's life when you know that life will never get better than this: twice miraculously blessed. That was one such moment. We had been supremely blessed. First, our little boy and now our darling little girl. I felt so blessed and vowed I would do whatever I could do to make sure our two babies would have every opportunity that I could possibly give them. My stars had aligned behind me, and I had been gifted with my dreams! We were holding our sweet, darling baby girl in our arms, and I was there in the moment. There were no longer dark clouds hovering about. I could dare to think about our future together. I glanced down at Sue, and unbelievably, I felt so drawn to her and knew I was even more in love with her than ever before. How could this possibly be? I had more than enough love to last a lifetime.

This time, I was determined not to make the same mistake as the one when our Timmy was born. So, just as soon as I left Sue's side, I called home to let Sue's mom know that everything had gone well. Sue was doing great, and everything was absolutely super. Now she was the grandmother of a darling little baby girl. She inquired as to what we were going to name the baby, and I took a quick sidestep and told her Sue and I were still discussing names, which may have been a little dishonest on my part.

In those days, we didn't know in advance the gender of the baby until it was born, so we had been discussing both boy and girl names. Matthew for a boy and Mary Elizabeth for a girl. Mary Elizabeth was my grandmother's name, and I always thought if I ever was fortunate enough to father a daughter, I intended to name her after my grandmother. Plus, Sue's aunt was named Mary, and Sue's mother's middle name was Elizabeth, so the name Mary Elizabeth seemed to be a perfect fit all the way around. However, Mary Elizabeth did not please Sue's mom. She wanted us to name the baby Elizabeth Ann. I was adamant and stuck to my guns, so the baby was named Mary Elizabeth, and so she is.

It was a joyful day when I brought Sue and Mary Elizabeth home from the hospital. Of course, we wanted to show Timbo his new baby sister, and he was OK looking at her and even letting us help him hold her. What he didn't like was to see one of us holding her by ourselves (it was OK for Grandma to hold her).

One morning, a few days after we had brought Sue and Mary Beth home from the hospital, Sue and her mother had gone for a short drive and a quick shopping trip. I was sitting in the overstuffed chair near the window, giving Mary Beth her bottle. Mary Beth was contently feeding. She had her eyes closed as she suckled on her bottle. Her tiny fingers were curled into balls, and her chest and tummy rose and subsided as the contents of the bottle slowly disappeared. Timmy was sitting in his small rocking chair, the same one that had been Sue's when she was a little girl, watching *Sesame Street*. Bert and Ernie were frolicking across the screen, interspersed by Kermit singing his *Green* song.

Not sure how closely Timmy was watching TV. Occasionally, he would sharply turn his head, and give Mary Beth and me a sharp glance with a bit of a pout. This went on for a bit until Mary Beth had almost finished her bottle. Suddenly, he arose from his chair, stalked over to us, and stood right in front of us with his lower lip partially sticking out, squinting up at us. He didn't say anything but just stood there and glared at us.

"Timmy, you want to come up here and help me feed your little baby sister?" I queried him. Timmy still didn't respond but batted his eyelashes a few times, but looked like he might be about ready to cry. I set Mary Beth's bottle down and picked him up with one hand while still holding her. "See, there's plenty of room up here for both of you," I told him as I gave him a quick little hug, leaned down, kissed the top of his head, and, with my almost free hand, tried to give him a little tickle. Timmy squirmed a little but still didn't say anything. Then, reaching around both of them, I finished giving Mary Beth her bottle. All of a sudden, Timmy started pushing the baby as if he was going to push her off my lap. Instead of making a fuss about it, I said to Timmy, "Hey, you know it's just you who will always be my Yo-Yo (That was my pet name for him). Only you! Would you like to hold your baby sister now?" However, that didn't seem to console him very much.

He sat like that for a couple of minutes but then glared up at me with those big baby-blue eyes, and I could see the moisture gathering in the corners of them. Then, he said, "Take her back, Daddy. Give her back to the hospital. I don't like her here. I don't want her here anymore. This is my place, not hers. I was here first." And a couple of big tears started trickling down his little cheeks. He quickly jumped off my lap, ran into his room as fast as he could, and I heard his door slam shut with a bang.

As soon as Mary Beth finished her bottle, I rested her over my shoulder, burped her, cradled her in my arms again, and as soon as she was asleep, I took her to her room and laid her down in her crib. I went into Timmy's room, picked him up, gave him a big hug, folded him in my lap, rocked him, called him my Yo-Yo, and told him, "Timmy, the hospital gave Mary Beth to us for us to keep and to love her, forever. She doesn't have anybody else to do that, only us. She is going to be your very own little sister to love and care for, forever, and for Mommy and Daddy to love her and care for her forever, too. So, I really need your help. I mean, you are a big boy now and you know I always depend on you for all the big important jobs, and this is really the biggest and most important job we've got now. You are my number one helper, and I need to depend on you. So, do you think you can help me with this one? Do you think you could take on this big responsibility of helping Mommy and Daddy take care of your little baby sister? It would sure help us a lot and make our jobs a whole bunch easier. Huh, what about it?"

He looked up at me, scolding me with just a hint of a frown, and nodded yes. Then he laid his head on my chest, and we hugged each other tightly. I started rocking him again and singing to him the song "Froggie Went A-Courtin," my own version, and he, too, was soon fast asleep. However, this could have been more of a drama. But I have always had plenty of love for both of them and always will!

Oh, and I enrolled Mary Beth in the payroll US Savings Bond program for $50 per month. When Mary Beth was ready, there would be funds available for her college, or at least to start college the same as Timmy.

Timmy holding Mary Elizabeth
(He 46 months) (She 1 month)

27. TRANSITIONS 1974-1975

In 1974, I applied for graduate school via the Air Force Institute of Technology (AFIT). I scored well on my Graduate Record Examination. I also applied for medical school after scoring well on the Medical Record Examination but failed to obtain admission to any of the schools I applied to. After being accepted into AFIT, I applied to the University of Cincinnati (UC) College of Medicine for their Master of Sciences Degree studies in industrial hygiene. I was to begin in late August 1975 as directed by AFIT (I was given a choice of the University of Cincinnati, Harvard, or Chapel Hill). Cincinnati was across the river from my folks and in fairly close proximity to Sue's folks as well. Cincinnati won, hands down. My application to UC was accepted, and that was that.

A few episodes with Timmy are worth mentioning. Whenever I was home, Timmy was almost an extension of me. Wherever I went, there went Timbo too. When he was smaller, we piggy-backed, or he rode on my hip, or I carried him in my arms almost everywhere. We read stories before bedtime; lots of stories. These included Dr. Seuss, Brothers Grimm, Hans Christian Andersen, Young Adventure Tales, ABCs, Numbers, etc. We practiced counting and the alphabet. By the time Timmy was a little over two, he knew his ABCs and could count up to ten.

Whenever I would be sitting in the house, Timmy claimed my lap for himself, and that was fine with me. When I worked in the yard, which I enjoyed (I won Yard of the Month several times), he would want to stay nearby and help. We had a big palm tree in front of the house, which I needed to trim. With new growth, old fronds tended to die and turn brown and were unsightly. To reach the offending fronds to trim, I had to climb up on a ladder about six or seven feet off ground level.

While I was attempting to trim the palm, Timbo was playing with a push toy up near the house, or so I thought. I sawed through the palm frond, and as it fell, I looked down, and to my consternation and horror, Timbo was right below me. The frond struck Timmy in the head, and a thorn spike tore through his skin right above his left eyebrow, coming out below just missing his eye by millimeters. The thorn had broken off and was still hanging there in his little face. Our poor baby Timmy was howling. I was afraid to remove the thorn for fear of doing more damage and didn't have the tools needed, for this could be a delicate operation with the thorn so close to the eye. I called Sue, and we quickly rushed him to the Wilford Hall Medical Center Emergency Room. Our striking, handsome, grown-up son still bears a hint of the scar over his eye, a reminder of my inattention. I still carry the regret for that moment that happened so many years ago.

On one of Sue's mother's visits from Ohio, we had a busy day sightseeing. The whole family took Sue's mother to the Farmers' Market in downtown San Antonio, and we visited the River Walk. We did just a little shopping and more sightseeing. Timmy was all excited, more excited than usual, just having his grandma there. He probably had more sugar than he should have had, as well.

When we got home (back to quarters; we lived on Medina Air Force Base), Timmy was tired and more than a little cranky. He was not willing to give up the ghost yet. He insisted that we let him color with Grandma, and it pleased her that he wanted to spend time with her. "Oh, just let him have a few more minutes," she pleaded. So, of course, I relented. I mean, what else was I to do?

After about thirty more minutes, when Timmy could barely keep his eyes open, I insisted it was time for his bath, his story, and time to get Timbo under the covers. The bath went pretty much without a hitch, but it seemed to revive him. I dried him off and got him into his jammies. I was reading him the *Jack and the Beanstalk* story, one of his favorites, but I could tell he really wasn't paying much attention.

"I want to go see Grandma," he piped up. Wrong response.

"No, Timmy," I responded in my best authoritative, fatherly voice. "You need to stay in bed, go to sleep, and get your rest, and tomorrow you'll see Grandma all day. You can color with Grandma, go for a walk, play, or do whatever you and she would like to do." But in spite of what I thought was my rather strong, commanding, no-nonsense voice, Timmy jumped from his bed, bounded past me, and headed out of his room.

"You, get yourself right back here this instance, young man!" I barked in my raised lieutenant's strong, commanding, stern voice.

"No!" Timmy sharply responded as he fled the room as fast as his little legs could carry him, and my best efforts to head him off at the pass were not nearly quick enough. His speed and agility, even then, were amazing. Not sure what it was—his inattention, his defiance to his daddy, or that he was going to get his own way—but before I could catch him, he ran smack into the hallway door frame leading into the living room where Sue and her mom were chatting and half-heartedly watching TV.

Timmy ran into the door frame so hard with his head that the force knocked him backward and he landed on his butt. Now he was bawling, and his grandma was sure I had almost killed him. Of course, it was my fault, like always. I swept him up in my arms to comfort him, and almost instantaneously, there arose this enormous goose egg that popped up on our poor baby's forehead. Oh, God, what had we there? Off to the USAF Wilford Hall Medical Center's Emergency Room we went.

Hours later (probably just a couple), our visit to the Emergency Room and X-ray department was completed. We were cleared to take Timmy back to quarters to observe with advice that the goose egg should be gone by morning and that our Timmy would be all right. We were supposed to watch him and make sure he had no untoward signs or symptoms. It turned out he was OK, and he still is.

On July 4, 1975, at Lackland Air Force Base's Medina Annex, we were all home and looking forward to celebrating Independence Day with our friends and neighbors. Our neighbors, the Coopers, were planning a cookout and invited us to participate and celebrate with them, along with some other neighbors and friends. Afterwards, we planned to go to the main base to see the fireworks show.

The day was starting out to be a typically hot and muggy San Antonio early July day. We could expect temperatures to soar towards 100 degrees by midafternoon. Timmy was getting a little excited. He always liked fireworks, and after all, the next day was going to be *his* birthday. I think he always believed the fireworks were a prelude to celebrate the anticipation of his birthday, or his birthday eve. Mary Beth was just three months old and, as usual, was being good as gold. And so, the day started and evolved.

That afternoon, our family was off to the Coopers. The group included Rob and Ming Cooper, along with their three daughters and a half dozen other couples and assorted kids. Rob was on flying status and had just returned from a mission (boondoggle) from Alaska and had a whole bunch of Alaskan King Crab. We also had goodies from all the other participants. It was a veritable feast! Everyone gorged themselves to the max.

The ladies were in a huddle, and Sue was holding Mary Beth while the ladies oohed and aahed over her. The men were over to the other side, discussing their favorite baseball teams and their stats. The kids were playing around, just having a great time. The Coopers' youngest daughter, who was about 8, had Timmy in hand. She liked to mother him like he was a real, live, walking, talking doll.

Some of the kids were on the Coopers' swing set, pumping and swinging away wildly. The Independence Day cookout was a great success. What a great day we were having, I thought to myself. I was thinking it wouldn't be too long before we should start preparing for the fireworks show when I heard this awful shriek! I looked towards the swing set, and there was Timmy in the back of the swing set, lying on his back, screaming at the top of his lungs with blood streaming from his forehead. He had inadvertently wandered into the arc of the swinger's path, and the swing seat had struck him right in the forehead, knocking him flat on his back, tearing a big gash in his little head.

I ran to him and scooped him up. Someone gave me a towel to wrap around his head. Sue handed Ming Mary Beth, and we raced for the USAF Wilford Hall Medical Center's Emergency Room once again. After what seemed like hours (probably only a couple) of X-rays and Emergency Room treatments with wound treatment and Timbo's head swathed in a cocoon-like bandage, looking like he was preparing to become a mummy, we were on our way home. It had gotten dark while we were getting Timmy treated, and before we could get off that side of the base, the fireworks started. I pulled off on the side of the road; we had a front-row seat for the fireworks show, much to Timmy's delight.

Now, it's a dad's job to protect his offspring, to keep them out of harm's way, to foresee lurking dangers, and always keep them safe. As shown by these examples, I hadn't done so well in my early parenting skills. As a matter of fact, it could be said I had failed miserably in keeping our baby boy from getting hurt. If all these ER visits happened today, we would be investigated for child abuse.

Timmy approaching his 4ᵗʰ birthday

July 5, 1975, Timmy's 4ᵗʰ Birthday

There he stood with the white turban wrapped around his head, looking like a zombie. This was long before the era of the zombie craze. However, all the little kids attending his birthday party were absolutely awestruck. The kids had never seen anything like Timmy's turban. They thought it was for dress-up. Was Halloween early this year, and had their mothers forgotten to dress them up in costume? Other than the bandage wrapped around his head, Timmy didn't seem fazed or have any aftereffects from the swing incident. The party went off without a hitch.

I might mention a word about the real estate where our house was located. Lackland Air Force Base's Medina Annex had its early beginning as the Medina

Base National Stockpile Site, built by the Atomic Weapons Project and the Armed Forces Special Weapons Project to stockpile nuclear weapons. This Medina site was a secret area where about a hundred humpbacked rectangular bunkers made of fortified steel and concrete, known as "igloos"—each roughly the size of four two-car garages—served as one of the country's largest nuclear weapons installations. On the clear, cool morning of November 13, 1963, a fire started in one of the igloos and caused a massive explosion, leaving nothing but a yawning hole in its place. Convoys flanked by blue Air Force police cars with flashing lights transferred all nuclear material from Medina, and its mission of storage of nuclear weapons was terminated and turned into a training arena.

Medina Base National Stockpile Site, 11/13/1963

On February 4, 1972, a little over eight years later, I entered Medina as a Technical Sergeant (E-6) mid-level non-commissioned officer, and upon graduating from Officer Training School at the Medina Annex,

Sue pinned on my uniform the gold (butter) bars of a Second Lieutenant (O-1) entry-level officer. After taking leave, I was transferred to the USAF Wilford Hall Medical Center, Lackland AFB, Texas, to manage their Environmental Health Services, and our family was assigned quarters on Medina Annex without knowledge of its extraordinary history. And there we were, living on the Medina Annex just a stone's throw away from what once was the largest nuclear storage area.

It was now August 1975. The movers came, and we hightailed it for our new apartment in Mount Healthy, a suburb of Cincinnati, Ohio, where we would reside for the next year while I completed my graduate studies. The nice thing about studying at the University of Cincinnati was that we were only about twenty miles away from my folks and about 150 miles from Sue's folks. For Timmy's birthday on July 4, 1976 (the United States' 200-year anniversary), we went to the Cincinnati Reds baseball game, and for dinner, we went to Johnny Bench's Restaurant accompanied by Sue's mom and dad.

Our apartment living in Mount Healthy was uneventful, as well as my time in graduate school. Our apartment was a three-bedroom, two-story building with a little less floor space than we previously had, but it was adequate. Sue and Timmy discovered good friends next door with a recent divorcee and her two daughters who were near Timmy's age. The girls became fond of Timmy and he of them.

Mary Beth, on the other hand, became even more clingy with me. Whenever I happened to be sitting, my lap was hers. (Sorry, Timmy!) It appeared she demanded almost all my attention and time if I happened to be in the apartment. Her room was on the second floor, facing the parking lot. One day, I needed to rush to the nearby 7-Eleven to buy some milk and a few other items, and I attempted to slip away. I no sooner got out the front door than I heard this banging on Mary Beth's window upstairs and this horrendous screeching.

When I looked up, our little baby, Mary Beth, was jumping up and down, as fast and as hard as she could, with her rattler in her hand banging on the window and screaming for me not to go or for me to take her with me. I couldn't tell which. It was absolutely heartbreaking. I could still faintly hear her screaming as I was preparing to get in my car, "Don't leave me, Daddy! Don't leave me, Daddy! Don't Go! Don't Leave me, Daddy!" I almost turned back around, but Sue was there, and I only needed to be gone for a few minutes. So, despite my angst, I hurried to the store and back as fast as I could.

Another time, in our living room downstairs, we had Mary Beth's playpen located fairly close to my stereo equipment. On that day, we had Mary Beth in her playpen. I had been playing with her, and we had been having the best time, but I really needed to study for an upcoming exam, so I put her back in her playpen, where she fussed a bit. She fussed and jabbered a bit more until I gave her her bottle. She could handle her bottle pretty well by herself by that time.

I settled down nearby, deeply engrossed in the exam material. Unknowingly, I had left my newly purchased Pointer Sisters album near her playpen. I had been playing the album earlier, so it was lying there outside of its cover. Mary Beth took her bottle and doused my new album with milk, nearly ruining it for my inattention. When I discovered what she had done, I was more than a little peeved, but then I had to laugh.

More fool on you, I thought to myself. That is just what you get. Next time you better learn to pay better attention.

Sue was a super trooper during this interim. I didn't have a lot of time to spend with her and the kids or to help around the house. It was almost like she was a single parent with extra duties, but she was a doting mom and wife in spite of it all. The apartment was always immaculate, and the kids always looked like a little prince and princess.

Graduate school was demanding. The class I enjoyed most was visiting the various industries: General Motors, Procter & Gamble, Eli Lilly, a coal mine in Kentucky, a foundry, a steel mill, and a whole lot more that I visited but they don't come to mind. The culmination of my master's program was to be my thesis on in-depth research of lead encephalopathy.

Anyone and everyone who has seen my handwriting will gladly tell you I will garner no awards in that endeavor. There even have been those who have taken a good look at my handwriting skills and have told me my script looked like that of a frustrated physician (no disrespect to physicians). Where am I going with this? Sue agreed to type my thesis for me, and because of my poor handwriting, we came to the closest point of divorcing over that than we ever did about anything else. I'm sure it was because of my illegible script.

In September 1976, graduate studies were completed. Despite my best efforts to get assigned to Florida (where the family was hoping we would get assigned), I received orders to the Royal Air Force Base (RAF) in Upper Heyford, England. To add insult to injury, housing was very limited there, so Sue and the kids could not go with me until I had found housing.

Which meant I would have to drive alone to Fort Dix and ship our small Ford Pinto to England.

Whenever I would be able to find a place to live, Sue would have to sell the Oldsmobile (my nephew was actually going to buy it), take care of getting our household goods shipped, make travel arrangements, fly from Cincinnati, Ohio (as it turned out she flew out of Columbus, Ohio), to London, England, with 5-year-old Timmy and 18-month-old Mary Beth.

28. JOLLY OLE ENGLAND 1976-1979

I'd been to London, England, before, crossing the English Channel from France when I was stationed at Chateauroux Air Force Station, Chateauroux, France. I had wanted to ensure I was able to visit England before my tour in France was finished. Unfortunately, none of my usual traveling buds were available to go with me, or they didn't seem to want to go at the time I had available. Therefore, I traveled solo. I took the train from Chateauroux to Paris and then waited to transfer (Gare Nord) to the connecting train to London. (This was long before the Chunnel was completed.)

When we got to the English Channel, we deboarded and were transferred to the Dover Ferry. It was smooth sailing across the Channel, and after leaving the shores of France, there was only water all around us. However, before we got to the English side of the Channel, a severe sudden storm appeared out of nowhere. We were hit with a deluge of rain and fierce wind. I was upside with many other passengers, all wanting to get a gander at the scenery and savor the experience as we crossed. The storm added a little extra excitement to the journey.

However, with the increasing wind, the ferry began to tilt and roll. It was no longer the gentle rocking to and fro we had been experiencing before. I was still good— until my fellow travelers began to have motion sickness and attempted to vomit overboard. However, instead of the vomitus following the normal gravitational trajectory, the wind was so strong it picked it up and whipped the vomitus through the air. It made a mess beyond imagination! It was weird to see strings of vomitus whipping in the wind. I had never seen anything like that before. I could feel my stomach beginning to get queasy. I almost lost it right on board the deck, too. Fortunately, the storm was short-lived, and soon, we were on solid ground in England and reboarded the train for London.

After arriving at the London Train Station, I took my suitcase and searched for the Tube (London Underground). There were signs directing me to the station, so it was easy to find my way. I had to figure out which line I needed to take. Maneuvering the Tube was easy after all the experiences I had with the Paris Metro. I found my way to the USO (United Service Organization), and the assistant there found me a sleeping room for my stay in London. I then began my London adventures.

I did the usual tourist sights: Windsor Castle, the House of Parliament and Big Ben, Buckingham Palace, the Tower of London (which dates back to the eleventh century after William the Conqueror's invasion of England), Trafalgar Square with Lord Nelson's Column, the Natural History Museum, Piccadilly Circus (London's Times Square), Globe Theater, and one of my very favorites, Hyde Park. I was also able to take in three theatrical productions: *Pickwick, A Funny Thing Happened On the Way to the Forum,* and the third I've long since forgotten.

Photo by Marcin Nowak on Unsplash

The nightlife, too, was interesting. When the locals found out I was a Yank, things began to get even more interesting. The birds (girls) were particularly intrigued by my Southern (hillbilly) accent. When I discovered they found my accent unique, I really poured it on and amped it up a notch. Well, let's just say I really enjoyed London.

Now, here I was (September 1976), twenty-two years later, being assigned to the Royal Air Force Upper Heyford Base, England, in what is called the Midlands, south of Banbury (of the nursery rhyme *Banbury Cross* fame), just north of Oxford (of Oxford University fame), and within an hour's drive to Stratford-Upon-Avon, Shakespeare's hangout.

As I got off the bus, I met my new boss, Lt Col (Dr.) Charles Bost, Chief, Flight Surgeon (another complete story in itself) and my new superintendent, Master Sergeant (MSgt) John Vance. When we first met—with some assistance on my part—I would like to think he would later be promoted to Senior Master Sergeant). They welcomed me to England, and

Colonel Bost drove me to my temporary quarters, the Officers Visiting Quarters nestled above the Officer's (O) Club. He told me to get some rest and to meet my staff the next morning after I got over my jet lag. It sounded like good advice, so I did just that.

The following morning, after chowing down for breakfast at the O Club, I met my new staff. In addition to MSgt Vance, there was Sgt Brough, a perky, good-looking female; Airman Koska; and Airman Curtis—four technicians, a far cry from the fourteen I had had under my tutelage at Lackland Air Force Base.

My first agenda was to complete mandatory clearing into the Upper Heyford USAF Hospital and the rest of the base. I wasted no time in completing those chores. My next priority was finding a place for us (Sue, the kids, and me) to live. There was no base or base-leased housing available. I was able to get on a waiting list, but the prognosis was not great. The forecast was that it would probably be several months before base-sponsored housing would become available.

I had only been gone four days, but I was missing Sue, little Timmy, and baby Mary Beth, something fierce. An intimate and necessary part of me was missing. My biggest problem was I didn't have wheels. Our little Pinto that I had shipped from the States wouldn't arrive in England for some weeks. I will always be grateful to MSgt Vance for he took me under his wing and chauffeured me around the surrounding area house hunting. He had only arrived in England a few months before me and had recently gone through the house-hunting ordeal. He had an advantage: his wife was English, and he had been stationed in England on previous assignments. The first one was when he met his wife, Annabelle.

He was familiar with the lay of the land. We went meandering about the local countryside, searching for a habitat for my little family. It seemed there wasn't a lot to choose from. Some folks didn't want to rent to Yanks, others' houses were too small, and some didn't take short-term rentals, which was a requirement because, hopefully, base-type housing would be available in the not-too-distant future. That left slim pickings.

It would normally have been a joy cruising around the picturesque English countryside, but I was feeling more desperate with each passing day to find us a place to live so I could send for Sue and the kids.

Despite my angst, I did find the English countryside fascinating. There were sheep pasturing everywhere. There were lush, green pastures spotted with slowly moving white dots, and narrow, winding two-lane highways through farmland or forested areas were the norm. I found the stone fences so neatly stacked along the highway particularly fascinating. *Where did all those rocks come from and who so fastidiously stacked them there?* and think about all the hours it took to stack them in place. There were even some bombed-out remnants left standing as ghostly reminders of the devastation of that terrible World War II.

The architecture followed no rhyme or reason. The spectrum went from thatched roof cottages to shanties to elaborate castles and modern apartments and estates all crammed together. I never knew what to expect that I would see around the next curve or rise of the roadway. Our daily travels took us through quaint villages with melodic names: Adderberry, Bicester, Banbury, Barford St John, Oxford, Godington, Woodstock, Wootton, Steeple Barton,

Hook Norton, Stow on the Wold, Burton-on-the-Water, Chippington Norton, Deddington, etc.

At last, we finally found a fairly modern two-story duplex in Charlbury that was available for us to rent by a young English dentist who was working in the Netherlands. The dentist's father, who lived around the corner, was managing the house and would act as landlord. The place would be a little small for our family, but I felt we could be extra friendly until something better came along. I was getting desperate, and it was getting to the point where my expectations were getting less and less. Besides, this was a relatively new place, and it was clean even though it had no closets, typical of English houses, because closets were taxed as rooms.

I was anxious to close the deal, call Sue, and tell her the good news so she could start the ball rolling. I knew she would have to arrange for our household goods to be packed up and shipped to England, as well as get plane tickets for herself and the kids. I knew she would be out of her comfort zone in doing all that and then flying with our babies across the Atlantic Ocean by herself. However, I had every confidence she would rise to the occasion! I was so excited that I would soon have them with me, that our little family would all be back together again. Without Sue and the little ones, there was a big part of me that was missing, and I wouldn't be whole again until I could have them near me and hold them in my arms again.

As soon as I completed the contract for the duplex, I took a copy to the housing office. That started the wheels in motion for Sue and the babies to join me. Unfortunately, Sue would have to go to the Lexington Army Depot (a 150-mile round trip) to arrange for household goods packing, pick-up, and shipment to

Upper Heyford, as well as arrange for tickets to fly from Ohio via Chicago to Heathrow Airport in London, England. This would entail taking Timmy (5 years old) out of kindergarten and toting Mary Beth (18 months old) across the great Atlantic Ocean to a new home, a new continent, and all kinds of new adventures. The plane ride over was somewhat hectic. The aircraft pressure seemed to bother Mary Beth and caused her discomfort, so she cried and screamed most of the way. Timmy, on the other hand, was a real soldier and a big help to his mommy.

There was a lot to do before Sue and the babies arrived. Our belongings were being shipped by ocean freighter, so it would take some time before they would arrive; therefore, I needed to locate some necessities before the family arrived. We would need to keep those items until our household goods were delivered. Fortunately, Family Services on base provided most of those necessities: cots, folding tables and chairs, some dishes and cutlery, linens, towels, etc.

Electricity was going to be another challenge. The British system was 220 volts versus the US's 110 volts. We would need converters for all of our electrical appliances. We would need to purchase a washer and dryer and an English refrigerator, but I would wait until after Sue's arrival for her approval before making any major purchases. Groceries were available from the base commissary as well as in the local economy.

MSgt Vance had been kind enough to chauffeur me around until we found a place to live. Now, he and his vehicle were no longer available. Everything on base was walkable—BX (base exchange), commissary, and Visiting Officer Quarters, where I was staying until the family arrived. My office had a vehicle to be used for official duties. The place in Charlbury was about fifteen miles from the base, and the Pinto delivery date was nowhere near. It was on a slow boat from Dover, Delaware. I needed to rent a vehicle in the interim!

I had always driven vehicles with automatic transmissions. Even my driver's training way back in high school was on an automatic. I looked into renting an automatic drive vehicle. It would have cost me 16 pounds (about $36.50) per day. However, I could rent a standard shift-drive vehicle for the same amount for a week. I had never driven a stick shift! But by golly, I was surely going to give it the old college try.

I was a newly promoted captain, and pay was much better than when I had been enlisted. But I was the only one bringing in a paycheck, and I had to think about supporting my wife, our two darling children, and myself, so I still needed to count pennies. I took the plunge and rented the stick shift. Here I was, a 33-year-old starting out driving in a vehicle using a stick shift and driving on the wrong side of the road! Talk about double jeopardy! You think I wasn't scared? My heart was in my throat for most of my first efforts.

I found all of the roundabouts to be particularly interesting because I didn't have to stop, clutch, and shift so much. I found my biggest challenge was stopping on a hill when there was a vehicle behind me, not to let my car roll back into it. Thankfully, that never happened. Before I picked up the newly rented car, MSgt Vance gave me some practice drives in his car, which had a stick shift, with a lot of patience and welcomed instructions. Fortunately, the route back to the base was not far, and in answer to prayers, there were no hills to maneuver. I had a little time to practice driving before I needed to go collect the family at Heathrow Airport.

In preparation for the big day, I had gone to Family Services and borrowed the bare essentials: a crib and cots with bedding and cookware with cutlery, a small table and four chairs, bath accessories, and a few other odds and ends. It would take some time before our household goods would arrive. I made sure utilities were turned on, and everything was working properly. I went to the commissary and purchased some basic food items. I knew that after she arrived, Sue would want to shop on her own. We would need to buy an English washer, dryer, and refrigerator. But Sue needed to have some input there.

I hardly slept a wink the night before Sue, Timmy, and Mary Beth were due to arrive. I knew that driving to Heathrow Airport in the rented stick-shift automobile would be a challenge, but I was so anxious to see my babies, all three. Maneuvering the endless number of runabouts took a bit to get the hang of, and the motorways and intense traffic entailed other challenges.

I finally arrived at Heathrow Airport, parked, and anxiously awaited the big arrival. After what seemed like an eternity, I spotted them. Timmy ran to me, and I swung him up in the air and gave him a big hug. Sue was carrying Mary Beth, who was reaching out for me. I was overjoyed to have my little clan by my side. The ride back to Charlbury was made without incident, but my nerves were on high alert all the way.

Eventually, the Pinto did arrive. I had to take the train to Felixstowe (all the way over on the east coast of England) to retrieve it and drive it back to Charlbury. The household goods made it too, even though a good proportion wouldn't fit inside our new residence, so our garage was stuffed full of overflow, wall-to-wall.

Our duplex mates were one of the local policemen, his wife, and two children, a boy and a girl. The girl was around Timmy's age, and their little boy was younger. The girl went to the local primary school, which was nearby, and she and her mother encouraged us to enroll Timmy there. And wonder of wonders, the school agreed to allow Timmy to enroll, and in no time at all, you couldn't tell he wasn't a little bloke. He completely lost his Yankee accent and anyone talking with him would have sworn he was British. He was and is very smart and took to school like he belonged. Why, he knew his ABCs when he was 2 years old, and I would take him to my office to show him off.

Mary Beth was still Daddy's girl. She loved to snuggle with me in the rocker while I read to her. She had some favorites, but it really didn't matter what I read as long as I held her tight and snuggled with her. She would interrupt me to reach up to hug me, give me a kiss on the cheek, and say, "I love you, Daddy."

Of course, I would respond with a little peck and say, "No, Mary Beth, I love you more."

Then Mary Beth: "No, I love you more."

Me: "No, I love *you* more." And after several iterations, we would collapse in giggles, and I would say we would have to continue with our story.

Shortly after my little family arrived in England, I went to the annual USAFE Medical Conference in Garmisch, Germany. Sue did not go, but this was an annual event and was mandatory for me to attend, which I did for the following two years. Sue did go with me in the second year. On the first and third trips, I rode with most of the other medical officers from the hospital via military cargo planes, somewhat rustic transport. We landed in Munich, Germany, with bus transportation into Garmisch.

The second trip with Sue was quite different, though. We drove the little Ford Pinto and crossed the English Channel by Hovercraft, which took about eight hours. We had sleeping quarters for the crossing, but sleeping was difficult. Sometime during the night, Sue felt the call of Mother Nature and somewhat sleepily staggered forward to ask one of the attendants (blokes) where the ladies' restroom was. In his brogue, he directed her to the lounge, where there were chairs to rest (a restroom, get it?). In Europe, it is safe to refer to toilet facilities as the WC. Fortunately, we didn't suffer from seasickness and finished the crossing without further incident.

Once we reached France's embankment, we reclaimed our Ford Pinto and were on our way to Germany. As usual, there was something about riding in a car that lulled Sue into a light slumber. This time was no different. When we got to the German border, I roused her because we had to show identification and papers. Her alertness didn't last long, though, because, before many miles, she was again lost in slumberland. I had driven for several miles, and sometime later, Sue became alert and glanced out the car's window. "Wiley, you have been driving in circles. This is the same city where we first entered Germany—*Ausfahrt!*" Ausfahrt is not the name of a city; rather, it is the German word for exit, so there were a lot of Ausfahrt signs all along the Autobahn during our time in Germany.

The USAFE medical conferences were held in Garmisch (in the west) and Partenkirchen (in the east). They have been separate towns for many centuries and still maintain quite separate identities. Partenkirchen originated as the Roman town of Partanum on the trade route from Venice to Augsburg and was first mentioned about the time of Christ. Garmisch and Partenkirchen remained separate entities until their respective mayors were forced by Adolf Hitler to combine the two market towns in anticipation of the 1936 Winter Olympic Games.

During our visits, the united towns were casually (but incorrectly) referred to as Garmisch, much to the dismay of Partenkirchen residents, we learned. Garmisch felt more modern, while the fresco-filled, cobblestone streets of Partenkirchen had a more ancient appeal.

Early mornings and late afternoons, we were pleasantly amused to watch the local traffic stalled or stopped while the dairy cows were herded to and from the nearby mountain meadows. The tinkling of the cow bells bounced around the village as the cattle were herded along their way.

During World War II, Garmisch-Partenkirchen was a major hospital center for the German military, the same place where Hitler held the 1936 Winter Olympics. The WWII NAZI hospital center was where the USAFE medical conferences were held.

The whole area was most picturesque. Flowers in pots and other containers abounded all around every cottage and from every terrace and window. The alpine type of architecture was the norm and was very photogenic. The people were friendly and encouraging, especially the shopkeepers. There were lots of medical officers' wives who had come along with their husbands, so there were activities for Sue's participation while I was engrossed with the conference.

We met Captain Frank Gardner, another bioenvironmental engineer, and his wife Becky, who were stationed in Germany and had been to Garmisch before. They took us under their wings, and we did a bit of sightseeing with them. One of the places we wanted to see was the Neuschwanstein Linderhaplace Castle, the model for Disney's Snow-White Castle in the Disneyland Parks.

The castle was built in a fairy-tale-inspired neo-Romanesque style. It was a breathtaking drive to the castle. Frank and Becky had a car and had driven from their base as well and were more familiar with the surrounding territory. They insisted on driving us, which suited us just fine. We toured the castle, and even though it was spectacular from the outside, inside, it was mostly bare. There was nothing inside there.

Photo by Felix on Unsplash

After we finished the tour of the castle, we met an elderly German gentleman who looked a lot like Santa

Claus with a long snow-white flowing beard with a matching full head of white hair. He was dressed in native German lederhosen—a cap and all-leather shorts with typical H-leather suspenders attached to the shorts and socks up to his calves. It appeared he spoke no English (at least he shared none), but with gestures, it appeared he was inviting Sue and Becky to be photographed with him before the Neuschwanstein Linderhaplace Castle. At first, the ladies were a little hesitant, but Frank and I thought it would make a wonderful photo op, so we urged our spouses on. They hesitantly agreed to pose with the old gentleman.

Unbeknownst to Frank and me, the old scoundrel, instead of offering a friendly arm around the ladies, was attempting to get a free feel; dirty old man! In spite of his age, I felt like smashing him in the face, but the ladies urged us to just let it go, which we did, and we got back in the vehicle and resumed our sightseeing.

Sue and I did quite a bit of sightseeing both in Germany and France before and after the conference. One of the highlights was a visit to Mad King Ludwig II's Linderhof Palace. (King Ludwig II was also responsible for the Neuschwanstein Linderhaplace Castle.) Linderhof Palace was King Ludwig II's favorite, and it was easy to see why. It glittered with lavish ornamentation; its size and its setting amid cool green forests gave it an intimate and livable quality. On the tour, we saw the Hall of Mirrors, the Audience Chamber that Ludwig used as a study, the two tapestry Chambers, the King's Bedchamber, and the Dining Room. There were lots of stories about this eccentric king. The gardens and grounds were superb and included fountains, pools, and the Moorish Pavilion.

Instead of retracing our trail back via the German autobahn, we decided to head towards France, crossing the Alps. Going up an almost straight-up incline proved almost too much for our poor little Pinto and her 22.0-liter engine. The motor power wasn't designed for the task. As soon as we started up one of the steep inclines, there would be a line of traffic behind us, and with every passing minute, it got longer.

To make matters more complicated, there were almost no places to pull over so that we could let the backed-up traffic pass us. On the plus side, we did get to see our first glaciers.

Sue's impression of the French was not great. She felt sure they all spoke English but just refused to speak it with us, so we had to depend upon my limited French vocabulary and American accent to get us by, and somehow, we did manage and were able to make our way back to our base in England.

At RAF Upper Heyford, I managed Bioenvironmental Engineering Services for a wing of F-111E aircraft, two tenant bases, and ten communication sites in the southern half of England. I provided consultation and assisted in preparing the environmental assessment for reactivating the Royal Air Force Base, Fairford. I performed baseline evaluations and collected data on potential deleterious conditions that could have detracted from the health of the command and advised on the best method for their control or elimination. I interfaced with the British Nature Conservancy Council, the local County Planning Board, and the Cotswold Environmental Health Office to develop operational plans to ensure current environmental conditions would be maintained. I was requested by the hospital commander to take on the additional duty as the hospital's disaster preparedness officer.

After assuming this responsibility, the hospital received ratings of excellent or higher on all aspects of the program from every team that visited the wing. The USAFE Operational Readiness Inspection/NATO Tactical Evaluation Team described the hospital's capability for detection of chemical agents as "best seen to date." The AF medical inspectors rated both the bioenvironmental engineering and the readiness programs as OUTSTANDING!

29. 7 PAYNES END, RAF BICESTER

The year 1977 provided new and exciting opportunities for our little family. First, we were offered base contracted housing at Royal Air Force (RAF) Bicester, at what was once British Officer Quarters. Our new residence at 7 Panes End was a detached, two-story brick house with a kitchen and a side laundry room, a formal dining room, and living room, and one bathroom downstairs. Upstairs had the master suite with two smaller bedrooms in the back and another (main) bathroom.

In addition to the house itself, there were two outside brick structures, a detached garage on the right and a large storage room on the left. In the rear of the house was a large yard for Timmy and Mary Beth to play to their hearts' content. At last, we would be able to spread out and use all our belongings (or at least display them)!

The Air Force moved us into our new quarters on the first of February. The move necessitated many changes for us, some welcomed and some not so much so. In the short time we had lived in Charlbury, we had made some good friends with our next-door neighbors and their kids, as well as with our childminder's (babysitter's) family and SSgt Newman and his wife, Emily.

SSgt Newman and I had carpooled to the base, alternating drivers and cars so as to allow our wives some freedom with transportation. It also meant leaving the Charlbury Primary School, where our wee chap had been progressing so well. We were so impressed with the Charlbury School that we wanted to keep Timmy in the British school system. The superintendent at the local British school adjacent to the RAF property was not nearly as accommodating or as understanding as the Charlbury primary one had been. Matter of fact, he strongly recommended we enroll Timmy in the American school system at RAF Croughton Base, where he would need to be bused. We were not enthused at the idea of our little offspring being driven back and forth some twenty miles each school day all by himself.

We persevered in our debate with the school superintendent, and he reluctantly agreed to let Timmy enroll, but still with some obvious reservations. He strongly voiced that Timmy would be better off with his American peers. Timmy still did well in the English system. The highlight of the year was participating in the school pageant for Queen Elizabeth's Twenty-Fifth Jubilee Celebration, where he played at being part of the Queen's court; he assisted in holding her train at the school's pageant parade! However, at the start of the school year in the fall, we did enroll him in the RAF Croughton Base Elementary School, where he remained until we were reassigned from England.

There were other changes involved with our new move. Both Mary Beth and Timmy were enrolled in horseback riding lessons. They both did well, but Mary Beth appeared more enthusiastic than her older brother. Mary Beth had her first haircut, which made her cuter than I

Mary Beth after getting her first haircut

thought possible. She wasn't so keen on having her locks shorn away, though. Sue bought her a pair of red boots that she seemed to dearly love and wanted to wear everywhere, causing Craig, my bioenvironmental technician, to name her "Miss Bossy Boots" because she certainly developed opinions of her own at that very young age.

We signed Timmy up for one of the base's little league soccer teams and later for T-ball. I was the assistant coach for his T-ball team, and I don't recall us winning even one game, but I would like to think we had fun. At least I was able to get into the spirit of things. Not being a sports-minded person or a person who was even very much interested in sports, it took extra effort on my part. I was, however, interested in our son and helping him have a good time and exploring different options as he was growing up.

After school, and when school was not in session, he found a buddy in Kirk Rieckhoff, who lived three houses down at the end of the street in a four-bedroom house. Kirk's dad was Lt Col Bud (Elmer) and the hospital administrator, who I often rode with to and from work. The second year we lived there, the Rieckhoffs moved into a five-bedroom house one street over, and our good friends Paul and Andrea Martin (and family) moved into the Rieckhoffs' vacant house. Now Timmy had a second chum to horse around with, Matthew Martin. I often referred to them as the three mighty musketeers. In addition, one of the two older Martin kids, Amber or Jason, sometimes babysat for us in the evenings if we went out to see a movie or to a social event.

Our family was doing well in our new home, settling in nicely. However, Sue and I discussed the fact that on one income, it would be difficult to take advantage of the opportunity to travel and explore Europe. The solution was for Sue to return to the workforce. We were not overjoyed about putting Mary Beth in daycare, and there would still be the problem of getting Timmy off to school and having someone there for him after school when he arrived home.

We started asking around, looking for a nanny. The answer just happened to be right under our noses—right in my own office, actually. Craig Koska, my technician, went home for Christmas vacation and returned with his delightful young bride, Nancy. Nancy needed to have income to help support their livelihood, but after intensive searches, she had been unable to find employment on base or in the surrounding area. Craig and Nancy loved children. It appeared the Koskas and the Taylors were the answer to each other's conundrum.

Sue returned to the civil service workforce, getting a job with one of the squadron commanders (Captain Schiener's Orderly Room), and later got promoted to be secretary to the chief of transportation. We hired Nancy to keep our kids while we were at work. Craig would drop her off on his way to the office. Both kids really loved Craig and Nancy. A huge plus was that whenever Sue and I traveled to see a little of the world, Craig and Nancy would stay in our house with Mary Beth and Timmy until we returned. House-sitters plus childminders!

On weekends, we attempted to spend as much time with Timmy and Mary Beth as possible. We visited nearby parks and recreation areas, the Duke of Marlborough's (Churchill) Blenheim Palace, Woodstock, Banbury, Oxford, Warwick Castle with its musty dungeons and torture apparatus still intact, the Roman city of Bath (the Roman baths still were in existence). Near the little church where we lived in Charlbury, there was an old stock with holes for placing the head and arms—yuck, can you even imagine? The churchyard's cemetery had headstones dating back to the 1200s and earlier. For the more ancient ones, erosion over time had mostly erased discernable details, and all that was left to view was some undecipherable indentations.

As I was the attending bioenvironmental engineer for the whole southern half of England, I was required to annually visit all of the radar sites located in the southern part of England. One of these sites was on St Mawgan on the Southwest tip of England, very close to Land's End. I decided to load up the whole family and take a few extra days of leave (vacation) along with my temporary duty (TDY). During my TDY, we were able to visit Land's End and the picturesque village of St Ives of the Nursery Rhyme fame "As I was going to St Ives, I Met a Man with Seven Wives...."

However, the most vivid memory of that trip, which I sometimes have nightmares about, concerns our family outing on the Atlantic Ocean Beach. Near St Mawgan, there was a really nice beach that was very popular with the locals. Now, the water wasn't quite as warm as we would have liked, but it was still tolerable enough for a short swim or a little romp in the ocean. Towards the back of the beach, there were small cabanas for changing into and out of swimwear. However, many people simply wrapped themselves in towels, and with a deft shake and a little wiggle or two, shorts and underclothes fell off, and with a quick step back, they were replaced with swimwear. With the ladies, it was a little more complicated—a little extra wiggle and some gymnastic contortions to remove tops, but basically, the procedure was pretty much the same. It was hard not to stare, for we had never seen such exhibitions in the States before.

But I digress from the situation from which I started to describe to you.

Sue was stretched out on the sandy beach on a towel with our belongings nearby, and Mary Beth was playing with her little bucket and shovel, digging in the sand, unmindful of us or anyone or anything about her, or so it seemed.

Timmy wanted to go swimming in the ocean. So, being an attentive dad, I took him to the ocean, and we played around in the water for maybe twenty or thirty minutes, certainly no longer than thirty minutes, for the water was pretty cold and Timmy and I both seemed to chill quickly.

When we got back to Sue and the blankets, Mary Beth was not in sight. I quickly looked around the immediate area, but Mary Beth was nowhere to be seen. Next, with Sue and Timmy's assistance we started scanning around us in widening circles. There was no Mary Beth! Sue and I both started to panic! Where in the H was our darling little baby?! Sue was sure that Mary Beth had gone with Timmy and me to dally in the ocean. I, on the other hand, had left her with Sue and was sure she would still be there.

We extended our search and hastily looked around us in the nearby and surrounding areas. We were calling out, "Mary Beth! Mary Beth!" No answer! No, Mary Beth! My heart was in my mouth and my stomach was in knots. Both Sue and I were then even more in the panic mode! What in the world were we going to do? What *could* we do?

I went dashing around looking everywhere I thought she might be or could be, or so I thought. Still no Mary Beth. I felt sure our darling little baby, our darling, beautiful girl, had been kidnapped by some deranged, mentally unstable person and was probably miles away by now. I had never been so scared or so desperate in my life as I was at that moment. We had no one around us that we knew that we could ask for help.

At that moment, I would have given anything to get our sweetie back. Our searches continued for maybe fifteen to twenty minutes more. It seemed like hours. I had just started out to find a policeman to report our baby missing when Mary Beth came casually strolling up carrying her sand bucket and shovel and very nonchalantly said, "I'm hungry, Daddy. Can we get something to eat? Can I have a hot dog?"

I felt I had aged ten years over the past several minutes, but with the safe and sound return of our baby, suddenly, all was right with my world once again! Mary Beth had simply been somewhere amongst the sunbathers, very nonchalantly building (or attempting to build) herself a sandcastle, and with all the ocean and crowd noises, had failed to hear our frantic calls for her.

In addition to our Garmisch adventure, there were four other major explorations we undertook: three in Europe and one in the Holy Land. The first one was to Amsterdam to see the tulips and the windmills. I had been to Holland before with my buddy, Ralph Gochenour, when we were both stationed at Chateauroux Air Force Station, France, but I wanted to show and share this experience with my bride.

We booked a tour with a local travel agency, and as it happened, we were the only Americans (Yanks) with all the rest of the English (bloke) travelers. However, we got along famously. The tulips were kind to us, and most were in full bloom while we were there, and with a couple of the local tours, we were even able to see a few windmills.

But mostly, our visit was confined to Amsterdam. We visited the Anne Frank house, took a dinner cruise (Valentine's and birthday celebrations for us) on the canal, strolled through the red-light district, and saw some of the window exhibits; they were very striking— colorful and educational. But we were strictly sightseeing and toured a diamond factory, having a great time while Nancy and Craig took care of our little ones.

When we returned home, we had a big surprise ourselves (at least it was for me). Mary Beth and her little friend next door had arranged an absolutely beautiful tulip and hyacinth bouquet for us. The girls had taken these beautiful blooms from the bulbs that I had so carefully amassed in front of the living room's bay window. They would have been at their peak of glory had they not been picked already. They were to have showcased the front of our house while they were in full bloom. When I saw what had happened, I took a deep breath and bit my tongue. I scooped Mary Beth up, gave her a big hug, and told her she had made a beautiful bouquet for her mommy and me and that she was my bestest girl. Then I kissed her. She, in turn, beamed all over.

The next grand excursion was a tour of Italy. We booked this tour with a local travel agency, and just as before, we were the only Americans while all the rest were English until we landed at Pisa, Italy, our embarkation city for Italy. This trip was taken in mid-April to celebrate our tenth anniversary.

Upon landing in Pisa, our tour was joined by two other Yanks who were taking the tour to celebrate their thirtieth anniversary on April sixteenth, the same day as ours. They hailed from Los Angeles, but both sets of their parents had migrated to the US from Italy.

We stopped in Pisa to take a sightseeing tour of the city and marveled at the grand Leaning Tower of Pisa. Most of the remainder of our trip was by motor coach.

The next stop was Verona, with the world-renowned balcony, which supposedly was the model used by Shakespeare for the grandiose scene in *Romeo and Juliet*. We enjoyed the Tuscany scenery on our way to Florence (Firenze), the city of Michelangelo,

Leonardo, Machiavelli, and Galileo. I had read the biography of Michelangelo when I was still a teenager stationed in France and was extremely impressed with this artistic genius. I had hoped that one day, I would be able to see in person some of his works. Michelangelo's work in marble was without peer. He carved four Pietas—two remains in Florence (the Cathedral of Florence and Academy Gallery), one in the Sforza Castle in Milan, and the fourth (and probably the most famous one) in Saint Peters in Rome, which we were able to view later in our tour. Michelangelo's most impressive piece was and still remains David, which stands guard at the Gallery of the Academy of Fine Arts in Florence. All the history, artistry, and architecture were overwhelming. Florence remains one of my very favorite cities.

Photo by Alex Ghizila on Unsplash

Rome, the Eternal City, the Capital of Italy was next on our agenda. Rome's history spans twenty-eight centuries. While Roman mythology dates to the founding of Rome at around 750 BC, the site has been inhabited for much longer, making it a major human settlement for almost three millennia and one of the oldest continuously occupied cities in Europe. Perhaps the most famous of all Roman myths was the story of Romulus and Remus, the twins who, according to the fable, had been suckled by a she-wolf. They decided to build a city, but after an argument, Romulus killed his brother, so the city took his name.

Unfortunately, time did not permit us to see all the highlights of Rome. We were rushed through, and I felt lucky we had as much time as we did. The most impressive remains from the ancient world, or time of the Caesars, were the Colosseum (Flavian Amphitheater) dating from 72–80 AD, the Pantheon dating to 27–25 BC, and the Roman Forums—mainly stark columns left upright with little else. Unfortunately, there wasn't time to visit the Roman catacombs (one of the landmarks I had read about and would have like to have visited.) The Catacombs of Rome were underground galleries used for centuries as cemeteries.

The most exciting part of the Rome visit was going to the Vatican and St Peters. Vatican City is an independent country inside Rome, the Eternal City. I was most impressed with the Sistine Chapel, particularly the Sistine Chapel ceiling and Michelangelo's interpretation of *The Creation* and *The Last Judgment*. In Michelangelo's biography, it detailed how he had to lay on his back on top of a crude scaffolding and enumerated the numerous hours it took him to paint the ceiling. How he was able to maintain his perspective on the multitude of figures was absolutely miraculous. Despite the renowned artwork in the Sistine Chapel, Michelangelo always proclaimed himself a sculptor, not an artist. St Peters, the heart of the Catholic faith, was breathtaking. Two of Michelangelo's masterpieces reside there, *The Pieta* (mentioned earlier) and *Moses*.

From Rome, we flew to Venice, the Heart of the World, seemingly afloat on a body of water. Venice, Italian Venezia, city, major seaport, and capital of both the province of Venezia and the region in northern Italy. An island city, it was once the center of a maritime republic. It was considered the greatest seaport in late medieval Europe and the continent's commercial and cultural link to Asia. Venice was unique environmentally, architecturally, and historically, and in its days as a republic, the city was styled *la serenissima* ("the most serene" or "sublime"). It remains a major Italian port in the northern Adriatic Sea and is one of the world's oldest tourist and cultural centers.

Venice, Italy
Photo by Damiano Baschiera on Unsplash

From the Venetian airport, we were bused to the outskirts of the city, where we were met with a flotilla of gondolas that carried us to our hotel room somewhere in the vicinity of St Mark's Square. To say Venice was unique was stating it mildly. Venice was the only city we visited where there were absolutely no mechanical means of transportation for sightseeing. It was either hiking and strolling through the streets and bridges, or we had to hire a gondolier to row us through the canals. The absence of overt noise was almost unsettling—no loud beeping car horns, no lawnmowers, no traffic noise. Occasionally, from our hotel room, we could hear the musical tones of a gondolier's serenade waffling from the Grand Canal. The calmness and quietness were heavenly.

I fondly recall Sue and I stopping at a little outdoor café on St Mark's Square for a bite of lunch, sandwiches, and Coca-Cola. While we were sitting there, a horde of pigeons were fluttering around us, looking for crumbs and begging for something to eat. It seemed like there were hundreds. Reminded me of the movie, *The Birds*. While we munched on our lunch, we had a wonderful view of the Clock Tower with the belfry and the two Mori, which have struck the hours for more than four hundred years. Next to them on the tower was the golden-winged lion, and just below the lion was *The Virgin and Child*. Our scrutiny was rudely interrupted by an unexpected spring shower, so we had to make a mad dash for the nearby awning and wait until the shower had passed before we continued our wandering. Venice was the last Italian city on our tour, and then it was back to RAF Bicester and our babies.

Our third expedition was an excursion arranged by the base's Officers' Wives Club. It was a trip to the Holy Land. In all of my exposure to the Bible through reading and religious services, Sunday School, and Bible Studies, I hardly dreamed I would be retracing the paths of Abraham, David, Jesus, and the multitudes of prophets, soldiers, heroes, and heroines described in the Bible. But there we were, landing in Tel Aviv, and after passing through the security checkpoint and collecting our luggage, we were off to a hotel in Jerusalem, where we were quartered for our stay in Israel.

In Jerusalem there was so much to do, so little time. And where to begin? This was a place that had been immortalized ever since the beginning of the Biblical written word. The Dome of the Rock seemed like the best place to start. One of the most spectacular buildings in the world, the Dome of the Rock, has dominated the skyline of the Old City of Jerusalem since its construction by Caliph Abd al-Malik in 691 AD—so identified with the city is the dome that it frequently served as Jerusalem's landmark. The site is considered the Most Holy (Sacred) to three of the world's major religions: Jewish, Christianity, and Islam.

Directly below the 108-foot-high dome laid es-Saldra, the rock mass from which, according to Muslim tradition, Mohammed ascended to heaven on his night journey to Jerusalem. Jewish and Christian tradition viewed the rock as the place where Abraham nearly sacrificed Isaac (Muslims counter that it was Abraham's other older son, their ancestor Ishmael, instead, that was nearly sacrificed). Almost everyone agrees, though, that Jerusalem's First Temple was built by King Solomon to house the Ark of the Covenant, and the Second Temple was greatly expanded by King Herod, and the temples stood somewhere on the same mount that now holds the Dome of the Rock. This was also the place where Jesus was reported to have chased the merchants and money changers from the temple. Sue and I were permitted to enter the Dome for a fee but not to pray, as only Muslims were allowed to pray inside. However, we did need to remove our shoes before entering. Fortunately, I had on new socks (no holes to expose!). As we looked around inside the Dome I was awed, overpowered by the sense of history that had taken place on the very place on which I was standing. What if I could have some kind of time camera that would simply slip through time and record the action that had taken place here, over the eons.

The Old City of Jerusalem was full of the historical and religious elements that make the city so special. The one-square-kilometer walled area is central to Judaism, Islam, and Christianity. The Western Wall in the Jewish Quarter was the last remaining wall of the Jewish Temple compound. There, we visited the Great Wailing Wall. Also, it is the holiest site in Judaism, and we observed men leaning against the wall, or nodding their heads or kinda rocking back and forth as I assumed they were in some kind of prayer.

Jesus died, was buried, and resurrected in Jerusalem. Jesus reportedly entered the city riding on a donkey from Mount Olives, leading his disciples to the place where he would meet his final earthly fate. Our visit to Mount Olives gave us a bird's-eye view looking down on Jerusalem and the Dome of the Rock.

Next, our tour included a visit to the Church of the Sepulcher in the Old City, which is still shared between many denominations. Then we went to the cave where Jesus was reported to have been buried and where the stone was found to have been rolled away. We also retraced the twelve stations of the cross where Jesus was led to his crucifixion.

Our tour included a visit to one of the local nightclubs, and after a couple of drinks, the chanteuse persuaded me to join their ensemble on stage, where I'm sure I made a complete donkey (spelled with three letters) of meself. Fortunately, we would never see these folks in this life again, with the exception of our fellow travelers.

We had signed up for several day excursions: Bethlehem with the stable and manager; Nazareth, Jesus's home growing up; Sea of Galilee, where Jesus was reported to have walked on water; and Jericho of Joshua and the tumbling-down walls. We were supposed to visit the Red Sea, but terrorist activity was reported in that area, so we were detoured to the Dead Sea and Masada. Most of us had a bout of floating in the Dead Sea. The Dead Sea's salinity was so concentrated that it would have been hard for us to sink; therefore, we floated.

Masada was an ancient fortress in southern Israel's Judean Desert. It was on a massive plateau overlooking the Dead Sea. Fortunately for us, a cable car, as well as a long, winding path, snaked up to the fortifications (no one elected to take the climb). According to Wikipedia, "It was built around 30 B.C. by the Romans as a winter retreat. Around 70 AD Jerusalem lay in ruins and the Jewish community was grossly abused and in disarray. It was reported that 960 Jewish extremists sought refuge at Masada. The Romans turned their attention to taking down Masada with those Jewish renegades, the last community in Judea not under total Roman control, including many women and children. Led by Flavius Silva, a legion of 8,000 Romans built camps surrounding the base, a siege wall, and a ramp on a slope of the Western side of the mountain made of earth and wooden supports. After several months of siege without success, the Romans built a tower on the ramp to try and take out the fortress's wall. When it became clear that the Romans were going to take over Masada, Ben Yair instructed everyone to take their own lives rather than live as Roman slaves. Two women and five children, who hid in the cisterns survived and later told their stories."

Interestingly, it was here in the mountains near Masada and overlooking the Dead Sea that the Dead Sea scrolls were discovered.

Our final adventure from Upper Heyford was to Paris, France, with half a dozen other hospital couples (fourteen of us in all). Paris, France, in my mind, is the most beautiful city in the world! As I was the one who was most familiar with Paris, I was selected to be our tour arranger and guide. I reserved a pension on the Left Bank just off St Germain Du Pres, not far from Notre Dame and fairly near La Sorbonne. It was a treat to revisit some of my old haunts and share them with our friends. There is nothing like sitting in one of the numerous sidewalk cafes munching on le Jambon (French ham sandwich on a baguette [French bread loaf]) and sharing a bottle of French Vin (or maybe bottles). Of course, we visited all of the tourist sites: Le Louvre, Notre Dame, Sainte Chapelle, Sorbonne (the College of Sorbonne established in 1257 as a medical school), Champs-Elysees, Arc de Triomphe, Place de Concorde, L'Opera, Le Jardin de Tuileries, Eiffel Tower, Montmartre, Sacre Coeur, Moulin Rouge, Lido de Paris, Palais Royal. Hotel de Ville, Invalides (Napoleon's final resting place), and there were many others. Our group became so adept at riding the Metro that we could navigate it almost as well as the natives.

While at Upper Heyford, I was selected to be the hospital's social coordinator. In that capacity, I arranged a couple of trips to London's West End to see *Annie* and *A Chorus Line*. These expeditions were open to all hospital personnel. The arranged coach picked us up at the base and delivered us to Piccadilly Circus (London's Times Square). In the evening, after the shows, we were picked up at Piccadilly Circus and returned to the base.

Too soon, our tour in England was over. Sue and our babies packed up and flew out of Heathrow to Columbus, Ohio, to spend the summer with her parents. I stayed behind until my tour was finished in late August. We purchased (ordered) a new Malibu Station Wagon to be picked up in Michigan. Therefore, I flew to Michigan and drove the new vehicle to Newark, Ohio, to be reunited with our little family.

30. CHARLESTON, SOUTH CAROLINA, Y'ALL

We got lucky in Charleston, South Carolina. We were assigned field-grade, almost-new housing that had three bedrooms upon our assignment to the Charleston AFB Clinic. Our house was extraordinarily nice, with a neat back porch, which I enclosed with Plexiglas and converted into a greenhouse. Sue became a woman of leisure again. That is, she resumed the full-time duties of mother, wife, and housekeeper. Timmy was enrolled in the local primary school adjacent to the base within easy walking distance. He also joined Cub Scouts. Mary Beth was enrolled in a small preschool not far from the base, where she learned all kinds of neat things, crafts, etc.

It wasn't long before we visited the humane society and adopted a cat, Taffy. Taffy probably had the most illustrious history of all the pets we have owned. While still a wee kitten, Taffy, unbeknownst to us, crawled up into the dryer vent to escape Sue's parents' dog, Scotty, who was visiting us for a short visit at the time. During the time, she was in the dryer vent, hidden away, someone added a load of wet clothes to the dryer and started the dryer. Fortunately, we were all at the kitchen breakfast table playing Euchre, and we heard this plaintive *Meow! Meow! Meow!* Scotty was up by the dryer, barking and growling and wagging his tail sixty miles a minute. We all thought the kitten was behind the dryer or washing machine or maybe in between the two, hiding away from

Scotty. However, the meows didn't sound like a hiding-away whimper but more like a desperate-call-for-help type of MEOW.

I got down on all fours with a flashlight. Our first intuition was incorrect. I traced the small meowing to the dryer's exhaust. I stopped the dryer, unhooked the dryer vent, and pulled out the soaked, almost-drowned little bitty kitty from the vent. Taffy was soaked through and through, and as I held the poor little thing in my hand, she looked up at me with those pitiful little eyes and gave me a breathy small meow as if to say thank you for saving me. There wasn't a dry hair left on her entire body, and it seemed she was having a hard time breathing. She seemed barely alive, but after a thorough drying off and a little rubbing and petting, she recovered and seemed almost as good as new and started in purring.

Timmy insisted Taffy was more for Mary Beth. He wanted a puppy for himself. As good parents should, we listened to our son's request, but we decided we would like a Lassie type of puppy for him (and us) and found a Collie breeder. We bought our own little Lassie and felt it only fitting because we were in the Deep South to give her a southern handle and called her Ginger Honey. Taking care of Ginger Honey was supposed to have been Timmy's (age 8) responsibility. Oh well. I think Ginger Honey may have had some beaver DNA in her blood because she made some short work of the legs of several of our antique furniture with her gnawing habits. I assume we didn't invest in enough rawhide for her, or perhaps we left her alone too often, and that upset her, and gnawing the legs of what she considered some of our favorite things was her way of getting even or perhaps it was her way to beg for attention.

Our second episode with Taffy occurred when she was a little older. I got this call at work from Sue that something was very wrong with Taffy. Sue thought Ginger Honey might have injured her while they were tussling around. Normally, in such an altercation, Taffy would just run off and hide. Sue told me, "I think Ginger Honey may have broken Taffy's back. Taffy is just splayed out on her stomach in the hallway, moaning, looking all wide-eyed. She seems to be in a lot of pain, and I just don't know what to do." I told Sue to hold on, and I would be right there.

When I got home, work was five minutes away, and taking a break was no problem; after all, I was the boss. I found Taffy in the hallway, all stretched out with her head down and her rear end sticking up in the air. I tried talking with her, but all I got was these pitiful meows and some kinda low moans (cats can moan). We were completely baffled. Dumbfounded. Our friend, the veterinarian, had an office very close to mine, so I called him and explained our situation. So, Dwayne Taylor, our friendly vet, told us to bring her right in to be examined. Dwayne did a careful exam on Taffy and kinda chuckled and told us Taffy was in heat. That was her problem. "But she's too young; she's just a kitten still. So how could she be in heat?" We responded because we were really flabbergasted, I didn't think Taffy was more than six or seven months old.

Dwayne told us, "That may be, but it doesn't take away from the fact she is in heat. Unless you want more little kittens, I would advise neutering her now." Which we agreed to. Even though there was more risk in doing the procedure during the time when Taffy was in heat, Dwayne agreed to do it for us. He operated, and there were no complications, and Taffy was fine for the time being (plus no new kittens, ever).

Next episode, Ann Taylor (Dwayne's wife) was down visiting Sue. Ann and Dwayne lived not far from our house, so she had walked down to our place. It was a pretty chilly day, especially for Charleston, so when their visit was over, Sue offered to give Ann a ride back home. Ann agreed. So far, so good; however, after they were all situated in the car and Sue attempted to start the engine, there was this God-awful noise and a thump. It scared Sue half to death. Sue got out of the car, raised the hood, and discovered Taffy barely hanging on to life. It appeared she had been lying on the motor where it was warmer, and when Sue attempted to start the car, she was hit on the head by the fan blade and suffered other trauma as well. Ann called Dwayne, and he told her to bring Taffy straight into his surgery. Sue called me, and I met them there. Dwayne was a super veterinarian, and after intensive surgery, he saved Taffy's life. She did lose one eye, though, and after that event, even though her name was still Taffy, we started calling her Tuffy. Tuffy was with us through three subsequent relocations: Nellis AFB, Nevada; Wright-Patterson AFB, Ohio; and Brooks AFB, Texas.

In December 1986, we were stationed at Brooks AFB in San Antonio by that time. We had bundled up the kids, packed the car, and set out to celebrate the Season with our folks in Kentucky and Ohio. Before we left, though, we boarded the animals, Ginger Honey and Tuffy, at the local kennel. The day we set out on our trek; the weather was abysmal. It was the worst winter blizzard the area had encountered in decades. My driving goal was to make it to the outskirts of Little Rock for our first night's layover;

however, the weather was so bad, and the highway was so treacherous that I settled for staying in Texarkana. Even though I had driven on snow and ice before, it appeared many of the drivers on the highway had not. Cars were spinning out in front of us, and that helped me to make my decision to stop early. Back in San Antonio, in addition to the snowstorm, they had an ice storm and lost power throughout most of the city, including Green Springs Valley, the neighborhood where we lived and where the kennel was located. It was during this outage that Tuffy escaped from the kennel, never to be heard from again, thus ending our saga with Taffy (Tuffy).

Timmy's introduction to scouting was when he joined the Cub Scouts at Charleston AFB. He had made a friend at school who was in the Cub Scout Pack, where he had joined, whose dad was the pack leader. This friend concocted with Timbo the idea of obtaining a magnifying glass. Timmy came home with the story that he needed a magnifying glass for this science project at school. Sounded logical to me; however, finding a magnifying glass was not an easy task. We couldn't do a Google search in those days. After much effort and searching, I did find the magnifying glass, which I proudly presented to our little boy.

When I got home the next day, Sue met me with the news that Timmy and his friend had been caught behind school using the magnifying glass to set fire to a bunch of leaves and grass. Tim hadn't needed the magnifying glass for a school project after all. I was disappointed. I felt deceived, and worse, I was angry. I mean the fire could have gotten out of control and become something really serious. Could have caught the schoolhouse on fire. I marched Timmy into his room and remonstrated on his behind with the Board of Correction (wooden paddle), an act that I have regretted for the rest of my life, but it can never be undone. At the time, I felt a great deal of remorse for what I had done, and I was hurt, too. I remember my dad would almost go into sobbing fits after giving one of us a severe beating, even though the paddling I had given our Timothy was nothing like what our dad metered out. I had always tried to avoid corporal punishment. I did not want to mimic my dad. I guess I should have applauded Timmy's and his friend's initiative and inventiveness in attempting to carry out a scientific experiment at their young age. But it was the deception, the lie, that I found so wrong. Perhaps I should have found a better method for remonstrating Timbo's indiscretion.

As a family, life for us was calm and peaceful. One or a couple of Timmy's friends had an Atari. That was the beginning of Tim's lifelong addiction to computer gaming and his avid interest in anything to do with computers. Charleston was a beautiful and unique city, and their downtown farmers' market was exceptional. Charleston had lots of good seafood throughout the area. We took the kids swimming in the Atlantic Ocean, went on picnics, and generally had a great time and made some pleasant memories. We were able to take the kids to Disney World in Orlando, Florida, not long after it first opened, and we all had a wonderful time there. Also, we especially liked Padre Island. Sue and I started a gourmet dinner group with the clinic officers and their spouses. Our first dinner was at our house with a French theme. Then, it would rotate to another couple's house. Our second dinner endeavor at our house was a Spanish-themed one. Our commander, Colonel (Dr.) Bargatsie and his wife brought menudo—our first encounter with menudo. The menudo generated a lot of talk (gossip), but usually whenever Dr. Bargatsie was not around. Needless to say, there was plenty of the menudo left over after dinner was over. Of course, almost everyone took some of the menudo leftovers home because after all Dr. Bargatsie, our boss had brought it.

As I mentioned earlier, Mary Beth started preschool shortly after our arrival in Charleston. In 1980, though, she started kindergarten at the primary school Timmy was attending. Towards the end of the school year, we were notified that Sue's dad's bladder cancer was getting progressively worse. In addition, Sue's mom had been diagnosed with breast cancer and needed to have a breast removed. They would both be in the hospital at the same time. Without hesitation, Sue and I both agreed she should go home and take care of her parents. I could and would cope! I could take care of our babies. I would prepare breakfast in the morning, and they would get lunch at school, and I would cut my days a little short so I could be home shortly after they got back from school. I would make sure they were properly dressed and presentable for school before I left for work in the mornings. They both rode their bicycles to and from school. Timmy would be responsible for escorting his little sister. So, Sue flew to Newark via Columbus, Ohio, and all was going as well as could be expected. Of course, we all missed Sue like crazy and were very worried about Grandpa and Grandma Rauch.

You know, in all situations, life is always ready to throw you a curveball. Despite everything going on, I was trying my best to be a good single dad. One afternoon, after getting home from work, I prepared dinner for us and, for a little extra treat, told Timmy and Mary Beth if they cleaned up their plates, we would all go to the Dairy Queen for ice cream. Dinner was progressing well. Timmy was well on his way to having a clean plate, but I noticed Mary Beth was carefully pushing her peas from side to side and then lining them up on one side of her plate in a row in a little design—eating none of them.

"Mary Beth, you have to eat all your dinner if you want ice cream," I told her kindly, hoping that would prod her into partaking of some of her peas. Usually, she was very good about doing whatever I asked her to do.

"But I don't like peas, Daddy," she almost whispered back all the while not looking at me while she left her fork lay idle on her plate with her hands in her lap.

"But peas are good for you. They will help you grow up big and strong and healthy and smart. Now I want you to eat those peas!" Not quite as kindly this time.

Then, she looked up at me with those big, sorrowful, glassy eyes that I so dearly loved, and I could see tears beginning to gather in their corners. Her little lower lip began to protrude and slightly quivered. I could almost hear her thinking, *Daddy, why are you doing this to me? Why are you being so mean to your little sweetie?* I almost relented, but I really felt Mary Beth needed to eat her peas. After all, vegetables were good for her, and if she would just try, I felt confident she would learn to like peas, like me and her big brother, who was cleaning his plate. See!

Seeing as how I was almost raised on a vegetable diet; I didn't think our kids ate enough vegetables. And besides, peas were one of my favorite vegetables. Wouldn't I have passed the taste for peas down to her through my genes? So, I kept insisting she eat at least some of her peas. Mary Beth very hesitatingly raised up a few peas and tentatively fed them into her mouth and gave me a wide-eyed stare. Her face turned a fiery red, and she began gagging.

OK, I was not going to win this one, and I was losing my cool. Was Mary Beth purposely defying me? Was she on purpose trying to make herself sick on those peas? That's what it felt like to me. So, we all went to the Dairy Queen for ice cream, but Mary Beth, my poor little sweetie, got none. Looking back over the years, I've kicked myself numerous times for being an insensitive, cold-hearted brute who mismanaged that situation so badly. To this day, Mary will not eat peas. She avoids them like the plague.

Here comes the next curveball while Sue was taking care of her parents, and I was single parenting. It was after work, and I was busy preparing dinner (but with no peas this time). The kids were out playing in the yard with a couple of little boys their age who lived a couple of doors down the street when, all of a sudden, they came running into the kitchen, Mary Beth bawling and clutching her arm.

"Daddy, it really hurts!"

I examined her arm. It was a little red, but there were no bruises or swelling and no breaks in the skin. I picked up Mary Beth and cuddled her and rocked her and told her she was my little sweetie, that she was OK, and that everything was going to be alright. I gave her a baby aspirin, put a small ice pack loosely on her arm, and laid her in front of the TV to watch cartoons while I finished dinner. We had dinner, but Mary Beth still complained about her arm hurting and she hadn't eaten very much.

After dinner, both kids had their bath—Mary Beth's somewhat gingerly as I was very careful while washing her, paying particular attention to her injured arm. Afterwards, we had bedtime stories and went to bed. The next morning, I prepared breakfast. We ate, and I helped Mary Beth to get dressed. She was still having a little pain, but not so much, but she seemed to have limited mobility in her hurt arm. After breakfast and making sure they were ready for school, all was not great, but it seemed alright, so I headed off to work and left them to get themselves to school.

I had not been at work for more than a few minutes when I got a call from Timmy.

"Daddy, Mary Beth can't ride her bike," Timmy worriedly told me.

This was going to be more serious than I thought.

I told Timmy to stay right there. I was on my way home. Before I left the office, though, I called one of our flight surgeons, gave her a thumbnail sketch of what was going on, and asked her if she could see Mary Beth. She quickly agreed and said to bring her right in. I found the kids in the carport waiting for me. I bundled Mary Beth into the car and sent Timmy on his way to school.

My flight surgeon friend examined Mary Beth very closely and told me she couldn't be sure, but we needed to have X-rays. When the X-rays came back, they showed a green split fracture of the humerus. Right there in my friend's office, I lost it. It was all I could do to keep from bawling, but in spite of my macho control, there were a couple of tears that trickled down my cheeks. What in the world kind of daddy was I to put my darling baby girl through such an ordeal and not recognize she needed medical help? I mean, I had had some medical training.

I was not doing well in Parenting 101. On the other hand, Mary Beth seemed OK except for her hurt arm; quite chipper, in fact. Actually, it appeared she enjoyed being the center of attention. We were sent directly over to the Navy's orthopedic surgeon across town to be reassessed. No arm in a cast, thank goodness, but Mary Beth had to wear a shoulder sling for the next several weeks.

Work for me went well. The previous bioenvironmental engineer had not fared well at Charleston. It was always easier to follow a poor performer than one who was really outstanding. One tended to be compared against one's predecessor. The whole bioenvironmental engineering program had been in shambles. With the cooperation of my staff, we started case files on each industrial shop with detailed data and sampled potential contaminants as required. Under my tutelage, the staff prepared reports, evaluations, and studies on environmental problems. My first efforts were to completely revamp the program and perform baseline evaluations on all the shops. We conducted a complete hazardous materials inventory and provided comprehensive evaluations so corrective actions was prioritized. With that new data, I was able to show that many of the occupational medical examinations being performed were not required and were unnecessary. Therefore, the clinic was able to eliminate nearly half of those examinations and devote those efforts to other more pressing programs.

Also, the clinic's disaster preparedness was itself a disaster and was floundering. I volunteered to take on the task and rewrote the guide and all the individual checklists. I started the clinic doing the mandated exercises, and we even did some joint exercises with the Navy, which got us some favorable press with the local news. It all paid off! When the Air Force inspector general's team arrived, we withstood their intense scrutiny and, for our efforts, were awarded Outstanding in both bioenvironmental engineering and disaster preparedness.

Additionally, I was selected as a seminar leader for the base's Air Command and Staff College Seminar. Everyone in the class finished the seminar and received their diplomas. But perhaps the most significant thing that occurred professionally to me at Charleston was that I was selected for Major two years before my peers; a real honor and completely unexpected!

Towards the end of the school year, we learned that when Timmy graduated from his elementary school for the next year, he would be bused to a school in the least desirable part of Charleston. The school had a terrible reputation for gangs and fights, and their academics were at the bottom of South Carolina's totem pole. At that time, South Carolina was ranked forty-ninth scholastically in the entire fifty states, only in front of Mississippi. That was just not acceptable to us, and Sue and I were not happy about the prospect of Timmy being bused away like that!

We searched for a private school and found one that was highly recommended by other officer couples of our acquaintance. Private schools would eat into our finances, and we would need to arrange our own transportation. However, we were looking out for the best interest of our Timmy. We visited the school and obtained the registration papers, which we took home with us. Over the weekend, I completed the registration, we both signed the forms, and I made out a check for the initial deposit. On Monday, I took the whole package to work with me to mail because the post office was near my office.

However, before I had the opportunity to mail the registration, I got a call from Colonel Bayer, our senior bioenvironmental (BEE) advisor at the Air Force's Surgeon General's Office. He told me he really needed me to be reassigned to Las Vegas, Nevada—Nellis Air Force Base—where there had been some difficulty with the current BEE and the environmental health officer. He needed someone of my temperament and reputation to be posted there to get things straightened out and get everything back on an even keel.

After consulting with Sue, how could I have said no? The school busing problem would be solved, and we would be on our way west to the desert one more time.

31. NELLIS AFB, HOME OF THE THUNDERBIRDS

On our way to Nellis AFB, we went via Ohio and Kentucky to visit our folks before taking our long journey West. Sue's mother appeared to be recuperating pretty well; her dad had his good days and not-so-good days. His prognosis was questionable. Going so far away with Sue's parents in their condition was our major concern.

The trip to Nevada was interesting with Sue and me, Timmy and Mary Beth, and Ginger Honey and Tuffy. Lots of potty breaks for kids and dog. Tuffy had a litter box, but when she did number two, it was suffocating inside the Malibu, so at our earliest convenience, we would stop and clean the cat box. Probably the most egregious thing was that Tuffy decided to serenade us almost the whole trip with her wailing, plaintiff meows, and unfortunately, we didn't have earplugs, and the radio did little to drown her out. I'm not sure why she felt she needed to be so vociferous. I guess she didn't like driving, or maybe it was the dry heat, or perhaps it was just being cooped up with all of us, or perhaps she just needed to make her opinion known.

We arrived at Nellis AFB on May 30, 1981, and boy was it ever hot. Daytime temperatures ranged up to 110, and it was rare for them to get down below 90 at night. If it was necessary to leave the car parked in the sun, we needed a towel to cover the steering wheel; otherwise, the steering wheel would be so hot it felt like your hands were being scalded whenever it was necessary to touch it. Therefore, we always used a sunscreen to cover the windshield and a towel to cover the steering wheel. Obviously, acclimatization on our part was required. Mary Beth and Timmy seemed to adapt better than Sue and I. Fortunately, we were able to get on base temporary family quarters, which were not great, but we managed. Permanent housing was another matter altogether. Even though I was a Major-select, we did not qualify for field-grade housing and were only offered company-grade housing, which, after leaving our spacious house in Charleston, felt like we were being sent to the slums. We would have tried to buy a house and even looked at some houses and some new construction, but prices were beyond my pay grade, particularly when one considered the interest rate was hovering around 17–18 percent at that time. So, we accepted a wee place, 1,250 square feet on base. The yard wasn't much bigger than the house. We were very close and more than a little friendly in that house on Nellis AFB. Cramped is a better description. One of the saving graces was the kids' school was just across the street from our housing unit, within easy walking distance.

Southern Nevada, Las Vegas in particular, was like no other place we had ever been stationed. It was almost like being in another country or another world. Even though we had lived in the desert in Arizona, this was even more drastic. The topography was alien. Vegetation was almost as scarce as hens' teeth, and most of what was there amounted to scattered creosote bushes and Joshua trees.

One-armed bandits (slot machines) were on the other end of the spectrum and had invaded the place. They were everywhere: in convenience stores, Kmart's, gas stations, grocery stores, not to mention the plethora of casinos. And it was the unseemly hot temperatures, as high as 100, plus the mid-teens, that made it an effort to even breathe. I guess Tucson had been a prequel, good training for the Las Vegas environment.

We hadn't settled in our new adobe long before Sue convinced me we needed a piano for Timmy and Mary Beth to start taking lessons, never mind that we already had wall-to-wall furniture. So, we went looking to purchase a piano. I thought because the Baldwin pianos were built in Cincinnati, it would be nice to own one of theirs; plus, their reputation was superb. We went to the Baldwin Piano Company store, found an upright piano we liked, and applied for a credit purchase. No deal! Baldwin turned our credit application down. It didn't matter that I had a secure, steady job employed by the U.S. Air Force, had been selected for Major, and had an unblemished credit report. It appeared the Baldwin Piano Company didn't consider military folks good credit risks.

Then we went down the street to the Yamaha store and bought their upright piano with no problem getting a credit purchase as easy as you please. Finally, the kids were able to start their music lessons. I'll have to admit, I shed few tears when, a few years later, the Baldwin Piano Company went bankrupt! I can carry a grudge as good as a hound dog carries fleas. Anyway, both kids did start their music lessons in Las Vegas.

There weren't a whole lot of family-type activities in the surrounding areas outside of scouting. We did explore Hoover Dam and picnic on Mount Charleston, where the temperatures were much cooler than what we were experiencing in the Las Vegas basin. Another interesting place we explored was Valley of Fire State Park, which was a vivid land of bold cliffs of red and white sandstone set amid the grandeur of the desert. The stories of powerful earth forces, adapting life forms, and early man were revealed in this unique parkland. We found one of the most fascinating aspects of the park was the many petroglyphs pecked into the joint faces and boulders throughout the Valley of Fire. These ancient pieces of rock, in which geometric and naturalistic designs were fortunately preserved, were the most prominent and startling of earlier cultures in existence.

The only kid-friendly casino in the great gambling empire at that time was Circus Circus. We did take the kids there a couple of times.

I mustn't leave out our trip to the Grand Canyon, one of the seven natural wonders of the world! I'm not sure what an impact the Grand Canyon made on the kids, but it certainly made a great impact on me, even though it was Sue's and my second trip to the canyon.

I would be remiss in leaving out a small incident that happened on our way to the canyon. We had only been traveling for a few hours. Two, three, or maybe even four through the deserted desert without a living creature in sight, less on any kind of human habitation. I do admit my foot was a bit heavy, but there was nothing there, almost no sign of traffic. It appeared we were lost from any kind of civilization. I looked over at the family, and everyone was snoozing. Perhaps I was lured into a false sense of security, for when I happened to glance in my rearview mirror, I saw emergency lights rapidly coming up behind me. At first, I thought there must be some kind of accident ahead. But nope, it was me. I was being pulled over for speeding in the middle of nowhere.

Long story short, I got a speeding ticket near what I was to later learn was the small town of Christmas, Arizona. It was certainly not a gift that I had been dreaming about or anticipating; actually, one I would have gladly done without. After returning from our little adventure, I had to report to my boss and explain about getting the speeding ticket. After my diatribe about the ticket, my boss, Lt Col (Dr.) Bell gave me a funny look and a small chuckle and then explained he also had been bequeathed a speeding ticket over the same weekend and near the same place where mine had been bestowed. It appeared the highway near Christmas, Arizona, was a well-known speeding trap; obviously not well known to us.

The Grand Canyon was an awesome spectacle of nature's grandeur, a classic example of erosion unequaled anywhere on Earth. The multi-hued cliffs and slopes of the tremendous chasm descended in a timeless panorama, culminating unbelievably in the dark and somber cliffs a mile below, where the Colorado River continued to carve deeper and deeper into the earth's crust.

During our tour at Nellis AFB, both kids joined the scouts. Mary Beth started Girl Scouts (Brownies), and Timothy graduated from Cub Scouts to Boy Scouts and, after two subsequent moves, would achieve his Eagle rank. I did some camping out with Timmy and his Boy Scout Troops, and before we left Nellis AFB, Timmy went by himself with his troop by bus to Utah for a big Jamboree-type campout for a week. On their return, Timmy's scoutmaster shared with me how well Timmy had done, how well he was adapting to scouting, and how mature he was for his size and age. He expected Timmy to have an Eagle Scout rank in the future. Turned out he was right.

On January 18, 1982, the four "Diamond" aircraft—Thunderbird #1, 2, 3, and 4 (tail numbers 68-8156, 8175, 8176 & 8184)—were training for an air show at Davis-Monthan Air Force Base, Arizona, flying over the nearby Indian Springs. Climbing side-by-side for several thousand feet in a slow, backward loop, then hurtling down at more than 400 mph, leveling off at about 100 feet. In a maneuver called a "line-abreast loop," a malfunction in the lead plane, Thunderbird #1, occurred. Instead of coming out of the dive as planned, the lead Thunderbird hit the desert floor and practically disintegrated on impact. At the speed they were going, the following three planes could not correct and followed in turn, hitting the desert floor and suffering the same fate. There were no survivors. It was reported by an eyewitness that it happened so fast he couldn't tell if one hit sooner because it looked like all of them hit at the same time.

One of the pilot's daughters was in Mary Beth's Girl Scout troop, of which Sue was co-leader. Her troop purchased a tree and planted it in honor of the pilots killed in this awful accident, particularly the father of the little girl in Mary Beth's troop.

During my tour at Nellis AFB, I was responsible for monitoring community and work environments for three wings and several tenant organizations serving a base population of over 11,000 military and 2,500 civilian employees. I provided medical reviews for all engineering plans and programs and ensured base potable water was free of impurities and met regulatory requirements. I conducted a special study on the residual effects of using spent (low-level) radioactive materials in munitions used for penetrating tanks and other armored weaponry. As the assistant medical readiness officer, I revised and updated hospital disaster response plans and annexes to base plans and response procedures to hydrazine incidents, ensuring appropriate responses to actual incidents with minimal impact.

One of the major ongoing exercises held at Nellis AFB was Red Flag, where military teams were challenged to prove their flying (fighting) prowess and expertise. This more than often caused flights to go supersonic, which in turn caused some window glass breakage and claims from assorted causes from ranchers, farmers, and villagers underneath the prescribed flying areas. Because I was the designated noise expert, I often got involved in these claims. Also, I augmented Air Force medical inspection efforts at three other facilities.

In April, we received a call from Sue's mother that her dad was losing ground. His prognosis had taken a turn for the worse. He was being assigned to Hospices, and it would only be a matter of time now. If we wanted to see him alive, we had better come back home, pronto. Sue and the kids flew back over spring break. In the interim, I applied for a humanitarian reassignment, which was approved.

On May 30th, 1982, we all departed with our cat and dog in our Chevrolet Malibu from Nellis AFB. One year to the day ended our stay at Las Vegas, Nevada, to be reassigned to Wright-Patterson AFB, Ohio.

32. 1982-1986 SECOND ASSIGNMENT TO WRIGHT-PATTERSON

We were overjoyed to get back to Ohio in early June 1982 and to be near our parents, especially now that Sue's dad's health had been deteriorating so badly and so fast. It was a real treat for the kids to enjoy their grandparents.

Before I started work at my new job at Wright Patterson AFB, we needed to find a place to live. Adequate base housing seemed to be out of the question. The only options left for us were to either rent or buy a place. We had been led to believe the best school district in the area was Beavercreek. Unfortunately, there didn't appear to be any place in Beavercreek for rent that met our needs. Our only option left was to purchase a home.

When we looked at buying in Las Vegas the previous year, the interest rate was 18 percent, which made payments beyond our reach. Thank goodness the rates had dropped to around 12 percent, which, if we found the right house in our price range, buying might now be doable, and also, if Sue rejoined the labor market, a requirement. We agreed Sue would rejoin the civil service cadre in order for us to purchase a home for the family.

However, when we found a house that we liked and could afford, we were still short five thousand dollars for the down payment. Sue agreed we could ask her parents for the loan (my parents wouldn't have that kind of money to loan us), so with much trepidation, considering the circumstances, we did. When we asked Sue's parents for the five-thousand-dollar loan, I made it quite clear we would be more than happy to repay the loan at the current rate of 12 percent interest. Sue's dad readily agreed to give us the loan. Her mother was a little more hesitant, though. We later learned she had told Sue's brother that would be the last she would ever see of that money. We were fortunate, though, to be able to pay off the loan in less than a year, including the 12 percent interest.

While we were waiting to close on the house, we drove Sue's parents to Beavercreek to see our prospective new home. Because we had not closed yet, we could only show them the house from the outside. Sue's dad seemed to take a real interest in looking at the house, and it seemed to perk up his spirits. He took his cane and measured the garage door to make sure that our cars would fit inside. Unfortunately, this would be his last car trip away from Newark. Circumstances prevented us from closing on our new home until September 30, 1982, too late to show it off to Sue's dad.

While we waited for our house to close, we took up temporary residence in a Beavercreek motel so that we could enroll the kids in the Beavercreek school system. I extended my leave time as long as I could but finally had to start work at Wright-Patterson AFB the first week in September.

On weekends, we visited Sue's folks. Per usual, on the 11–12 September weekend, we went to Sue's parents' house. Sue's dad's condition had continued to deteriorate. He was now bedridden, on a heavy dose of pain medications, and was barely coherent. I think he was able to recognize Sue, but I'm not sure he recognized the rest of us.

It seemed we had hardly settled in for the night, and I was really having difficulty finding sleep. I may have dozed off in the early hours of Sunday morning, September 12th. All I know is that I heard this agonizing moan from Sue's mom in the next room. "He's gone!" she cried out. I hurriedly pulled on my trousers and rushed into Sue's parents' bedroom to see if I could revive her dad or help in any way at all. Unfortunately, he was not breathing and had no pulse. I attempted CPR to no avail. Sue's mom was right: Sue and Bob's dad was gone.

A special sensitive memory remains somewhere in the back of my mind. It occurred shortly after the passing of Sue's dad. There were a lot of arrangements to be made before the funeral, so we decided Sue would stay and help Bob and her mom with whatever needed to be done. I needed to return to work (even though I could have taken emergency leave) and the kids needed to be out of underfoot and in school.

Mary Beth's class was scheduled to have their annual pictures taken that particular week. Oh boy! Sue had instructed me how I was to dress Mary Beth: dress, shoes, socks, etc. I mean, I was OK with the idea. I had had the kids by myself before. I could cook for them, feed them (even take them out to the local McDonald's if necessary), but what I was not, was a beautician-type hairdresser by any stretch of the imagination. So, getting Mary Beth ready for her class photo went pretty smoothly, all things considered, until we came to her hair.

Mary Beth had a full head of hair (thicker than blackberry brambles in a briar patch), and no matter what I attempted to do with it, it just wouldn't take any kind of shape that I was intending or attempting. I tried and tried as time was running out too quickly. It was time for Mary Beth's bus. I did the best I could, but my best efforts left a lot to be desired. When I was just a kid, one of my favorite stories was *The Little Match Girl*. Well, I kinda felt that Mary Beth's hair musta looked somewhat like I envisioned the Little Match Girl's hair looked like, much to my consternation, and unfortunately, Mary Beth's school pictures kinda proved that assertion.

Household goods were delivered to our new home in Beavercreek, and then we began the chore of unpacking and getting everything into some kind of sequence and order. The kids continued in school and Sue returned to working in the civil service arena in Area B near my office. However, Sue's return to the workforce necessitated adding another automobile to our inventory: a Toyota Corolla for a whopping $6,000-plus. The little Corolla proved to be a worthwhile investment, as it became Mary Beth's car to drive when she much later enrolled in College at Texas A&M University, and then we later sold it after her graduation. It proved to be a real workhorse.

There are a few things that occurred in Beavercreek worth mentioning. Both kids continued piano lessons until Tim decided piano lessons were no longer for him. He joined the orchestra in middle school and took up the violin. Mary Beth, though, did continue piano lessons and also continued horseback riding, which she had started in England. Tim joined the Flying Fish at the Wright-Patterson Youth Swim Team, so began his interest in swimming. Tim also joined a softball league. And Tim became gainfully employed. He had a paper route where he managed to deliver the *Dayton Newspaper* on his bicycle around the neighborhood. The most challenging part of the job was making deliveries on the Sunday paper early (and I do mean early) and adding all the advertisements and supplements to the paper, which I always helped him do. The papers had to have the advertisements and supplements added before the papers could be delivered. Tim also complimented all these activities by mowing a few lawns as well.

It was July 1983. Tim and I were camping with the Boy Scouts. The first night, I felt something bumping me under my cot, and lo and behold, a big raccoon was fervently scratching at my duffel bag, which I had stored under my cot. Silly me, I had brought some peanuts to share with Timbo and his friends and had packed them in my duffel bag. Well, obviously, the raccoon wanted to be cut in as well. At first, I wasn't sure what was going on beneath me but suspected that I might have a black bear under my cot, which gave me an acute case of tachycardia. The critter was attacking my duffel bag with such frenzy that I was sure the bag would soon be scratched to tatters, plus the thing was so rambunctious I was feeling all these bumps and grinds beneath me. I must say I was quite alarmed!

But, upon getting my flashlight out, I discovered it was not a bear but a raccoon who was not easily deterred. He obviously had been around the block a few times before and was not easily hustled off. It appeared he was used to us humans invading his territory and knew we usually carried goodies in our possession. Goodies in which he would gladly share, even help himself to. I was somewhat leery of the raccoon. You never knew about rabies. However, by waving my flashlight at him and whacking him with my pillow, he finally gave up, but not before bellowing a few evil, unsolicited growls back at me before he scurried off.

I had not planned to stay for the whole outing, so after four days, I drove back home, where I received a telephone call from our 8-year-old daughter, Mary Beth, who was enjoying some time with her grandparents in Newport, Kentucky. She told me my Aunt Cassie, my mother's maiden sister who lived a couple of doors down from my mother, who was a little slow mentally and had had some mental concerns, and had been in and out of hospitals for most of her life (because of them) had been discovered unconscious, had been taken to the hospital and was in a coma.

Mentally, Aunt Cassie had been more like a child and was almost like one of my siblings during all the time I had spent with her and Grandma and Grandpa. During her mental lapses, she was not always coherent. I recall on one of my visits to her in the hospital, she kept rambling on about how they had killed her dead—they had killed her dead, she kept repeating. Around the time she had been committed was a Fourth of July holiday, and there had been a lot of fireworks being let off around her house which had bothered and confused her in her agitated state. I believe she thought she had been shot. Hence the statement, "They killed me dead." To make a long story short, one of my favorite people in the world, Aunt Cassie, passed from this life on July 17, 1983.

Back to raccoons. Mary Beth was in Girl Scouts and was on a campout with her troop. Unfortunately, it was mating season for raccoons. Mary Beth needed to visit the little girl's room, which was some distance from her tent, and on her way, she managed to interrupt an amorous raccoon. The raccoon, displeased by the invasion, attacked Mary Beth and bit her. We were concerned about rabies, and Sue was pretty adamant that I should take Mary Beth to the base and get her rabies shots.

When I worked in the Emergency Room nearly a decade previously, giving rabies shots was an excruciating process. It was the old duck embryo series of fourteen injections administered into the abdomen and was very painful. Therefore, I was a little more cautious about rushing her to the hospital. Sue prevailed, and we did go to the hospital's ER, where I received a good scolding from the physician for even hesitating to bring Mary Beth in for the rabies series. Rabies prophylaxis was, by that time, a much simpler series of five injections of intramuscular shots (deltoid and was almost painless.)

I began my assignment as deputy director of bioenvironmental engineering services for one of the largest bioenvironmental services in the Air Force but was soon promoted to director upon the reassignment of the then-current director and almost simultaneously pinned on Major. This was a big time of transition for the bioenvironmental engineering career field, as the Air Force needed to quickly comply with expanding Environmental Protection and Occupational Safety and Health Standards.

The enormity of the scope of the workload to accomplish these tasks was almost mind-boggling. My first effort was to devise a plan, establish goals, assign responsibilities, and measure progress. On our Air Force inspector general evaluation, our team received high marks for leadership and progress but outlined that the workload was simply overwhelming for the number of assigned personnel, which resulted in us almost doubling our assigned staff sometime later after the inspection was over.

Some of the more interesting areas we were responsible for were the Air Force Material Headquarters, a large division that required a top-secret clearance for entry and for performing assigned duties; acquisition for all Air Force weapon systems and related materials; Research and Development; the Air Force Institute of Technology; the Aerodynamics' Laboratory; the Inertial Guidance and Calibration Center for guided missiles; and the Air Force Museum, which not only rivaled what the Smithsonian in Washington, DC, offered, but substantially exceeded it.

Additionally, I was selected as a seminar leader for the base's Air War College Seminar. Everyone in the class finished the seminar and received their diplomas. Then, in early 1986, I received notification that I had been selected for promotion to Lieutenant Colonel and also received a call from our associate chief telling me he needed me to head up the Industrial Hygiene Branch at the Air Force Occupation and Environmental Health Laboratory in San Antonio, Texas.

33. SAN ANTONIO
9/1986–3/1991 OEHL

Our moving truck delivered our household goods to
our new home in San Antonio in early August 1986,
and it was stiflingly hot. We had purchased a new two-
story home in Green Springs Valley a couple of miles
north of the San Antonio airport. I helped sort,
unpack, and place most of the delivered items and
then returned to Wright-Patterson AFB to finish my
tour there. We wanted to get the kids moved in before
the school year started so we could get them enrolled
in school. Timmy started off as a freshman at
MacArthur High School, and Mary Beth enrolled as a
sixth grader at Bradley Middle School.

Timmy continued participating in the orchestra with
his violin, joined the MacArthur swim team, at first
quit the Boy Scouts, and later rejoined the Boy Scouts
and went on to earn his Eagle badge. In 1989, Timmy
graduated from high school and enrolled at Texas
A&M. I kinda insisted he declare his major in
electrical engineering upon entering the university.
He tried it for one semester and then told me the
electrical engineering curriculum was not for him. He
wanted to declare his major in computer science. I
wasn't totally convinced but relented, and it has
turned out to be the right choice and has been a real
blessing, for he has excelled in his chosen specialty
beyond our wildest expectations. During summers, he
worked as a lifeguard at the Brooks AFB Swimming
Pool. We let Timmy take our old Malibu to college to
drive until his final year when we bought him a small
Ford truck on credit with the stipulation, he would

take over payments whenever he became gainfully employed. After college, he got his first full time job at Radio Shack Headquarters in Fort Worth, Texas.

Mary Beth continued horseback riding, took up the flute at Bradley Middle School, and joined Flags at MacArthur High School. In 1993, Mary Beth graduated from MacArthur High School and also enrolled at Texas A&M with her older brother Timmy. Mary Beth was pretty adamant that her major was going to be genetics. She had originally played with the idea of veterinary medicine and had even volunteered time to assist our local veterinarian. Her next thing was pharmacy, and she again volunteered some time at the Kelly AFB Clinic Pharmacy, but after a chat with a former boss of mine who shared with us his prediction that the future world of pharmacy would all be run by robots, she turned her goal to genetics. She has kept her goal and, like her older brother, succeeded in her chosen field and has done really well and made us proud, a real professional and expert in her field.

During summer breaks, Mary Beth worked at Burger King and then at Jack-in-the-Box. I had told Mary that I expected her to obtain her college degree before she could even consider marriage. Oh well, so much for that. She met her future husband, our dear son-in-law, in her first year at Texas A&M. Curiously, they both had attended Bradley Middle School and MacArthur High School together even though they did not know each other then. Craig, our son-in-law, was on the same swim team as Tim during their high school years. Mary completed her degree requirements in record time, three and one-half years, so that she and Craig would graduate together in December 1996, and then they got married on

December 28, 1996, a couple of weeks after their graduation. Craig was a year ahead of Mary Beth but extended his tenure to four and one-half years, so he and Mary would graduate at the same time, I'm guessing. Mary did get her degree before tying the knot, and I was so proud of her and Craig. For a wedding gift, we give them Sue's Celica.

After the dust settled on our move back to San Antonio, Texas, Sue rejoined the civil service workforce as administrative assistant to Dr. Leo Cropper, a veterinarian who worked at Brooks AFB as well. Leo, his wife, and three daughters were all stationed with us at RAF Upper Heyford, England. At Upper Heyford, they were members of our little Gourmet Group. Leo and his wife had gotten divorced in the interim, and Leo had custody of their three daughters. Sue worked there for about a year, but when she had an opportunity for a part-time position as an editorial assistant with the Army Audit Agency, which was located much nearer to our home, she took it. When the Army Agency's editor retired, Sue applied for the editor's job and was promoted to the editor's position, which was a big boost for her career and provided her with much better pay.

I enjoyed my new position as a branch chief at the Industrial Hygiene Consultation Branch at the AF Occupational Environmental Health Laboratory (OEHL) Branch. Shortly after my assignment to AFOEHL, I assumed the grade of Lieutenant Colonel (LT Col). I had about twenty-three young, very bright engineers on my staff as consultants ranging from Lieutenants to Majors to provide assistance to all of our AF bases, which might be having industrial hygiene concerns. This included directing technical and administrative activities for engineers and technicians responsible for providing industrial hygiene consultative services to bases, major commands, and Air Staff offices.

I planned, scheduled, and directed field surveys to meet customer needs. I reviewed/rewrote Air Force Occupational Health standards for noise, hydrazine, and JP-8 jet fuel and ensured those standards met or exceeded regulatory requirements. I managed the Industrial Hygiene Equipment Loan Program, including the selection, evaluation, procurement, calibration, and maintenance of survey equipment necessary for the AF's industrial hygiene programs. Also, in my branch, we had the genesis of the Computerized Occupational Hazardous Materials Program, which was later adopted Air Force-wide.

Midway through my tenure at the Occupational and Environmental Health Laboratory, I was asked to assume the duties of the assistant division chief of the Analytical Services Division, where I took on many of the administrative duties, parceled out special assignments, and generally monitored the workload for the lab. Then, towards the end of that assignment, I was asked to take on a new challenge: as division chief of the Fiscal and Administrative Division, when the current chief was unexpectedly reassigned. This was a bit of a new ball game for me, but by that time, I had had a lot of experience managing and handling people, and even though paper pushing was not my favorite thing to do, I felt complimented that our commander had enough trust in me to select me for the position.

When the lab received a tasking for a senior representative to act as a consultant for the USAF Surgeon General for Team Spirit in South Korea, our commander selected me. Team Spirit was a joint tactical training exercise held between US forces (Navy, Marine Corps, Army, and Air Force) and South Korean Forces that ended in the mid-1990s. My instructions were to fly from San Antonio, Texas, to Offutt AFB, Nebraska, to meet up with the hospital cadre that would be OPR for the month-long effort in Korea.

The next evening, after I arrived in Nebraska, we boarded a C-141 with net sling seats crammed together, and I was seated next to the commander (another Lt Col), where we had just a little more leg room. First stop at LAX Airport, California, then Hawaii, and next Midway Atoll, with our final stop in Seoul, Korea. From Seoul, we were bused to Busan (pronounced Pusan), where we would be living for the next thirty days in large government-issued tents (Tent City). We had one tent that functioned as our BX, and there were two other large tents—one for men and one for the ladies—containing toilet and showering facilities. Oh, joy. The latrine facilities were a brisk walk from the Command Tent, where my cot was stationed by the commander's.

The hospital commander had been in Korea before; actually, his wife was Korean, and he dearly loved garlic, which abounded in abundance in Korea. Garlic was a seemingly necessary ingredient to the local diet as it was used freely in Korean diets/recipes. We did have a permanently installed hospital that was used for the exercise and would be available should there be an actual conflict and the hospital be put in operational status.

For the Team Spirit Exercise, the pretend war was ensuing, and patients were brought to us for triage, treatment, and even surgery. Also, within the hospital facility, we did have a kitchen and dining facility, where we took most of our meals. As the Surgeon General representative, I had a vehicle and two technicians assigned to me, so I was able to visit and evaluate most of the military (Army as well as Air Force) in South Korea and, in doing so, was able to view a large portion of the South Korean topography. Curiously, burials were done vertically rather than horizontally, and in most backyards, I saw rather husky, tethered, big dogs that I was told were being raised for consumption. The stench from the fields was a bit overpowering. Again, I was told toilet refuse was scattered over the fields to supplement fertilizer. One highlight of the mission: I was able to take a tour up to the demilitarized zone and hear the propaganda din being bellowed across from the North Korean side.

During Desert Shield/Desert Storm, I was tasked to substitute for the Tactical Air Command (TAC) bioenvironmental engineer who had been deployed to the desert. It was certainly an interesting time. My biggest challenge was finding backfills for bioenvironmental engineering officers and technicians who had been deployed to the desert. It was a matter of calling up bioenvironmental engineering specialists from the Air National Guard and Air Force Reserve Units.

For the most part, everyone was cooperative and was more than willing to jump right in and serve their country wherever they were needed. I had several volunteers who wanted to go to the desert itself. Then I still had the normal duties of taking care of command duties and found out I was pretty good at that, too. The worst thing was being away from my family, even though the TAC surgeon general was generous with giving me time off to return to San

Antonio, even going so far as to give me a ride on his plane whenever he had meetings or business in the South Texas area. (I guess it's beginning to sound like I couldn't hold down a job, or they didn't know where or how to best use me?)

While living in San Antonio, both Tim and Mary reached their 16th birthdays and obtained their driver's licenses. Tim obtained his driver's license in July 1987, which was a big relief, for it meant I no longer had to get up and chauffeur him to his 6 a.m. swimming practice every weekday morning. As I have mentioned before, we had always tried to make birthdays special in our family, so for Tim's 16th birthday, we planned a trip for the whole family (we were concerned that this might be our last opportunity to include Tim in the family outings, for kids tended to grow away from parents as they grew older; thank goodness for us, that has not occurred) to Yellowstone National Park. We took I-10 through El Paso, New Mexico, to Tucson, Arizona, where Tim was born and spent the first five months of his life.

We visited Davis Monthan AFB (Tim was born in the hospital on the base), drove by 4945 Adams Street, the house where we lived when Tim was an infant, and then visited the Grand Canyon National Park, which was considered to be one of the Seven Wonders of the natural world and was home to much of the immense Grand Canyon, with its layered bands of red rock revealing millions of years of geological history.

Just north of the Grand Canyon, we drove through Zion National Park, a southwest Utah nature preserve distinguished by Zion Canyon's steep red cliffs. Our Zion Canyon scenic drive cut through its main section, leading to forest trails along the Virgin River. The river flowed to the Emerald Pools, which had waterfalls and a hanging garden, and then on to Salt Lake City, Utah, and the Mormon Tabernacle, followed up by the Great Salt Lake.

Before we knew it, we were in Jackson, a town in Wyoming's Jackson Hole Valley, home to three ski areas: Jackson Hole Mountain Resort, Snow King Mountain Resort, and Grand Targhee Resort. The Town Square featured arches made of shed antlers from the nearby National Elk Refuge. The National Museum of Wildlife Art had works by Andy Warhol and Georgia O'Keeffe. Northward were the peaks of Grand Teton National Park, as well as the vast Yellowstone National Park Great Salt Lake. Following on, we checked into our lodging inside Yellowstone National Park.

Yellowstone National Park was the US's first national park and was considered the flagship of the National Park Services. It was a nearly 3,500-square-mile wilderness recreation area atop a volcanic hot spot. The park is located mostly in Wyoming; however, the park does spread into parts of Montana and Idaho, too. Yellowstone's most famous geyser is Old Faithful, but it had what seemed to be hundreds of other geysers (actually more than 300).

In addition to the geysers, there are a lot of hot springs, some bubbling, one of the world's largest calderas with over 10,000 thermal features, dramatic canyons, alpine rivers with some breathtaking waterfalls (nearly 300), lush forests, and home to a whole bunch of critters. Some of these include bears, wolves, bison, elk, and antelope. We encountered herds of bison and had to dodge these huge elk who were meandering practically at the front door of our lodging.

By driving the Grand Loop Road, we were able to view the park from the comfort of our car. The park had thousands of miles of trails, from day hikes to back-country explorations. We took advantage of only a few—not enough time. We only took a few of the less challenging ones. The main attractions were all located on the Grand Loop Road. The park had one of the world's largest petrified forests. Yellowstone Lake was the largest high-altitude lake in North America. Yellowstone was like no other place we had ever seen, and the drive around the park was spectacular, with something new and exciting almost around every curve. Before we left, we drove over to Montana for lunch.

Old Faithful spouting off, Yellowstone National Park, Wyoming

Photo by Donna Elliot on Unsplash

We decided to take a different route to get back home in order to see a little more of the country. From Yellowstone, we headed southeast to Casper, Wyoming, where we picked up I-25 and followed it to

Douglas and Cheyenne, Wyoming; Fort Collins, by Boulder, Denver; to Colorado Springs, all in Colorado, where we stopped to visit Jim and Linda Rotge. Jim and I had been in the Airman's Education and Commissioning Program at the University of Arizona, and then we had been through the Officer's Training Program at Lackland AFB, Texas, together. Jim had completed his commitment to the Air Force and had gotten out and was then working as a physicist for a contractor in the Colorado Springs vicinity. Jim and Linda now had a parcel of kids—four or five, if I remember correctly. After our visit with them—it was great catching up—we were back on the road after first visiting the Air Force Academy, Pikes Peak, and the Garden of the Gods, to Albuquerque, New Mexico, then on to El Paseo, Texas, where we picked up I-10 that took us back home.

Figure 7 Tim's Senior Photo

Tim was off to Texas A&M to start his college career in the fall semester of 1989, leaving us with the first half of an empty nest. Tim had his heart set on going to Texas A&M and would not even consider or apply to any other university. I insisted we visit the University of Texas on their open house day. Tim reluctantly agreed to go but his heart just wasn't in it. He refused to talk with anyone or to visit any of the departments. I again insisted we tour the campus, but it was futile, as Tim just briskly walked straight through, looking neither left nor right but straight ahead. His argument was that he had already been accepted to Texas A&M, and that was where (he had made his mind up; my input) he wanted to go—and as far as he was concerned, the case was closed. And as far as I was concerned, I might as well have been spitting in the wind.

Anyway, our first nester was spreading his wings, and it was a mixed blessing. It was with a certain amount of sadness to see our firstborn leave us, but I was thankful that we had gotten him this far and prayed we had sufficiently guided him so that he would be able to make his mark in the world, to build his future and find peace and happiness in whatever that future might bring. No worries, for he has exceeded all our prayers and dreams for him!

Mary's sixteenth birthday came around far too quickly, too. My little baby girl had before our eyes grown into this very beautiful, sophisticated woman. And probably the hardest thing for me to accept was that soon I would no longer be the only, or main, guy in her life. Our joy was to see how smart and mature she had become, and getting her driving license gave her some freedom to get out on her own.

So, for her 16th birthday, we had decided to go to Carlsbad Caverns in New Mexico. Tim was finishing up his sophomore year at Texas A&M and was not able to get away for this family outing. So, similar to Tim's trip, we started on I-10, heading west. Carlsbad Caverns National Park was in the Chihuahuan Desert of southern New Mexico. The park contained over 119 caves. Three caves were open to public tours. Carlsbad Caverns was the most famous and was fully developed with electric lights, paved trails, and elevators. Slaughter Canyon Cave and Spider Cave were undeveloped, except for designated paths for the guided "adventure" caving tours. Guano mining occurred in the pit below the entrance to Carlsbad Cavern in the 1910s.

We were able to participate one evening in the bat-flight viewing. It was a program that started in the early evening at the amphitheater near the main entrance prior to the start of the flight, which varied with the sunset time. At first, there were a few bats flying out of the cave, and then more and more until it was like a black cloud overhead, and even though it was just past sunset, the sky above us was darkened. Wow, most spectacular. Mostly, these were Mexican free-tailed bats emerging from the natural entrance and flying to the
nearest water. We were told there were seventeen species of bats that lived in the park, including many Mexican free-tailed bats. It had been estimated that the population of Mexican free-tailed bats once numbered in the millions but had declined drastically in modern times. The cause of this decline was unknown, but the use of organochlorine pesticides (specifically DDT and dieldrin) was likely a contributor.

Unfortunately, during our trip to Carlsbad, we received word that Leticia Martin, my beloved landlady from Newark, Ohio, had passed away. We had been very close, like family. Also, during our absence, while out driving, Tim was sideswiped by a hit-and-run driver. Fortunately, he was not seriously hurt—shook up more than anything else. Damage to the car was not insurmountable, thankfully.

I received an assignment to the USAF Medical Inspector General's Team at Norton AFB, California. Because Timmy was going to be in his junior year at Texas A&M University, and Mary Beth was going to be in her junior year at MacArthur High School, and because Sue had gotten this really great promotion to be editor at the Army Audit Agency (GS-12), we decided I would be going solo to California and would try to make it home as often as I possibly could.

34. CALIFORNIA, HERE I COME!

I was able to find a small (600 square feet) one-bedroom apartment close to Norton AFB in a not-so-nice neighborhood, but it did have a gated community, which made it more acceptable, and the price was right. The Air Force had shipped basic furniture for me—one twin bed, a card table and four chairs, an easy chair, a TV, minimal cooking utensils, and silverware, along with necessary clothing. As it was just going to be me, I didn't need a lot. The USAF Medical Inspector General component was divided into command and three inspection teams: A, B, and C. I was assigned to the A-Team, and as it turned out, I was the senior biomedical service officer assigned during my tenure there.

During my assignment in California, Tim completed his third and almost his fourth year at Texas A&M and had found his groove in computer science. Why did I ever insist he start with electrical engineering? Dads don't always know best. Tim was earning good grades and worked as a lifeguard at the Brooks AFB pool during the summers. I was really proud of him. He was developing into a responsible young adult, I would say, right under my own eyes, but because I was away most of this time, in reality, it was pretty much on his own recognizance. He had made a good friend at the university, Roy, a previous Marine, who was residing in San Antonio during the summer as well. We hired Roy and Tim to paint our house, and they did a really decent job of it.

Mary Beth was in her junior and senior years at MacArthur High School during this time and really missed her dad (and he, her). I think it was a difficult time for her. She was growing and needed more independence, and Sue was stuck with being a single parent and seemed to have difficulty in loosening the reins, or so it seemed. Therefore, I tried to be a peacemaker as much as I could and mediate each viewpoint to the other party. There were mixed reviews of my successes.

It was almost 5 a.m. Sunday morning, June 28, 1992, when I was awakened from a deep sleep by my bed shaking. I mean, it was like someone was picking up the bed and setting it down hard over and over again. It was almost like someone was lifting the bed up and attempting to shake me out, literally. Everything in the apartment was shaking, rocking, and rolling. Pictures were falling off the wall, and things were falling off the tables and counters. I felt like the whole apartment was about to take off to the unknown, or collapse.

I suddenly realized this was not a dream. I thought this was the big one. I had been hearing about the BIG earthquake for years. I had had it for sure. I didn't have time to think. There wasn't enough time to replay my life before me, but I was confident this was it. I was a goner. This was the big California earthquake that I had heard so much about. But after a few more shakes and tremors, things quieted down, and I was still alive. Thank the Good Lord! There was a bit of a mess on the floor from the falling debris, but I was still there, and in one piece.

Except for being scared half out of my wits, I didn't seem much the worse for wear. I shakily got out of bed to assess what had happened. I learned there had been a magnitude 7.3 earthquake, and even though the shaking lasted only for two to three minutes, it seemed a lot longer to me. Fortunately, I had no real damage from the earthquake, even though the epicenter was relatively close. Tremors kept occurring over the next several days, but after a while, I tended to ignore them.

I tried to make it home as many times as I possibly could. It was lonely living by myself, doing my own cooking, laundry, and housekeeping. I had lived alone before Sue and I were married when I rented a room from the Red Cross Manager in Newark, Ohio. But that was before I had my own family.

I really missed them—just being there for them. It wasn't like Tim hadn't been away at the university for a couple of school years before I was transferred to California, and everyone seemed to be doing their own thing even when I was home. So, whenever we (my IG team) had an inspection in Europe, the East Coast, or even the Midwest, as long as we flew through Dallas, I would take a few days off and fly from Dallas to San Antonio, and when my leave was over, I would then fly back to California. That way, I only had to pay the difference in airfare costs over and above what would have been airfare for the inspection trip. That way, I was able to minimize my out-of-pocket expenses. Still counting pennies; a necessity.

An inspector's duties were completely different from anything I had experienced before in my Air Force career. We were on the road conducting inspection evaluations for two to three weeks at a time. Usually, inspections took one week per base, but two weeks for the larger facilities, and it was a hectic schedule and required burning the midnight oil almost every night. It was stressful, too. I was evaluating many areas outside of my area of expertise in the Biomedical Science Corps (BSC) multiple disciplines. My training and experience as a medical technician helped a lot.

Too, I took my duties very seriously because my findings would, in all probability, enhance or detract from the evaluatee's career. During evaluations, I attempted to provide as much staff assistance and career guidance as I could in the limited time, I had available. I felt this was crucial in that most BSC officers were one-deep in their positions and had little reliance on outside assistance, so I felt a little mentoring was the least I could provide.

During my tenure on the inspection team, I was recognized for my professional skills and astute insights into key factors in the extensive transition from a comprehensive-based system of medical oversight to a more efficient and effective results-orientated process. I was also recognized for expert assistance to the Headquarters Air Force and the bioenvironmental engineering associate chief in updating Air Force Occupational Safety and Health Standards and revising Air Force policy to incorporate new regulatory requirements of our specialty. When I wasn't on the road for inspections or doing temporary duty, assisting some other function between trips, I would be stuck at Norton AFB for two to three weeks at a time doing mostly staff work, pushing papers—BORING! This was the biggest downside to the assignment, along with the separation from my family and the loneliness that it entailed.

While assigned to the Medical Inspector General's Office, I was notified of my selection to colonel (O-6) and actually assumed that rank on December 1, 1992. It turned out to be a nice pay raise and tended to open certain doors.

In the summer of 1993, the whole inspector general's team was scheduled to move to Kirtland AFB, as Norton AFB was scheduled to be closed. As it turned out, this was good and bad. The good part was that I was released three months early from a two-year controlled assignment and was able to return to my family in San Antonio, as I had lobbied and been selected for an assignment back to San Antonio, Texas, as chief bioenvironmental engineering at Kelly AFB. The not-so-good part was that I had been scheduled for a three-week inspection tour to Turkey, a country I had always wanted to visit; not to be, though, and it appears I will probably never make it there. A visit to Turkey had always been on my bucket list.

35. KELLY AFB, TEXAS 1993-1996

The Kelly AFB assignment turned out to be an interesting one in that I replaced a former boss who then remained part of my staff until he retired. The first big event after returning home was Mary Beth's graduation from MacArthur High School. Later, I was able to take Sue with me to New Orleans (our second visit to New Orleans) to the Industrial Hygiene Conference, where we were able to chum around with Vic and Chris Dunn. (Vic Dunn had been on my staff at Wright-Patterson AFB.) After I left WPAFB, Vic up and got married. I had thought he was a confirmed bachelor. But after Sue and the kids left for San Antonio, Vic was kind enough to let me stow away at his place until I had finished my commitment at WPAFB.

And the one night when Vic didn't come home, and I was worried sick and was about to start calling the local hospitals and the police, he finally came dragging in towards noon on a Sunday morning with a sh-t-licking grin, looking like the cat that had just eaten the canary. I finally pried it out of him that he had spent the night with a lady friend. Whoops! It was then I suspected things were getting serious. It wasn't an awfully long time before it was Vic and Chris followed by wedding bells. Vic had since left WPAFB, and he and Chris lived in Las Vegas, where he had a position working at the Nevada Test Site. In addition to my conference, Sue and I had a great and memorable time in New Orleans.

Now, the search was on for Mary's college. Her mom took her to Oberlin, and I took her to Rice (Houston, Texas) for interviews, and I think we both took her to Texas A&M. On Mary's and my trip to Rice, I attempted to explain to her that Ivy League schools were very competitive for entrance because they drew on the brightest of the bright. Now, I knew our Mary was (and is) as sharp as a tack and could hold her own with anyone. But I attempted to share with her that sometimes it is better to be at the top of the heap intellectually wise (Texas A&M) than to land towards the bottom or even in the middle (Rice or Oberlin). Plus, there was the matter of tuition. (Perhaps from my angle, it was MORE about the matter of tuition). While Sue and I could probably scrape up the cost for Texas A&M University, there was no way we would be able to afford Rice or Oberlin without the assistance of her getting student loans or some rather lucrative scholarships. As it turned out, Mary wound up going to Texas A&M, so all my angst was for naught.

Figure 8 Mary's Cap and Gown Photo

Now, I had to ensure Mary knew that she was not to even consider or think about wedding bells until after she had received her degree. Truth was, though, she was 18, and legally, there would have been little or nothing we could have done had she not carried through. She had dated somewhat sporadically during high school but didn't seem particularly smitten with any one dude, even though she was dating this one kid who was also going away to university at the same time to the University of Texas. It didn't last long, thank goodness. There is a bit of a story there, but perhaps I will leave it for later.

Late in her freshman year at Texas A&M, she met Craig Pritzlaff, a young man who, with his parents, lived close to our neighborhood. Interestingly, they had both attended middle and high school together, and Craig and Tim had been on the MacArthur Swim Team together. I first heard of the new boyfriend while I was attending an industrial hygiene conference in Anaheim, California, with a frantic phone call awakening me from a deep REM sleep. Sue was on the line and was in a panic mode because Mary hadn't returned home yet. It was past midnight, and she had just found out that Mary was locked up in some park with this guy, and they couldn't get out—or so they had reported. She called Tim, who was still at Texas A&M, nearly three hours away. Tim jumped in his truck and rushed to the rescue anyway. In the interim, Craig (the boyfriend) and Mary were able to locate the parking attendant at his residence, who came and unlocked the gate to let them out. Call out to the FBI averted!

My assignment at Kelly AFB had some good, some bad, and some great aspects. I managed one of the largest bioenvironmental programs in the Air Force. Later, I was appointed as the first medical operations commander at the base for 175 personnel under my command. Thirty military members were formally recognized for mission excellence at base and command levels. Under my tutelage, my squadron achieved significant professional recognition. The largest occupational residency program in the Department of Defense received national accreditation. Headquarters, Air Force Inspection Agency, rated all functional areas of the squadron as "Outstanding" or "Excellent" while recognizing the Domestic Violence Response Team as an Air Force benchmark.

The Food and Drug Administration certified the Kelly Mammography program as the only certified Food and Drug Administration, military or civilian program in San Antonio. These were examples of the great things that were accomplished, mostly by helping people manage themselves, encouraging them to excel and succeed by handing out accolades, awards, and promotions, and yes, atta boys/girls.

A couple of not-so-great examples... The worst one was four of our bright, talented, and overachieving young Air Force members were on their way for a jaunt in northern Mexico when their automobile, for unknown reasons, veered off the road and hit a rare tree (for vegetation of any kind at the area in question was very sparse) head-on. My young lieutenant, bioenvironmental engineer, and one of my outstanding bioenvironmental technicians were killed outright. Another public health technician was fatally injured and hospitalized at Wilford Hall Medical Center and unfortunately passed away just a few days later. One of the hardest things I ever had to deal with was to watch life slowly fade from this robust, intelligent youngster despite the best efforts of the latest medical technology and superb medical care, and prayers of family and friends.

The fourth victim was another bioenvironmental engineering technician, who was also badly wounded. She had a broken neck, which wound up in her being a quadriplegic for the rest of her life.

The second example was that in my other role as commander, I found discipline somewhat distasteful. While it was enjoyable to hold out the carrot, it was far less so to wield the stick. But I always tried my very best to be fair, reasonable, and equitable.

Other achievements at Kelly AFB included setting up new operations complex for both Bioenvironmental Engineering and Public Health Services, developing a lead-based paint removal approach that served as the Air Force model, and providing oversight for the

Health and Wellness Center to be retrofitted into the old arts and crafts building, which stood as a first-class nexus for prevention and wellness.

Tim had graduated from Texas A&M in late spring 1994 and secured employment with Radio Shack at their Headquarters in Fort Worth, Texas, and departed our little nest forever, it appeared. His expertise with computers has served him well. He quickly advanced at Radio Shack, earning several well-deserved promotions. It was a treat for Sue and me to visit him in his new digs and for him to show us around the Ft Worth/Dallas area and his new workplace in Fort Worth. I must admit, though, it was a bit bittersweet seeing our little boy all grown up and making it on his own and doing it all by himself without any help or advice from Mom or Dad. But then, this was what we had raised him to be and prepared him for, wasn't it?

After I returned from California, Mary brought her new beau over to meet us. *Not bad,* I thought. Tall, suave, nice-looking, and there was even some resemblance of appearance between him and Mary. I thought the resemblance was interesting. He seemed very polite, articulate, and perhaps a little nervous. Understandable. It was quite evident that Craig was somewhat nervous about meeting us. But I had the feeling he was somewhat intimidated by me. Imagine!

As we sat there that evening, I looked over at Mary and Craig and thought they really made quite a remarkable couple, and somewhere in my subconscious, the thought popped into my head: *Those two would make handsome babies.* So, in order to try to lighten the mood in our little environment, I announced, "Mary's initials are M E T, or "met" for Mary Elizabeth Taylor, but were you and

Craig to marry," I told them, "They would become M E P." And I repeated several times, "MEP! MEP! MEP! MEP!" I'm not sure that broke the ice, but I'm sure that Craig had a new perspective on me. He probably thought I was a little nuts, and maybe he still does. My intent was to shatter the image of this old, cold-hearted, distant Colonel. Maybe I succeeded a little. Who knows?

Craig and Mary became engaged in the summer of 1995 and married on December 28, 1996, a few days after they graduated from Texas A&M. Their wedding was a memorable occasion for us. My brother Bobbie and his wife Eddie were there, as well as Sue's brother, Bob, and her mother and Aunt Sissy. Craig had his mother and father and several of their relatives from out of town, and friends and neighbors from both sides were in attendance.

As I slowly escorted my beautiful grown-up baby girl down the aisle, out of nowhere came this vision of Mary when she was a chubby little cherub jumping up and down at our upstairs window while holding on to the window frame, screaming and crying, "Don't leave me, Daddy! Don't go! Daddy don't leave me! Don't go! Don't leave me!" I recall the tears streaming down her little cheeks as she begged me not to leave her. This time, it was not me leaving her. It was **she** who was leaving **me.** I felt a small tear tickling my left eyelid, attempting to escape, and I had to bat my eyes quickly to prevent it, but I had to smile for appearance's sake and also felt a catch in my throat. At the point we reached the altar, I took her veil, smoothed it over her brow and behind her head, and gave her cheek a gentle pat and a quick kiss. A farewell kiss? I took her hand and placed it in Craig's outreached, expectant hand. Giving her away? It was a little hard giving her up, but they made such a handsome couple, and there was a world waiting for them to conquer. I had really become attached to Craig and was confident the two of them would make a go of it. I knew being newly married and freshly entering the business world would keep them very busy. I only hoped they would still find some time for us, and they always have.

Mary & Craig's Wedding....Wiley, Sue, Mary, Craig, Sue's Mother, and Tim

36. TINKER AFB, OKALHOMA 1996-1998

I really wanted to stay in San Antonio as long as I could. I applied for the position to manage the Bioenvironmental Engineering Program at the School of Aerospace Medicine but obviously didn't have the necessary political pull. It appeared my next assignment would be at Tinker AFB while they dangled the carrot that my final assignment would be for the command position at the AF Logistics Headquarters, Wright-Patterson AFB, Ohio. It was a solitary and lonely drive by myself from San Antonio to Tinker AFB with the Camry crammed full of essentials that I would need to batch it by myself, AGAIN! I was able to find a small furnished apartment fairly near the base, which was sufficient for my needs. Sue remained behind in our home in San Antonio and continued in her position with the US Army Audit Agency.

Highlights of my assignment to Tinker AFB included arranging for an evaluation of a new isocyanate sampling method and an ergonomic evaluation process, decreasing potential personal injury, and increasing productivity Air Force-wide. I spent countless late-night hours orchestrating efforts to complete a ten-month backlog of indoor air quality assessments in a record-setting two months, which I inherited upon my arrival at the base. I garnered an overall "Excellent" rating from the 1997 Operational Readiness Inspection Team. Also, I was honored to be selected to serve on the Air Force Major's Promotion Management Review Board and the National

Engineering Advisory Committee during my tenure at Tinker AFB.

After graduating and tying the knot on December 28, 1996, Mary and Craig returned from their honeymoon and found employment in Austin, Texas, Craig with the State's Environmental Directorate and Mary with Icon. Shortly after they moved there, they made the executive decision and bought a house in the Austin suburbs.

In February 1997, the US Army had a draw-down in personnel allotments, and subsequently, Sue was offered an early retirement from Civil Service. She barely made the length-of-service requirement but not quite the age requirement, so she subsequently needed to take a small cut in her retirement pay. Sue was still minding the house in San Antonio, so this was most fortuitous for us, as we were planning on Sue transferring to Tinker AFB had this golden opportunity not been offered. We put our house on the market for sale, but unfortunately, the housing market was in a slump, so we wound up renting it until our tour at Tinker AFB was finished. Then we were able to sell it, and we about broke even, for the housing market still seemed to remain in a slump. We did not get the price I felt we deserved, but at least the house was off our hands and was no longer our responsibility.

I was fast approaching four years remaining in the Air Force until I would be facing mandatory retirement: thirty years as an Air Force officer. I really did not want to spend my final years in the military at Tinker AFB, even though I liked the job well enough. I had a great staff and a super rapport with my management. I also had been managing junior bioenvironmental engineering assignments for some time as well. With my experience, rank, and accomplishments, I felt I deserved a major command position. And seeing as how my friend was going to be retiring from the Air Force Material Command position that summer, I lobbied for and was able to get the assignment back to Wright-Patterson AFB, Ohio, near Sue's and my folks. This would put us in a good place to retire.

37. BACK TO OHIO— 3RD ASSIGNMENT & RETIREMENT

I really wanted my last assignment to be in Ohio, where I could retire so Sue and I would be near our folks. Now, the kids had a life of their own. Both still lived in Texas. Tim lived in Fort Worth, and Mary and Craig lived in Austin. So, my lobbying had come to fruition, and I was assigned to be the Air Force Material Command (AFMC) Bioenvironmental Engineer at Wright-Patterson AFB, Ohio. That would be my last assignment, as my thirty-year point as an officer was rapidly approaching. We could have gotten base housing for the brick housing, colonels' and generals' quarters were available, but we elected to stay on the economy since we planned to remain in the area after my Air Force career was terminated.

It made sense to buy a house. We didn't have to be nearly as concerned about the local schools, as there were no kids needing schooling. So, after much searching, we found a one-story home that we both liked in Enon, Ohio, and it had a great big yard. It was large enough for lots of flowers (roses) and even a vegetable garden. The house was only about seven miles from the base, and being somewhat out in the country, traffic was almost nonexistent.

We missed our kids. It was much harder being so far away from them, but they had their own lives and were doing well. I seriously doubted if they missed us as much as we missed them. But so goes life. Tim was able to secure a new position with PepsiCo and continued to advance his career. He had proven to be smart, ambitious, and a hard worker. We were, and still are, really proud of him. He subsequently invested in a new three-bedroom house that was being built in The Colony, Texas. Well, actually, the third bedroom he converted into his office after his move-in. The kitchen, dining, and living area was a grand open space. His furnishings, though, tended to be rather sparse. However, his big screen TV and all his computer equipment were state-of-the-art!

In 2002, Tim had torn the meniscus in his knee and needed surgery. He was living alone at the time and obviously needed assistance after the surgery and during rehab. I was honored that I could provide that assistance. Made me feel needed. I tried really hard to take good care of him until he had sufficiently recovered from being on his own. At that time, I had recently retired from the Air Force.

Mary and Craig were prospering in Austin. However, Mary wanted to pursue her dream of becoming a genetic counselor. To make a long story short, she applied for and was accepted to the master's program at the University of Cincinnati, the same university where I had earned my master's degree. This was heaven-sent. It was going to be an opportunity for all of us. They would be living far enough away that we wouldn't make a nuisance of ourselves by camping out on their doorstep but close enough for us to be available whenever they might need us and close enough for visits whenever their schedules permitted.

While Mary pursued her graduate studies, Craig secured employment at the Fernald Site. The Fernald Preserve, where Craig found employment, was a former nuclear production facility located in a rural residential area eighteen miles northwest of Cincinnati, Ohio. The site had gone by many names over the years, including Feed Materials Production Center, Fernald Environmental Management Project, and Fernald Closure Project, but was most often referred to as Fernald. Uranium metal products for the nation's defense programs had been produced at Fernald, including slightly enriched and depleted uranium. Smaller amounts of thorium metal also had been produced. Unfortunately, uranium, radium, and other radioactive materials contaminated the soil, debris, groundwater, and surface water during that time. Production stopped in July 1989 to focus resources on environmental restoration. The Ohio EPA and U.S. EPA oversaw cleanup activities at the site. All remediation, except for ongoing groundwater pumping, was completed in 2006. Restoration returned natural plant and animal communities to the site. The Fernald Preserve is now a green space park with wetlands, ponds, prairies, and upland forest areas created based on original land surveys and post-excavation topography.

As Mary's graduation from her master's program neared, Craig decided he, too, would like to pursue his dreams as well and applied to law school. We were ecstatic when we learned one of the first schools to accept Craig was the Ohio State Law School, less than 100 miles away from us. Our elation was short-lived because Craig was also accepted into the more prestigious Southern Methodist University Law School in Dallas, Texas, which he subsequently accepted.

Mary's graduation from her master's program was grand. Now she was a codified genetic counselor ready to go out and conquer the world. Sue and I were so proud of our little baby girl, who had grown up to be a smart, savvy, intelligent, beautiful person who was ready to establish her niche in this grand old world.

Now that Mary's graduation was history, the kids, Mary and Craig, were anxious to continue their lives in Dallas, Texas, far away from us again. With a little trepidation, Sue and I jumped right in and helped them with their packing up, loading their rental truck, and away we all went to their newly rented apartment in Allen, Texas, where we reversed the procedure and helped Mary and Craig complete their move. Craig started law school, and this time Mary went to work to support them while Craig took on the arduous task of becoming an attorney.

Back at Wright-Patterson AFB, a special morning that occurred at the headquarters when our daily routine was so harshly interrupted is worth mentioning. We, the executive staff, were all in the surgeon's conference room waiting for the command surgeon to finish the AFMC general's briefing. We were all gathered for the command surgeon to conduct our daily 8:30 a.m. briefing. The date was September 11, 2011. We were chatting, visiting, and sharing antidotes with each other, and all the while, the oversized TV was tuned to CNN when the news reporting was interrupted by a Special News Bulletin. An airplane had crashed into the North Tower of the World Trade Center complex in lower Manhattan! Almost immediately, we were shown a video of the plane approaching and crashing into the tower. Was this some kind of a joke? Fake news? An accident? What the H was going on?

We all sat around the conference table, stunned into complete silence. One could have heard a pin drop. The time the plane crashed into the North Tower was

8:46 a.m. While we sat transfixed, watching the news, a second plane crashed into the South Tower seventeen minutes later at 9:03 a.m. These planes were later identified as American Flight 11 and United Flight 175, respectively. Both 110-story towers collapsed within an hour and forty-two minutes, leading to the collapse of the other World Trade Center structures, and significantly damaging surrounding buildings.

A third hijacked flight, American Airlines Flight 77, crashed into the west side of the Pentagon (the headquarters of the American military) in Arlington County, Virginia, at 9:37 a.m., causing a partial collapse of the building's side. That was not the end yet.

The fourth and final flight, United Airlines Flight 93, flew in the direction of Washington, D.C. The plane's passengers, alerted about the previous attacks, attempted to regain control of the aircraft and prevent it from crashing into its intended target. A struggle broke out in the aircraft, and the hijackers crashed the plane in a field in Stonycreek Township, Pennsylvania, near Shanksville, at 10:03 a.m. Investigators determined that Flight 93's target was either the U.S. Capitol or the White House. Was this to be the start of World War III? Armageddon? That day has certainly given the world pause and brought home to those of us in the United States some of our vulnerabilities.

Ending my career as a headquarters staffer proved to be an exciting and sometimes challenging assignment, even though I had already backfilled a similar position at Tactical Command Headquarters during Desert Storm/Shield and had worked on a temporary basis at the Air Force Surgeon's Office in Washington, DC, in a staff position before.

Along with AFMC duties, I was asked to continue the role as advisor to the junior cadre of the Bioenvironmental Engineering Corps, which mainly consisted of assignment duties, professional guidance, and enhancement, and just being a sounding post for our younger bioenvironmental engineers. The juggling act there was to match the right person for the right job at the right time. I was also the AFMC Senior Biomedical Service (BSC) Advisor, and in this capacity, I was invited to sit on Graduate Education Selection and promotion boards for the entire BSC cadre.

I was honored to be selected to be the first director of the Command Surgeon's Occupational Health Division and was applauded for doing a "yeoman's job of melding Flight Medicine, Public Health, and Bioenvironmental Engineering as well as the Air Force Occupational and Environmental Health Laboratory under one umbrella." I received high marks from my senior management for managing programs and policies in these areas to minimize health risks and promote healthier lifestyles for over 188,000 employees at twelve AFMC installations and organizations. As the command advocate for integrating health needs in weapons system development and sustained activities, I was able to garner $416,000 for initial implementation and redirected $514,000 to identify shortfalls to reduce health risks in the weapon system acquisition process. My thirty-year point—i.e., mandatory retirement— came much too quickly.

It has been great, and it has been fun, but there too, comes a time to say farwell to it all. This is me after forty one plus years of Air Force service, having the opportunity to say thanks one last time to friends, family and comrades.

Wiley's Retirement Photo

My family and friends did a bang-up job of giving me a memorable retirement send-off. The auditorium was filled. Most of my family was there: Sue, Tim, Mary and Craig, my mom and dad, most of my siblings, Fern and her son, Robbie, William David and Martha Lou, Mary Jane, Henry, Barbra and Agustin, Bonnie Lou and Bobby Jean and Eddie. Sue's family consisted of her mom, her brother Bob, and Aunt Sissy. Almost the entire staff of the AFMC surgeon's staff were in attendance, as well as a large number of bioenvironmental engineers, as they had been having a conference at Wright-Patterson AFB in the days before. Attending also were neighbors and friends from church and our local community.

I was honored with special guests from out of town: Paul and Andrea Martin, our good friends from undergraduate days when Paul and I were in the Airmen's Education and Commissioning Program together, Ralph and Helen Gochenour (Ralph had been my best man and roommate in France), John Vance, my NCOIC at RAF Upper Heyford, Chris and Vic Dunn (Vic had been a good friend since our days working together at Wright- Patterson AFB but had since gone to work at the Nevada Test Site), and

Nancy and Craig Koska. Craig had been my outstanding technician at RAF Upper Heyford, and Nancy had been our babysitter. They were more like family. We had unofficially adopted them. We were also stationed together at Brooks AFB a few assignments later.

There were many special points and accolades during the retirement ceremony, but one of the most touching ones to me was when our environmental health officer gave a brief summary of my forty-one-plus years in the Air Force. As she recalled my assignments, the bases on which I had been stationed, and my grade, the American Flag was held by the corresponding bioenvironmental environmental representative. First holding the flag was a one-striper Airman Third Class. All the airmen were standing on the left side of the podium. As the reading continued and I advanced in rank, the flag continued to be handed off to the next higher enlisted rank until it was handed off to the Technical Sergeant (TSgt). From TSgt, I transitioned over to the officer ranks. At that point in the summary, the TSgt crossed the stage where the officer bioenvironmental engineers were aligned and passed the flag to the second lieutenant. Thereafter, the flag passing continued up through the officer ranks until it stopped with the Colonel (my retiring rank).

After the retirement ceremony was completed, we all meandered over to the Officer's Club for the retirement luncheon. The most memorable and endearing portion of that event occurred as we were finishing the meal, and everyone had been served dessert—retirement cake and ice cream—when Tim and Mary presented a slideshow. This wasn't just any old slideshow. This was a professional Hollywood-type presentation of "THIS IS YOUR LIFE" set to music. It was even better than a Hollywood presentation because it was of us, and it was done by our kids. Even though Mary had been snowed under with studies and her part-time job, she obviously had sorted through a multitude of family photos and slides, and she, Tim, and Craig had then sorted out pertinent ones for the presentation. Tim, the computer whiz kid, had assembled all of that for us and our guests. It was better than any documentary movie. Sue and I were touched to the bone.

The icing on the cake, though, was a small presentation that Mary made. Somewhere in my hidden treasures of memorabilia (or my "junk stuff," as Sue often referred to it), Mary had retrieved a little silver cap pistol a little 8-year-old boy (mentioned earlier) had given me almost forty years ago at the time of my farewell party when I had left the hospital at Chateauroux, France. He had been in and out of the hospital a lot with some kind of immune disorder, and he and I had gotten quite close. He kinda looked up to me like an older brother. Mary shared the story that when he presented the pistol to me, he presented it to me with the caveat that it was the weapon to help keep all the girls off me.

Mary paused, cast around the audience, smiled, and said, "I guess with all the years, the magic on the pistol wore off, thankfully. Otherwise, Tim and I wouldn't be here!"

After the slideshow, there were several presentations and gifts—all greatly appreciated. Sue, though, had outdone herself and gave me this beautiful quilt she had designed and made for me of eagles. The untold hours she had spent on it represented to me all the years that she had spent caring for me and our little family—the love, devotion, and patience she had given to us over the years. Words are hardly adequate to tell how much it touched my heart. Choosing the eagle as the emblem for the quilt was spot-on. The eagles not only represented my retiring AF rank, the emblems I wore on my uniform, the symbol of our country, but also the great bird that soared in the boundless sky. The sky, the eagle's purview for me, was not the boundary for hopes and dreams, nor did it set restrictions, standards, or expectations, but offered a beacon to reach for encouraging dreams beyond the ordinary and to stretch towards infinity. That is what the quilt represented to me, and I will treasure it until I draw my last breath.

Mary, Craig, and Tim surprised us with a retirement gift of a Caribbean Cruise, our first-ever ocean cruise. When I considered it, Mary was in graduate school, working a part-time job, Craig was working a job that he was not overly enthused with, and Tim was branching out into new territory—he had left Radio Shack. They weren't exactly destitute, but they were a long way from being financially secure. Therefore, this was a big financial sacrifice for them to give us this luxury for our retirement. I mean, it was Sue's retirement as well as mine. I may have served over forty-one years, but Sue had been there with me for over thirty-five of those years.

Growing up, I had always dreamed of traveling and seeing and sampling a bit of the world, and we had done that, just not by ocean cruises. Never even considered ocean cruising. This was a totally new ballgame. Turned out the cruise was absolutely wonderful. We had a great time on the mammoth ship with all the activities on board and the sightseeing tours of all the places where we stopped before the cruise ended.

Too soon, it was our last day, and it was time to get ready to disembark. The night before we were to disembark, we were told to pack up our suitcases and place them outside our cabin doors for the porters to pack them away for delivery to Immigration the following day. While Sue was completing her toilette for the evening, I finished packing everything up in our suitcases and placed them outside our cabin door as instructed; good trooper that I was.

We had our last blissful night aboard the ship, and I claimed the bathroom first upon awakening in the morning. When I was finished, I gently awakened Sue and told her it was her turn to get ready. She groggily got up and started to do her bathroom thing, and it wasn't long before I heard the bathroom door bang open, and she kinda barked, "Where are my clothes that I am supposed to wear today?"

What in the world was amiss? Was this going to be my fault again?

We hastily searched our cabin to no avail. That is, we did not find Sue's clothes. Had someone stealthily sneaked in during the night while we were asleep and stolen Sue's clothes and not taken mine? That really didn't make much sense. When Sue pointed out where she had purposely stowed her clothes, it dawned on me those were the clothes I thought she had left for me to pack! And pack them I had. I had very carefully, precisely folded them neatly, making sure that I had pressed out all the wrinkles before stowing them away and closing the suitcase. Actually, I had been very proud of my attention to detail and packing prowess and thought that Sue would be very proud of me for taking such good care of her things.

At that moment, though, she really didn't look too proud, or so happy either, for that matter! Well, she still had on her pajamas, and she was just about the cutest thing in them. I thought that maybe I could just buy her a new outfit from one of the ship's stores. Then, of course, it dawned on me. That was not going to happen, for all the stores aboard the ship were already closed for deboarding. Perhaps we could stop at a store just as soon as we were away from the ship.

Those were not viable solutions, per Sue. Did I think for one moment she was going to walk off that ship in her pajamas? Well, I better have another thing coming! The real solution was for me to find one of the ship's porters, rummage through tons of baggage, and rescue the suitcase that held Sue's belongings that I had so grossly mistakenly packed. And I had better hurriedly do so!

Fortunately, I was able to find a kind porter who took pity on me and escorted me to the bowels of the ship and undid this large net that seemed to hold hundreds of pieces of luggage. We dug through the lot until I discovered ours, retrieved the suitcase in question, took it back to our cabin for Sue to unpack her day's outfit, and then returned the suitcase to the ship's bowels. (Do ships really have bowels?) Anyway, it was a great adventure despite my faux pas!

I found retirement life different; quite a challenge, to be truthful. No more uniforms, saluting, and all the other military stuff. But we still had the base exchange (BX), commissary privileges, and, thankfully, retirement pay. I now had to try and coordinate clothes every day.

I was soon involved in church activities. Sue and I enrolled in Bible Studies, and I volunteered to chaperone the homeless sleepovers at our church, which included feeding them, providing sleeping quarters (setting up and making beds, then stripping them and laundering bedclothes), and security (guard duties).

I was also induced to manage the Ohio Reads Program for the local elementary school, which entailed securing volunteers to assist the young children in helping them improve their reading skills. Of course, I joined in with the volunteers with the readings as well. It was a most rewarding and satisfying experience. I've always loved kids, and it was a treat to work with them. Most of them just needed a little attention and seemed to thrive on the little extra attention we were able to give them. In truth, I received more attention than I gave.

Too, I was an avid volunteer with the AARP's free tax preparation program. Not only did we set up and prepare folks' income tax forms for them, but we usually actually submitted them to the Internal Revenue Service. In those instances where an individual (or family) was unable to come to our site, we actually made house calls. This was a new aside in my tax preparation ventures, and the house calls were only done for my volunteering in Ohio.

After church on January 5, 2003, Sue and I did a little run to the base commissary to pick up a few groceries, and we visited the BX for a little shopping. While we were there, Sue happened to pick up a base newspaper. This was very unlike Sue, for usually she didn't care a whit about the base newspaper. Later, while Sue was perusing the base newspaper—again, uncharacteristic for Sue—she discovered an advertisement for an industrial hygienist (my specialty) located in what appeared to be Bonham, Texas. In actuality, Bonham, Texas, was where the Human Resource Division for the Texas Veterans Affairs was and is located, hence the advertisement, from Bonham, Texas. The actual position was to be located in Dallas, Texas.

There was one minor problem. The position announcement was scheduled to close on January 8, 2003. I did have a resume, but it was one I had compiled before I retired from the Air Force and was mainly slanted toward senior management/leadership positions. Therefore, I would be required to make major revisions to my resume, as this position was more technical and hands-on. However, to my credit, I was a certified industrial hygienist.

On Monday, January 6, 2003, I called the number listed to query them about the position and was told if I faxed them my resume by the close of business on January 9, 2003, I would be considered for the position. I had my resume on a disc, so with major revisions (and I do mean major), I printed out the new resume, took it to the Wright Patterson Air Force Base, and faxed it off to Bonham, Texas. I doubted if there was little probability that I would be hearing from the Texans.

Life went on as usual for the next couple of months, and I had almost forgotten about the application when, on April 2, 2003, I got a call from the Texans inquiring if I would be available for a telephone interview. What could I say? So, I agreed with little hope of being selected. I knew I was getting a little long in the tooth. A few days passed, and I received another call, and wonder of wonders. I had been selected for the position, except they needed me to start work on April 21, 2003, at the Dallas Veterans Hospital.

Sue and I had to think fast. This would mean leaving Sue behind until we could sell the house in Enon, and I would need to hoof it to Texas by myself, pronto. Well, maybe not exactly by myself, for Tim lived in the Colony, Texas, as he at that time worked for PepsiCo. Mary and Craig lived in Allen, Texas, where Craig was enrolled in law school at Southern Methodist University. Both kids lived in the Dallas suburbs, within commuting distance of the VA Hospital. Tim had almost three bedrooms (one room had been converted into his office, remember?) to himself, so we decided collectively it would be better if I stayed with Tim until our house was sold and Sue could join me. I set out on my own and drove from Enon and arrived at Tim's house on April 20. 2003, one day before I was scheduled to start my new job.

38. DALLAS, TEXAS
04/03–10/14

I enjoyed living with Tim, and it was a great pleasure to prepare a Sunday dinner and have Craig and Mary join us and watch TV or play some games and just relax. Usually, we didn't have a lot of time because of Craig's studies. Missing from our little core family was Sue.

The most difficult challenge about my new job was the traffic to and from work. I found the drive to work to be really off-putting. Traffic was horrendous, almost like a busy parking lot, and needed a lot of getting used to. Getting settled at work was a breeze, except for my assistant industrial hygienist, who felt she should have been promoted into my position and seemed to carry around a chip on her shoulder. I divided up the duties in what I felt was a fair and equitable fashion, and we mostly stayed out of each other's way until, after just a few months of this (about four), when the assistant transferred laterally to Louisville, Kentucky.

I hadn't been in Dallas for very long until Mary and Craig announced they were going to be Mommy and Daddy! Sue and I, and Tim, were overjoyed. Now we just needed to get the house in Enon sold and get Sue to join us. And finally, Sue was able to find a buyer for the Enon house and we were all set to close in late July 2003. I was allowed one last move at government expense as part of my retirement package. The next order of business was to arrange for packers to come in and pack everything up and then for the movers to come in and pick up all our worldly goods and haul them to the Dallas area, where most of it would be stored until we could move into our new home whenever it was completed.

Sue and I had decided to build a house in Grand Prairie on the south side of Dallas. I had had my fill of fighting the northside traffic from H. We had found a builder with a floor plan we liked and who would modify his plans to meet our requirements. Most builders would not do so. They were pretty rigid about sticking with their standard floor plans. We settled on a two-story, four-bedroom (one room converted into an office), three bathrooms, and a large playroom on the second floor with built-in window seats. Sue would later convert that room into her sewing room. In the interim, we also contracted to rent a small apartment that permitted dogs and cats on a monthly basis near our new home. Things were progressing well.

Sue, all by herself (perhaps with a little help from the realtor), sold our Enon house and arranged for the movers to come in and pack us up on July 21, 2003, and to have everything loaded up for shipment to Grand Prairie on July 23, 2003. I returned to Ohio to help with the move on Friday, July 18th.

Sue had taken care of everything. Bless her heart. The yard was immaculately trimmed and mowed; everything was in its place outside; inside, everything was sorted and labeled *Ready for Packing*. Boy was I ever a lucky man to have such a beautiful, loving, and efficient wife. All of those preparations, Sue had done on her own. I was pleasantly and thankfully surprised.

Unfortunately, Sue's Aunt Sissy, who lived in Newark, Ohio, was found unconscious and rushed to the local Emergency Room, where she was hospitalized on Sunday, July 20th. She had had a massive heart attack. Sissy was able to hang on for several days, but then she simply gave up and passed from this life on July 23, 2003.

This, however, left me in a bit of a quandary because the packers were scheduled for the following day after Sissy's attack, and we had sold the house and needed to be out of the house. Therefore, we could not postpone the move. Sue needed to be with her aunt during this critical time (Sissy had been in a coma-like stage after the attack), which meant I would need to handle the move all by myself.

I must admit, I did feel a little panicky because Sue always knew where everything was, what went with what, and how to keep everything sorted. She was a great traffic controller. I knew I would be lost without her. I always have been. I mean, she has always been the glue that held me and everything else together.

I did, though, in spite of the situation and my self-doubts, persevere. The packers came and packed up all of it, and the movers emptied the house on the same day we learned Sissy passed. I called the kids, so Mary and Tim flew into Dayton Airport, where I was able to pick them up for the funeral, and we were able to stay at the Wright Patterson VIP Visiting Officer Quarters because everything had already been removed from our house. After the funeral, the kids flew back to Dallas, and Sue and I started on another chapter of our lives as we started our drive to the Dallas/Fort Worth area with our Collie and two cats in tow.

Sue and I settled into a small one-bedroom apartment alongside Interstate 10 in Grand Prairie, Texas, with easy access for me to get to the VA Hospital and also close by where we were having our new home built so that it would be convenient for us to keep tabs on the house's progress as it was being built. To say we were a close family living in the tiny apartment is a bit of an understatement. To complicate matters, Reveille, our Collie, was having urinary tract problems and had difficulty walking. We had to keep a diaper on her. Had she been human, she would have qualified for hospice care.

Fortunately for us, we were able to take possession of and move into our new home by mid-November 2003.

Work was going well, and Sue was getting to know a group of folks she had met at the local YMCA. We were still getting things sorted and put away at our new house while also preparing for Christmas.

My whole division at work was having their annual Christmas Party on December 17, 2003 (WEDNESDAY). It was planned for 11:30 a.m. I had prepared my Punch Bowl Cake to share, and everyone was just getting ready to sit down to devour our Christmas feast when I received a call that Mary had been taken to the hospital and was expecting our first grandchild momentarily. Needless to say, all thoughts of participating in our office Christmas party's feasting flew right out the window.

I hurriedly excused myself and headed up north to the hospital to wait, and wait, and wait. But you know, part of our military life was having instilled in us the innate ability to hurry up and wait and to take it in stride! So, waiting was not an alien requirement for me.

At 4:30 p.m., our first grandson, Riley James Pritzlaff, made his entrance into the world, and what a blessing he was and is. Sue, Tim, and I, along with Craig's parents, anxiously awaited our first glimpse of the wee darling when his grinning, bursting-with-pride papa exhibited him for the first time behind the Nursery Room window for us all to take our first look-see. Here he was in all his little glory, an early Christmas present for all of us!

The next big event was Craig's graduation from Southern Methodist University Law School in late May. After graduation, he joined this high-powered law firm and started putting his lawyerly skills to practice. Now that law school was over, and Craig was pulling down big bucks, he and Mary felt the need to increase the size of their living space to accommodate their growing family, so they bought this really fantastic two-story home in Coppell, Texas, a grand chateau.

In April 2006, Tim managed to find a new beau. In June of that year, he brought him (Jimmy Speed) down to meet us, another lawyer. (*Lord,* I thought to myself, *as if what this world needs are more lawyers*).

I was attempting to install a ceiling lighting/fan fixture in our guest bedroom. Jimmy pitched right in and helped me install the darn thing. I was struck by how friendly and accommodating Jimmy was, and he was not shabby in the looks department either. *Maybe Tim will be able to hang on to this one for a while,* I thought—and he has. Wasn't long before the two of them became an item. Tim bought a new two-story home (another chateau) on the outskirts of Frisco, Texas, and Jimmy moved in with him, and so their journey and life together began.

On July 26, 2006 (WEDNESDAY), Mary and Sue were out shopping at Target when our second grandson decided he wanted to see what was going on in the world outside. I guess he felt it was time for him to join the rest of our family. This was a little surprising because, according to Mary's physicians, our second grandson's expected arrival was not due until early August. However, what did they know?

Sue and Mary quickly truncated their shopping spree and made a mad dash to the hospital, notifying the rest of the crew (us) while on their drive to the hospital. It was another bouncing baby boy, August Reed Pritzlaff. Was this the beginning of Mary and Craig's start of their very own football team? Sadly, it was not to be, for August was to be the finale.

Interestingly, August's and Riley's temperaments are significantly different. It seemed Riley and I had an instant rapport. I could cuddle him, give him his bottle, rock him, and hum him to sleep in no time at all. August, on the other hand? I could rock him and give him his bottle, but he was quick to let everyone know it was his mommy he preferred. He never took to me that much, or it seemed to me or as much to anyone else as he did to his Mommy. Maybe later, his dad. I must share how much Sue and I admire the parenting skills of both Mary and Craig with our grandsons. If things could have been inverted, they would have made good mentors for Sue and me. However, needless to say, we are very proud of the lot of 'em—our kids, our grandkids, and our sons-in-law.

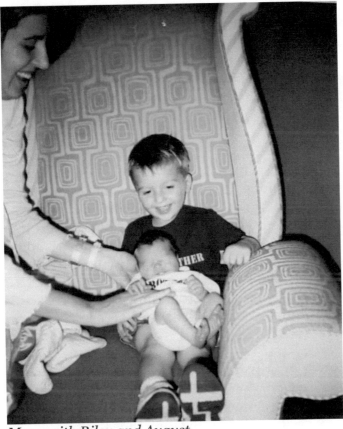

Mary with Riley and August

Within a two-and-a-half-year timeframe, Sue and I lost our remaining parents. My dad passed away on

February 24, 2006. Sue's mom passed away on August 2, 2007. Bob, Sue's brother, discovered her mom still in bed after going up to her house to see why she wasn't answering her phone. Sue's mom had lived in the family home until the day she died. Bob had lived nearby and had been a great support for her in her final years.

My mom passed away on September 10, 2008. She had moved to a nursing care facility shortly after Dad passed. She refused to live with either of her remaining nine children. She had taken care of both of her parents as they neared their final days and was very adamant that she was not going to be a burden on any of us, not that she would have been. She wasn't. Also, my beloved sister, Fern, passed away on September 27, 2006.

Sue and I accompanied her brother, Bob, on a trip to England (September 2010) to revisit some of our old haunts and explore some new ones with him. We rented a two-bedroom flat in Central London near the Natural History Museum from friends of our friends Paul and Andrea Martin, which was located near the Underground, allowing us quick access to all of London and the nearby surrounding areas. We also purchased rail passes, which gave us access to most of Southern England.

Our biggest limiting factor was time. Of course, we, at breakneck speed, shared with Bob the Tower of London and the Crown Jewels, Hyde Park, Trafalgar Square, Piccadilly Circus, Big Ben, the House of Parliament, Saint Paul's Cathedral, Buckingham Palace, Tower Bridge, etc. I won't go into a lot of detail here, for I have shared most of these already elsewhere.

Our visit to Salisbury and Amesbury was mainly to see and pay homage to Stonehenge, a prehistoric monument on the Salisbury Plain in Wiltshire, England, two miles west of Amesbury. Archaeologists believe Stonehenge was constructed from 2,000 to 3,000 years BC and is aligned towards the sunrise on the summer solstice.

Figure 11 , Stonehenge, England

Day Trips, Mostly by Train, Included...

Canterbury is known as a cathedral city in Southeast England and was a pilgrimage site in the Middle Ages. The most well-known cathedral is Canterbury Cathedral, one of the oldest and most famous Christian structures in England. Thomas Becket, the archbishop, was murdered there in 1174 by knights of King Henry II. Becket and the King were known for being at odds with each other. The King is said to have said, "Will no one rid me of this turbulent priest?" Four of the King's knights took him literally and did just that.

The University of Cambridge was one of the highlights of our visits. Their alumni and faculty have won 121 Nobel Prizes over its eighth-century existence. Its founding followed the arrival of scholars who abandoned the University of Oxford after some difficulty with the local townspeople. Their notable alumni are extensive: Sir Isaac Newton, Stephen Hawkins, Francis Bacon, Alan Turing, Charles Darwin—just to name a few. We had lunch at the *Eagle*, where on February 28, 1953, Francis Crick announced he and James Watson had discovered the secret of life, DNA.

Another day trip (not by train) was the day we hired a driver to take us to share some of our old haunts with Bob that were not easily available on the train schedules. We revisited RAF Bicester—7 Payne's End, where we used to live—and drove through RAF Upper Heyford, where we both used to work (at the time of our visit a ghost town), Charlbury, where we first rented upon our arrival in England, Stratford Upon Avon, Shakespeare's birthplace and where he kept his family while he was out in the world with his theatrical troupe. Blenheim Palace, Winston Churchill's homeplace, and then to his burial site and finally to Oxford for a quick drive-through of the university before heading back to London. What a day!

One of the greatest joys in my life has been the times spent with our little family. I realize when one's kids grow up, get married, and strike out on their own, they have their own lives and responsibilities. So, it has been a real treat for Tim and Mary to make an effort to share some of their time with us.

After we moved to Grand Prairie, we had a lot of Sunday family dinners/cookouts together, rotating between the three houses and the two big holidays. Christmas and Thanksgiving were almost always celebrated together in some fashion or another. Birthdays, too, were big events, and we always attempted to make a big to-do for the birthdays in spite of my never celebrating a birthday as I was growing up (and my messing up Sue's first birthday celebration after our marriage when I didn't get her a cake).

As a family, we also had some exciting adventures together. We rented a cabin alongside the Little River in Broken Bow, Oklahoma, where Mary had a run-in with a black bear. Craig, Riley, August, and I had a fishing bout in the Little River (Craig was a bit laid up with an injured foot); I don't remember anyone having bragging rights about any great catches.

Tim, Mary, Jimmy, and Sue went kayaking on the Mountain Fork River. Sue managed to turn her kayak upside down, with her inside it and had to be rescued by Tim.

Another excursion took us to Lake Tahoe, where we rented another cabin in the forest. This must have been around Tim's birthday, for I recall fireworks over the lake and dinner on a boat ride out in the lake, hiking in the woods immersed in Mother Nature, the guys (Tim, Jimmy, and Craig) paddle-boarding in the lake, and all of us taking an Aerial Train to the top of the mountain—what a view!

Then we got to 40th birthdays. Tim was first and wanted to go to Laguna Beach, so we did. We rented a house within a couple of blocks off the beach, easy walking distance. But first, we all flew into San Diego, where we took some time to visit before we set off for Laguna Beach. Most of that time was spent exploring the *USS Midway* aircraft carrier, which had aircraft exhibited from WWII, the Korean War, and Operation Desert Storm.

Tim and Jimmy had rented this snazzy little sports car. Sue and I attempted to fit in the cramped back seat along with our luggage; no way was that going to happen. We wound up piling in with Craig, Mary, Riley, and August in their rented SUV.

We spent a few days on the beach, and I, of course, despite lathering on globs of sunscreen, managed to get a terrific sunburn. I looked like a pickled beet.

Everyone else did great. The guys (Craig, Tim, and Jimmy) did their paddle-boarding thing.

The sunsets were magnificent, awesome from the beach. On Tim's actual birthday, we were off to Disneyland for breakfast with Minnie Mouse and friends; it was an absolute blast. It was difficult to tell who enjoyed it the most. And the rest of the day was spent enjoying the thrills at Disneyland. The following day, we went to Universal City, and the day after to LEGOLAND, and then it was back to Dallas.

For Craig's 40th we went on a Disney Cruise, leaving Port Lauderdale for the Caribbean, including Saint Thomas, Virgin Islands, Bahamas, and the Disney Castaway Cay. One of the most memorable events of the cruise was a whisky-tasting challenge with my beloved sons-in-law. Maybe there is something to be said for age and experience, for *I* didn't appear to be much worse for wear and tear afterwards. Nuff said.

Mary's and Jimmy's 40th birthdays occurred within two weeks of each other, so we headed out to Hawaii to celebrate. We started our celebration on the Big Island, Hawaii, where we rented a neat house built by WWII Japanese prisoners of war on the Kilauea Military Camp on Crater Rim Drive within the Hawaii Volcanoes National Park.

Within the park abounded endless hardened lava flows stretching from the crater all the way to the Pacific Ocean left over from major eruptions, one of which had occurred a few months before our excursion. The residual had left a bed of black basalt that stretched for miles as far as the eyes could see. The largest eruption of lava ever recorded occurred in 2018 when Kilauea erupted again, three years after our trip. The crater was within easy walking distance of our house and was fairly dormant during our visit. As a matter of fact, not only could we walk around the rim of the crater, but we could actually walk down inside it (but not too close to the cauldron) because there was still some activity going on with the molten, boiling lava within the cauldron. Lots of emitting steam. We had to be particularly careful of all the steam vents surrounding the volcano, too.

There was a lot for us to see and do in Hawaii—the largest, youngest, and still growing island of the Hawaiian chain of islands. The Big Island was the home of Pele, the volcano goddess (we didn't get to actually see her). It encompassed all four climate zones and was a tourist paradise crammed with history. We hiked trails in and around the volcano and the lush rainforest, waterfalls, and black-sand beaches, swam in the Pacific Ocean, and did as much sightseeing as we could get in within our allotted time.

Craig and I visited the Mauna Kea Summit and viewed the thirteen telescopes funded by eleven countries. The view from the summit gave us the feeling of being on top of the world for good reason. Actually, it appeared we were pretty close. We were standing at 13,796 feet; the mountain is Hawaii's tallest and the highlight of many visitors' trips to the Big Island of Hawaii. The Mauna Kea Observatories (MKO) featured some of the world's largest telescopes, including equipment from Canada, France, and the University of Hawaii. For these many reasons, it was on many lists as an unparalleled destination for stargazing. Craig and I even attempted to make snow angels in the snow atop Mauna Kea.

Another interesting site was the area where Captain Cook, in 1779, reached his final destination, where he had abducted and was holding the island's King Kalani' Opu for ransom, and in retaliation, the King's tribesmen killed Captain Cook and ate most of him. One could say that was one kidnapping that went wrong.

For the second part of our Hawaii soiree, we stayed on Oahu Island at the military's Hale Koa Hotel on Waikiki Beach. The hotel was in a prime location for enjoying the beach and ocean and sightseeing. We were able to drive all around the island and take in the views. The waves on the Northern end were huge and awesome. Great for surfing, which we were not able to do. --not enough time

Photo by on

Figure 12 USS Battleship Missouri, Pearl harbor, Hawaii

Our most memorable visit was to Pearl Harbor. Of particular interest was a visit to the *USS Battleship Missouri* where the Japanese signed an unconditional surrender for WWII in 1945.

In early June 2012, Mary was able to get us reservations using Groupon at the four-star Lajitas Golf Resort and Spa, which we used as our headquarters for exploring the Big Bend National Park and surrounding area. Big Bend National Park had been on my bucket list for a long time, and it turned out to be as magnificent as I expected. The park was the largest protected area of Chihuahuan Desert topography and ecology in the United States and was named after a large bend in the Rio Grande/Rio Bravo. The park protects more than 1,200 species of plants, more than 450 species of birds, 56 species of reptiles, and 75 species of mammals. We saw a lot of vegetation, some birds, but no mammals that I recall—and thank goodness, no reptiles. The area has a rich cultural history, from archeological sites dating back nearly 10,000 years to more recent pioneers, ranchers, and miners. The Chisos Mountains, located in the park, are the only mountain range in the United States to be fully contained within the boundary of a national park. Geological features in the park include sea fossils and dinosaur bones, as well as volcanic dikes.

The park encompasses an area of over 800,000 acres, entirely within Brewster County. The mountains, the crevices, the canyons, the sinkholes, the arroyos, and the river were all extraordinary. Most of us tried hiking barefooted up and down some of the slippery canyons to keep from slipping. We kayaked on the Rio Grande in teams, Tim and Sue, Craig and August, Jimmy and Riley, and Mary and me.

Mary and I were the only ones to survive the rapids without tipping over. Once we came to the end of our kayaking journey, we all waded over and back across the Rio Grande to Mexico. For at least a few minutes, I guess we were illegals in Mexico. We had a jeep tour to give us a better perspective of the Texas southwest. We investigated the Terlingua Ghost Town and Cemetery, all the while somehow surviving the 116-degree heat. The trip included a visit to Marfa, Texas; Fort Davis, Sandhills State Park; and the McDonald Observatory.

39. TRAVELING SHOES

East Europe

Sue and I decided after I had retired for the second time (first from the Air Force, then from Veterans Affairs) that if we were going to do any traveling in what was left of our lives, we had best get started.

While stationed in England, we had opportunities to explore some of the United Kingdom, a little of France, Italy, Germany, and the Netherlands, and we were even fortunate enough to be able to visit the Holy Land.

While I was stationed in France, I had been able to see a bit more of Europe, but there still remained so much we had not seen, and most were awaiting our exploration.

Sue had met these folks at the YMCA. There were a lot of couples in that group who were planning a river cruise to Eastern Europe to mostly areas I had never been to but places I had read about, and they were certainly on my list of places I would like to see, so we decided to join the group. It was a nineteen-day trip that covered five countries along the Danube River; three of these countries had been behind the Iron Curtain from 1945 until the late 1980s. History goes back to some of these countries being part of the Roman Empire, then the Holy Roman Empire, the Ottoman Empire, under Attila the Hun, the Hapsburg Empire, then under Hitler's Fascism and some later under Communism. All were deeply affected by WWII.

On our trip, guides explained all aspects of what we encountered. Our first stop was in the Czech Republic's capital, Prague, or Praha—the city of a hundred spires. Charles IV, the Holy Roman Emperor, ruled from the castle in Prague dating from the 9th century and basically put Prague on the map. There was SOOO much to see and our time was SOOO limited. The first university north of the Alps was founded there, and that was where we started our walking tour on day one.

Cobblestone streets were evident throughout the city. We crossed the Charles Bridge, completed around 1400, across the Vltava River. We meandered into the Jewish Quarter (or Joseph Town), which told the moving story of the region's Jews, also called the Ghetto. (The ramshackle Joseph Town was razed and replaced with a then-modern town in the 1800s we were told). Hitler's goal was to leave a museum of the extinct Jewish Race. Less than 10 percent of the Jewish population in the city survived the Holocaust!

The Jewish Quarter included six sites: the Town Hall and the old and new synagogues to the side with five other synagogues; the Jewish Cemetery—12,000 evocative tombstones, one almost piled up on top of the next one, with many layers. They were so jumbled it looked like an earthquake had struck. The Jewish believe "death is the gateway to the next world" (over 100,000 had been buried in the relatively small cemetery); from 1439 to 1787, this was the only burial ground for the Jews of Prague.

The Pinkas Synagogue's walls were covered with handwritten names of the 77,000 plus Jews who were sent from here to the gas chambers—a chilling and sobering thought. While scanning the walls of all the names we could hear the somber reading of their names alternating with the Canto singing of the Psalms. It was enough to send chills up and down my spine. Upstairs was a display of art drawn by the Jewish children imprisoned at the Terezin Concentration Camp, who all later perished before the war ended.

Our walking tour next led us to the Old Town Square, Powder Tower, and Jan Hus Memorial. Jan Hus, before the time of Martin Luther, was a college professor as well as a priest. He condemned church corruption and promoted local religious autonomy, and for his effort was burned as a heretic. Behind Jan Hus stood a monument of a mother and child. They represented the ultimate rebirth of the Czech Nation.

Also in the Square was the Church of St Nicholas, originally Catholic, now Hussite; Gothic Tyn Church with distinctive spires; St Vitus Cathedral in the distance; Charles Bridge; Vitava River. The Medieval Astronomical Clock's outer ring showed the time (Bohemian time was indicated by gold Gothic numbers; modern time by Roman numerals). At the top of the hour, on its very top, the twelve Apostles paraded around. On the right, Death tipped his hourglass and pulled the cord to ring the bell, causing the rooster to crow and the hour to be rung. At the bottom of the clock were the signs of the Zodiac and scenes from a peasant's life, and on the left was a vanity figure holding a mirror and Greed, a Jewish moneylender. So much was going on that it had to all be interpreted by the guidebook; otherwise, it would have been a complete mystery to me.

Figure 13 Medieval Astronomical Clock, Czech Republic, Prague

After Prague, we were off to visit the Nelahozeves Renaissance Castle, which was built in 1593 on the banks of the Vltava, thirty minutes from where we were staying (one of the finest in Bohemia, according to our guide). It was used only as a summer home, for it had no heat except in the dining room. The art was impressive and included works by Brugel, Rubens, and Veronese, among others. We were told Nelahozevea was Protestant and supported the 30-Year War against Catholicism. However, the Protestants were defeated in 1620 at White Mountain; therefore, the owner had to sell out and flee the country. The castle had then been in the Labkowicz family ever since, except for the period from 1945 to

1989, when it was taken over and controlled by the Communists. Post the Communist's seizure, the castle was returned to its rightful owner, who, at the time of our visit, was living in Boston. Just down the street from the castle was the birthplace of the composer Antonin Dvorak, most notably known for his New World Symphony.

From Prague, our tour party was bussed to Nuremberg to join the rest of the cruise (Prague was an additional pre-side trip). Nuremberg was the German city that played a crucial role in Hitler's accession to power. It was there that some of his party's major rallies took place. During our visit, it was eerily so quiet one could almost hear the ghosts of those hordes from the past being baited into believing every lying, hateful word (fake news) being spewed from Hitler's mouth as we solemnly walked across the parade fields where the throngs gathered to hear Hitler's fiery speeches denouncing the Jews, Gypsies, mentally/physically handicapped, asocial elements, sexual deviants; anyone who didn't meet the Aryan image (or ar least Hitler's version). This was Hitler's rallying call to Make Germany Great Again. (Sound familiar?)

Six million Jews, a half-million Gypsies, and untold numbers of others were murdered during the Nazi regime. It was also Nuremberg where the Nuremberg Trials occurred, the military tribunal that was followed by twelve American military tribunals. There were four counts of Crimes Against Peace, Humanity, Common War Crimes, and a Conspiracy to Commit those crimes. However, no number of judgments could ever erase those atrocities committed by those brainwashed, mindless Hitler followers who had so besmirched the plight of so much humanity.

Once we were on the Danube River, we were in our cabins at night, recuperating from all our daytime sightseeing/exploring while the ship sailed down the Danube to our next adventure. Breakfast and dinner were normally served on board and were exceptionally good.

From Nuremberg, we took a small cruise up the Danube to the Weltenburg Asam Monastery, which was founded by Irish (or Scottish) monks in about 620 AD and is thought to be the oldest monastery in Bavaria. The monastery courtyard was surrounded by Baroque buildings, the highlight of which was the abbey church dedicated to Saint George, built by the Asam Brothers between 1716 and 1739. According to our guide, Weltenburg Abbey Brewery (Weltenburg Klosterbrauerei) was by some reckonings the oldest monastery brewery in the world, having been in operation since 1050.

We sailed on to Passau, the "City of Three Rivers," because the Danube was joined at Passau by the Inn from the south and the Ilz from the north. Passau's population hovered around 50,000, of whom about 10,000 were usually students at the local University of Passau. Our guide shared that Passau was an ancient Roman colony of ancient Noricum called Batavia, Latin for "for the Batavi." The Batavi were an ancient Germanic tribe often mentioned by classical authors, and they were regularly associated with the Suebian marauders, the Heruli. During the second half of the 5th century, St. Severinus established a monastery there. The organ at St. Stephen's was long held to be the largest church pipe organ in the world and was, at our visit, second in size only to the organ at First Congregational Church, Los Angeles.

Next, we toured Salzburg. It was the location where *The Sound of Music* was filmed. Places we visited, many of which were shown in *The Sound of Music*: Mirabell's Palace: Prince-Archbishop Wolf Dietrich von Raitenau had Altenau Palace built in 1606 as a token of his love for Salome Alt. The palace fulfilled its purpose: fifteen children were born of their union.

The Hohensalzburg Castle (Festung Hohensalzburg) on a hill dominating the old town is one of the largest castles in Europe, with views over Salzburg. The entire Old Town of Salzburg was nominated as a World Heritage Site in 1996.

Birthplace of Mozart: Melk Abbey or Stift Melk is an Austrian Benedictine Abbey and one of the world's most famous monastic sites. It is located above the town of Melk on a rocky outcrop overlooking the River Danube in Lower Austria, adjoining the Wachau Valley. So many breathtaking historical views to absorb!

On to Vienna and the Hofburg Palace/Apartments. We were welcomed to the Spanish Riding School in Vienna! The Spanish Riding School in Vienna is the only institution in the world that has practiced for over 430 years and continues to cultivate classical equitation in the Renaissance tradition of the Haute École. A few of the highlights in Vienna include St. Stephens Cathedral, Imperial Castle, Vienna Boys Choir, Schönbrunn Palace, and the Albertina Museum.

After Vienna, we cruised into Lower Austria, a peaceful, bucolic region and home to some of the country's best wines. By now, the stresses of everyday life seemed distant as we absorbed the ever-changing scenes, we floated past: children playing on the riverbanks, young couples strolling arm in arm like generations before them, vintners carefully pruning their vines, and cobbled quaysides lined by half-timbered buildings. We marveled as the captain skillfully navigated the ship along the serene river and through locks whose mechanisms never ceased to fascinate us as we cruised towards Dürnstein during dinner.

We started passing by Slovakia, officially the Slovak Republic, a landlocked country in Central Europe, bordered by Poland to the north, Ukraine to the east, Hungary to the south, Austria to the southwest, and the Czech Republic to the northwest. The capital and largest city is Bratislava. On our first morning in Slovakia, we explored their fast-emerging capital city, Bratislava, on a guided tour starting in its beautifully restored Old Town, where most of the historical buildings were concentrated. The Town Hall was a complex of three buildings erected in the 14th–15th centuries and, at the time of our visit, hosted the Bratislava City Museum.

While in Slovakia, we were bused to a remote village to have a Slavic meal prepared by local inhabitants. Our hostess spoke no English, but she had her daughter assisting, who spoke a limited amount of English. The lunch was quite different from the food we were used to, but it was quite good, and the experience was notable.

The final stop was Budapest, Hungary's capital (Queen of the Danube), bisected by the river Danube. Budapest was widely known for its well-kept pre-war cityscape, with a great variety of streets and landmarks in classical architecture. The most well-known sight of the capital was the neo-Gothic Parliament, the biggest building in Hungary with its almost 900 feet in length, also holding (since 2001) the Hungarian Crown Jewels. Saint Stephen's Basilica was the most important religious building of the city, where the Holy Right Hand of Hungary's first king, Saint Stephen, was on display as well. The tour also included a visit to a diamond factory, where I bought Sue a diamond ring to replace her engagement ring that had been stolen some years before.

We were fortunate to have in our party a gentleman who was born in Budapest and had spent his early youth there but had escaped from the approaching Nazi regime at an early age. He was Jewish. He and his wife befriended Sue and me and gave us a behind-the-scenes tour of Budapest. He showed us the house where he was born and where his first years were spent and then took us to this local partial inside/outside market where all the locals shopped and where it seemed everything was sold. We bought a leather belt and a couple of bags of paprika.

Photo by Dan Novac on Unsplash

Then he took us to the Dohány Street Synagogue, the largest synagogue in Europe and the second-largest active synagogue in the world. The synagogue was located in the Jewish district, taking up several blocks in central Budapest bordered by Király utca, Wesselényi utca, Grand Boulevard, and Bajcsy Zsilinszky road. It was built in the Moorish revival style in 1859 and had a seating capacity of 3,000. Adjacent to it was a sculpture reproducing a weeping willow tree in steel to commemorate the Hungarian victims of the Holocaust.

ALASKA

With our good friends Paul and Andrea Martin, we took an Alaskan Cruise with the Holland American Cruise Lines. We flew to Vancouver, British Columbia, where we spent a couple of days before we boarded our ship before actually setting out on our cruise.

Vancouver, a bustling West Coast seaport in British Columbia, was among Canada's densest, most ethnically diverse cities. It was purported to be a popular filming location and is surrounded by mountains, and also had a thriving art, theater, and music scene. We were provided with a grand tour of the city and an impressive looksee of Victoria and Butchart Gardens; absolutely awesome! Then, after boarding the ship, we sailed through the Icy Strait Point to Juneau.

The City and Borough of Juneau, more commonly known as Juneau, was the capital city of the state of Alaska and was located in the Gastineau Channel and the Alaskan panhandle. It was a unified municipality and the second-largest city in the United States by area. Juneau has been the capital of Alaska since 1906 when the government of what was then the District of Alaska was moved from Sitka per the U.S. Congress. Because of where it is situated and its surrounding terrain, Juneau is considered an island city in terms of transportation. All goods coming in or going out must go by plane or boat, as there are no roads to the rest of the mainland.

The next stop was Skagway, which we found to be a compact city in southeast Alaska, set along the popular cruise route, the Inside Passage. It was and is home to gold-rush-era buildings we found preserved as part of the Klondike Gold Rush National Historical Park. We discovered the White Pass & Yukon Route Railroad, which still ran vintage locomotives past the famously steep Chilkoot Trail and still offered sweeping mountain views during its climb toward Canada—not included in our cruise. We had another walking tour, and then it was back to the ship.

Figure 15 Hubbard Glacier

The next day, we visited the Hubbard Glacier, one of the biggest glaciers we could get to, which was enormous. The calving face was something like seven miles long and 1,100 feet high. We saw chunks of ice falling that were the size of football fields. It was weather-dependent on how close we could get, so on our day, it was a pretty nice day with fairly calm winds; therefore, we were able to get pretty close. It was one of the trip's highlights and not to be missed. Afterwards, it was back to the ship.

On to Seward, a port city in southern Alaska, set on an inlet on the Kenai Peninsula. Seward is a gateway to Kenai Fjords National Park, where glaciers flowed from the Harding Icefield into coastal fjords and were surrounded by peaks. We were told the fjords were the habitat of whales and porpoises. The city's Alaska Sea Life Center had seals, puffins, and fishing boats that filled Seward Harbor. To the west, a trail led to the summit of Mount Marathon. Fresh salmon, as well as dried salmon, were featured on almost all menus throughout our Alaskan trip. It was great for me. Maybe not quite so much for Sue, as she was not a great seafood enthusiast.

We disembarked our cruise ship and began our land tour portion of the trip at Anchorage. Anchorage, Alaska's largest city, is in the south-central part of the state on the Cook Inlet. It was known for its cultural sites, including the Alaska Native Heritage Center, which displayed traditional crafts and stage dances and presented replicas of dwellings from the area's indigenous groups. The city was also a gateway to nearby wilderness areas and mountains, including the Chugach, Kenai, and Talkeetna. It was one of the largest cities in the world located that far north. Our guided tour of the city and some of the surrounding environs was most interesting but did not include nearby Elmendorf Air Force Base. I would not have liked to have been stationed there, nor would I have liked to take up residence there, much too cold for my taste.

From Anchorage, we took the domed McKinley Explorer Train to Denali National Park, where we were housed at the McKinley Chalet Resort. Denali National Park and Preserve encompasses six million acres of Alaska's interior wilderness. Its centerpiece is the 20,310-foot-high Denali (Mount McKinley), North America's tallest peak. With terrain of tundra, spruce forest, and glaciers, the park is home to wildlife, including grizzly bears, wolves, moose, caribou, and Denali sheep. An impressive sight from our resort. Popular activities in summer included biking, backpacking, hiking, and mountaineering. We had two guided day tours into Denali Park and saw moose, Denali sheep, goats, and, in the distance, one black bear, and the topography was amazing.

We left Denali by train and headed for Fairbanks. At 65 degrees north latitude, the sky took on a capricious life of its own; a canvas for the aurora borealis, the midnight sun and sunsets and sunrises that lasted forever. (Unfortunately, the aurora borealis was not visible during our visit—at least not that we observed.) At its peak, Fairbanks enjoyed seventy straight days of twenty-four hours of daylight. There were serious mountain ranges, pristine rivers and lakes, abundant wildlife, and a certain poignant solitude that was found nowhere else on Earth.
Locals embraced the natural world and had created a vibrant river city in the far north. Where else could we travel to such a remote locale and still enjoy all the amenities of a charming downtown, a thriving arts community, rich Alaska Native culture, authentic Alaskan activities and attractions, and endless

opportunities for exploration? Still, not my ideal place to take up residence, but a neat place to visit; chalk it up on my bucket list. In addition to our normal guided tours, we observed a dog sled race. This concluded the end of our Alaskan adventure, so we jetted back home.

San Francisco

Sue and I had an exciting trip in and around San Francisco with our friends Paul and Andrea Martin. We stayed at the Marines' Memorial Hotel, centrally located in San Francisco, as both families were members of the Marines' Memorial Association. A couple of very steep blocks above the hotel was Chinatown, where we enjoyed their cuisine a couple of times. Also, cable car routes ran on both sides of the hotel just a few blocks away, and taxis and public transportation were easily available. Of course, we had to ride the cable cars at least a couple of times.

We took in the usual tourist attractions: the Golden Gate Bridge, Fisherman's Wharf (where we dined), Pier 39 (where we shopped and dined and watched the nearby California sea lions) and took cruises through Nob Hill and Telegraph Hill. I had my first view of the giant Redwood trees when we visited the Muir Woods National Monument, where the Redwoods extended forever—breathtaking views and lots of trails. Again, limited time.

Then we took a tour down Coastal Highway One, with our first major encounter being Santa Cruz, a city on central California's coast. Its long wharf, with eateries and shops, stretched into Monterey Bay. Nearby, the Santa Cruz Beach Boardwalk's vintage rides included the 1911 Looff Carousel and the Giant Dipper roller coaster. Downtown Pacific Avenue had vintage clothing stores, cafes, and galleries. Along West Cliff Drive, Natural Bridges State Beach was known for its bridge-shaped rock formation.

Santa Cruz was followed by Monterrey, a city located on California's rugged Central Coast. Its Cannery Row, the one-time center of the sardine-packing industry, was immortalized by novelist John Steinbeck. During our visit, it was a popular strip of gift shops, seafood restaurants, and bars inside converted factories. Next on to Carmel-by-the-Sea, a small beach city on California's Monterey Peninsula, known for its museums and library of the historic Carmel Mission, and the fairy tale cottages and galleries of its village-like center. The Scenic Bluff Path ran from surf spot Carmel Beach to bird-rich Carmel River State Beach, with a scuba entry point. South lay the sea animals and whaling museum of Point Lobos State Natural Reserve. It was here we visited Dr. Seuss's shop, where we purchased a lithograph of one of his paintings.

We ended our trek on Highway One at Big Sur, a rugged stretch of California's Central Coast between Carmel and San Simeon. It was bordered to the east by the Santa Lucia Mountains and the west by the Pacific Ocean, and it was traversed by narrow, two-lane State Route 1, known for winding turns, seaside cliffs, and views of the often-misty coastline (even though it was fairly clear on our travel day, thank goodness). On our way back to our hotel, we passed several roadside stands selling garlic—a big garlic farming area, it seemed.

Australia and New Zealand

Sue and I had planned a trip to Australia and New Zealand with Paul and Andrea Martin around their 50th anniversary. However, they had a change of heart and decided to take their whole family, kids, and grandkids back to England to celebrate their anniversary. Well, we had already made plans and decided to go ahead with our agenda to explore the great Down Under.

We signed up for a twenty-five-day cruise with Royal Caribbean Cruises but had to make our own flight arrangements. We had a four-hour flight on American Airlines from Dallas to Las Angeles's LAX Airport with a three-hour layover, then a fifteen-hour-plus flight on Qantas Airlines from LAX to Sydney. Our plane was late getting into Sydney, and we had to make a mad dash to get through Customs and almost missed our connecting flight to Perth, another four-hour flight. Thank goodness Royal Caribbean had a bus waiting to pick us up at the airport to take us to our hotel. (We had several other Royal Caribbean cruisers on our flight who made it through Customs with us, and there were several other cruisers on our flight who didn't make it through Customs and had to take a later flight.)

To say we were somewhat exhausted would have been a gross understatement, so the first thing we did was to freshen up the tiniest bit and quickly hit the rack for some badly needed snooze time.

We awakened sometime around 9 p.m. (Perth time), hungry and hoping we could still find someplace nearby where we would be able to get some vittles. We stopped to ask the desk clerk, and she advised us the hotel's restaurant was closed, but there was a moderately priced restaurant just a couple of blocks away. We decided because we were just starting this adventure, we would stick with the basics and ordered hamburgers, French fries, and cokes—not too much different from what we were used to having in the States. What was different, though, was the price. Our bill for hamburgers, fries, and coke amounted to over $75, tip not included. (Culture/inflation shock?)

We had an extra day to meander around Perth on our own before we were escorted to the ship to begin our actual cruise. We discovered although the Colony of New South Wales had been established as a convict-supported settlement at King George's Sound (later Albany) on the South Coast of Western Australia in 1826 in response to rumors that the area would be annexed by France, Perth had been the first full-scale settlement by Europeans in the western third of the continent.

From our ship, we were given a guided tour of Perth and the nearby Swan Valley, which included a couple of wine-tasting stops. (We had numerous excellent wine-tasting opportunities throughout our Down Under visit.) We toured around the city center, Fremantle, the coast, and the Swan River. In addition to the Perth Cultural Centre, there were dozens of museums across the city (which we unfortunately did not have time to visit).

We passed many heritage sites: Fremantle and other parts of the metropolitan areas. Some of the oldest remaining buildings, dated back to the 1830s, included the Round House in Fremantle, the Old Mill in South Perth, and the Old Court House in the city center. We were allowed a couple of hours to peruse the retail shopping in Perth, which was focused around Murray Street and Hay Street.

Then we were off to the Swan Valley, with its fertile soil—uncommon in the Perth region, we were told—which featured numerous wineries, such as the large complex at Houghton's, the state's biggest producer, Sandalfords, and many smaller operators, including microbreweries and rum distilleries. The Swan Valley also contained specialized food producers, many restaurants and cafes, and roadside local produce stalls that sold seasonal fruit throughout the year. Tourist Drive 203 was a circular route in the Swan Valley. We passed by many attractions on West Swan Road and the Great Northern Highway.

Our ship sailed at night, so we tended to stop at cities along the way, some small and some larger, and during our stops, we were always offered guided tours inland to get a flavor of Southern Australia. We were able to see firsthand some of their agricultural endeavors: fields of wheat, barley, canola, cotton, sugar cane, orchards, and varieties of vegetables, oats, and rice. We occasionally got a view of the native flora and fauna, as this would occur throughout our experience.

I will just mention some of the more common ones here: kangaroos—the largest marsupial in the world; herbivores—mainly ate grass; emus—the second-largest marsupial next to kangaroos and lived in pairs of families (youngsters stayed with adults often up to two years); duck-billed venomous platypus—of two only known monotremes or egg-laying mammals in Australia (only five in the world), koala—lived mainly in gum tree forests and woodlands and usually found in tall eucalyptus trees; bandicoot—nocturnal marsupials; gray-headed flying fox—largest Australian native bat; spotted quolls—Australian mainland's largest carnivorous marsupials; Tasmanian devil—the size of a small dog, could hunt in packs, and was the largest carnivorous marsupial, and only found in Tasmanian; two types of crocodiles,—freshwater and saltwater (saltwater, the largest crocodiles in the world); laughing kookaburra, with its distinctive riotous call, and other native species introduced by human settlement. The most well-known were dingoes (dogs) and rabbits.

Our first major port of call after leaving Perth was Adelaide, the capital city of South Australia, the state's largest city, and the fifth-most populous city in Australia. "Adelaide" may refer to either Greater Adelaide (including the Adelaide Hills) or the Adelaide city center. Until the post-war era, it was Australia's third most populated city. It had been noted for its leading examples of religious freedom and progressive political reforms and became known as the "City of Churches" due to its diversity of faiths. During our visit, it was known for its many festivals and sporting events, food and wine, coastline and hills, and its large defense and manufacturing sectors.

Our next major stop was Melbourne, the second-largest city in Australia. The discovery of gold in Victoria in mid-1851 sparked a gold rush, and Melbourne, the colony's major port, experienced rapid growth. Within months, the city's population had nearly doubled from 25,000 to 40,000 inhabitants. Exponential growth ensued, and by 1865, Melbourne had overtaken Sydney as Australia's most populous city. South Melbourne's "Canvas Town" provided temporary accommodation for the thousands of migrants who arrived each week during the 1850's gold rush. (Note the time nearly coincided with the California Gold Rush.)

During World War II, Australia was fully involved in the war effort, and as part of that effort, Melbourne hosted American military forces when the government requisitioned the Melbourne Cricket Ground for military use. While successive contingents of Yanks passed through Melbourne, it was the lengthy nine-month stay of the Marines during 1943 that was distinctive and particularly memorable. They considered Melbourne their second home, even adopting the traditional Australian folk song "Waltzing Matilda" as their "battle hymn" and have continued to sing it at every annual reunion since the war ended. The US servicemen's music, food, language, and everyday modes of behavior influenced Australian culture more broadly.

Then, we were off to Tasmania, which was an island south of Australia. Tasmania seemed to be a world unto itself and most fascinating. Tasmania is renowned for its unique wildlife and spectacular natural sites and national parks, which cover vast amounts of land on all ends of the island. Hiking trails leading to majestic waterfalls were not uncommon, we were told, and we crossed paths with rare species of birds (pointed out by our guide) and saw the iconic Tasmanian devil in an enclosure! They (there were several) did not care for tourists and thank goodness they couldn't get to us!

Photo by Michael Jerrard on Unsplash

The Tasmanian devil became the largest carnivorous marsupial in the world following the extinction of the thylacine in 1936 and was now found in the wild only in Tasmania. Tasmania was one of the last regions of Australia to be introduced to domesticated dogs. Dogs were brought from Britain in 1803 to hunt kangaroos and emus. This introduction completely transformed Aboriginal society, as it helped them to successfully compete with European hunters and was more important than the introduction of guns for the Aboriginal people.

Tasmania had extremely diverse vegetation, from the heavily grazed grassland of the dry Midlands to the tall evergreen eucalyptus forest, alpine heathlands, and large areas of cool temperate rainforests and moorlands in the rest of the state. Many species were unique to Tasmania, and some were related to species in South America and New Zealand through ancestors who grew on the supercontinent of Gondwana 50 million years ago.

Back on our ship, we sailed across the Tasmanian Sea to New Zealand. The mountains protecting the New Zealand shores were stark and seemed to rise straight up from the sea as we eked our way through one channel after another. The mountains rose up on both sides of the ship, almost occluding the light from the sun, and were assisted by a dense fog that hovered somewhere beneath the mountains' rooftops. The constant cold, wet drizzle did not help matters, either.

Figure 17 New Zealand Gorge

Our first major stop in New Zealand was Queenstown, which was on the shores of the South Island's Lake Wakatipu, set against the dramatic Southern Alps. It was renowned for adventure sports. It was also a base for exploring the region's vineyards and historic mining towns. There was bungee jumping off Kawarau Gorge Suspension Bridge and jetboating on the Shotover and Dart Rivers. No one on our tour, to my knowledge, partook of either, at least that I was aware.

Then we sailed around the southern portion of New Zealand's South Island, stopping to explore the Slope Point End 46,40" South Latitude 2,985 miles north of the South Pole, New Zealand's southernmost tip. Interestingly, some of the flora, small trees, and shrubs were severely bent in the opposing direction from the prevailing wind.

Then to Dunedin, a city in New Zealand, at the head of Otago Harbor on the South Island's southeast coast. It was known for its Scottish and Māori heritage, Victorian and Edwardian architecture, and a large student population. Hiking and cycling trails crisscrossed the dramatic landscape of the adjoining Otago Peninsula, home to colonies of albatrosses, sea lions, and rare, yellow-eyed penguins. It was the closest major city and port for the 1861 Otago Gold Rush, and the gold rush was the actual genesis for Dunedin. Matter of fact, during the height of the gold rush, Dunedin grew to be the most populist city in New Zealand.

From Dunedin, we took an excursion to visit the old mining town, more like a ghost town. The day trip included a visit to a working sheep farm, where we witnessed sheep dogs in action herding sheep being directed by tweets of a whistle on which way to herd the sheep and then when to bring them home (and also an exhibition of sheep shearing). This was followed by a barbecue of a roasted sheep feast with all the trimmings, where we watched sheep on the spit actually being roasted!

Last on our tour of New Zealand was Christchurch, the largest city in the South Island of New Zealand

and the seat of the Canterbury Region. Christchurch lay on the South Island's East Coast, just north of Banks Peninsula on Pegasus Bay. The Avon River/Ōtākaro flowed through the center of the city, with an urban park along its banks. The city's territorial authority population was somewhat less than 400,000 people and included several smaller urban areas as well as rural areas.

Christchurch was the second-largest city by urban area population in New Zealand, after Auckland. It was the major urban area of an emerging sub-region known informally as Greater Christchurch. Christchurch became a city by Royal Charter on 31 July 1856, making it officially the oldest established city in New Zealand. The city suffered a series of earthquakes between September 2010 and January 2012 (one to three years after our visit there), with the most destructive occurring at 12:51 p.m. on 22 February 2011, in which 185 people were killed, and thousands of buildings across the city suffered severe damage, with a few central city buildings collapsing. By late 2013, 1,500 buildings in the city had been demolished, leading to ongoing recovery and rebuilding projects. The city later became the site of a terrorist attack targeting two mosques on 15 March 2019, in which fifty-one people were killed, and which was described by Prime Minister Jacinda Ardern as "one of New Zealand's darkest days."

The water cruise portion of the trip, both for Australia and New Zealand, ended with the disembarkation of all passengers at Sydney. There was a small contingency of us who had signed up for an extended internal land tour. Those of us in the extended tour were bused from the ship to the Sydney Airport and flown to Cairns, located in their tropical Queensland territory, gateway to the Great Barrier Reef. From Cairns Airport, we were driven to our luxurious hotel and, the following day, drove to the Rainforest Station Kuranda, where we had this fantastic tour through the jungle in a WWII Duck, an amphibious tank-like thing-a-ma-jig. Back at the station, we were treated to some native food and entertainment as well, and we got to encounter some of the native wildlife. The park was sort of a breeding station. Sue got to hold a koala; there seemed to be a lot of them there. There were also wombats, wallabies, dingoes, and even crocodiles, and there were probably a lot more of which I just don't recall.

The following day, we were bused out to the Great Barrier Reef and took a large boat to this huge man-made platform that was located quite a distance from the land, where we spent most of the day. On the platform, there was a historical museum explaining all facets of the reef. Also, we were able to take a submarine that was equipped with these neat viewing windows down inside the reef to view the coral beds and the activity within and were able to view schools of fishes darting around and many species of fish lazily swimming by the sub. I guess with all the tourists visiting, the fish were used to intruders.

Back at the topside, the weather on the platform was remarkably coolish, and because I guess I was expecting tropical weather, I hadn't dressed too warmly; in other words, I was cold.

A grand buffet consisting mainly of seafood was offered with lots of plump shrimp, one of my favorites. However, when we sat down on the park-like benches to eat, I must tell you I was still cold, and my fingers were stiff and somewhat shrunk. I found that peeling the shrimp became a bit of a chore.

Two things I should mention here. The platform floor consisted of spaced planking with spaces about three-fourths of an inch between each plank. The second thing was that when Sue put my wedding ring on my finger in 1967, I had never taken it off until a year or so before this trip. I had to have surgery on my left hand to correct a trigger finger problem, and the surgeon insisted I had to have my wedding ring removed. Well, with the ensuing years and my gaining some weight, the ring would not come off despite the surgery staff's best efforts, so they had to cut it off, much to my consternation. After surgery, though, I took the mangled, severed ring to a jeweler and had him add some gold so that it would fit back on my finger. Needless to say, it was much looser than the original ring that had been on my finger and easily came off and went back on again.

Photo by Shaun Low on Unsplash

The boiled shrimp was excellent but somewhat greasy, and somehow, to my dismay, I felt my wedding ring slip off my finger. It didn't even bounce on the floor but went right through the crack at my feet. I could see it hit the ocean water beneath my feet, not even making a tiny splash, and then it ever so slowly dipped and swirled, almost in ringlets, slowly sinking into the Coral Sea and disappearing into the colorful waters below. And there it remained with the fish and coral. Is it still there? I don't know, but it no longer sits around my finger.

Next, we flew from Cairns to Alice Springs and then took a long bus ride to visit Uluru, or Ayers Rock, which is a massive sandstone monolith in the heart of the Northern Territory's arid "Red Centre." The nearest large town was Alice Springs, about 305 miles away from Uluru. According to the guide, Uluru was thought to have started forming around 550 million years ago. It was within Uluru-Kata Tjuta National Park, which also included the 36 red-rock domes of the Kata Tjuta (colloquially "The Olgas") formation. Uluru was sacred to the Pitjantjatjara, the Aboriginal people of the area, known as the Anangu.

Photo by Michael Jerrard on Unsplash

The area around the formation was home to an abundance of springs, waterholes, rock caves, and ancient paintings. Uluru is listed as a UNESCO World Heritage Site. Uluru and Kata Tjuta, also known as the Olgas, were the two major features of the Uluru-Kata Tjuta National Park. Uluru was one of Australia's most recognizable natural landmarks and has been a popular destination for tourists since the late 1930s.

That night, we had a magical candlelight dinner under the stars a few miles away from Ayers Rock, enveloped by the darkness around us except for the sparse candlelight on the elaborately set dining tables with their stark white cloths. The canopy overhead was like a humongous soup bowl turned upside down with twinkling stars glued to its underside. In the extreme darkness, it was like seeing stars stacked behind each other and the Milky Way stretching above us, best described as if someone had painted a great swath of a somewhat fluorescent glow stretching across a portion of the sky and sort of an afterthought someone had scattered in some twinkling stars hither and yon. It was almost like being set down in another world.

The meal was an exciting adventure, and I don't recall all that it entailed, but I do remember two of the main course items—kangaroo and alligator. There were also native fruits, vegetables, and salads.

We were entertained while dining with several selections on the didgeridoo. The didgeridoo is a wind instrument played with vibrating lips to produce a continuous drone while using a special breathing technique called circular breathing. I could feel the vibration in my body. It was like my bones were humming along. I could even feel it in my teeth. I don't think I've ever heard anything quite like that before.

After our dining experience, we were invited to trek away from the dining area to another space where a group of telescopes had been arranged for a star (or planet) gazing experience. Each telescope had been set up to view a particular star or planet, and our guides quickly pointed out particular details of each and also constellations and stars (including the Southern Cross, which was only visible below the equator) easily seen with the naked eye.

The next morning, we were roused at O dark thirty in order to be at Ayers Rock to see the sunrise over the rock, quite a spectacular view! However, we were outfitted with head nets, much like those beekeepers wear to protect themselves from bee stings. Ours, however, were to protect us from the thousands of fly-like gnats that swarmed everywhere. I was reminded of the biblical passages from Exodus regarding the swarming locusts. In addition to the spectacular sunrise over Ayers Rock that morning, we were also greeted with a stupendous rainbow that stretched across part of the rock.

From Ayers Rock, we were bused back to Alice Springs and then flew back to Sydney for the final days of our trip. Sydney was the capital city of the state of New South Wales and the most populous city in both Australia and Oceania. It was located on Australia's southeast coast. The metropolis surrounded Sydney Harbor and extended about 43.5 miles towards the Blue Mountains to the west, Hawkesbury to the north, the Royal National Park to the south, and Macarthur to the southwest.

Photo by Kevin Murray on Unsplash

Aboriginal Australians had inhabited the Greater Sydney region for at least 30,000 years, and we were told Aboriginal engravings and cultural sites were common throughout Greater Sydney. The traditional custodians of the land on which modern Sydney stands were the clans of the Darug, Dharawal, and Eora peoples. During his first Pacific voyage in 1770 (War of Independence 1776), Lieutenant James Cook and his crew became the first Europeans to chart the Eastern Coast of Australia, making landfall at Botany Bay. In 1788, the First Fleet of convicts, led by Arthur Phillip, founded Sydney as a British penal colony, the first European settlement in Australia. After World War II, Sydney experienced mass migration, and by 2021, over 40 percent of the population was born overseas. Foreign countries of birth with the greatest representation were Mainland China, India, England, Vietnam, and the Philippines.

Despite being one of the most expensive cities in the world (which we can attest to), Sydney frequently ranked in the top ten most livable cities in the world. The city had over 2,500,000 acres of nature reserves and parks, and its notable natural features included Sydney Harbor and Royal National Park. The Sydney Harbor Bridge and the World Heritage-listed Sydney Opera House were major tourist attractions. The guided tours of Sydney were very impressive, with the highlight being the tour inside the opera house itself. Our stay in Sydney was at the same hotel where General MacArthur resided during his command of the Allied Pacific Forces during WWII.

After Sydney, it was back to LAX for us—possibly the worst, most frustrating airport in the world. The airport attendants were just mean, not helpful at all.

And then home.

40. KEPT ON TRAVELIN'

Christmas Marketing in Germany

When we landed in Munich, Germany, it was snowing, and by the time we got to our bus waiting to take us to Nuremberg, where we would be starting our Christmas Marketing Tour, it was really beginning to snow hard. This was certainly a lot different from the weather we had left back in Texas.

We hadn't gotten but a few miles out of Munich when we drove into a real blizzard. The snow was coming down in billowing sheets, and the visibility in front of the bus was practically nonexistent. Then, of all things, the bus's windshield wipers froze and stopped working, so the driver had to pull over, stop the bus, and treat the blades to unfreeze them before we could continue our trip.

The snow continued falling in almost blinding gusts all the way to Nuremberg, causing traffic to slow to almost a crawl in some places. Needless to say, it took us a lot longer to get to Nuremberg than was originally planned. However, the snow was gorgeous. Actually, it was kinda eerie. This was a winter storm we hadn't expected but were delighted to participate in as long as we were inside the bus, warm and fairly comfortable. The snow continued to accompany us for the rest of our tour, making the markets—and all of Germany, for that matter—a beautiful winter wonderland, and we got to see it in all its splendor.

All of the markets contained the flavors of the individual areas, their crafts, foods, drinks, costumes, and music. It appeared each market had outdone the previous one. Nuremberg was our first Christmas Market stop with all the Christmas lights and the festive spirits. It was hard to imagine this was the city where Hitler had preached his propaganda to the masses, spewing out his venom, lies, and hate that caused millions to be sacrificed in the Holocaust that preceded and led to WWII. Also, this was the city where the Nuremberg Tribunal was held at the conclusion of the Allies' laborious, hard-earned, and frightfully costly victory over the Axis Forces to mete out at least **some** accountability for the atrocities committed.

From Nuremberg, we boarded our riverboat on the Main River through Frankfurt, where we hooked up with the Rhine River, and we had our next Christmas Market in Mainz, a German city on the Rhine River known for its old town with half-timbered houses and medieval market squares. Many of the houses could have been used as models for the houses pictured or described in the Grimm Brothers' fairy tales. In the center, the Marktbrunnen was a Renaissance fountain with red columns. Nearby, a distinctive octagonal tower topped the Romanesque Mainz Cathedral, built of deep red sandstone. The Gutenberg Museum honored the inventor of the printing press with exhibits, including two of his original bibles. We purchased a copy of the smallest bible in the world, a real miniature.

On to Koblenz, a German city on the banks of the Rhine and of the Moselle, a multi-nation tributary. Per our guide, Koblenz was established as a Roman military post by Drusus around 8 B.C. Its name originated from the Latin confluence. The actual confluence was known as the "German Corner," a symbol of the unification of Germany that featured an equestrian statue of Emperor William I. The city celebrated its 2,000th anniversary in 1992. Koblenz lay in a narrow flood plain between high hill ranges, some reaching mountainous heights, and was served by an express rail and autobahn network.

Next, we visited Bonn, a city in western Germany that straddled the Rhine River. Most of our time was used up in the different Christmas Markets, but we did have guided tours of each city we visited. Bonn was known for its central Beethoven House, a memorial and museum honoring the composer's birthplace. Nearby was the Bonn Minster, a church with a Romanesque cloister and Gothic elements, the pink-and-gold Altes Rathaus, or old city hall, and Poppelsdorf Palace, housing a mineralogical museum. Haus der Geschichte had some fascinating post-WWII history exhibits. During the Second World War, Bonn acquired military significance because of its strategic location on the Rhine, which formed a natural barrier to prevent easy penetration into the German heartland from the west. However, the Allied Forces (US 1st Infantry Division) captured the city during the battle of 8–9 March 1945. After the Second World War, Bonn was in the British zone of occupation.

Our final Christmas Marketing adventure was in Cologne, a 2,000-year-old city spanning the Rhine River in western Germany. It was the region's cultural hub, a landmark of High Gothic architecture set amid the reconstructed old town. The twin-spired Cologne Cathedral was also known for its gilded medieval reliquary and sweeping river views. The adjacent Museum Ludwig showcased 20th-century art, including many masterpieces by Picasso, and the Romano-Germanic Museum housed Roman antiquities. From simply a tourist point of view, it was the most interesting stop on our itinerary. The city's medieval Catholic Cologne Cathedral (Kölner Dom), the third-tallest church and tallest cathedral in the world, constructed to house the Shrine of the Three Kings, was a globally recognized landmark and one of the most visited sites and pilgrimage destinations in Europe. The cityscape was further shaped by the Twelve Romanesque churches of Cologne. Cologne was also famous for Eau de Cologne, which had been produced in the city since 1709, and "cologne" has since come to be a generic term.

Prior to World War II, the city had undergone occupations by the French (1794–1815) and the British (1918–1926) and was part of Prussia beginning in 1815. Cologne was one of the most heavily bombed cities in Germany during World War II. The bombing reduced the population by 95%, mainly due to evacuation, and almost the entire millennia-old city center was destroyed.

While we were in Cologne, Katrin (the exchange student who lived with Sissy in Newark while she went to school in the US) and her new husband Mik met us for a visit, and we took them to lunch. After lunch, we presented them with the Dallas sweatshirts we had brought for them. Too soon, it was time to head back to Texas.

Presidential Tour of South America
Sue and I signed up for a twenty-seven-day Presidential Tour of South America, and after departing the U.S. from Miami, Florida, we landed in

Santiago, Chile. We were taken from the airport to our hotel, where we had our welcoming dinner, slept the night, had an early breakfast, and bright and early in the morning, we were bused to San Pedro de Atacama, at about 8,000 feet elevation, which included many of the small towns in that sparsely inhabited area of Chile.

Before the Inca Empire and prior to the arrival of the Spanish, the extremely arid interior was inhabited primarily by the Atacameño tribe. They were noted for building fortified towns called pucarás, one of which was located a few kilometers from San Pedro de Atacama.

The town's original church, located just a block or so from the hotel where we were lodged, was built by the Spanish in the mid-1500s (was later rebuilt) and was located on the west side of the tree-lined Plaza de Armas and near the town's oldest building, Casa Incaica, which dated back to 1540—just a little over fifty years after Columbus discovered the Americas. I was absolutely fascinated that it existed and was still there in a usable condition.

The church was constructed of adobe material; there were three doors, an arched stone lintel, and a beamed ceiling. Both the interior and exterior were painted white, while the altar was of bright colors. The walls, roof, and entrance door were built with Algarrobo wood and cordon (cactus wood) and bound together by llama leather, in the technique traditional to the altiplano. The roof was made of large rafters of Algarrobo wood that were overlaid with slices of cactus logs. Algarrobo trees were seen along with the pepper trees next to the church. The altarpieces inside the church were carved and painted, and the statues were of St. Mary and St. Joseph and contained fluorescent lighting features. The church was a designated National Monument. San Pedro de Atacama Hotel was located in the Atacama Desert and was used as our base station for exploring the surrounding environments.

The Atacama Desert is a desert plateau in South America covering an approximately thousand-mile strip of land on the Pacific Coast, west of the Andes Mountains. According to our guide, the Atacama Desert is considered the driest non-polar desert in the world, as well as the only true desert to receive less precipitation than the polar deserts. And while we were there, it was hot and dry! It had been used as an experimentation site for Mars expedition simulations. Most of the desert was composed of stony terrain, salt lakes, sand, and felsic lava that flowed towards the Andes. The desert owed its extreme aridity to a constant temperature inversion due to the cool north-flowing Humboldt Ocean current and to the presence of the strong Pacific anticyclone.

The most arid region of the Atacama Desert was situated between two mountain chains (the Andes and the Chilean Coast Range) of sufficient height to prevent moisture advection from either the Pacific or the Atlantic Oceans, a two-sided rain shadow. The Atacama Desert may be the oldest desert on Earth and has experienced extreme hyperacidity for at least three million years.

Photo by Florian Delée on Unsplash

Death Valley, also known as Mars Valley, was in the middle of the Cordillera de la Sal, just a little over a mile from San Pedro de Atacama. Its name was because, formerly, whoever dared to attempt to cross the Valley died in the attempt. Proof of this was in the remains of bones of animals and of people that had been found in the place, in addition to pieces of natural plaster that were often confused with these vestiges. No type of plant or insect could live there because of the lack of moisture. Death Valley has been called by many as the most inhospitable place on the planet, although for recreational purposes, its dunes were highly appreciated by those who practiced trekking and sandboarding—of course, on a limited basis.

For us, it was up at O' dark thirty for a bus ride through the up and down mountainous terrain to El Tatio to see the peak activity of the geothermal field with its many geysers (over eighty), which began just before sunrise. The El Tatio geothermal field was located in the Andes Mountains of northern Chile at 14,170 feet above mean sea level and lay at the western foot of a series of stratovolcanoes that ran along the border between Chile and Bolivia. It was the third-largest geyser field in the world (next to Iceland and Yellowstone) and the largest in the Southern Hemisphere. The geothermal field had many geysers, hot springs, and associated sinter deposits.

Figure 22 El Tatio Geothermal Geyser Field, Chile

We had been encouraged to bring bathing suits to take advantage of the hot springs. However, in spite of the warm, even somewhat hot, temperature of the hot springs, the ambient temperatures were pretty frigid, and we were thankful we were wearing our coats, so we did not participate in bathing in the hot springs, even though there were others there who were soaking/playing in the springs.

On our return trip, we drove through Los Flamencos National Reserve, a nature reserve located in the commune of San Pedro de Atacama, Antofagasta Region of northern Chile. The reserve covered a total area of 286 square miles in the Central Andean dry Puna ecoregion and consisted of seven separate sections. It housed and protected a rich diversity of flora and fauna in the middle of the Atacama Desert. And yes, we did see a whole bunch of pink flamencos.

We also traversed Valle de la Luna (Valley of the Moon), a valley within Los Flamencos National Reserve. It was known for its moonlike landscape of dunes, rugged mountains, and distinctive rock formations—weird topography. To the southeast, the turquoise water of the Laguna Cejar sinkhole had an extremely high salt concentration. On one of our day trips, we ascended somewhat slowly to the Edwardo Avaro Andreau Fawna National Reserve in Bolivia.

Our destination was an area of inactive volcano sites that harbored two salt lakes—Laguna Verde (green) and Laguna Blanca (white) at an elevation exceeding 14,000 feet. However, on our visit, both lakes

Figure 23 laguna Verde, Boliva 14,000 feet

appeared to be as blue as they could possibly be. Interestingly, on our
way to the lakes, we passed through a few villages and were exposed to poverty and squalor firsthand at its least desirable, making us wonder how these people managed to survive. Just a few miles before we

reached our destination, we stopped at a roadside café for lunch and had…I'm not sure what. It was a challenging combination, and almost nothing was discernible.

However, to my knowledge, none of us got sick, so I guess it was all OK. Sue hardly tasted anything. Also, the numerous flies were big pests, lunchtime challengers, were swarming everywhere, and had to be fought off.

The night before we left the Atacama Desert, the tour guide arranged a cookout on a peak overlooking the desert, and after stuffing ourselves and sharing probably too much wine, we watched this glorious sunset gradually fade into the desert—even before the last shades of the sun had disappeared, stars began to burst out of the sky everywhere. As more darkness crowded in, the sky became alive with billions of stars, each seeming to out-glow the next—they were producing their own set of fireworks—and the star (no pun intended) of the show was the great Southern Cross. It was like a net of brilliant stars had been cast over the entire earth. Brilliant! The Atacama Desert was advertised as one of the best places on Earth for stargazing, and after our soiree, I agreed, as did everyone on our tour.

From the Atacama Desert, we were bused back to our original hotel in Santiago, where we toured the city and the surrounding area. Santiago was Chile's capital and largest city and sat in a valley surrounded by the snow-capped Andes and the Chilean Coast Range. Plaza de Armas, the grand heart of the city's old colonial core, was home to two neoclassical landmarks: the 1808 Palacio de la Real Audiencia, housing the National History Museum, and the 18th-century Metropolitan Cathedral. Santiago was founded in 1541. We had an all-day tour of the city and environs and a second-day tour of some of the surrounding area, which included a couple of vineyards and some excellent wine tasting. Then, we flew off to the southern tip of South America.

Punta Arenas (historically Sandy Point in English—latitude 53.16 S) was the capital city of Chile's southernmost region, Magallanes and Antarctica, Chile. It was the largest city south of the 46th parallel, and at the same time the most populous southernmost city in Chile and in the Americas. Due to its location, it was the coldest coastal city with more than 100,000 inhabitants in Latin America. It was one of the most southerly ports in the world, serving as an Antarctic gateway city.

The temperatures were frigidly cold, and the wind was fierce and seemed to never stop blowing, and we were grossly underdressed and under-prepared for the cold. It felt like we were never going to get warm again. We saw many objects tied down or secured so they would not be blown away by the gale-like winds.

Located on the Brunswick Peninsula north of the Strait of Magellan, Punta Arenas was originally established by the Chilean government in 1848 as a tiny penal colony to assert sovereignty over the Strait. During the remainder of the 1800s, Punta Arenas grew in size and importance due to the increasing maritime traffic and trade traveling to the west coasts of South and North America. That period of growth also resulted from the waves of European immigrants, mainly from Croatia and Russia, attracted to a gold rush and sheep farming boom in the 1880s and early 1900s. The largest sheep company, controlling 3,863 square miles in Chile and Argentina, was based in Punta Arenas, and its owners lived there. The geopolitical importance of Punta Arenas remained high in the 20th and 21st centuries because of its logistic importance in accessing the Antarctic Peninsula. One of our day-trip excursions was to visit a penguin colony. Again, it was very cold. We saw a few penguins, but most of the penguins had already migrated elsewhere. Our tour was a little late for good interactions with the penguins.

We were bused from Punta Arenas to El Calafate, a small town located on Lake Argentina, where we boarded our ship to tour the lake to visit the land of the glaciers, the third-largest collection of glaciers in the world only exceeded by Antarctica and Greenland. Los Glaciares National Park was in the Austral Andes of southwest Argentina, near the Chilean border.

Our boat amenities were first class. The boat's owner was also the chief chef, and her desserts were to die for. All other menu items offered were superb as well. There was no lack of great food, and if anyone went hungry, it was not for lack of availability of the mouth-watering cuisine. All beverages, including alcoholic ones, were included.

The ice cap accounted for about 30 percent of the national park area. The ice cap of Los Glaciares National Park was unique, with the glaciers starting at 4,900 feet above sea level as compared to most other glaciers that began at elevations from 8,200 feet and higher.

The parks' many glaciers included Perito Moreno, best known for the dramatic icefalls from its front wall into Lake Argentina. Perito Moreno Glacier was considered one of the leading attractions of the national park. Although it was located in one of the most remote parts of the world, Perito Moreno Glacier was accessible from the land and was accessible by a short hike. Visitors traveled the world to see this exquisite glacial landscape, us included.

To the north, Mount Fitz Roy's jagged peak rose above the mountain town of El Chaltén and Lake Viedma. The name was derived from the ice cap located in the Andes of that part of the range. This Andes ice cap served as the source for forty-seven large glaciers, with thirteen of them flowing eastward toward the Atlantic Ocean. Los Glaciares National Park was a UNESCO World Heritage site displaying an excellent example of the Magellanic subpolar forest as well as featuring the Patagonian steppe biodiversity. The arid Patagonian steppe was created from the barrier of the Andes mountains, which prevented moisture from the Pacific Ocean from reaching the other side of the range.

Figure 24 Los Glacier National Park, Argentina

The park was home to many birds, such as condors and black-chested buzzard eagles, which I assumed we saw many times circling overhead but was not able to identify or even differentiate them. And much to everyone's delight, we had a couple of families of dolphins racing our ship on at least two occasions as they flipped and bobbed alongside our ship racing us and making a game of it. Too, early one morning as we scurried around the lake and got a little close to shore, we surprised a nest of walruses sunning themselves peacefully who in no uncertain terms let us know that they did not welcome our intrusion with some wild barking and flapping around as if to warn us to get the heck out of their territory. All too soon it was time to depart the lake and to leave the land of glaciers behind.

After heading out towards Bueno Areas, we stayed at an extravagant resort at the foot of the spectacular Fitz Roy Mountains in El Chalten. El Chaltén was a village within Los Glaciares National Park in Argentina's Santa Cruz province. It was considered a gateway to trails surrounding the peaks of Cerro Torre and Mount Fitz Roy to the northwest. Near Fitz Roy, a path led to the Laguna de los Tres viewpoint. Just northwest of the village, the shores of Laguna Capri offered mountain views. Shops lined San Martín, one of the village's main streets. The day trips from the resort to viewing the local topography were breathtaking. Then, we were back on the road to Bueno Aries.

Figure 25 ,Mt Fitz Roy, Argentina

Buenos Aires, officially the Autonomous City of Buenos Aires (Spanish), was the capital and first city of Argentina. Its center was the Plaza de Mayo, lined with stately 19th-century buildings, including Casa Rosada, the iconic, balconied presidential palace where the song *"Don't Cry for Me Argentina"* was sung in the movie *Evita*. Other major attractions included Teatro Colón, a grand 1908 opera house with nearly 2,500 seats, and the modern MALBA museum, displaying Latin American art.

In 2012, it was the most visited city in South America, and the second-most visited city of Latin America. Since the 19th century, the city, and the country in general, had been a major recipient of millions of immigrants from all over the world, making it a melting pot where several ethnic groups lived together. Thus, Buenos Aires was considered one of the most diverse cities of the Americas.

An exciting historical event occurred while we were visiting Buenos Aires. Their Jesuit Cardinal Jorge Bergoglio was named Pope and took on the name Pope Francis. The whole city just went crazy. Pope Francis was the first Pope named from the New World and was the first Jesuit (actually many firsts). The whole city was jubilant, or so it appeared. He was dearly loved and respected. Overnight, all kinds of souvenirs for the new Pope were available to purchase, and of course, we were right in line to visit the cathedral where he had been presiding.

In addition to the definitive and enlightening day tours with all the historical information, we were also treated to some fairly elaborate dinners and evening entertainment. One such evening affair was an evening filled with an exhibition of tango dancing by a professional troupe. After their finale, one of our Canadian passengers even got a chance to join the professionals (one professional) and strut her stuff. Actually, she wasn't half bad. Guess all those lessons paid off.

We left Buenos Aires and were loaded back on our trusty bus to Iguazu Falls, where we checked into our five-star hotel adjacent to the jungle within a short walk to Iguazu Falls—a World Heritage Site. Iguazu Falls was the largest waterfall system in the world. Depending on the definition of a waterfall, there were either 85 or 275 individual waterfalls that were part of the larger Iguazu Falls system. The Falls spanned 1.7 miles along and over the border between Argentina and Brazil.

Devil's Throat measured 269 feet and was the tallest drop across all the falls. The various falls varied in height from 197 feet to 269 feet. This highest point was locally called Garganta del Diablo, which translated as Devil's Throat. The collective span was wider than Victoria Falls, located on the border between Zambia and Zimbabwe. Iguazu Falls had an average flow rate of 62,010 cubic feet per second. Niagara Falls, on the border of Canada and the United States, had a higher volume of water, but Iguazu Falls was wider and taller. Many would claim that Iguazu Falls is the most beautiful waterfall in the world, and from those I have seen and experienced, I would agree. It was certainly most impressive!

The jungle we encountered around the Falls was not much like the ones portrayed in the movies because of all the tourists that had and were still visiting the area. There were lots of well-worn paths leading all over the place alongside the jungle that covered the sides of the Falls. Too, there was lots of fauna to be encountered; monkeys, toucans, and coati were everywhere, and so many birds and butterflies we couldn't keep track of them all. Trails leading to the Falls allowed stupendous views.

I also took a boat trip right into some of the Falls, and despite having rain gear, I got soaked (Sue declined to participate with me in this endeavor even though I had purchased her a nonrefundable ticket as well—go figger). After challenging the Falls, we floated down the Iguazu River and were given an open-air Jeep tour of a different part of the jungle and passed an eagle perched in the overhead canopy of the jungle on our way back.

Iguazu Falls, Photo by Jaime Dantas on Unsplash

Before we left the Argentinean side of the Falls, we had a day trip to see the Brazilian Side of the Falls. Even though from our hotel and our side of the Falls, we could look directly over to the Brazilian side and what looked like half a mile or maybe even a mile across; however, to get there by motor vehicle was another matter. We had to head west to follow the Parana River, which separated Paraguay from Argentina Before we left the Argentinean side of the Falls, we had a day get there by motor vehicle was another matter. We had to head west to north to three points where Paraguay, Argentina, and Brazil confluence. That is where the Iguazu River emptied into the Parana River. The Iguazu River separated Brazil and Argentina, and then we followed the Iguazu east to the Falls on the Brazilian side. The trip took about two to three hours there and the same time back. The view of the Falls was quite different but still spectacular and well worth the trip. Iguazu Falls ended our South America adventure and from there we flew back home.

41. THE ARC (Army Residence Community)

After living in Grand Prairie, Texas, for ten years, Sue and I had a sinking feeling both kids had abandoned us. Tim and his partner Jimmy had been lured away to Chicago, Illinois, in 2012, and Mary's husband, Craig, was hired in the Texas Attorney General's Office in Austin, Texas. They bought a home and moved to Cedar Park in 2013. Sue and I decided it was fruitless to try and tag along after the kids (as much as we would have liked to). They both had busy, successful, rewarding lives, and even though we hated to admit it, they no longer needed us. But in spite of ourselves, we must have done a pretty good job in getting them to that point. Of course, most of the credit was theirs.

With our good friends Paul and Andrea Martin, we looked at retirement facilities in 2004. They, at that time, were living in Sun City, Texas, where we had considered moving until I obtained the position with the Veterans Administration. Paul had done quite a bit of research as to which retirement facility offered the most amenities and the biggest bang for the buck and had decided that San Antonio was the best place for all of us.

The two main draws in San Antonio were the Air Force Village and the Army Residence Community, with the availability of all the military facilities in the general area. After all, San Antonio wasn't called Military City for nothing. Paul and Andrea put down deposits for both places in order to hold a spot for themselves. Sue and I, on the other hand, were not as enchanted with the Air Force Village, so we only made a deposit for the Army Residence Community (ARC). The Martins actually moved into the Army Residence Community in 2010 and encouraged us to follow suit. I was not quite ready to isolate myself with a bunch of old folks, just yet. However, as it happened, we did join them in October 2014.

In 2013, we were notified the ARC was planning on expanding new spacious duplexes with larger/nicer landscaping with up to 2,100-feet-plus floor plans (that would be their third expansion at that time; we had also been offered an opportunity to buy in at their earlier expansions). Were we interested? I was still not convinced the ARC was the place for us at each period and also was still hesitant with their latest offering. Plus, I wasn't sure I was ready to leave our nice, spacious home in Grand Prairie. However, in early summer 2014, we did visit our friends, the Martins, at the ARC, and on the one morning when they both had medical appointments, we decided to fill in the time by checking out the lay of the land with the ARC Marketing Department.

Sure enough, all the new duplex houses that were in the process of being built were sold. However, if we were amiable to accept an existing smaller cottage under renovation, scheduled to be ready in the fall, we would be placed at the top of the list to get a house on Lakeside, which had some of the housing plans we desired as soon as one became available. I was still slow balling it, not completely convinced. But, because the ARC offered independent living that graduated to assisted living that graduated to health care with another unit devoted to Memory Care, it did appear to cover all the bases.

Sue and I had discussed how we needed to be independent in our advancing years, and what the ARC offered seemed to fit the bill. So, I somewhat hesitantly agreed to accept this offer with the caveat that we would need to sell our house first. As the housing market in our area was pretty slow at that time, I was fairly confident the exercise was going to be a mute effort or at least a somewhat long delayed one. To my surprise, however, after we put our house on the market, almost the first person who viewed our house made us an offer. The closing—move-out—for us coincided with the date the ARC cottage would be available for us to move in. The major obstacle to overcome was we had way too much baggage (stuff) to fit into the San Antonio quarters, even should we eventually manage to get the larger duplex.

Sue managed to engage a lady to have an estate sale to get rid of most of our excesses, but then she canceled us at almost the last minute. Then we (Sue mainly) had to scurry around to find a replacement, and Sue did find a person who would come to our home and take all items we had declared excess, store them at her storage facility, and sell them at a later date with some other major production(s) of hers. The lady Sue had contacted had her staff come and collect all the items we had indicated were excess, but it was ages before we heard anything from her. Well, we felt that the enterprise was turning into a real debacle. After a great deal of time had elapsed and much haranguing and a threat to file a legal suit, we did recover a small portion of what we felt the items were worth. After that we didn't feel it was worth the hassle to pursue the matter further. Another lesson learned.

With Mary's and Tim's help, we did all our own packing, but we did hire movers to pick up everything. They dropped off the daybed, the chopping block table, and the piano at Mary and Craig's on their way to San Antonio on October 14, 2014. It seemed the majority of everything we had left we had to put into storage because it just would not fit in our small two-bedroom cottage. But we still managed somehow. No cooking, no yard work, and we had housekeeping services along with several planned activities. We lived like that for seven and a half months until we were offered and moved into the ARC's Lakeside Model Home. As the ARC did not plan on building any more of these types of homes in the foreseeable future, we were offered their Lakeside Model Home. We moved into the Model Home on the first of June 2015. And here we still are as of this writing.

Sue has had her quilting, sewing, and Mahjong, with some quilting retreats thrown in. I have substituted working at the ARC Library and prepared their calendar. I helped manufacture handicap ramps until my hip replacement, chaired the ARC Movie Committee, and worked for AARP each tax season. We have been able to do some traveling since we have lived here. Otherwise, we have been enjoying the ambiance here along with our fellow ARC'ers.

On November 7, 2015, Sue and I, along with Mary, Craig, Riley, and August, attended Tim and Jimmy's wedding at Tim's boss's house. It was quite the ceremony and celebration. Tim and Jimmy had been together for some time by then (nine years), but with the Supreme Court decision allowing same-sex couples to marry, Tim had popped the question asking

Jimmy to marry him, and Jimmy had accepted, hence their wedding. And with the grand fete approaching, the guys had invited Sue and me to tag along on their honeymoon to Key West, Florida. They barely had the invitation out of their mouths before we agreed to accompany them. Key West had been on my bucket list for a long time to visit, and that could well be our only opportunity. We were flattered and honored to be invited and had a great time.

Figure 27 Jimmy and Tim's big Wedding Day

We flew out of Chicago to Miami, where Tim rented a car, and we drove down US Highway 1 with water on both sides of us stretching beyond the horizons. We discovered the keys were hardly more than wide places along the highway with lots of boats attached and also lots of boats in the water along the way. Key Largo, our first key encountered, was perhaps somewhat larger than most of the rest of the keys until we got near the end of the highway.

Our destination, Key West, had palm-lined streets with gingerbread mansions and tin-roofed conch houses, which had been homes to Ernest Hemingway, Tennessee Williams, Elizabeth Bishop, Robert Frost, and Jimmy Buffet, to name a few of the famous people who discovered solace and inspiration in the island city whose Bahamian and Cuban heritage in large part was inspired by Bahamian wreckers, commercial fishermen, spongers, and Cuban cigar-makers. Otherwise, the people there looked much like people anywhere else in the US with lots of tourists thrown in.

Almost everything to do and see was within walking distance of our rental. Chickens were everywhere, underfoot, and otherwise. They were all free range, somewhat of a spectacle, and almost a nuisance.

Watching sunsets from the west side of the keys was glorious. We never got up in time to see the sunrise from the east side, therefore I'm unable to give you my impressions of the Key West sunrises. We had a pleasant boat tour around Key West, and it was a nice stroll to the southernmost point of the US. I guess we could call it our Land's End. We visited Truman's Little White House and the Lighthouse.

One of the more interesting places we visited, though, was Ernest Hemingway's Home and Museum. Supposedly, sixty polydactyl (six-toed) cats resided there. We may have seen a dozen. Cats normally have five front toes and four back toes. About half of the cats at the museum had the physical polydactyl trait, but they all carried the polydactyl gene in their DNA, which means that the ones that had four and five toes could still mother or father six-toed kittens. Most cats have extra toes on their front feet and sometimes on their back feet as well. Sometimes, it looked as if they were wearing mittens because they appeared to have a thumb on their paw.

Jimmy and I feasted on seafood, which was plentiful. We pigged out on hogfish. Seafood was not quite Tim and Sue's cup of tea, so they diversified. We tried dessert at a little place called Better Than Sex (I think it was Key Lime Pie, and it was really good; not sure it was *that* good, though!) We had chicken dinners at a little place called Blue Heaven, with a lot of chickens running all over the place. I wondered if our dinners had recently lost their places in the yard outside but didn't dare say anything to Sue. Tim and Jimmy did some athletic stuff like snorkeling, jet skiing, or parasailing while Sue and I meandered around and did a little souvenir shopping, otherwise we took it slow and easy.

Return to Spain

I retraced my steps in reverse order. Ralph and I had visited Spain in the early sixties when we were stationed in France. We had started in Spain's northwest, going down the west side, crossing the southern portion along the Mediterranean Sea, and then up the eastern side.

Here, Sue and I, and Tim and Jimmy, along with our friend Andrea Martin, were starting in Barcelona and reversing my original trip back to Madrid. Tim and Jimmy had taken a pre-trip to Ireland and met us in Barcelona. As I have spent some detail on Ralph's and my visit to Spain, I will be somewhat briefer on this visit.

In Barcelona, we visited the Pablo Picasso Museum and bought one of his prints that had been used by August's first-grade art class as a model. August's rendition had garnered a write-up in the local paper and was exhibited in the local library.

We spent one morning investigating and admiring Antoni Gaudi's Sagrada Familia. His minor basilica was a project of incredible scale and ambition that was still only around three-quarters complete more than 140 years after Gaudí first became involved. When its spires are finished, it will be the tallest church building in the world and hardly resembles any religious structure you'll have seen in your life. The Sagrada Família combines several architectural styles, including Catalan Modernism, Art Nouveau, and Spanish Late-Gothic, but Gaudí's masterpiece defies these kinds of definitions when you look up open-mouthed at the ceiling of the nave.

We flew from Barcelona to Malaga, a seaside city located on the Coda del Sol. It was one of the oldest continuously inhabited cities on Earth, some 3,000 years of civilization. It was also the hometown of Pablo Picasso.

We were bused from Malaga to Granada (described in some detail in my previous trip to Spain), then to Seville. In Seville, we had a pleasant horse-drawn carriage ride amongst the busy downtown traffic. It was a bit daunting, but the horses at least seemed used to it, so why should we have been alarmed? Seville was also the final resting place for Christopher Columbus. Seville was visited on my earlier adventures in Spain.

After Seville, we were bused to Cordoba, where we caught the bullet train to Madrid. Zippity-zip, and we were there.

In Madrid, it was great to revisit the Prada and some other old places whose familiarity had dimmed with the elapsing of time. In one of the main squares, Tim, wearing his A&M cap, was mobbed by a bunch of A&M students who were studying in Madrid. Small world.

During spring break 2018, Sue and I drove up to Mary and Craig's house and joined them on their trek to the Grand Canyon. Riley had had his 14th birthday in December, and August was approaching his 12th birthday in July. Our first stop for exploration was at the Petroglyph National Monument, New Mexico.

Petroglyph National Monument protected a variety of cultural and natural resources including five volcanic cones, hundreds of archeological sites and an estimated 24,000 images carved by Ancestral Pueblo peoples and early Spanish settlers. Many of the images were recognizable as animals, people, brands, and crosses; others were more complex. Their meaning was, possibly, understood only by the carver. These images were the cultural heritage of a people who had long since moved on through history for many reasons. The monument was intended as a protection for those lands and sites from and for visitors to see and appreciate for generations to come.

Next, we discovered the El Malpais National Monument on our journey. The area around El Malpais was used for resources, settlement, and travel by Oasis America cultures, Native Americans, and

Spanish colonial and pioneer exploration. Archaeological sites remained in the park. In the 1940s, the Malpais lava field was one of the eight candidate sites considered by the Manhattan Project to test the detonation of the first atomic bomb. Instead, the White Sands Proving Ground nearby was the site selected for the Trinity nuclear test. The Department of Defense did use the site as a bombing range to train pilots during World War II. After the war, the Bureau of Land Management became the administrator of the area. In 1987, President Reagan signed Pub. 100–225, which created El Malpais National Monument and designated it a unit of the National Park Service.

Then, we visited the Painted Desert and the Petrified Forest. The desert got its colorful broad strokes because of its stratified layers of siltstone, mudstone, and shale of the Triassic Chinle Formation, which eroded easily. These fine-grained rock layers contained abundant iron and manganese compounds, which provided the pigments for the various colors of the region. The erosion of these layers resulted in the formation of the badlands topography of the region.

Remnants that made up the Petrified Forest evolved over millions of years, in the southern portions of the desert. These remains of a Triassic period coniferous forest had fossilized. Evidence of early human habitation, as well as ancient dinosaur tracks and an assortment of fossilized prehistoric plants and animals, were found in the region as well.

We had managed to reserve cottages within the Grand Canyon National Park Reserve for our visit there. As awesome as the Grand Canyon is, one can't just observe its splendor without understanding a little of its history. Nearly two billion years of Earth's geological past had been exposed as the Colorado River and its tributaries cut their channels through layer after layer of rock while the Colorado Plateau was uplifted. Several recent studies supported the hypothesis that the Colorado River established its course through the area about five to six million years ago.

For thousands of years, the area had been continuously inhabited by Native Americans, who built settlements within the canyon and its many caves. The Pueblo people consider the Grand Canyon a holy site and made pilgrimages to it. Even though it was not the deepest canyon in the world (Kali Gandaki Gorge in Nepal is much deeper), the Grand Canyon is known for its visually overwhelming size and its intricate and colorful landscape. Geologically, it is significant because of the thick sequence of ancient rocks that are well preserved and exposed in the walls of the canyon. These rock layers recorded much of the early geologic history of the North American continent. To those in the know it is like looking at an open book.

Photo by Donald Teel on Unsplash

After leaving the Grand Canyon, our next major stop was Montezuma's Castle National Monument. Montezuma Castle was situated about ninety feet up a sheer limestone cliff, facing the adjacent Beaver Creek, which drained into the perennial Verde River just north of Camp Verde. It is one of the best-preserved cliff
dwellings in North America. Access was thought to have been permitted by a series of portable ladders, which could have been easily withdrawn in the likelihood of an attack. This would have made the site much easier to defend. Flooding was also thought to have been a factor in the cliff-dwelling sites.

Our next big stop was Tucson, Arizona, where we had hoped to visit both Davis-Monthan Air Force Base's Boneyard and the Saguaro National Park. Unfortunately, we had not made advance reservations to visit the Boneyard, so all we could do was drive around its perimeter.

Davis-Monthan was the location of the 309th Aerospace Maintenance and Regeneration Group (AMARG), the sole aircraft boneyard and parts reclamation facility for all excess military and government aircraft. Aircraft from the Air Force, Navy, Marine Corps, Coast Guard, NASA, and other government agencies were processed at AMARG, which employed over 500 people, almost all civilians. It was the largest airplane boneyard in the world. Another role of AMARG was to support the program that converted old fighter jets, such as the F-4 Phantom II and F-16, into aerial target drones. It also served as an auxiliary facility of the National Museum of the United States Air Force and stored tooling for out-of-production military aircraft. AMARG's typical inventory comprises more than 4,400 aircraft.

However, we had better luck with the Saguaro National Monument. Saguaro National Park was in southern Arizona. Its two sections were on either side of the city of Tucson. The park was named for the large Saguaro Cacti, native to its desert environment. In the western Tucson Mountain District, Signal Hill Trail led to petroglyphs of the ancient Hohokam people. In the eastern Rincon Mountain District, Cactus Forest Drive was a loop road with striking views of the desert landscape.

The last major exploration on this road trip was the Gila Cliff Dwellings National Monument. Considered by archaeologists to be on the northernmost portion of the Mogollon people's sphere of influence. The Gila Cliff Dwellings National Monument was home to two prominent ruins sites among a collection of smaller sites located within the Gila Wilderness inside the Gila National Forest. The terrain around the ruins was rugged and arid and contained steep-sided canyons cut by shallow spring rivers and mesas and bluffs forested with Ponderosa pine, Gambel's oak, Douglas fir, New Mexico juniper, pinon pine, and alligator juniper (among others). Climbing to the actual sites was somewhat challenging for Sue and I. Less so for the rest of the crew.

For Riley's Golden Birthday, which was delayed until late July and early August 2021, the whole family went to California. A large portion of the time, we were able to get a suite at the Marine Hotel in San Francisco, which we used as our base of operations. We all did the touristy things in San Francisco. We took in the usual tourist attractions Golden Gate Bridge, Fisherman's Wharf (where we dined), Pier 39 (where we shopped and dined and watched the nearby California sea lions), took a drive on Nob Hill and Telegraph Hill, and drove by where Craig's parents used to live.

Craig, Riley, and I hiked up the hill near the hotel to Chinatown to sample the Chinese cuisine. The remainder of the crew were not so much Chinese cuisine aficionados. Then, we all took a leisurely drive along Coastal Highway One. In addition, Craig, Mary, and the boys took in a baseball game at Candlestick Park and did the Trolley ride. Riley wanted to see Stanford and Berkeley Universities' campuses, which we were able to accomplish, and we also took a tour of the Napa Valley and had an interesting wine-tasting event while we were there. While we were in California, Craig rented a van and chauffeured all of us to two of the National Parks that had been on my bucket list forever, Sequoia and Yosemite. Both exceeded expectations.

The amazing giant sequoia is one of the largest organisms on earth and grows from a seed less than half an inch long! When fully grown, the sequoia pushes its craggy treetop more than 250 feet into the sky. A few rare specimens have grown taller than 300 feet. But it is the sequoia's huge girth that sets it apart from all the other trees. Sequoias are commonly more than twenty feet in diameter, and at least one has grown to thirty-five feet across. Six people would have to lay head-to-toe to match this width.

The Giant Sequoia National Monument was designated by President William Jefferson Clinton in April 2000. The monument now encompasses some 328,315 acres.

The giant sequoia (Sequoiadendron giganteum) is the world's largest tree. It grows naturally only in a narrow sixty-mile band of mixed conifer forest on the western slopes of the Sierra Nevada Mountain range in California. There are thirty-three giant sequoia groves in the Giant Sequoia National Monument. We were enthralled by numerous giant sequoias, but the grandfather of them all was General Sherman, the world's largest tree, approximately 2,000 years old. The grandest of them all!

Sequoia National Forest, Photo by KC Welch on Unsplash

Driving and hiking through the monument was a great adventure. The hiking trails were numerous and offered a plethora of exploitative sites to visit and wondrous sights to behold. Sue and I managed a few of the less challenging ones but let Mary, Craig, and the boys explore to their hearts' content those steep, winding, challenging, breathtaking ones regardless of whatever they might offer. Sue and I were simply content to relax beneath the shade of the giants and enjoy the refreshing breeze while listening to the surrounding solitude and watching the sequoias grow, waiting for our little tribe to return.

On one of our evenings, we decided to have our evening meal at the café down by the nearby lake. The café included outdoor dining with picnic tables shielded with huge umbrellas for shade. We were hurriedly finishing our meal when it appeared there was a storm threatening us, moving fast off the lake. We were in the process of collecting leftovers, disposing of them, and making a quick dash for shelter. The wind at our backs was swiftly picking up velocity, almost like it was telling us to get the heck out of there. All of a sudden, the wind picked up one of the giant table umbrellas, took careful, almost specific aim, and hit me smack in the back between my shoulder blades. I went over like a struck bowling pin, face first. Fortunately, we were still on the grassy portion. Unfortunately, I was getting to the point where, once I was down, it became difficult to get back up. Again, fortunately, Craig and Riley, one on each side, hoisted me up. Piece of cake.

The café manager came rushing over to see what had happened and to assess the damage. He asked if I was all right. I was a little shaken, and it occurred to me to tell him we had everything under control and specifically because I had my attorney with me (Craig, my son-in-law). However, I managed to smile weakly at him and told him I was okay. Except for a bit of bruised pride and being a little shaken up, I was alright and did survive nature's unexpected onslaught.

On another of our expeditions, we even paused to observe a mama bear and her two cubs foraging nonchalantly in the woods, and then they calmly strolled across the highway in front of us, halting traffic in both directions. We pulled right over from the highway to watch them pluck berries from some nearby bushes calmly as you please, completely ignoring us and the rest of the tourist onlookers. A big plus was seeing those bears and rainbows to boot (a triple rainbow, much to our amazement). It was almost like the Sequoia Forest was putting on a special show just for us.

In Yosemite, it was awe-inspiring to stand amongst the granite cathedrals and appreciate the true miracle of Mother Nature. Yosemite boasted some of the best views, hiking trails, and family vacation opportunities we'd encountered. Yosemite was a land where history was made—our nation's first land dedicated to recreation and enjoyment. It was the precedent for all future American national parks.

Located in Central California, Yosemite National Park was established in 1890 and drew four million annual visitors. Almost 95 percent of the park's nearly 748,000 acres (roughly the size of Rhode Island) was classified as wilderness. The Valley was a seven-mile-wide canyon with incredible rock formations, including El Capitan, the world's tallest granite monolith and one of the world's top rock-climbing destinations. It appeared to have been standing there through the ages.

Yosemite National Park, Photo by Casey Horner on Unsplash

Yosemite Falls was the largest waterfall in North America, with breathtaking views. Unfortunately, during our visit, because of the last few years of drought, the water flow was so low it was not that spectacular. We were told peak visitation at the falls occurred in the spring, as the falls were comprised entirely of melting snow. The park was also known for its giant sequoia trees, which were estimated to be over 3,000 years old. It was a wonderful trip, and the best part about it was enjoying it with family.

China

Our most recent trip was with our good friend Andrea Martin to China. We landed in Beijing, China's sprawling capital, its history stretching back three millennia. Yet it's known as much for modern architecture as its ancient sites, such as the grand Forbidden City complex and the imperial palace during the Ming and Qing dynasties.

Nearby, the massive Tiananmen Square pedestrian plaza was the site of Mao Zedong's mausoleum and the National Museum of China, displaying a vast collection of cultural relics.

In Beijing, we had tea with a local family, had a rickshaw ride, and visited the Forbidden City, a palace complex at the center of the Imperial City of Beijing. It was surrounded by numerous opulent imperial gardens and temples, including Zhongshan Park, the sacrificial Imperial Ancestral Temple, Beihai Park, and Jingshan Park. The Forbidden City was constructed from 1406 to 1420 and was the former Chinese imperial palace and winter residence of the Emperor of China from the Ming dynasty (since the Yongle Emperor) to the end of the Qing dynasty, between 1420 and 1924.

The Forbidden City served as the home of Chinese emperors and their households and was the ceremonial and political center of the Chinese government for over 500 years. Since 1925, the Forbidden City has been under the charge of the Palace Museum, whose extensive collection of artwork and artifacts was built upon the imperial collections of the Ming and Qing dynasties. The Forbidden City was declared a World Heritage Site in 1987. The complex consisted of 980 buildings, encompassing 8,886 rooms. It was listed by UNESCO as the largest collection of preserved ancient wooden structures in the world. In 2018, the Forbidden City's market value was estimated at 70 billion USD, making it both the world's most valuable palace and the most valuable piece of real estate anywhere in the world. Outside of the Forbidden City, there were tables of local Chinese playing Mahjong. They all appeared completely absorbed in their games, oblivious of the traffic and activities surrounding them. I teased Sue and asked if she didn't feel like she needed to join in. I told her I would either wait for her or come back for her later.

Included as part of our visit to the Forbidden City was Tiananmen Square, a city square in the city center of Beijing, China, named after the eponymous Tiananmen ("Gate of Heavenly Peace") located to its north, which separates it from the Forbidden City. The square contained the Monument to the People's Heroes, the Great Hall of the People, the National Museum of China, and the Mausoleum of Mao Zedong. Mao Zedong proclaimed the founding of the People's Republic of China in the square on October 1, 1949; the anniversary of this event is still observed there.

The size of Tiananmen Square was about 53 acres. It had great cultural significance as it was the site of several important events in Chinese history. Outside China, the square was best known for the 1989 protests and massacre that ended with a military crackdown, which was also known as the Tiananmen Square Massacre or the June Fourth Massacre. While we were there, there were a lot of visitors, and in one area, there was a grandiose ceremony taking place. I attempted to get a little too close—I just wanted to see what was going on, I guess, for a better look-see and a photo but was quickly shooed off.

On our last day in Beijing, we took a day trip to see the Great Wall of China, a series of fortifications that were built across the historical northern borders of ancient Chinese states and Imperial China as protection against various nomadic groups from the Eurasian Steppe. Apart from defense, other purposes of the Great Wall have included border controls, allowing the imposition of duties on goods transported along the Silk Road, regulation or encouragement of trade, and the control of immigration and emigration.

Furthermore, the defensive characteristics of the Great Wall were enhanced by the construction of watchtowers, troop barracks, garrison stations, signaling capabilities through the means of smoke or fire, and the fact that the path of the Great Wall also served as a transportation corridor. Collectively, they stretch from Liaodong in the east to Lop Lake in the west, from the present-day Sino–Russian border in the north to Tao River in the south, along an arc that roughly delineates the edge of the Mongolian steppe, spanning 13,170 miles in total. Today, the defensive system of the Great Wall is generally recognized as one of the most impressive architectural feats in history.

The Great all of China, Photo by <u>William Olivieri</u> on <u>Unsplash</u>

The great Wall was steep and rugged in places but proved some awesome views of the surrounding valleys. On one of the steep climbs Sue fell and injured her leg and made walking difficult for her. As a matter of fact, her leg tended to bother her throughout the remainder of our trip. After the Great Wall, we visited Xi'an, the capital city of twelve Chinese dynasties, and its history went back over 3,000 years. Xi'an was also the starting point of the famous Silk Road, a trading route that linked China with Europe. The Silk Road brought wealth and a mix of different cultures to Xi'an that continues even today due in large part to the Mausoleum of the first Qin Emperor's Terracotta Army, a collection of terracotta sculptures depicting the armies of Qin Shi Huang, the first emperor of China. It was a form of funerary art buried with the emperor in 210–209 BCE with the purpose of protecting the emperor in his afterlife.

Terracotta Amy, Photo by Manoj kumar kasirajan on Unsplash

The figures, dating from approximately the late third century BCE, were discovered in 1974 by local farmers in Lintong County, outside Xi'an, Shaanxi, China. The figures varied in height according to their roles, the tallest being the generals. The figures included warriors, chariots, and horses. Estimates from 2007 were that the three pits containing the Terracotta Army held more than 8,000 soldiers, 130 chariots with 520 horses, and 150 cavalry horses, the majority of which remained buried in the pits near Qin Shi Huang's Mausoleum. Other terracotta non-military figures were found in other pits, including officials, acrobats, strongmen, and musicians.

From Xi'an, we flew to pick up our Viking ship in Chongqing, a sprawling municipality at the confluence of the Yangtze and Jialing rivers in southwestern China. In the city center, the large, domed Great Hall of the People complex stood above the pedestrianized People's Square. On the other side of the square, the Three Gorges Museum features artifacts from the construction of the Three Gorges Dam as well as ancient art.

Then we were on our river boat on the Yangtze River. The most dramatic part of the river was the Three Gorges region, a 150-mile stretch. The three larger gorges on the Yangtze were the Gorge, the shortest and narrowest of the three with the most spectacular scenery; the Wu (Witches) Gorge, noted for its magnificent lush green mountains frequently shrouded in mist; and the Xiling Gorge, at forty-seven miles, was the longest of the three, with narrow, precipitous cliffs.

In addition to the three large gorges, we took a special cruise boat up the Daning through the Lesser Three Gorges. Narrower than the great gorges, the canyon scenery was even more dramatic. We saw several historical sites along the way, like hanging coffins and the ancient plank road carved into the cliffside. The Three Gorges experience also included a visit to the dramatic twelve-story red Shibaozhai Temple perched alongside the Yangtze and a tour of the immense Three Gorges Dam project site and museum.

Wuhan, the sprawling capital of Central China's Hubei province, was a commercial center divided by the Yangtze and Han rivers. The city contained many lakes and parks, including the expansive, picturesque East Lake. Nearby, the Hubei Provincial Museum displayed relics from the Warring States period, including the Marquis Yi of Zeng's coffin and bronze musical bells from his 5th-century B.C. tomb.

Unbeknownst to us, while we were there doing our minor investigation of the city, a worldwide plague was brewing and about to be released. A teeming, monstrous threat was beginning to hatch and brew over in Wuhan while we were innocently taking in Wuhan's sights. We later learned this plague would be called the COVID-19 virus, which would follow us back to the States a few months later and then spread like wildfire over the entire world.

After Wuhan, we traversed through Nanjing, Zhenjiang, Chinghai, and Nantong, with our final stop and stay in Shanghai. Obviously, there were many sites to see and savor—with lots of photo ops and all kinds of local foods to sample along the way—such as the flowers, temples, gardens, art, theatrics, etc. We were even treated to a local Chinese grammar school, and our tour was divided into separate classrooms, and we were treated with a visit with the young Chinese students—it was a major highlight of our trip—most impressive. But Shanghai was a good departure point.

Shanghai, on China's Central Coast, is the country's biggest city and a global financial hub. It was also the most populous urban area in China, with a population of nearly twenty-five million. Its heart was the Bund, a famed waterfront promenade lined with colonial-era buildings. Across the Huangpu River rose the Pudong district's futuristic skyline, including the 2,073-foot Shanghai Tower and the Oriental Pearl TV Tower, with distinctive pink spheres. Sprawling Yu Garden had traditional pavilions, towers, and ponds. From our hotel, there were lots of touristy things to see and lots of shops to purvey in case we had forgotten to buy anything and still had any money left over.

Back on the home front, we continue to bask in the successes of our offspring. Tim and Jimmy are firmly settled in Florida in their spacious dwelling. Jimmy's law practice flourishes, as well as his internet sales enterprise. Tim, the workaholic, has been and is quite a success. Tim and Jimmy had a new house built on the land where Jimmy grew up (his homestead).

Mary's family are all all-stars. Mary was recently promoted to be the Manager of Oncology Reporting for her genealogy firm, and Craig was promoted from the Texas Attorney General's Office to be the Texas Director of Office Compliance and Enforcement.

August is now a high school senior and is the policy director of the student council, captain of the school's debate team, and co-captain of the school's water polo team. And is excelling in his studies. And more recently elected to be student body president.

Riley recently graduated from high school, having served as class president for his first three years in high school and in his senior year as student body president. He is now enrolled at Texas A&M University, excelling in his studies, and was also voted in to serve as his class senator and in the school's fish council. Earlier, there had been rumors about Riley's latest flame, and on one of our visits to Cedar Park, Riley actually brought her over to meet his grandparents (us). However, he had forewarned her about me. Her name was Bella, and true to her name (in the Romantic language, Bella means beautiful), she was (and is) cute as a button. No sooner had we been introduced than I told Bella that I was so glad to meet her because I had been hearing so much about her. There had been all this talk, and I just wanted to make sure she actually existed and was not merely a figment of Riley's vivid imagination. And that if she did exist, I wanted to make sure I included her in this book I was writing because Riley was loath to share his personal soirees with us—or much else, for that matter.

I could see there was a bit of a blush arising in her cheeks, and she appeared a bit dubious as to what I was telling her. But I assured her it was all true with the straightest face I could muster. Riley was glaring intently at me but took it in stride. Both Riley and Bella, as well as August, were members of the teen court, and we got to see them all in action: Bella was the presiding judge, Riley was the prosecuting attorney, and August was a member of the jury. Bella managed the court in a no-nonsense, judicious manner, and Riley was a self-assured, dogged prosecutor who held the court's attention and managed all points of evidence against the defendant. I actually felt a little bit sorry for the defendant. After witnessing Riley in action, I've decided I don't want him to ever prosecute a case against me—Heaven forbid.

At the end of May 2022, the whole family gathered for Riley's graduation from high school. Of course, the highlight was watching him march across the podium and accept his diploma, but more importantly was observing him in action as he delivered his finely honed address to his fellow graduates as the student body president, challenging each of them to take up the baton and press forward with their best efforts to make their world a better environment in which to live, to work, and for the future generations that would follow behind them. After all, the results would be their responsibility. It was their opportunity to make it better.

Sitting there in the bleachers, looking at and listening to Riley, and thinking that this outstanding young man was our grandson made me so proud. I would have been proud of him no matter what, but he and his younger brother August have so much going for them. They are both bright, ambitious, and hardworking. I know they can and will achieve whatever they set their minds to. The sky is not their limit. But whatever they might choose in life and whatever successes they may accomplish; I hope they will always choose happiness first.

Sue and I have been truly blessed!

42. LE FIN

What a wonderful, marvelous journey it has been! There have been the ecstatic peaks and the sometimes-low valleys with a lot of plateaus in between. Eons ago, in another lifetime, it almost seems I recall myself, this skinny, probably somewhat malnourished kid helping my grandparents hoe their cornfield and, after finishing several rows of corn, finally taking a break at the end of the cornfield under the old elm tree with its low hanging branches providing sufficient shade and shelter from the blistering sun, with the cicadas screaming overhead and the bobwhites and cardinals joining the chorus nearby, wondering what did the fates have in store for me. Even though I tended to be a dreamer, never in my wildest imagination would I have imagined the journey that my life has taken. All for the good!

When we would take our little break, I would often stare up at the sky and watch all the clouds lazily crawl across the heavens and try to figure out what all the shapes represented, and dream about what my life was going to be like when I grew up and where my journey would lead me. I yearned to see some of the world that we had explored in our geography class and to meet some of the folks we had read about in foreign lands, and I thought I wanted a family, a wife, and lots of kids. And I hoped that maybe one of those kids would be a tow-haired boy that maybe looked a little like me. Would that be too much to ask?

I dreamed a lot in those days, for life was hard, and helping to eke out a living with my family was difficult, at best. As it has happened, I have been fortunate to exceed even my wildest dreams. I have traveled the world and experienced cultures I didn't know existed even though I had read a lot, read almost everything I could get my hands on. To borrow a line from *Auntie Mame*, "I have lived!" So many wonderful people have come into and out of my life—a few I might not have missed **too** much, but everyone is part of my amazing memory puzzle. Every person has been a part of my experience, and for that, I am and will be forever grateful, for they are and have been the reasons for me being the person that I am. In many ways, I feel like I have led a charmed life because I have been so lucky. It was like the gods, spirits, or fate were looking out for me. Of all the things I have experienced and that I am most thankful for are:

1. In 1966 (a September evening, I think), after taking my date, Sue Ann Rauch, for dinner and plying her with wine (she actually had maybe half a glass), I asked for her hand under the table, and I slipped an engagement ring on her finger, and when she withdrew her hand she didn't say no, nor did she remove the ring, which I took to mean Sue was accepting my proposal! I could breathe again. My heart had been in my mouth, and my whole body was in a quiver—like jelly. This was one of the most exciting moments of my life! When I had purchased the ring set, the wizened elderly (at least to me at that time) salesman had told me that this purchase was probably the best or worst transaction I would ever make in my entire life. He was right; it was the most fortuitous investment I have ever made. I was in Seventh Heaven to think this beautiful, intelligent, graceful lady was agreeing to share her life with me. I

loved her so much that I thought I wouldn't be able to breathe and that I was going to burst with happiness—and I still love her even more as I reminisce about those early days we shared together. I felt like I had just won the grand lottery, and I guess I had! But she did agree to share her life with me, and we were married on April 16, 1967; we celebrated our 56th Anniversary in 2023. We're still going strong as of this writing.

2. On July 5, 1976, Sue gave birth to our most handsome and beloved son, Timothy Francis Taylor. Growing up in a large family (I had nine siblings and was number five in the lineup), I always dreamed of having children of my own, so when our Timothy Francis was born, it was such a miracle, and I was just over the top. Words can't describe the joy of caring for and watching him mature from a wee baby into a crawler and then a walker. Before we knew it, he was in preschool, on the soccer team, T-ball, baseball, elementary school, high school, college, and then out into the business world, where he made a name for himself. I am so proud of our Tim. I'm not sure our parenting skills were that great, but we must have done something right, for he is just an awesome person, and I couldn't ask for a better son.

3. On April 1, 1975, Sue gave birth to our most beautiful and talented daughter, Mary Elizabeth Taylor (Pritzlaff). Mary Beth was our second miracle. I didn't believe I could be more overjoyed by anything than I had been by the birth of our firstborn, but I was wrong. With Mary's arrival, I was bursting with pride—we (Sue and I—well, maybe more Sue than I) had done it again. I was just as ecstatic with her arrival as I had been with Timmy's. Almost from the

beginning, Mary Beth was Daddy's girl. When she was awake, she didn't like for me to be out of her sight and could have a real conniption fit when I would leave her. Once, she got back at me for my inattention by dousing one of my LPs with her milk bottle, which I had inadvertently left too close to her playpen. Parenting, caring for, and watching over Mary Beth paralleled that of Timmy, except she was a girl, and there tended to be some sibling competition. There were Brownies, piano lessons, T-Ball, gymnastics, flags, preschool, elementary school, high school, college, marriage, and career woman, and then mother to our two awesome grandsons. I couldn't be prouder of our Mary. Again, I'm not sure our parenting skills were that great, but again we must have done something right, for she is just an awesome person, and I couldn't have asked for a better daughter.

This is a love letter to my family. Sue and I had, at times, discussed jotting something down for posterity but kept procrastinating. Tim was the impetus for this effort when he gifted me a program that got me started. I have always been the family's historian because there are many stories and innuendos that would have been lost had I not committed them to paper. The danger in doing this is leaving someone out who felt they should have been included versus including someone who felt they should have been left out. Too, there is the argument that I may have remembered an incident somewhat differently than someone else or even purposely expounded a bit. Whatever the case, there was never any intent to bruise anyone's feelings or to make anyone appear in a bad way.

Made in the USA
Columbia, SC
23 December 2023

29408498R00313